PILGRIMAGE

PILGRIMAGE

Adventures of a Wandering Jew

Perle Epstein

Houghton Mifflin Company Boston 1979

Library of Congress Cataloging in Publication Data

Epstein, Perle S
    Pilgrimage: adventures of a wandering Jew.

    1. Epstein, Perle S. 2. Hasidim — New York (State)
— Biography. 3. Mysticism — Judaism. 4. Mysticism —
India. I. Title.
BM755.E77A36   296.8'33 [B]   79–15688
ISBN 0–395–27620–9

Printed in the United States of America

H 10 9 8 7 6 5 4 3 2 1

FOR ALL MY TEACHERS

With wisdom you don't eat bread.
— HEBREW SAYING

Acknowledgments

SINCE MOST of the names of the people who appear in this book have been changed, I would like to express my gratitude to them en masse at the outset. The couple who live behind the blue gate must be singled out, however, for their boundless generosity and affection.

I would like to thank Rabbi Aryeh Kaplan, whose translations and discussions about Kabbalah have proven invaluable. The quotation from the Maggid of Mezerich that appears in the Introduction comes from an unpublished manuscript by Rabbi Kaplan entitled "Sparks in the Night."

Thanks are also due Janet Wolfe for her poetic rendering into English of a selection from the *Zohar*.

Without my Jerusalem friends, guides, translators, and rabbis, there would have been no pilgrimage at all; the same is true about my dear teachers, friends, and fellow seekers throughout the United States and Europe. To those who do not appear in the book, I extend my gratitude as well. For any distortions of events, conversations, and lectures recognizable to those who do appear, I shall place the blame on the subjectivity of dualistic experience.

I wish to thank the state of Kashmir for providing me with official hospitality during the conference on Mind that I attended in 1977.

Jonathan Galassi, my editor, deserves special thanks for his gentle demeanor and unyielding good taste.

The spiritual presence of my family is the very foundation of this book. My father and mother encouraged me from the first, even in the face of ideas and experiments inimical to their traditional beliefs. For their loving acceptance, no expression of thanks is sufficient.

My brother Larry provided me with characteristic humor, insight, and brilliance during the difficult times. His wife Jane generously provided a home and hearth during my wanderings and rapid solutions to artistic dilemmas.

My fellow pilgrim on the way, my husband, taught me how to "bind one soul to the other with common intention." For this rarest of gifts, I thank him.

Contents

PILGRIMAGE

Introduction

An Aberration in Judaism

I HAD BEEN SEDUCED by mysticism and Oriental philosophy as a college student when Dr. Yiu, my Chinese comparative literature professor, introduced me to the Eastern classics. From the day she read the first enigmatic Taoist lines of Chuang-tzu's parable about the man dreaming he was a butterfly and then wondering when he awoke whether he was not indeed a butterfly dreaming he was a man, the world was never the same for me. I talked about Dr. Yiu's class incessantly with my best friend, Sue, who corroborated my enthusiasm when she told me that she'd grown teary-eyed over the first pages of D. T. Suzuki's treatise on Zen.

Intellectually, I suppose, Dr. Yiu was my very first "guru." Emotionally, I was a mystic by birth, my father's family having planted firm Hasidic roots in eighteenth-century Poland. My own upbringing was what in Jewish religious circles is called moderately Orthodox. This meant that my father did not wear black Hasidic caftans or a beard and sidelocks, and my mother did not wear a wig or kerchief to cover her hair. At home it meant punctilious observance of the Halakha (the Law and precepts set down in the Old Testament and talmudic codes), which meant refraining from work on the Sabbath, eating kosher food, and performing ritual obligations like praying daily and celebrating the holidays. By some

inexplicable quirk of fate, this moderately Orthodox child was enrolled in the most rigidly Orthodox girls' yeshiva at the tender
age of eight. My skewed picture of religion — and of Judaism
specifically — I attribute to my five otherworldly years at the Beth
Rachel School for Girls, which tried hard (but failed) to mold me
into a "modest Jewish wife and mother," an emblem of ritual purity — as far removed from my beloved secular world of books, art,
and foreign adventure as a *glatt* kosher kitchen is from a China-
town noodle house.

Perhaps it was my parents' avid intellectual and social curiosity
that created the Jewish "menace," for that was how I was characterized by the rabbi's wife, who was my teacher. I even remember
the rainy winter day with the scabby Brooklyn trees swaying disap-
provingly at me from beyond the window in tandem with her shrill,
scolding voice when she said, "You are a menace!" after I had
asked her to explain clearly a physical detail she had glossed over
in translating the Hebrew word for begetting.

I have been searching for my proper identity ever since. That
"menace" who dared to question the Holy Scriptures and swallowed
great gulps of Dickens on Sabbath afternoons when it was sinful
to be reading secular literature developed into a bundle of paradoxes. The rebbitzen's shrill Torah and Dr. Yiu's melodious
Chinese aphorisms continue to resonate side by side in my pulse. I
often profess to long for the ideal community of mystics where I
might settle down to a life of contemplation, yet I still harbor the
old secret pull toward religious anarchy. With the archetypal rebbitzen forever peering over my shoulder, I have agonized over
the "irrelevant" Judaism practiced in America and yearned more
than ever to inject my profane life with a sense of the sacred. To
reconcile the struggle, I settled for a career of writing about
mysticism.

One day in the late nineteen sixties I looked up and found that
an entire generation around me was gazing eastward and inward. I
had been reading Indian philosophy and practicing yoga for so long
by then that the "new consciousness" took me by surprise. Were
the current idealists merely escaping from too much luxury, too

much violence? Or did they, like me, suffer from religious troubles? A cynical psychiatrist friend assured me that all belief systems were mad and prescribed dedication to work as an antidote to "fuzzy mysticism." I grew worried. Perhaps people like Chuang-tzu and Gautama Buddha did indeed represent a conspiracy of self-deluded neurotics whose delusions were powerful enough to cross centuries, borders, and oceans, inspiring ever-new generations of escapists like me. Or maybe it was an Asian plot designed by the Communists to soften further the decadent minds of the American bourgeoisie. I sat across from that skeptical psychiatrist in the lotus position and pondered the phenomenon but got no closer to understanding what I, who blandly called myself a mystic, really did about it beyond reading prolix English commentaries on the Bhagavad-Gita. At last I concluded that I was not a practicing mystic but a scholar of mysticism and that I was cheating in order to hold on to my respectability. I was certainly not an ascetic, nor was I even traditionally religious, but in my heart of hearts I knew that I was at the same time Dr. Yiu's spiritual child and the rebbitzen's stepchild — a Jewish-Oriental mystic — and that made me uncomfortable.

Something about the suddenness of the eastward turn in the sixties made me uncomfortable, too. Despite their positive thrust toward universalism, Oriental spiritual disciplines were alienating many seekers from everyday American life. As a mystical writer, I had to be careful not to obscure the concrete truth about cultural differences; if we tossed aside our jeans for robes and our peanut butter for lentils and rice, if we no longer thought of ourselves as Jews and Christians but went around painting saffron dots above our noses, would that bring us any closer to enlightenment? On the contrary, I feared it would only alienate us from our productive diversity, our healthy pluralism. Secluding ourselves in religious enclaves and closing off the rest of the world, as they had done at the Beth Rachel School for Girls, could only breed cultism, xenophobia, and strife.

In 1972 I was working on a book about Oriental mystics, which forced me to think very carefully and critically about the intense and sometimes comical pilgrimage I and so many others had embarked on. Indeed, Indian gurus were being passed in the night by American adepts flying eastward; borscht-belt hotels were making way for monasteries housing sleek-headed Buddhists and tantric Babas. We were being bombarded by paradoxes. I could no longer avoid unearthing and examining my own familial traditions, nor could I hide from the reflexive Jewishness I had come to regard as nothing more than a childhood tic.

Three years later I had worked my way around to writing about Jewish mysticism; armed with a notebook full of questions, I journeyed to Israel. The first person I interviewed was a rabbi who had forfeited his rights to dynastic succession in a renowned miracle-working Hasidic family to become a rational Zionist. From him I hoped to get an overall picture of both worlds.

The road to Holon was pitted with deep holes that gouged the springs of my rented Volkswagen. A wasteland of auto collision yards and single-story factories fronted by great rubber corpses and belching sulfur converged onto a sudden paved highway leading to the center of town. Coming down from Jerusalem meant entering the "real world" again; but the real world loomed ahead like a Dickensian nightmare. The road out of Jerusalem, city closest to heaven, her golden vision disappearing in noxious yellow fumes, had led me directly into the modern hell of an industrial town. No time to shift gears in the car or in the mind. I drove along a palm-lined street of stucco houses and pulled to a stop in front of number 20.

Rabbi Zitomer was seated in his typically book-lined rabbinical study waiting for me. Though he wore a skullcap and his wife's hair was covered by a recognizably Orthodox kerchief, there was nothing Hasidic or particularly spiritual about the atmosphere in the house.

Bearded, soft-spoken, and comfortable in English, Rabbi Zitomer sat with his hands folded on the table between us and asked what I wanted to know.

"Is there a place in Judaism for mysticism?" I asked.

"Jewish mysticism — Kabbalah — has no practical meaning for

real life; it's an escape. Mysticism, with its goal of returning to God, is not necessary for the life of faith. For the Jews, the Covenant is sufficient; we serve Him but we do not have to merge with Him."

Disheartened, I interrupted with a question about his own mystical family tree.

Rabbi Zitomer lit a cigarette, frowned slightly, and decided to ignore the question.

"Being close to God as one would be to his best friend is all the Jew requires. Mysticism deprives us of responsibility in the world of action, where the individual Jew only achieves importance as a member of the community of Israel. The Torah is not a mystical but a sociological document enabling human beings to live together in harmony. At its best, Kabbalah is a *philosophical* adjunct to Judaism. It makes no compromises with the imperfect present but always looks toward the redemption of Israel. Yet, no matter how deep its thoughts, Kabbalah is essentially an aberration in Judaism." The rabbi stopped, leaving the room so deadly quiet that I could hear the fluorescent bulb buzzing overhead. From across the table, his eyes seemed to be searching mine with infinite pity. "I have nothing more to tell you," he finished.

Later that autumn, when I was busily scouting the libraries back home, I received an urgent call from my old friend Sue, now a sculptor. In a Greenwich Village falafel café, against a cascading backdrop of Arabic music, she informed me that she had decided to go to India and study Vedanta philosophy in an ashram. Her eyes brimming with tears, she confessed to being shaken by a previous day's meeting with a fellow named Ben, who had only a month before returned from that same ashram a confirmed materialist.

"Ben is a brilliant philosopher; if he became disillusioned, who knows what will happen to me? What do you think I should do? What if he's right, if the Vedanta *is* flawed? What if it's all self-delusion, needing to hold on to the idea of oneness because of some infantile neurotic fantasy?"

Remembering that Sue had spent a long time in psychotherapy, I said nothing. Then, sitting across the table from her, I suddenly recalled Rabbi Zitomer's pitying look. Had he, like the Jewish philosopher Ben — similarly possessed of an obsessively inquiring talmudic mind — also found the flaw in the soothing ointment of mystic absolutism? Had the son of miracle workers fled in despair to the ethical materialism that today passes for Judaism to escape his "aberrant" blood? Until that moment I had never thought of mysticism as inimical to Judaism. But with Sue's dilemma in front of me, I realized that I was engaged in searching for a chimera.

"Forget about Ben and go to India," I said.

All that winter I cursed and raged at myself for digging around in such a stale, misogynous tradition when my friends were chanting to the sound of bells at the colorful shrines of Tibetan lamas. I had grown illiterate in the face of Buddhist smugness, been smothered by the all-encompassing vedantic embrace. But I had a contract to fulfill, and I doggedly continued reading dusty microfilm at the Jewish Theological Seminary. In the ragged, obscure manuscripts of the kabbalists I began to find tantalizing glimpses of the "holy sparks" that I had intuited in the Scriptures as a child. I marveled at the powers of obstruction that had hidden the ecstatic teachings from Jews like Sue who were so hungry for them that they would travel to dusty Indian villages, contract dysentery, and even die to find them.

For two hundred years Jews had ignored their mysticism in the hope that it might go away. And now, dropping plumb lines fashioned in the East, I was trying to dredge it up alone. After months of work, I even managed to convince myself that the Kabbalah was meant to be discovered by aberrant individuals like me. I came to see that all mystics deviated from the norm, that they were basically agnostics, passionate inquirers who would willingly experiment on their own bodies and minds in order to test what the Orthodox passively accepted as authority and the skeptics denied out of hand. Mystics were essentially anarchists, explorers, scientists of the soul who were never satisfied with anything short of immediate existential experience. In this way they transcended all religious hierarchy, law, culture, and national barriers, forming a kind of international brotherhood whose different customs were subsumed by the quest for what some of them called liberation and others called yoking.

Whether monist Hindu, nontheist Buddhist, or monotheist Jew, mystics of all stripes and traditions shared the common aim of direct, subjective knowledge of the Absolute. "To know" in Old Testament Hebrew also means "to merge with."

When he had exhausted all his doubts and questions, confronted despair, and released his limited time- and spacebound sense of himself, the Jewish mystic discovered the point at which knowledge and existence coincide and reveal the Infinite. And that made him a dangerous force among an exiled people so preoccupied with nationalism and scholarship that they had exchanged God for a book.

Learning these things in secret only made me more argumentative in public. On another trip to Israel, I challenged a very brilliant and dogmatic young rabbi on his rationale for the proscription against unkosher wine.

"How does not drinking unkosher wine with Gentiles bring a Jew closer to God?" I asked.

The question apparently infuriated the rabbi, for he immediately snorted back at me, "If you want to know God, go to India and become a Hindu! Judaism is concerned with the laws that operate between man and man!"

Frustrated by the living rabbis, I returned again and again to the words of the dead master kabbalists. For long hours I contemplated the writings of the Maggid of Mezerich, an eighteenth-century Hasidic genius whose uncompromising mysticism so touched me that I felt my body grow hot and cold by turns and my head grow light.

"I will teach in what disposition one can best speak about the Torah," I read once, in direct answer to a question I had been pondering about the true meaning of the words "Torah study."

It is in the state in which one no longer has any sense at all of one's own self, is all ear, so that it is not the speaker himself who speaks, but the world of speech in him ... The human being reaches this level only after he has freed himself from the bonds of the senses. He must think of himself as if he had no more connection with this world. Then he becomes united with the innermost reaches of his thought and the height of his divine nature, so that he no longer perceives his own self. A man should actually detach his ego from his body till he has passed through all the worlds and has become one with God.

Dialogues with the Maggid convinced me that contemporary Judaism represented but half a tradition, that its mystical portion had atrophied after "knowledge" of God had taken second place to "service." Invested with a power of concentrated intention the kabbalists called *kavanna,* the most ordinary daily event could free us from the bonds of the senses. Masters like the Maggid of Mezerich taught their disciples how to pray, walk, eat, make love, sleep, and dream with the intention of raising sparks of holiness from their every action. In the eyes of the rabbis who worshiped only law and reason, the Maggid, too, was an aberration, and they excommunicated him. I vowed not to rest until I had found such a teacher.

ONE

1

Looking Around

YOGI BANDHU AND YOGI WALTER were both Jewish. Bandhu's real name was something like Murray Shwartz. Whenever he greeted me at the door, he was barefoot, barechested, and clothed only in flouncy white cotton pantaloons. His hair was white and flouncy, too, and his high beaked nose and blackbird eyes always reminded me of my favorite grandmother. Bandhu was a health food fanatic; meals with him, like those I took with my father's eccentric mother, always consisted of raw spinach, wheat germ, and dark-floured crackers. Some gristly, unsalted vegetable stew usually completed the dinner. At Yogi Bandhu's incense pervaded everything; at Grandma's it was lilac and camphor. Going to see him was just like going to see her: secret, weird, cut off from "real," everyday experience. Grandma had been surrounded by mystics all her life; uncles on both sides were princes in saintly Hasidic dynasties that reached all the way up to the Baal Shem Tov himself. She believed in the rebbes' powers; one saintly Polish uncle had prayed and saved my father from dying of sleeping sickness. The miracle worker had even predicted the exact time of day when the child would wake up.

The holiest Hasidim had eaten at Grandma's Passover table. Yet she was a self-styled "intellectual" feminist who would sit me down in front of the piano and entertain me with ditties from the *Burl Ives American Folksong Book*. When I was nine I spent almost every weekend at her house, listening with mouth agape to her miraculous tales of escape from the anti-Semitic hordes as she smoked mauve gold-tipped cigarettes "for asthma."

Yogi Bandhu, too, was surrounded by mystics. His one-room studio near Carnegie Hall was plastered from floor to ceiling with snapshots of bearded Indian gurus seated with folded hands and legs in inextricable lotus postures, their eyes half-closed and blissful grins on their lips. Bandhu never stopped talking about his year in India under his own special "swamiji." This one, enshrined in fresh flowers, burning ghee lamps, and dropcloths embossed with OM, was a little dark elf with shoulder-length black hair that looked like it needed a shampoo. I could never explain to myself what I was doing at Yogi Bandhu's place, yet it bore such an uncanny resemblance to Grandma's that I never missed a Friday.

I saw Yogi Walter on Wednesdays. He was about forty, and he always wore black tights and a raw silk kurta. Walter Berger was the antithesis of the hyperactive Bandhu. He had a domed forehead, cropped black hair, Oriental features, and was always calm. While Murray Schwartz went begging for students, Walter Berger was cornering the market in hatha yoga. Pet store proprietors, housewives, and illustrious neurosurgeons were flocking to his classes in the Washington Hotel. I had found him through a friend who recommended that I do something physical lest I decay in the stacks of the Columbia University library, where I was writing my doctoral dissertation. I detested exercise then and still do now. But I must have been ripe for the message from the East; from the moment I was instructed to bring my head to my toes in the Mahamudra position, my body sprang into action and smoothly accomplished the feat without so much as a snap.

Walter glided down, pantherlike, from his platform in front of the class. Up close he didn't have a wrinkle; his Japanese rice-paper face and saintly calm enfolded me as he leaned down and whispered, "You've done yoga before."

Still engaged in the posture, I shook my head. The redhead from Great Neck sitting next to me was breathing like an overheated kettle.

"No, never."

"I mean in a past life," he said. "See me after class." And he slipped away as soundlessly as he had come.

It was Walter who flattered me into teaching hatha yoga for him on Wednesdays, and Yogi Bandhu who "initiated" me — for seventy-five dollars and a bunch of marigolds — into the secrets of meditation.

For a year I divided my time among the dark library stacks, the locker room and banquet hall of the Washington Hotel, and the cluttered studio on Fifty-seventh Street. Walter's wife, Phoebe, ran a special class for yoga teachers, which exposed me to really serious practitioners of the art for the first time. There was a giant Parthenon-thighed girl who walked with downcast eyes and could get up on her head without so much as making the wooden floor creak under her mat, and a sylphlike English ballet dancer who'd been born in India and could balance herself off the ground on her palms and read Indian texts that had Sanskrit on one page and English on the other. All the "advanced" people talked in low voices and made no noise as they walked. They were miniature Walters in the way they ate their avocado salads for lunch and in the spiritual earnestness with which they conducted their classes.

I soon began shopping on Broadway for soya bread, raw milk, and cheese, and bought organic fruits and vegetables at outrageous prices from a belligerent arthritic. It never occurred to me to ask either Walter or Yogi Bandhu why the people who sold health foods were so often crippled, poxed, sallow, and mean. On Tuesday nights I studied Walter's booklist in an effort to familiarize myself at least with what I was supposed to be teaching the next day. A world inhabited by Zen Buddhists, organic gardeners, and communal Sufis unraveled before me. For twenty minutes each morning and evening, I sat cross-legged and recited Yogi Bandhu's Shayam mantra until purple lights swam before my closed eyes.

In the summer of 1963 I decided to drop in on Walter in his Monterey headquarters; it was my first trip to California and I was excited about being part of the now world-famous Berger Yoga School. Walter had been interviewed on television, and, dressed in a black leotard, with appropriately downcast eyes, I had demonstrated the postures. Phoebe usually accompanied him, but she had put on too much weight to appear on television.

Bob Canfield, Walter's new production manager, picked me up in quaint and spotless Carmel Village, driving past Robinson Jeffers's retreat and pointing out the homes of all the reclusive movie stars who lived en route. Instead of going directly to Walter's, as I had expected, he took me to his own house, a sinuous glass and stone affair cluttered with angry African masks and crucified totems. The bar, contrary to the rules of yogic discipline, was stocked with liquor. He opened the glass doors and led me out across the patio. We picked our way down the rough-hewn stone steps and gazed at the Pacific.

"Like stout Cortés," I said, expecting a jaunty reply and getting none from the distracted Bob. Bubbles of spray curled against the rocks, seals flapped themselves with pleasure, and I sat peacefully contemplating Kim Novak's palace in the cliffs across the water.

When we returned to the house, Walter was waiting in the living room. A stringy-haired flower child with bare feet and bells around her ankles, not Phoebe, clung to his arm. Smelling of incense and marijuana, dressed in a bright orange robe, Walter offered me his usual distant embrace.

"So good to see you here," he said, not meaning it. His robe had slipped open at the chest, revealing an enormous pewter ankh. His body appeared wraithlike, floating and insubstantial. The flower girl stared wonderingly at us all and giggled at nothing in particular.

"How about dinner?" Walter offered awkwardly.

"Great!" said Bob, rubbing his hands nervously. "Steak or lobster?"

That Monterey steak and Bloody Mary dinner topped off with

brandy was the very first time in a whole year that I had touched meat or drunk liquor. It alienated me from health food lovers ever after.

Yogi Bandhu, in the meantime, was preparing the real test of my contemplative life. Each week I would return to the studio, sit cross-legged on the floor in meditation with him, eat Venus wafers and mixed green salad (how I hungered in those days for a hard-boiled egg or a slice of Camembert cheese), and describe what had "happened" during my meditation. How to describe nothing? Could I tell him that Shayam always made me think of Shazam and Captain Marvel?

"Well, there are these flashing purple lights . . ."

"Hmm . . ." he said meditatively, holding his finger to his cheek. No doubt a sign of great spirituality, purple lights, I thought.

"And sometimes my body goes numb." That was true.

"Does the guru ever appear?" he asked eagerly, pointing to the oily-haired elf above the shrine.

"I'm afraid not." It has always been very difficult for me to tell an outright lie.

"Sounds like you're ready for the test of detachment."

For one startling moment I thought he meant leaving my body or levitating from my meditation mat. I'd learned from Walter how to stand on my head and found it exhilarating.

"Is it a new posture?"

"What do you feel most obliged to do?" Yogi Bandhu, typically Jewish, answered my question with a question.

He often seemed unnecessarily querulous, flitting about the tiny studio like a nervous bird. It was then that he most reminded me of my grandmother, on her "bad" days, which she spent complaining that her spiritual and intellectual depths went unappreciated by the world outside. Murray Schwartz appeared to be getting himself into such a state just then. His gestures betrayed the high-strung flailings of a racetrack regular whose horse was lagging behind; even his speech slipped back into its natural Coney Island intonation.

"You heard me. What are you most obliged to do?"

"Go to my parents' Passover Seder next week," I blurted out just to say something.

"Den dat's it. You'll come here on dat night, and we'll have dinner, chanting, and meditation!"

On Wednesday nights I worked as an usher for Walter's lecture series, "Yoga and the Spiritual Life." Brimming with good will, my head full of Alan Watts and Swami Nikhilananda's Sunday discourses on the Vedanta, I prepared incense, made flower arrangements, and helped Phoebe paint great golden OMs in Day-Glo on oaktag posters. Phoebe was my spiritual ideal. She floated like a vision of health and serenity through the crowd, greeting students at the front door of the hotel banquet room with her ethereal head poised like an Athenian marble, the blue vein in her forehead throbbing under the saffron dot that marked her "wisdom eye." She was something I had always wanted to be: intense and far away at the same time. In her long, slitted Indian robes, Phoebe Berger truly resembled the Devi, the Indian goddess her worshipful student presumed her to be.

Every Wednesday night for six weeks that spring, the faithful gathered. I was delighted to find that my hatha yoga students made up the lion's share of Walter's audience. In only a matter of weeks I had cultivated a following of my own. Even now, after all those years, I am amazed at how easy it is to become a guru. Study hard enough, emulate every facial quirk and gesture of your favorite master, speak in high terms that describe even the most mundane kidney stone as a symbol of "spiritual hardening," every inch of waistline fat as part of the "grand cosmic design," and burn a lot of incense. It works! Even college professors will listen, I found. I got my first teaching job at NYU because some fellow with a Ph.D. in philosophy had backed out of a Humanities course at the last minute. He was headed for Arizona immediately, he told the dean, because the Guru Maharaji had ordered him there. Giving up house, job, family, car, and gold watch, the detached philosopher fled into the arms of his spiritual master.

And I had spent my first Seder night that year listening to Yogi

Bandhu's guru singing recorded chants in unintelligible Sanskrit.

Phoebe withdrew from classes one day without an explanation, but she left us with the name and address of an Indian instructor, a man she oddly referred to as "a *real* yoga teacher." The implications of that "*real*" escaped me until a week later on the subway, as I read the television page of the *Daily News* over my neighbor's shoulder. A small paragraph near the bottom of the page, under some salacious headline like TV YOGI REFUSES ALIMONY TO ESTRANGED PREGNANT WIFE, contained the intimate details of the scandal that was to end my career as a yoga instructor for the Walter Berger School.

Disgusted with myself for having created idols of vulnerable human beings, I cleared out my locker at the Washington Hotel without giving notice, threw Walter's philosophical pamphlets into the trash, and telephoned Yogi Bandhu, saying that I would no longer be coming on Fridays. I'd had my fill of phony Eastern philosophy and wished to continue practicing the physical exercises with a *real* Indian yogi. Tradition has it that you get the teacher you need and deserve according to your level of spiritual understanding. It was Narendra's amused, almost ironic presence that divested me of my preoccupation with exotic meditative techniques and my "mystical" aspirations. He was of medium height, very brown, with aristocratic Bengali features. He wore turtle-necked polo shirts, slacks, and brogans and was of indeterminate age. Nothing like my idea of a yogi.

His studio in a small Upper East Side flat resembled my dissertation adviser's study, with its book-lined walls and business-like desk and typewriter. Narendra supervised my yoga exercises with brusque humor, occasionally quoting Tagore's poetry at me as I handed him his five dollars at the door before we parted. I liked his classes so much that I brought friends and introduced him to my husband, Noah. Illustrating his remarkable suppleness with a rather cocky headstand, Narendra stunned us all one evening when he informed us that he was sixty. Another time, he spontaneously serenaded us with Hindu chanting. Within a year, Narendra and I had become good friends. His European wife invited Noah and me to dinner. We exchanged house gifts and ate curry together. The four of us sat out in the country on weekends discussing Judaism, Buddhism, and Vedanta.

Narendra taught me how to divorce the attitude from the goal — and how to bring it back again. Meditation became life, not something especially reserved for sanctified moments. Prayer, walking, cleaning out a barn, were meditation. Under his guidance, I simultaneously cleared the cobwebs and became the spider who spins its identity from the core of itself. Physical exercise put me in touch with my body in the physical universe; meditation, used in this new way, reintroduced me to that person I had accumulated over the years and called myself. Otherwise it became a hobby, like gathering decals and plastering the mind over with other people's visions. Authentic meditation was first a way of *looking,* then a way of *being,* in the world.

Narendra never demanded that I assume his tradition. He readily accommodated every Jewish holiday and changed his classes. Sometimes, instead of meditating, we just sat in his study and talked about politics. Nothing special happened — no flashing lights, no ecstasy. Other friends who were turning toward Eastern disciplines castigated me for sitting in New York with a teacher who gave you nothing: no initiations, no rosaries, no real disciplines. Edith went to him once and found him the vainest man she had ever met. Nora accused him of banality. Sue complained that he was curt and didn't clear up a thing about Vedanta. Indeed, there were times when Narendra's cool detachment lapsed into boredom. I would try to engage him in some definition of my meditative "experiences," and he would hold back, or reply with a generalization, or even look at his watch.

One morning I was sitting at home and reading a book about the Kabbalah written by an eccentric English theosophist. I decided to sit in a corner of the dining room and test one of the mental exercises described in the book. Tucking my legs under my body and loosely resting my right hand in my left palm, I gazed at the white wall in front of me and recited one of the Hebrew names of God. After a few minutes I lost consciousness of everything but my breathing, which seemed to be coming from the wall. The color of the room around me had changed, and I, like the furniture, was invested with an electric blue light that turned burning Nile green, then blue again. Outside the open window the sun disappeared and a sudden flash of lightning crashed into the room where I continued to sit, repeating the name. The distinct scent of some flower or spice pervading the room was the last thing I noted before Noah bolted through the swinging doors separating my end of the railroad flat from his office.

"What's that smell?" he shouted, shaking me. "Are you all right? Did you hear that incredible clap of thunder? What are you doing here on the floor?"

I blinked and looked up at him, still uncertain about the location of my body, which seemed to have come unstrung from my mind. The sun was shining, and the birds were singing outside as if nothing had ever happened.

"I was just trying out an exercise from this Kabbalah book," I said.

"What have you been burning in here, then? Incense?"

"No." But I, too, smelled the lingering fragrance of burnt flowers.

"Well, stop it," he said. "It's creepy."

I was still slightly dazzled when I left the house to mail a letter. The sun appeared too bright and hurt my eyes. I carried the envelope in my bag and crossed Fifth Avenue, which was a two-way street then. A bus going uptown was coming along very fast. *I think I'll go uptown* was the thought that popped into my head. The bus suddenly pulled to a stop where I was standing, at least two blocks from the bus stop. The driver waved me on without a word. I paid the fare and was about to sit down when he pulled up to a mailbox and, nodding his head, said, "Go ahead and mail your letter. I'll wait."

I got off, mailed the letter, and got back on the bus. It seemed perfectly natural that the bus driver should know exactly what I wanted and comply with it. At Forty-second Street I got off and walked into the public library. There was definitely something there I had to see. When I entered the front hall, I saw a sign announcing an exhibition of William Blake's etchings. Instantly, I knew why I had come. I walked around and around, looking into the glass cases at the now familiar electric blues and burning greens of Blake's visions. It was as if I were continuing the experience on the floor of my dining room back on Tenth Street. The difference was that I could feel my heart pounding violently with a weird kind of mental excitement I couldn't define. My own consciousness seemed to be creating the world outside. It was like stepping out of time into a science fiction vision where everything happens as you think it, or rather, *because* you are thinking it. Briefly, as I left the exhibition and walked over a sleeping derelict on the library steps, I thought I had become somehow dislocated, schizophrenic.

When I told Narendra about the experience, he seemed unimpressed. He was Indian, after all, and telepathic events are an acceptable part of life in that corner of the world. He used to enjoy telling stories about the yogis he had seen bearing elephants on their chests and the swamis he had known who could tell you who you were by merely looking at the shape of your feet. Just another part of the many-leveled "reality" we call the world. It would be better, he said, not to bother with such phenomena because they would only divert me from seeking the Truth, which is shapeless and formless, unbounded by color or time.

"When a bear hibernates all winter, it still comes out of its den a bear and not an enlightened saint," he used to say about people who tried to induce paranormal mental states. "These psychic phenomena are no less a game than your stockmarket. It's okay to play games occasionally but not to the point where they become business."

Walking into the mind can be a terrifying, unhinging experience. People come down with all kinds of fears and delusory symptoms when they go to see psychiatrists. Imagine, then, what it is like to pass through the levels of your own individual mind into the vast open courtyard of universal consciousness. The notion itself is staggering, like turning yourself inside out and seeing yourself as just another object in the world. That merging sensation is usually identified with psychosis in the West. However, what Freud pejoratively referred to as oceanic consciousness was precisely what Eastern sages called enlightenment. And my head was definitely turned eastward.

I noticed after that disruptive experience that I would have to walk the psychological tightrope very carefully. It was one thing to play games and another to fool around with my sanity. Narendra was the perfect teacher at this stage. He helped me negotiate the shoals of too much self-observation when I complained of feeling disassociated and provided me with just the right posture in the face of too much engagement. Everywhere and every time of day or night became appropriate for this attentive observation called meditation.

I was intrigued by Narendra's capacity for enjoying the material world. I bought him a fine cotton pullover from Bergdorf Goodman for his birthday, and he put it on immediately, laughing, "Oh, how expensive! I'll wear it with the label showing." Having forgotten the key to his studio, he would show up at our apartment early in the morning and sit with us over coffee, beaming as he showed us photographs of his new baby.

I had found what I was looking for: being intense and far away at the same time, for that perfectly characterized my relationship with Narendra. When new swamis and Tibetan rinpoches came to town, I always went to see them and came back to tell him about the experience. I went through a "shopping" phase, hungrily searching out other disciplines, eager to try everything in the great bag of Eastern goodies that was traveling through America during that crazy decade.

Our home became a way station for Taoists and Tibetans; I developed an entirely new network of friends who themselves were eagerly reaching in all directions for the final message that would put their inquiring minds at peace. For a time, it seemed that everyone I knew was uprooting and heading for India, Ceylon, and California. Itinerants bearing letters from someone I had met and spoken to vaguely at a yoga retreat appeared on my doorstep, looking for a stopover on the way to enlightenment. I attended innumerable group meditation sessions with theosophists, kabbalists, and assorted madmen. A psychiatrist at a party tried to introduce me to "chaotic meditation" by rubbing my temples; another appeared at a Waldorf-Astoria conference in Tibetan garb and played bells to an audience of astonished therapists. A theatrical friend of many years was "touched" by a local guru and suffered electrical shocks in her spine; Buddhist monks showed up at birthday gatherings on Central Park West with invitations to join them in Kyoto. They all came and went, but Narendra somehow remained. His "ordinariness" kept me from flying off the ground. His honest though testy commitment to truth kept my search for a spiritual way station from disintegrating into a fad.

Gene Arnold, an active participant in the guru grapevine, called me one day to say that I would be missing the greatest teacher of our time if I did not come to see and hear the hundred-year-old Sri Singha at a church on East Sixty-second Street the following Sunday morning. How could I resist a spiritual master reputed to be one hundred years old?

The church was filled with Sri Singha's followers, a mixed bag of Americans and dark-skinned Asian devotees. All of them were smiling blissfully, a community of absolutely contented, busy human bees whose entire life's work centered on the guru. Sri Singha, wrapped in a white turban and white robes, was seated on a raised platform. I was not particularly interested in hearing a Sufi discourse in Tamil, but when I looked into the smooth, radiant face of the tiny brown cricket-man whose nimble black eyes and unearthly smile were beckoning only me, I sat down close by. I hardly heard what he was talking about; the translator seemed to be reiterating something about "stilling the monkey mind" and was mechanically illustrating the discourse with stories about jungles in Southeast Asia, where the naked Sri Singha had performed miracles for aboriginal villagers. None of it was important, only the rising lump in my throat each time I looked into the old man's face.

At the end of the discourse, Sri Singha began chanting Sufi

hymns in a sweet piping cricket's chirp. The entire audience was rapt; some were crying unashamedly. As the meeting dispersed, Gene rushed over to me, his angelic blue eyes full of mystic tears, his face flushed and ecstatic. "Come on out to my house with Sri Singha and his party. I'll get you a lift."

Disoriented, I followed a group of people I barely knew outside into the warm, noisy street. New York had been transformed by Sri Singha's chanting; automobiles and gray garbage pails and soot had all been infused by the ancient Sufi's blessed presence. Two tall American devotees hustled the master into a waiting car. The cluster of brown disciples and a heavy woman, whose folded flesh was escaping from her sari at the waist, aggressively crammed themselves in alongside him. Assuring me that they would drive me out to his house and back to the city afterward, Gene hurriedly introduced me to Philip and Sandy Weisman. Philip, who didn't look too happy about it, laconically waved me into the back seat. Sandy was friendly but visibly troubled.

We made small talk all the way up to Rye. The two of them were writers, with long experience on the "spiritual scene." I had heard of their books, and, of course, they hadn't heard of mine. Philip had traveled far across the world doing research for his work on Sufism. His silent, morose exterior held me back from prodding him about his enviable experiences. He had actually camped in the desert with the guardians of the innermost secrets of Sufi mysticism, but he wasn't saying a word. Sandy talked almost apologetically about her on-again-off-again interest in Judaism. She considered herself "a kind of disciple of Nissan Rosenberg, the singing Hasidic rabbi." I had vaguely heard of Rosenberg, but wasn't interested in pursuing the subject. My brain was still too full of Sri Singha's hypnotic chanting; I could barely focus on Sandy's vulnerable, freckled face.

Gene Arnold's pebbled driveway was full of VW buses and mandala-stickered station wagons. We entered the big white house through the kitchen, where six dark women in saris were preparing pasty rice and vats of vegetables. The entire house smelled of turmeric and incense. People lined the hallways and stairs leading into the vast, open living room. Gene and his wife had removed all the furniture and all the pictures of other gurus in deference to Sri Singha, whose strict Moslem creed forbade the reproduction of human images. Seated on a white daybed above us, the old master gazed rapidly around the room, stopping at each face as if to absorb the very essence of its owner. Philip and Sandy and I were ushered around the fifty or so American Sufis seated on the shiny floor. Not unnoticed by Master Singha, we tucked ourselves into position one row from the back wall, where the empty square that had until yesterday borne a giant photograph of the Indian saint Sri Rama-krishna now formed a mystic frame encompassing nothing but space.

The session was open to questions, which the translator quickly sent back to the smiling master. Philip asked about the Zikkr, which, I learned for the first time, was the Sufi mantra believed by the faithful to connect man and God. Moslem mystics repeat the saying: *La ilaha Il Allahoo* (There is nothing other than You. You are Allah). Sri Singha was more interested in Philip, however, than in Philip's problems with his Zikkr.

"Guru wishes to know what work the gentleman does," repeated the translator phlegmatically. The alert cricket-man peered over the crowd with a beatific smile. I caught his eye, and he nodded, again acknowledging my being. Sandy pinched me in the ribs so hard I nearly cried out.

"A writer!" shouted the translator consecutively with Singha's delighted Tamil reply. "Something for all the writers in the room," announced the now interested translator. With that, the old master reached into his robes and removed three oranges. In three light-ning-quick movements, he tossed one to Philip, one to Sandy, and one to me. A satisfied murmur escaped from the crowd on the floor around us. Again the old man nodded in my direction.

"Singha wishes you to come and sit up front," said the translator.

Hands pushed and prodded me from every side. An immediate path opened between the raised daybed and myself. I rose with great embarrassment at the display that I, a stranger to Sufism, was making in front of all these knowledgeable adepts and walked to the front of the gathering. Philip looked at me sourly as I picked my way over his long legs.

"Sit," said the translator in English. Singha was gesturing with his perfect, chocolate-colored hands and simultaneously urging me to sit in whistling Tamil.

"Guru wishes to know your question," said the translator, gazing at me from behind thick, tortoiseshell glasses. He had a magnificent shock of black hair, I noticed, and was wearing a very expensive Scottish tweed jacket.

"I have . . . no . . . no question," I stuttered.

The old man threw back his head with delight and laughed. I almost expected the translator to laugh in consecutive translation; instead, he hung back respectfully, waiting for the master to reply.

"Very good, very good — no questions," came the approving answer. "I will sing to you, child of my eyes, dear one, child of radiance. I will sing."

I had always considered myself a bad subject for hypnosis, but Sri Singha's chanting captured me entirely. For three days after our meeting, I could barely eat, sleep, or work. Sufi mystics, I later learned, establish a link with their students by capturing their hearts through music and dancing. Unarmed and unforewarned, I had wandered into a Sufi camp ready for the taking.

From within my trance I forced myself to walk up and down Lexington Avenue, stopping at various restaurants along the way and drinking hot black coffee whenever I felt myself drifting off. My senses were entirely focused on Sri Singha; every time I closed my eyes I saw his loving cricket-face; day and night I heard his lilting song. It was worse than falling in love at twelve. Part of me never wanted to see him again; the other part threatened to die if I didn't arrange another meeting. At last the numbness melted into pure exhaustion. On the fourth day I could not lift myself out of bed. Fifteen hours later I awoke refreshed, myself again, as if nothing had happened.

Narendra laughed harshly when I related the episode to him. "It's amusing to see how all your American rationality disappears with your first glimpse of a singing Tamil Mohammedan," he said, then dropped the subject. Narendra's unsympathetic response only goaded me to return to the Sufis again to see for myself whether I had indeed been duped. This time I took along Noah and a clever redhead from one of my Eastern philosophy courses at NYU. Jennie had studied yoga intensively in Holland. Though only in her mid-twenties, she was no stranger to the many Eastern disciplines we had been discussing that semester. Besides, she had a refreshing sense of humor and a gift for caricature that could liberate me from the danger of falling into a trance again. We borrowed a friend's oversized Pontiac and, at six o'clock on a Saturday morning, drove to Baltimore, the location of Sri Singha's American ashram.

The sprawling Tudor-style mansion housing the ashram stood on a residential street lined with stately pin oaks. It was fall, and the sidewalks and porch were blanketed by flame-colored leaves. Above the front door lintel hung an unobtrusive sign: SRI SINGHA ABODE. The first floor had been converted into a meeting room of sorts; its drab pews had probably been salvaged from an old church. To the left of the meeting hall was a modest-sized communal kitchen, whose shelves were neatly stacked with jars of herbs and spices. The once grand staircase in the entrance hall wound all the way up to an open gallery, which gave onto a series of rooms. Sri Singha, we were told, would be receiving guests in his private chamber in half an hour.

Less than half an hour had gone by when a plump, cheerful woman introduced herself to us as "the bookkeeper" and led us upstairs into Sri Singha's bedroom. About twenty people were gathered at the foot of the bed where the old man sat. I shuddered at the display of open-mouthed obeisance I saw on the faces around me. These people were not pimply runaways searching for soup and Daddy; most of them were in their thirties, professionals of one sort or another — physicists, doctors, engineers, mathematicians. Others were successful artists, dancers, television directors. As we drank coffee earlier that morning, one man had confessed to me quite uninhibitedly that he had met God in the person of Sri Singha. Another, a mathematician who said he no longer believed in the efficacy of science, had left his lucrative government job to join the Sri Singha Abode permanently. Were they all hypnotized? I wondered. Sri Singha did not hesitate to present himself as an avatar, yet his discourse that day in Baltimore reminded me of the sectarian carping that passed for Sabbath sermons in my parents' synagogue.

I had lately detected the shrill note of exclusivity in many such discourses. Remarks like "Meditation is maditation" and interguru badmouthing were not uncommon at the tail end of the mad rush toward spirituality. The invisible split in the mystics' camps was quickly widening into a chasm during the desperate search for American disciples that marked the early nineteen seventies. Those who had attended the discourses and meditation sessions of almost every representative master then passing through began to wonder if any valid tradition even existed. So much subtle and not-so-subtle abuse went flying around our heads, so many slick brochures and fund-raising letters cluttered our mailboxes, that many, finding themselves spiritually stuffed, exchanged meditation for jogging.

"Guru asks if the young lady has read the *Puranas*," said the translator.

All heads turned in my direction. Guru obviously had me at the end of his pointed stick.

"Not all, but I'm acquainted with them."

"Sri Singha sees that the young lady is interested in Brahmanism. Does she know that in their ritual worship the *Puranas* prescribe the drinking of blood and cow urine?"

Two very specific implications had been presented to me: one, that Sri Singha could "see" clairvoyantly into my mind and inclinations, and two, that I ignorantly observed the religious customs of the ancient Hindus because I did yoga exercises and studied with a Brahman teacher. When I didn't answer, the old man repeated his question more insistently in Tamil, urging the translator to repeat it to me. For the first time in our brief acquaintance, Sri Singha was frowning. In fact, the entire exchange had begun to echo the intolerant ring of less saintly masters.

I wriggled uncomfortably in my seat on the floor.

"I study Vedanta," I replied feebly, somewhat beside the point.

The old man quickly rejoindered, the translation now coming consecutively with much heat.

"Does the young lady wish to see with her own eyes the blood-drinking, orgiastic feasts of the Brahmanists in South India? Sri Singha is now, at this moment, inviting her to accompany him back to India next week. He wishes to take her with him so that she can see with her own eyes the sexual orgies of so-called yogis. Has the young lady heard of tantra?" The interrogation went on.

"I have read tantric texts in the course of my studies, but —"

"If you were not a woman, Sri Singha says he would have read out loud to you from the *Puranas* the explicit sexual rituals indulged in by these 'holy men.' "

"I don't see what this has to do with the Vedanta, which is, after all, a philosophy and not a religious practice."

"Tell the young lady that she is deluded, the guru says. Tell her that I mean what I say about inviting her to come with me to India. We will provide the airplane ticket. Does she wish to come?"

I could feel the devotees jostling expectantly around me.

"He means it. He never asks anyone to come with him unless he means it," whispered a barefoot scholar in a white cotton djellaba. The challenge had been thrown, but I did not have the courage to pursue it.

"I can't . . . I can't leave my work," I said, eliciting groans of disgust from my neighbors on the floor.

Sri Singha's interrogation stopped abruptly. He wrapped one shoulder more snugly into his fringed white shawl, adjusted his turban, and turning his gaze away from me, called out sharply in English: "Lunch!"

Sandy Weisman and I had exchanged telephone numbers, but I never really expected to hear from her again. Seven months after my trip to Baltimore, however, she called and, breathily apologizing for her distracted behavior during our last meeting, invited me to spend an evening with Rabbi Nissan Rosenberg. It was spring, and I had already entered into a diffident relationship with Zen. Nothing was further from my mind than Hasidic ecstasy. It was only simple courtesy, I told myself, that had brought me to the basement on the Upper West Side that housed Nissan Rosenberg's gathering.

The stark room was filled with very young hippie Hasidim, some barefoot girls, one or two Sufis in Islamic costume, and no sign of Sandy. Loving chaos prevailed everywhere: youngsters hugging and kissing, befeathered boys tuning up exotic stringed instruments, and, finally, the rabbi, Nissan himself, bursting through the door late, guitar in hand, fingers shaped into an outdated V-for-victory salute. (Was he so outmoded as to be unaware of its Nixon associations?)

"Greetings, little holy brothers and sisters," he shouted, flashing a warm, toothy, red-faced grin. Had the Baal Shem Tov been like this? Had he, too, surrounded himself with such a motley, ragtag bunch of nomads? Perhaps that was why the studious Vilna Gaon refused to have anything to do with him. And why today's establishment rabbis always sneered when Rosenberg's name came up.

A boy in a checkered shirt and peaked cap tinkered with two speakers and a tape recorder at the far end of the basement. There was one ear-splitting squawk from the equipment and, without further introduction, Nissan launched into his disjointed, inspired Hasidic lesson.

"Approaching Mount Sinai required preparation for three days before . . . there are no boundaries dividing people from that place."

I craned my neck, looking for Sandy. Still not there. Feeling cheated, I tried to concentrate on what Nissan was saying.

"The Torah says only so much in teaching man how to connect with God. One half in black and white, and the other half, unknown, requires intensive, devout prayer . . . David's prayers over the five Books of Moses resulted in the Psalms. The unrevealed Torah requires prayer in order to get behind its literal laws. Searching beyond the written words of the Torah is one's manner of connecting oneself to God . . . returning one's portion to God. He, in exchange, returns His portion. You can only reach this level of exchange with God through preparation. Those who search only for the highest, most Absolute light reach a high level of preparation — like Rabbi Akiva. They taste not only the words and letters of the Torah, but much more deeply than this . . ."

The talk spilled out in an unrehearsed torrent whose inner meanings were later to become very familiar to me — words like "preparation," "unrevealed Torah," even "prayer," were to assume undreamed-of significance in my life. But that night Nissan only drew a blank with me. I was bored and restless, curious about the gypsy folk who were swaying with their eyes shut as Nissan talked. I also was annoyed with Sandy, who at that moment was sliding unobtrusively into a seat near the entrance.

Nissan paused, closed his eyes, and swayed as he savored his own words. Suddenly he broke into a wild grin and spontaneously burst into song. The boy in the checkered shirt signaled the audience to join in; three other hippie Hasidim jumped up from their seats and began clearing the chairs from the floor. Soon everyone was dancing. A trio of ragged young girls linked arms and beat out a hora with their feet at the center of a larger circle formed by the men. Accompanied now by a ponytailed, heavily moustached guitarist with a feather in his cap, Nissan played, stamped his feet, and sang still louder and faster, urging his circling followers into a frenzy of chanting and singing. Some of them closed their eyes; others stepped back, allowing the inspired ones more space, clapping their hands and swaying their bodies in ecstasy. A few older guests forgot their self-conscious dignity and joined the whooping, leaping inner circle. Sandy waved me into the dance, but I held back, leaning against the wall, a tourist. Was I witnessing a Jewish version of the *bhakti* that was now impelling Sri Chaitanya's twentieth-century followers to dance in front of Saks Fifth Avenue, chanting "Hare Krishna"? Nissan appeared to be doing his best to provide his little, holy Jewish brothers and sisters with the opportunity to dress their need for ecstasy in skullcaps and fringes. Indeed, he had dedicated his life to drawing them back into the Jewish fold by using the same exotic ritual gestures that had taken them away. Nissan's naiveté endeared him to me. He was distracted, chaotic; when we spoke, he gazed ahead of our conversation in another direction, but I believed him to be sincere.

On my second visit to the same Upper West Side basement, I found a sparse audience and a more somber, reflective mood. Nissan had decided to organize his talk — as far as he could organize anything — around the esoteric nature of the Jewish holidays.

"God gives us a taste of His plan when we suffer. When we cry and are angry at Him, He gives us a taste of what He really wants of us . . .

"Why Death? God gives Pesach [Passover] to counteract it. Pesach is freedom, the revival of the dead, spring. God opens the gates of heaven on Passover . . .

"Why does the Torah prohibit a crippled priest from serving in the Temple? God gives us Shevuoth as the answer, a taste of how complete we can be, how perfect . . .

" 'Why did I not complete my life's deeds?' Blowing the shofar on Rosh Hashana shows that we have always been where we were supposed to be.

"Yom Kippur means leaving everything behind, giving up the world and serving God . . .

"In answer to the fact that there is no guarantee of permanency and perfection, God gives us Succoth, His own guarantee that He will always be where we are . . .

"Shabbat is the acceptance of the world with detachment because we are on such a high plane of consciousness.

"Mount Sinai is a sign of the real existence of the world; the holiness of utmost existence. The knower of One God is he who has directly heard the voice on Mount Sinai . . . The Torah is words on the level of the mundane world and letters that give the relation of God to man . . . Utmost existence allows man to taste what is beyond existence . . ."

Nissan delivered his litany with much swaying, pausing, and head-shaking. Yet none of its pieces seemed glued together. Like his movements, his perpetual lateness, and his distracted conversation, Nissan's profound kabbalistic seeds would never successfully take root. Only the sincerity of his dancing and singing, his touching attempt to pump ecstasy into our jaded hearts, kept Nissan's brand of mysticism from alienating me from Judaism once and for all. That, and three further events in which our paths crossed again.

One of Noah's medical colleagues, a likable Yiddishist with a penchant for Jewish culture, invited us to hear Nissan sing at a Progressive synagogue. Nissan Rosenberg was for a while, the "show Hasid" among the Jewish haute bourgeoisie of New York's Upper West Side. Though only six or eight blocks from his ratty basement meeting place, the synagogue in which Nissan was scheduled to appear that Saturday night was centuries distant. For the first time since I had begun attending such "spiritual" gatherings, I noticed that the audience was dressed in suits, ties, jewelry, furs — not a sandal, bead, or feather in sight. After greeting a few acquaintances, Noah and I took seats in a pew to the left of the vast podium. There were embossed Oriental carpets strewn on the highly polished wooden floors, and fine oak beams held up the spacious, well-appointed structure. I felt terribly out of place. The large brass menorah before the sanctuary housing the Torah scrolls did nothing to assure me that I was not, in fact, in a Unitarian church. Well-heeled synagogues always make me feel pugnacious and a little sick to my stomach. Curled under my grandfather's prayer shawl as a child, I used to fly through the worlds within worlds on the wings of Ofanim in a poor little Brooklyn house that doubled as a synagogue for pious old men. But I have grown tense and suspicious in modern synagogues ever since I heard my first organ recital rendition of the Friday night prayers in a Reform cathedral in suburban New Jersey during a ghastly group bat Mitzvah, where ten pubescent girls in white and pink organdy were given miniature Torah scrolls by a Mephistophelean rabbi and Sabbath worshipers gathered immediately afterward for a huge, drunken, initiation orgy. My pugnacity I attribute to being unceremoniously tossed out of two Kol Nidre services on the eve of Yom Kippur because I had not bought a ticket.

With such a case history, it was no surprise, then, that my hands turned clammy and my stomach, hollow, the moment I heard the dissatisfied murmuring of the jeweled crowd around me. Nissan, as usual, was over an hour late, and the ladies and gentlemen who had no doubt paid him handsomely to entertain — and simultaneously connect them with their "Jewish heritage" — were fuming. I felt personally responsible, as if some unspoken force were blaming me for Nissan's outrageous lateness; every raised eyebrow demanded that I explain the typically "uncivilized" behavior of the Hasidim whose blood ran in my veins.

Nissan finally arrived, and his concert was a success. His poignant Hebrew songs melted ever the hardest rationalist hearts among the Jewish Progressives. Those who had complained the loudest about the typically "uncouth" behavior of Rosenberg's bunch were the first to snake through the aisles with his ragtag boys; huffy matrons removed their gloves and clapped their hands with the same uninhibited enthusiasm as the barefoot girls now swaying alongside them. There was no question about it: Rosenberg had a talent for bringing Jews together in song and dance.

My next encounter with Nissan Rosenberg took place on the street in front of Yeshiva University at midnight. I had accompanied his band of followers to a concert there in the hope of finding a greater sympathy toward mysticism among traditional Jews. The dancing was wilder, the room hotter and more cramped, the participants more casually dressed, but the feelings I left with were not much different from those following my confrontation with the Progressives. Though Orthodox, Nissan's yeshiva audience exhibited no comprehension of why, and what, they were observing. What's more, it was clear to me that they lacked the social refinement of the Buddhists with whom I had meditated and the profound devotion of the Hindus I had come to know through Narendra.

"Why do you bother?" I asked Nissan, as we headed for his station wagon and the tightly crammed ride downtown.

"They are my little Yiddishe souls," Nissan replied, his enveloping smile signaling an end to the discussion.

"What do you mean, *your* Yiddish souls?" I persisted. "Who appointed you?"

Nissan stopped in his tracks and handed his guitar to his nearest disciple, a charismatic, black-bearded young man in a beret.

"If I don't get them back from the swamilas and the yogilas, who will? And then there won't be any Yiddelach left to greet the Meshiach when he comes!" Nissan shouted, flailing both hands at the impassive moon above us.

"What does it matter anyhow? If the Jews go to swamis and yogis to find God, it means that the rabbis haven't succeeded as well in introducing Him to them. It doesn't make any difference how you get to Him anyway . . ."

"Oh, but it makes a big difference, a big, big difference!" Nissan wagged his forefinger at me, his silver beard spreading like a peacock's tail across his massive chest. "You don't see the rabbis running around India gathering little Hindulach and converting them to Judaism. How many Yiddelach do you think are following the holy swamis — God forbid I should cast aspersions on them — in America? Sixty percent of their flock is Jewish! Do you hear that, Jewish!" Nissan screamed, raising his finger threateningly close to my face.

"Oy, *Gott in himmel!*" he exclaimed, again raising his head heavenward. "What should we do, lose them entirely? There weren't enough little Yiddelach wiped out in the crematoriums? What do they want from us? How many are we, hundreds of millions maybe, like the Arabs? Have we so many to spare that we should give them away to the Hindus and the Tibetans? Tell me!" he cried.

"Maybe you don't want me to ride home with you, Nissan. I'll take a taxi," I said quietly. "I just can't go along with your elitism."

"Of course he won't let you take a taxi home," interceded the handsome disciple as Nissan stalked off ahead. "Come on, he always gets excited like that when anyone has this discussion with him. He's a great friend of Swami Ananda and Sheik Ali, and Samdup Rinpoche, you know. And it hurts him like hell when he sees all those Jewish followers of foreign disciplines."

Though unconvinced of the necessity to retrieve the Jewish souls from their Eastern diaspora, I rode home with Nissan in silence. He insisted that the driver drop me off at my door, and he sprang out of his privileged rabbinical seat up front to plant a forgiving kiss on my cheek as we parted.

I saw him again in Jerusalem in 1974, on the day following the first and most deadly summer bombing of Zion Square. Still sick and miserable over the carnage and numb at the thought of being alive after strolling there invulnerably almost every day, Noah and I found ourselves walking with the crowds to Nissan's concert on Mount Zion. The streets were crawling with army vehicles; soldiers in full battle dress patrolled every corner, shouting into portable wireless sets. A long, dark, uphill trek led us into the lighted square at the heart of the Diaspora Yeshiva. The courtyard was packed — standing room only, squatting room on the cold, stone floor. Hippies, American tourists, white-haired men sporting lanyards and cowboy buckles, Israeli teen-agers, and black-frocked Hasidim of every variety elbowed each other for space near the elevated platform. The inevitable barefoot girls dangled their legs from the ancient parapets above the square; recently "returned" Jewish women in Indian garb held babies in slings across their chests, balancing themselves precariously at either edge of the platform where the Mount Zion Band members (their husbands) now arranged their electronic instruments. Some of them still wore the wooden Hindu rosaries of their discarded yoga days.

The Jerusalem sky was filled with a billion dazzling stars.

Nissan arrived an hour late; here, too, he whipped the gathered crowd into a frenzy of dance and song. Tourists and hippies and Orthodox Hasidim joined arms in defiant celebration of their Jewishness; jumping up and down, they shouted their broken hearts out against the electrified strains of the Psalms in folk-rock English. Everyone was sweating and panting and crying and laughing crazily. It became contagious. Even the manicured matrons were dancing. For the first time since I had begun attending Nissan's concerts, I found myself out of my seat and jumping up and down a little, too — jumping on Mount Zion for the dead of Zion Square, shouting the Psalms for the Jewish dead. *"God gives us a taste of His plan when we suffer,"* Nissan had said. Were those killed the day before suffering for Him? For Nissan's Pesach, which would revive them when the Messiah came and recalled all his Yiddelach from the yogis and swamis?

"Why does the Torah prohibit a crippled priest from serving in the Temple?" Nissan had asked metaphorically. Were those maimed by the terrorists' bomb being given a taste of Nissan's Shevuoth, *of how complete we can be, how perfect?* Why all this anthropomorphic rationale for suffering? Why couldn't we just leave it alone and accept it, like the Buddhists?

Still jumping in place, I resolved to corner Nissan after the concert and force him to answer me without metaphors. Why did the Jews, even the mystics, have to apologize for God? But I never did get to see him. Nissan merely dissolved into a crowd of loyal followers and swayed off into the Jerusalem night.

On Yom Kippur, in his crowded New York synagogue, after flashing me a heroic smile of recognition and a V-for-victory salute, he again dissolved into the mob of disciples.

By Simchat Torah, Nissan didn't recognize me at all.

I had tasted enough of ecstasy and was now ready for the cold light of pure philosophical discourse. Convinced that reasoning, rather than dancing, would bring me closer to Truth, I attended a series of talks by H. J. Shastri, the eminent Indian spiritual iconoclast. Shastri's audience consisted of a number of reputable scientists, artists, and assorted academics. At last, I thought, I could feel at home: no adolescent love fests, no West Side snobs, no trances — only a group of dispassionate scholars determined to explore the meaning of consciousness.

For three days preceding Shastri's arrival, about fifty invited participants gathered around a conference table to be primed by his ranking disciple. During the sanest and soberest of boardroom-like meetings, where the words "God," "love," and "enlightenment" were not mentioned even once, Henry Wilkes, a prominent scientist, delivered his extended, brilliantly organized paper on the nature of consciousness. I found myself totally aware, involved, and alert during these lectures; none of the usual distractions penetrated my mental field. Yet, by the time Shastri arrived, I was in a state of hopeless despair. Wilkes had carefully and most ably constructed a picture of human functioning that allowed no room for divine or transcendent experience. His gloomy picture of consciousness demanded only perfect attention to a mechanistic, almost demonic structure whose inherent instructions not to deceive itself had no choice but to deceive itself. Since all projections of mind were part of an overall process of self-deception, the desire for the mind to know itself was also part of the grand delusion that had led humanity into its present morass of guilt, conflict, and social fragmentation.

According to Wilkes, we had to begin by understanding this process of self-deception, thereby drawing on an energy more intense than what we normally experience as thought. The only slender thread of hope he managed to inject into his entire three-day presentation was the notion that there did, however, exist a universal consciousness, on which our own floated like an abstracted bubble. This concrete reality, as opposed to individual, transitory consciousness, could be known if we transformed our limited awareness into a new map for understanding ourselves and the universe. But this process could only begin when we came to realize the innately self-deceptive structure of the human mind.

"If consciousness is always self-deceiving," I scribbled in anguish on my note pad, "then how do I know that these instructions for a new map are not merely further exquisite, even Satanic, bits of misinformation to drive me mad?" There was no way out of the Chinese labyrinth of boxes into which Wilkes had crammed us. Judging from the wrinkled discerning brows around me, I was not alone in my despair. A spark of cold comfort appeared on the second day in the form of a discussion on matter. Here at least we were on common ground. We were all experiencing the table in front of us and the solid assurance of the padded chairs under our buttocks.

Subatomic physics, said Wilkes, had revealed the dynamic nature of form. Matter could no longer be regarded as something static, but was now seen as constantly dissolving, dynamic, a continuous moving field. Neither table nor chairs nor buttocks, for that matter, were trustworthy. Having established the impermanence of matter, however, man still continued to search for the chimera of permanence, or Ultimate Reality. Here I perked up. Perhaps Wilkes was hinting that the physicists, after finally locating the Ultimate Reality, had appointed him to reveal it to this distinguished gathering in New York — a scientific (and appropriately twentieth-century) version of the theophanic Revelation at Sinai. Yet the most he could deliver was the notion that matter shades off into the unknown, beyond the reaches of space and time. Like thought, or consciousness itself, matter, too, was continually dissolving according to pattern. Perhaps redefining Ultimate Reality would make things simpler, he postulated.

"Is consciousness," Wilkes asked provocatively, "manifesting a greater energy? Can it, when transformed into objective awareness rather than subjective thought, become *higher* energy, part of the ground on which all abstractions float? Are we not perhaps seeing only irregularities against an energy field that produces matter and consciousness between which there is no gap? Is our consciousness not merely content that is foolishly trying to analyze itself with tools not designed for the job? Like trying to see your own eyes. Since what it is and what it knows are identical, consciousness is therefore simultaneously information *and* existence. So, a new form of order, deeper than consciousness, must break through this mechanical process we have identified as thought, and that new awareness we call insight.

"The consciousness of mankind is one, although it is — with tragic results — trying to treat itself as separate. Only insight, which is nonmechanistic, unbounded by space or time, is capable of knowing this unity; only awareness is aimed at the survival of mankind."

So "insight" and "higher energy" had replaced "vision" and "God." That was all right with me. My self-deceiving consciousness had been pacified for a time.

On the final day before Shastri's much-awaited arrival, Wilkes focused his flawless intelligence on the problem of the observer and the observed. "The instructions of consciousness are fast and habitual, programmed from time immemorial not to destroy itself. How, then, can it achieve the condition of one mind? If all instructions to the mind are irrelevant, we must deal a death blow to consciousness as it now exists, using the flawed mechanism itself, since we cannot change it from without. We must inject silence into the babbling flow, not by methods or external techniques that try to seize and arrest thoughts, for there is always a time lag between fact and our cognizance of fact. Rather, when the mind sees the absolute necessity for silence, it may subdue thought. Meditation and other such techniques only counterfeit such 'high energy' awareness or the insight marking real transformation. *There is no technique for bringing the mind to order.* Only the intensity characteristic of high energy awareness may break through the superficial self-deception that marks the habitual mental process."

I was beginning to feel almost hopeful when Wilkes delivered yet another blow. "Feeling is nothing more than a product of thought, which says, 'Feeling existed here all the time and I am merely thinking about it.' Thus we are deluded by the imprint of feeling on memory. When we feel that something is missing, we are led immediately to desire, hope, and belief, which are based on the initial desire."

There was a slight pause, during which Wilkes waited for our faulty minds to overcome their time lag. I was on the verge of casting my head on the table and resigning from the fight. Belief, hope, and desire were my watchwords; what else had motivated me to come here but the feeling that such a conference would assuage my desire for belief in some Ultimate Reality that promoted the hope that there was indeed meaning to our puny existence?

Since belief, hope, and desire were all part of the vast network of self-deception I had come to identify as myself, it was now necessary to *watch* the process as it took place. Wilkes seemed indeed to be telling us to turn ourselves inside out and look at our eyes.

"Remember," he warned, "there is no *I* inside *having* or *experiencing* all the ups and downs of feeling, only consciousness in all its self-deceptive phases of material content. *I* is constructed and programmed to propagate this notion of itself. To be truly aware means to know the limitations of thought, which can only be creative not when it is generative, but rather when it is used — like the tool that it is — in dealing with the phenomenological world."

From here Wilkes led us deftly through the swamps of differing "realities." Defining reality as "things," or the content of consciousness, he advised us to regard Truth as that which is. "Whatever we think is reality — correct or incorrect; therefore reality, like thought, is limited. Actuality is that which is fact or happening. The field, or immeasurable truth, against which fact occurs cannot enter into the content of consciousness, but resides in silence. Thought is merely an echo."

The impeccably elegant Shastri was about eighty years old and had blue-tinted hair that matched his suit. He took his place at the head of the table, looking neither left nor right and acknowledging no one. With stunning alacrity, he launched into an attack on our illusory identities. Without so much as a reference to the introductory lectures, Shastri castigated us for the corrupt society in which we had chosen to live, think, and work. Urging us to change the nature of the world by working on our individually fragmented minds and hearts, he chided us for our fearfulness, our smugness, and our suicidal passion for thinking. Though many of us had never laid eyes on him before, he seemed to know us thoroughly: we were gripped by fear of the future and rumination over the past. We were marchers in an inexorable parade toward death that made the future a grim reality only because we hadn't the courage or the insight to end it by decapitating desire. Like dogs in the laboratory, we were behaviorally bound to reward and punishment.

Suddenly his cold stare came to rest at a point on the swinging doors at the rear, and he addressed the invisible presence between the doors. "What happens when the past meets the present and ends there? What would happen if you were to live only in the present, in immediate reaction, without habitual conditioning from the past?"

Like all instinctive students, we tried hard to reach for the answer that would halt the teacher's disdainful barrage. We grew increasingly embarrassed at our incompetence. Shastri, after all, knew the answer. Why, with all our Ph.D.'s and M.D.'s, didn't we? None of our answers suited him. The class, growing desperate, started guessing wildly.

"*No! No! No!*" Shastri rose, shaking his fist, shouting, spittle forming at the corners of his mouth. He shook his head furiously, then grabbed his temples in both hands, as if the effort had dislodged his head from its delicate stalk. Then he sat down and wiped his mouth with a monogrammed handkerchief.

"If you have no reaction stemming from the past, you have ended the process, liberated yourself from the accumulation of centuries, enabled yourself to see, truly *see* the world as it is, and so die to psychological time," he finished softly. Crumpled in his chair, his elegantly shod feet crossed on the floor close to his body, Shastri now appeared vulnerable, a testy old man given to fits of verbal abuse. Though he spoke later of compassion, I sensed none coming from him, only incurable displeasure at our human condition, frustration at his inability to communicate his vision reasonably to reasonable men and women, and, finally, contempt.

"Words, thought, image, all serve to differentiate between *I* and *they*. And that is the beginning of fragmentation. If this is actually realized, I can meet the present. Do you see?" he cried.

"Yes." We nodded obediently, as one.

"No, you don't see!" he screeched at us. "You don't see at all!"

Thought was generating a stomachache. My self-deceptive search for compassion had met only a well-dressed skeleton. Shastri seemed all bone, no flesh, no vital organs, no heart. I later learned that he hardly ate more than a few grains of food a day; and, when I approached him to shake his hand in the corridor, he recoiled as if I had offered him a snake. Aaron Breit, a Shastri disciple of many years, thought he was reassuring me when he said, "S. doesn't like to be touched by anyone — it's not you."

Between seminars I walked around with a splitting migraine headache. At night I tried to remain "aware" of my delusory dream life; I awoke gray-faced, choked off, and tearful.

"You are merely the victim of the brain's pursuit of pleasure and its avoidance of pain," Aaron joked on seeing my vexed face and baggy eyes as we stood together near the coffee urn on the morning of the final seminar. Try as I might, I could not make distinctions between perfect awareness and the normally skewed messages from my deceitful brain. On the night of Shastri's final assault, I lay in bed staring fixedly at the ceiling and experienced my thought flow. For a moment it seemed that I had fallen asleep, but I knew immediately that I was awake when I felt my heart cave in, as if an enormous fist had clenched inside, refusing to open and let me breathe. Sure that I was about to die, I relaxed my body and watched the process. The event was remarkable for its lack of images or words, only the vast, crushing sensation of sadness, a black hole of sadness into which I and the entire Creation had marched to our passive extinction. For a quarter of a minute in the sequential time of my bedroom life and in the timelessness of subject-object annihilation, I *was* "sadness" itself. All that remained was death.

Shastri would have been disgusted with the animal that held me back from following "sadness" into the "high energy" void. My physical heart, by unclenching and recalling me into life — which distinguished between my pillow, the room, the Creation, and myself — had forfeited the opportunity to see and be free.

I find myself sitting cross-legged on the floor of a large, bare hall smelling of pine and miso soup. Seated everywhere around me is an incongruous mix of white American faces; some wear the coffee-colored robes of Zen monks, others are draped in ponchos. A balding stockbroker in a blue blazer sits, shoeless and motionless (like the wild-haired teen-ager with the holes in his socks in front of him), beside his Sunday school wife in her cameo-pinned silk blouse. I am squeezed between Sue and Noah, our backs against a smooth wooden wall. In front of us, a chic media type is silently and efficiently arranging her equipment. The whirring of her camera is the only sound in the hall. Not even a baby's whimper (and there is a healthy sprinkling of babies and preschoolers among us) breaks the pine-scented calm. Sue's stomach gurgles with pleasure at all the food we have just consumed. She turns to me and smiles. Nobody enjoys food like Sue, my oldest friend. Everything about her is original, her art as well as the alternate life-style that she evolved as naturally as the life that evolved from the sea. Before anyone, male or female, had been "liberated," Sue was living alone in a tenement above a hero sandwich shop in an industrial district beyond NYU that was light-years away from calling itself fashionable SoHo.

We had rushed a square, snobbish sorority together at college, and Sue was accepted because she was "arty" and wore a huge artificial red flower on the cinch belt above her crinoline-based, quilted hoop skirt. I was voted in because the grade level of the sorority was as low as its beauty level was high, and a test-grubbing, academic type like me was just what they needed to keep from being suspended by the Pan-Hellenic Association.

I feel Sue's itchy sweater sleeve against my face as she shifts to a more comfortable position. She's never done a day of exercise in her life, yet she's slim and graceful. Only recently, since her visit to India, her back has gone bad. I am, as always in these meditation sessions, placid, an organic part of the floor, with my legs tucked into the familiar lotus that I have learned to endure over the past eight years as well as any Asian yogi. The other young people around me are equally comfortable. Even the gray-hairs don't seem to be suffering. Noah fortunately has the wall to rest his back on. He's been practicing hatha yoga with Narendra for nearly two years, and although it's shown some improvement, his bad back can tolerate Eastern sitting for short periods only. He props himself against the wall and gazes around the room with his pensive, all-seeing lizard slits, then past the elevated platform with its burning incense fonts, toward the glass wall, where he stops and fastens his attention for a moment on the raindrops plunking soundlessly into the lake beyond a wet silver birch tree that looks like it's bowing in at us. A rabbit hops across the white pebbles. Noah blinks once or twice, then looks at me and smiles, his face a living embodiment of his favorite jazz tune, "When Buddha Smiles."

Someone is beating a wooden gong in slow, steady time. A few of us are shaken out of our reveries; the regulars at the zendo are unmoved. Now the rapping is louder, a woody arpeggio that sends shivers down the spine. It's all so effective, this sparse Zen ritual: just a few bells and wooden castanets, a little incense, a lone tree, and a rain-soaked pebble garden are enough to stimulate the spine. It's the foreignness of it that appeals to you, I reason with myself. Remember Chuan, the frail, tiny ex-monk from Thailand, and his stories about twelve-year-old, shaven-headed boys nodding with sleep and boredom over these same enchanting bells? Just like the yeshiva, where you were stuffed into a row of folding chairs in the part-time synagogue, part-time assembly hall, bored and fidgety, stepping on Nina Quetzel's toe or singing the Hebrew morning prayers in jazz time to confuse priggish Mutzie Miller on your left and, you hoped, to get her into trouble so there'd be a break in the services and some excitement out in the lobby, where the rabbi's wife deported the "punished girls." Mutzie Miller was a math genius; now she's married to a rabbi and has eight children.

At least it smells nice in the zendo meditation hall. At the Beth Rachel Yeshiva for Girls the synagogue always smelled of tallow, old books, and the whisper of little girls' farts. The monks don't fart; they have been taught absolute control of their bodies and minds so that they may sit in uninterrupted *sesshin* for as long as four hours at a time. Even the Saturday morning prayers never lasted that long. Besides, in *shul* you could sing off-key to amuse yourself, or count ladies' hats, or stare down sullenly at fat boys your own age who surreptitiously peeked up at you in the women's section over their heads. The altar curtain at the yeshiva — I remember suddenly, as the roshi steps silently out of nowhere onto the platform and seats himself on a pillow — was always wrinkled, a washed-out mauve velveteen cloth embossed in gold with the prancing lions of the tribe of Judah.

The roshi has a shaven dome and an intelligent, witty, oddly Western air about him. Softly, he tells us that Zen Buddhism is perfectly tailored for Americans, that we are hard-working and pragmatic, and that Zen Buddhism is, too. My ears are with him, but my mind is carried away on the memory of a recurring image that broke through while I was meditating with Narendra one morning the year before. Sometimes it comes back with such alarming clarity that it makes my eyes water. There are days when only thinking of it without imagining it visually makes my right eye twitch; yet at other times I can humorously discuss it with Sue, pretending I don't believe in its symbolism.

I sit with the Zen master, waiting for the itinerant thoughts to cease. As he directs us in meditation, I wait for the buzz to fade away and the quiet stage of attention to begin. This is the hardest place, because I am somewhere between the hypnagogic state that precedes sleep and the mirage that tells me I am no longer thinking when I really am, and I go on and on in that way until I trap myself in a vortex of thought from which I can't emerge no matter how hard I try. Breathing rhythmically, I watch the thoughts run down as I would a movie going into slow motion; they get fewer, sparser, become the barest needle pricks into consciousness, and almost fade entirely when — damn — the familiar three-dimensional scene springs up full-blown before my mind's eye.

A group of young and middle-aged swamis in saffron robes are making their way in single file up a treacherous mountain pass. The peaks in the distance are frigid white; lesser peaks and valleys below are not as cold — dry greens and browns and a rocky carpet of parapets mark the course of the journey. The swamis are following an ancient white-haired master, who, although he carries a staff as a prop, is making his way nimbly (at an unnaturally fast pace for such an old man) up the mountain face. As each swami progresses to the level above him, he extends his hand back, assisting the person behind him. In this fashion, all of the swamis manage to stay only a few feet behind the master. The last swami, however, is having difficulty in crossing a narrow ravine dividing two peaks. He is obviously an inexperienced novice who is not as surefooted as the rest. At one point he stretches his hand and body so far in order to reach the swami above him that he nearly topples head first into the ravine. The older, more experienced swami above him encourages him to continue by motioning with his hand. Again and again he offers the young novice his hand, stretching it as far below him as he can without falling himself. In the meantime the swamis up ahead are gaining ground, moving higher and higher behind the old man with the staff. The young novice strains a last time, sweat beading up on his forehead, pain and frustration clouding his bright, dark eyes. Finally, he takes a deep breath and bids his brother swami to continue without him. At that moment I become frightened; my body shudders as I look into the face of the monk who has failed to keep up with his master and realize that he and I are one person . . .

A baby in the room grows restless and gurgles out loud. I open my eyes and see the roshi, a father himself, smiling in the child's direction. Suddenly he changes into the scowling rabbi of my youth, a man whose grandiose sermon was so much more important in the eyes of God than the contented gurgle of a child that he once actually interrupted his service to ask mother and child to leave. I blink, and the roshi becomes himself again. He has resumed his spiel on Buddhism for the West. Somewhere in all this there is sure to be a call for funds. Shortly, an unobtrusive disciple will appear with a bamboo basket. Many here are well dressed, probably very rich. Will they slip us envelopes on our way out the door? After all, they went so far as to provide us with free transportation all the way from New York. They must want something in return.

"Pledge!" I see the pacing sexton in his prayer shawl, his red face bobbing underneath, holding up ten fingers, the fringes of his shawl lifting to reveal the gold cuff links on his shirt, the natty beginnings of his blue suit sleeve. *"The Rothman family, one thousand dollars!"* (Odd, hearing money mentioned out loud in the synagogue on the Sabbath, the day of perfect rest and detachment from the material world.)

The roshi ends his talk ambivalently and motions for his chief monk to lead us in chanting. A curly-haired American boy rises and points to a thick, black Japanese inscription on a rice-paper wall suspended from a beam in the ceiling.

"Please let us repeat the prayer together after the roshi," he says, tucking his hands into the loose, flowing sleeves of his robe. His master turns to him, nods and smiles, then, closing his eyes, intones the chant.

As usual, I don't like reciting prayers (especially not foreign ones) out loud in the company of large groups of people I don't know. For me, prayers are silent, personal. In huge gatherings they become nothing more than background buzzing, associated always with old, hungry men who hurry the last of the Sabbath service into a garbled roar so they can get home to dinner faster. Or with spiritual "freaks" who celebrate masses of erotized love for God as "theater."

Noah and Sue are reciting loudly and fervently. They are both enjoying the quirky lilt and rhythm of the Japanese language. He likes to shout and clap when he listens to jazz; she spends her free time uninhibitedly performing as a star-spangled singer in an artists' rock group. Noah and Sue have no early memories about prayer, since neither of them was raised to perform it every morning as I was. Though they nod and bend and close their eyes now, neither knows the sanctity and the boredom of it as I do. I move my lips to be sociable. When the roshi's booming voice stops, I lower my eyes and focus on the reddish whorls in the wooden floor. My mind goes blank. My heart is calm but unresponsive to prayer in any language. It has been knocked out of me for good, I fear. Fortunately, the silence is brief; the wooden clapper bell signals the end of the meeting. Monks scramble to their feet and rush to the kitchen to resume their chores.

The roshi does not ask us for money. He invites us instead for tea and sweets. Smiling, he shakes our hands and speaks of the dharma, relating the legend of the Buddha's future rebirth in the West.

"From the moment Maitreya the Compassionate One appears," he says, "Buddhism will reign in the world for seven hundred years."

When the roshi clasps my hand, I find his dry and cold.

2

Through the Blue Gate

I N ISRAEL, it was sunny and very hot every day during the summer of 1974. Noah and I stopped before the lively café where, two years before, we had hired an English-speaking redheaded Lebanese guide to escort us around the holy places. Now that café was vacant; two Arab boys in oversized pants sat smoking lethargically at a rear table. They might have been waiters. Directly across the street, gunslinging Israeli soldiers patrolled the Citadel of David. The Old City seemed abandoned. It gets like that on lazy summer afternoons in Jerusalem, particularly after bomb scares. Even the flies had deserted the fresh-grapefruit-and-orange-drink stand flanking a souvenir shop on one side and what appeared to be a pool hall on the other. The only remnant of our past visit was the outdoor shoeshine man, a Circassian in embroidered vest, tasseled hat, voluminous puffed trousers, pointed shoes, and moustache. He sat cross-legged behind his miniature Gaudi shoeshine cathedral, waiting for no one in a half-doze.

Opposite a Christian religious bookstore we found a telephone booth. Two stray dogs with interlocking tails crisscrossed our path as we approached it. I put a telephone coin in the slot and dialed the number I had scribbled on the creased and sweaty piece of paper that had accompanied me for a week. An announcement appearing in a small blurb in the Jerusalem *Post* had caught my attention in flight: "Zen Center Opens on Mount of Olives." The venerable abbot of a Zen monastery in Japan had arrived a week before to invest his disciple, a Jerusalem-based teacher, with the revered title of roshi. The ceremony and attending company were briefly described, and, at the end of the announcement, the telephone number where further information could be obtained was given.

Noah and I were both working in Jerusalem for two months: he, at a hospital; I, interviewing Israeli women for a post–October War piece in a magazine dedicated to Jewish affairs. We had left New York reluctantly, with false cheer and a flimsy shield of confidence; it was the day after the Maalot Massacre, and threats of retaliation and renewed war hung over the El Al terminal like a thick smog.

Moreover, leaving Narendra and yoga classes behind bothered me — mostly because I was forced to admit that I was more dependent on the routine than I had thought.

When I approached Narendra with my fears about a trip at such a time, he said, "Go, there are probably good experiences awaiting you in Jerusalem. You needn't be afraid." He offered advice or opinions only reluctantly, and I had never thought of him as omniscient, but his encouragement strengthened my decision not to cancel the trip. Seeing the Zen announcement while still in the air over the Atlantic gave me further "proof" that I was not breaking the connection, that, indeed, there were teachers all over the world, a great network perhaps, who took care of seekers by some vast mental satellite.

The woman who answered the telephone after five long rings had a German accent and was terribly eager to hang up. Yes, there was a Zen center, and the roshi did teach a beginners' class, but only on Sunday afternoons at four and only to truly dedicated students, not just the curious. Yes, today *was* Sunday, but did I have any knowledge of Zen or what "sitting" entailed? I answered that I had written about various mystical disciplines, that I had sat with the New York roshi, and studied hatha yoga and meditation for more than ten years.

"Yoga has nothing to do with it," she snapped. "This is nothing like yoga. Why do you bring that up?"

I was taken aback by her outburst — and became more determined to discover who this roshi was. What was his singular method of meditation that had nothing to do with yoga — beneath which, judging from her tone, nothing in the mystic's hierarchy could be lower?

"Meditation is meditation," I retorted angrily.

"And what makes you think that writing books about the subject prepares you for sitting?"

I was amazed at the turn of the conversation — no, the *argument* — I was having with this faceless German stranger across from the Citadel of David, before a window featuring a great bronze crucifix and a set of Saint Thomas Aquinas's writings, while my husband paced in circles on the other side of the smeared plastic booth.

"Listen, you said the Sunday class was open to beginners. Let's say I'm a beginner, a foreigner who's new in Jerusalem and who wants to learn about Zen meditation. Forget the yoga, forget the books. Where do I go?"

"The House of Hussein, on the Mount of Olives. The first lesson is free. If you wish to continue on to the more advanced training, you must contribute toward a fifty-dollar membership for the year. On Tuesdays and Thursdays the roshi is in Haifa and there are no classes."

"The time, and the number of the house," I insisted, sending a mental blessing to the inefficient Jerusalem telephone operators, who hardly ever cut you off after the first five minutes.

"Four o'clock, and there is no number. Just ask for the House of Hussein, and anyone can show you where it is." She hung up.

We took a taxi to the major cross street on the Mount of Olives and got out in front of the Victoria Hospital. A donkey hitched to a broken cart gazed at us with interest. The neighborhood was otherwise deserted: To our left and below, the sun was setting in a nimbus of orange fire; to our right, the Dead Sea loomed like a blue mirage out of the parched Jordan Valley. We walked up and down the street facing the hospital several times before noticing the small cardboard sign on the screen door of an otherwise typically Arab house: ZEN MEDITATION CENTER. From the basement came the sound of a plaintive Arabic wail on the radio. A white curtain billowed out of an open window of the darkened Zen center; a wind chime played against the rafters of the front porch. Suddenly, as we were standing there, the door opened, and the roshi himself stepped out.

"Come in," he said.

We followed him into the darkened zendo. As we did, I caught a glimpse of the three of us in the hallway mirror; unconsciously, Noah and I had both bowed our heads.

"You ah ehly." The accent made the roshi's English almost unintelligible. I looked more closely at the back of his shaven head, then down at his receding shoulders; the rest of him was lost in a flowing black robe. The man I followed into the silent house was small, wiry, and tough, not particularly gracious and not particularly mean. Narendra's attitude, to be exact, and by now a familiar one. Tireless searching had disclosed that all good teachers were equally indifferent to approval or blame. They were simply, unobtrusively there; the door was open, and you could come and go as you pleased. So, too, the Jerusalem roshi, who, without formal introduction, turned toward us and said what, in his comical English, sounded like: "Take off yu shu and come insigh."

It was the Jerusalem roshi who unwittingly introduced me to the Jewish mystics. Noah and I sat with him every Sunday afternoon, absorbing his calm, drinking his green tea, taking pictures of him that somehow never came out, and finding in his discourses a singular intelligence that both of us knew we had never come across before in any teacher. Everything about the roshi was right — from his elfin face to his rubber thong sandals. He was a hidden gem waiting to be mined. When I asked him once why he had chosen to sit in isolation on the Mount of Olives, of all places, he replied, "I am in eye of storm." And he seemed to enjoy being there. Once, after a long walking meditation, I became fretful and nervous about terrorists. At that very moment the roshi opened his discourse on "the terrorist within." He had the most delicate invisible antenna that picked up just such unspoken frets. On another occasion, when Noah was suffering from a week-long stomach upset, the roshi greeted us at the door with a pot of green tea and said, "We drink tea fuhst; green tea good for stomach."

The Jerusalem roshi had only about ten regular students, three of whom we met at the beginners' class on Sundays: a bulbous woman who had to sit in a chair, a neurasthenic French boy, and a green-eyed, high-strung South African girl. There were few distractions as we meditated in the sunroom, only the swish of white curtains blowing about over our heads, an occasional chicken squawking and pecking in the dirt outside, and, when we rubbed our eyes and looked up, the misty horizon marking the point at which the Dead Sea met the sky. The imperturbable roshi emerged from his meditation, clapped the wooden castanets, rang the bell, and talked extemporaneously, uncannily, about what we had on our minds.

One day he asked Noah if he would mind giving the three other students a lift into town. It was the first time he had ever requested anything, and as it gave us a small opportunity to pay him back for all he had given us, we did it gladly. On the way out the door, the roshi took Noah and me aside and said, as if parting with us for a long time, "Because of your grandparents and great-grandparents you both get enlightenment." We thought it a curious remark, especially since he had spoken within earshot of his three permanent students, and we mulled it over in silence as we walked to the car.

It was an uncomfortable downhill trip; little was said until the fat woman had been deposited at her bus stop a mile before the center of town. Noah went out of his way to drive the South African girl to her door because she seemed depressed and lonely. The French boy lived en route to our apartment; he spoke very little

English, and Noah didn't speak French, so the conversation was sparse. Nonetheless, we learned that his name was Jean and that he studied Zen on Sundays and saw "a very special woman psychologist" during the week. When I mentioned that I was interviewing women for my article, Jean suggested that I make it a point to see his psychologist; she was a most unusual person, he promised, an Algerian who represented a rare Jewish minority, a woman most worthy of being interviewed. Intrigued, I agreed to meet him at the Algerian psychologist's home the following Thursday afternoon.

"She has no telephone," said Jean. "I must take you there."

The sun was still high over the Judean Hills when we pulled up to number 36 Bar Yohai Street the following Thursday. Madame Ariel's house stood on a hill overlooking a valley of pines, cheek by jowl with all the other unremarkable, middle-class houses characteristic of the neighborhood. Only the Mediterranean blue gate leading into her garden distinguished it from the rest, and, I noticed as we descended the uneven stone stairs, a sprawling pomegranate tree covered the entranceway. Two elegant black cats sat licking their paws on the cement ledge that divided the garden proper from a tiny sitting area.

Without knocking, Jean gently turned the front doorknob and let us in. Noah and I were instantly dazzled by the sight of ourselves in a long, gold-framed mirror reflected against a minuscule hallway, the walls of which were literally pasted over from floor to ceiling with thousands of snapshots. I barely had time to adjust my eyes to the darkness of the hall before finding a path through the maze of silk-covered sofas, gimcracks, eighteenth-century French chairs, books, antiquities, statues, and Oriental carpets that comprised Madame Ariel's mazelike entrance. Room after room led us deeper into an Arabian Nights of velvet wall tapestries, carved treasure chests, Moorish wedding dresses, and haphazard stacks of books. At the end of the labyrinth stood an enormous, old-fashioned bed with a hand-painted landscape on the headboard and a jumble of pillows. The windows to the left of the bed were draped with exotic shawls; an immense television set rested on a thick tree trunk stationed at the end of the bed, on which I could now see a figure nestled among the pillows.

"Who is that?" a weak voice called in French.

"Me, Jean, and the people I told you about," the boy timidly addressed the heap of pillows.

"Come closer. I am not well today. You've come at a bad time," said the melancholy voice in heavily accented English.

This was surely the most eccentric "psychologist" I had ever come across. When we were two feet from the figure, a hand reached out from under what I now made out to be a purple afghan and motioned me to a Moroccan leather hassock at the side of the bed. In front of it was a small table covered with thimbles, thread, and fabric. For one crazy instant I thought the voice was going to ask me to sew. But it only bade Noah sit down on what looked like a vinyl kitchen chair to the right of the hassock. Obediently we sat down, folded our hands, and awaited further instructions.

The pillows moved slightly, revealing a handsome woman in her sixties with a high forehead, a sharp nose, girlish lips, and thick, silver hair swept up in a French pompadour. Most remarkable were the mica chips for eyes that peered across the covers at me, piercing my forehead.

"Forgive me, it is the memorial day of my father's death, and my dog, my Koka, died only this morning. I am very sad," said Madame Ariel, never once removing her extraordinary gaze from my face. Then she turned to Jean and peremptorily dismissed him in French.

When he had gone, she asked Noah to show her his hands, which he politely did. When she had finished looking at them, Madame Ariel urged me to come right up to the bed so that she could see my eyes better. Jean, it was obvious, had mistaken a gypsy fortuneteller for a psychologist.

"You have the eyes of my late daughter," said Madame Ariel, holding my chin between her short, strong fingers. "What do you want?"

To this day I do not know what prompted me to answer "illumination" instead of "an interview." What made our intimate exchange even more unusual was my instinctive distaste for the woman's theatricality and my suspicions about the occult chaos surrounding her. Yet her question, so simply and directly put, must have touched the root of my search at exactly the right moment, for it was Madame Ariel who first permitted me to voice out loud what had been obscured by ten years of spiritual restlessness.

She looked at me quizzically, let go of my chin, and said, "We'll see. Come back tomorrow morning at nine and a half."

Stung by her arrogance, resentful of having been drawn out so easily, I immediately resolved never to come back. But by that time she had turned her attention to Noah, and the two of them were chatting amiably about medicine. Her father, said Madame Ariel, had been a neurosurgeon in Algiers. The Adret family had been noted Sephardic physicians for hundreds of years. Madame Ariel, I noticed, spoke very graciously to Noah, only reserving her melancholy gypsy air for me. Now I was doubly angry at myself for having been tricked by her bizarre setting and her esoteric trinkets.

When we left, it was dark outside. Noah cheerfully informed me that he had every intention of going back to visit the fascinating Madame Ariel.

"I thought you were just being polite," I snapped as we walked back to the car.

"She's weird, but she knows a lot about medicine — from her father, I guess. Anyway, I want to find out more about Near Eastern approaches to illness, herbs and things like that. I'm thinking of writing a paper. You're not the only one who writes, you know. I enjoy talking to her; it's as if she's known me forever," said Noah, cementing our relationship with Madame Ariel then and there.

I was petulant about being forced, as I saw it, to return the next day. But, unknown to myself, I must have really wanted to see her again because I am frequently stubborn and hard to move once I have fixed my mind against pursuing a new acquaintance. Madame Ariel's discerning eyes compelled me to return as much as her studied oddness put me off.

Our conversation the next morning was more acceptably "social"; Madame Ariel presented herself as a housewife and grandmother who enjoyed cooking and entertaining as much as she enjoyed working with pupils — her charming euphemism for patients. When I arrived at nine-thirty, I found her dusting the windowsills with an enormous, multicolored feather duster. Her face was glossy with perspiration, and she was breathing heavily.

"I have a congenital heart defect," she explained, pointing to her chest. "During the *hamsin* I cannot breathe."

"Have you seen a specialist?" I asked awkwardly.

Madame Ariel emitted a charming musical laugh and said, "I have never seen the end of doctors. My body is no longer my own, I have taken so much medicine. And I have been on the verge of death more times than you can imagine. But that is not important." She stopped abruptly, put her arm around me, and ushered me into what I had mockingly labeled "the mystic boudoir" during our tempestuous ride home the night before. Convinced that I had only returned because Noah (who was admiring the view from Madame Ariel's back terrace and drinking Algerian tea with her austere Russian husband) had developed a perverse attraction for Sephardic Jews, I meekly followed her inside.

Noah had lectured me into the morning hours on the color, heart, warmth, and cultural superiority of the Oriental Jews over our own Ashkenazi "ghetto mentality." Without Madame Ariel, he warned, my article would be drab. His intuition told him that it would be good for both of us to return to her home. But no amount of intuition could now assuage the uncomfortable feeling that I was being totally consumed by a woman two heads taller and (though supposedly on the verge of death) infinitely more powerful than I. Outwardly deferential, I vowed to resist her to the end.

Churning with conflict, I sat on the red vinyl kitchen chair opposite Madame Ariel on her bed, interviewing and being interviewed in turn. Two people inside me listened to Madame Ariel's dramatic stories about her life. One me called her grandiose, self-congratulatory, and given to fabricating for effect. The other person, who listened and dutifully wrote things down, was fascinated by the heroic woman who had fought in and survived two wars, taken her psychology degree when forty and a mother of four children, and worked fearlessly with the most violent and hopeless mental patients.

Human beings were her favorite subject, the meat and salt of her existence. When she was not seeing "pupils" by day, she and her lawyer husband were entertaining hordes of international guests at night. On Sabbath afternoons her tiny garden was crammed with forty or more diplomats, professors, children, writers, princesses . . .

Although she disclaimed being a "mystic," preferring to be "a woman in life," as she said, Madame Ariel proved in our deepening conversation to be efficiently educated in all the spiritual disciplines of the Far and Near East. "I never practiced any. Only from the people I have worked with, that is how I learned."

"And your system of meditation?"

"It merely came from watching my children and from living for the first four years of my life without speaking because that was the treatment for such a heart condition as mine in those days. I lived with a plaster over my mouth which only came off at mealtimes. For the rest of the day I only listened," she said mischievously, eyes glinting.

No matter that she had probably constructed an elaborate fantasy to accommodate my magazine piece; I was enjoying myself immensely. Her quaint English pronunciation and some undefinable magnetism in her presence more than compensated for her exaggerations. Moreover, I had never in my life met anyone who could be with me so completely, as if she had entered my very being and was experiencing the pulse of my life with — and through — me. What appeared on the surface as Madame Ariel's unmitigated egotism abruptly dissolved as she merged her identity with mine. For as long as we sat there together we seemed to be breathing, talking, and feeling as one. That was her great and uncanny talent, what she called her inborn ability to "listen." Shastri had instructed me to "see" and thereby "know" the Absolute. Madame Ariel, in the way of the Jewish mystics, emphasized "listening" with concentrated intention to the life inside. Unlike the other teachers I knew, she had no patience for discourse or theory. As "a woman in life," she preferred *doing* rather than *talking*. Therefore, without introduction or elucidation, even before I realized that we had moved from conversation into meditation, Madame Ariel plunked me head first into one of her "exercises."

After briefly quieting my mind and body with simple instructions in rhythmic breathing, she guided me for twenty minutes through an interior world I had never confronted in all my years of studious contemplation. Freed of all mental constraints, even of the self-conscious observer present in all previous meditation sessions, I roamed across meadows, climbed trees, traveled sunbeams, and called upon mystics long gone. For a few moments even Rama-krishna appeared on the ground in front of me, wearing the rosary of Hindu beads Sue had brought me after her first trip to India. I followed ancient sages I had never found in books and drank with them from ancient wells. Presently I stopped at the Western Wall, where someone whispered to me in Aramaic, a language I once understood but had long since forgotten. When I opened my eyes and saw myself in the red chair, I experienced a shock. "I" had plunged so deeply into the complex of thought pictures that passed for "me" that it no longer seemed possible to glue the pieces of my identity together again. My disorientation did not faze Madame Ariel, however; she sat on her bed stroking one of her cats, a huge, contented smile spreading across her face.

"Very fine. Very fine. You return tomorrow again at nine and a half?"

Not exactly sure *who* would be returning, I nodded my head.

I spent four weeks being reintroduced to my mind and reconciled with my past in the same fashion, unaware that my conversations with Madame Ariel had become indistinguishable from meditation. Amazed that I could suspend the omnipresent "witness" who lived inside without forcing images out of consciousness, I explored with meticulous care the subjective worlds within worlds. Gradually a pattern emerged: I was a checkerboard amalgam of spoiled and chauvinistic American individualism and skeptical monism, with a healthy dash of Hindu ritual thrown in for good measure. I was everything and everyone at once; I embraced universes and slithered wormlike under rocks. Angels were at my beck and call. Alternating paths lured me; I would try anything once. Competing choruses strained to catch my ear. I was everything but Jewish. Ten years of meditation had only prepared me to "listen" to the noise.

On the Sunday after my first morning with Madame Ariel, I returned alone to the zendo on the Mount of Olives. A neat, handwritten sign on the screen door informed me that the roshi had left for England and would not be back before fall. Invisible Jewish forces were at work.

In my last early morning "meditation" with Madame Ariel, I climb upon a great white and silver wheel. Suddenly the wheel turns color; now green outside and purple inside, it develops flaming orange spokes and a jewel-encrusted hub. It pulsates from the middle and breathes as it rotates. I know that it is Ezekiel's wheel, with its huge white wings and its host of faceless angels gazing over the top, and I jump on fearlessly, no longer a novice afraid to leap the space of the ravine. I am absorbed in the whiteness of the wheel, which rotates and turns silver as it moves simultaneously inward toward the center and outward toward the world. The wheel changes from white to rainbow color; it is jewel-encrusted and then pure white again as it turns. Clutching its outer rings, I leap to the center. Madame Ariel intervenes. "Open your eyes." And I begin to weep so hard that I feel I will never stop. We are sitting on garden chairs under the pomegranate tree; the perfume of tiny white jasmine flowers pervades the air. A man on the street stops, peers in at us over the blue gate, and says something very quickly in Hebrew.

"I'm sorry, I don't understand," says Madame Ariel.

The man, whose face is gentle, wears a light blue skullcap and carries a briefcase. He leans in closer over the gate and repeats in English: "This reminds me of the days of the prophecies." Then he simply smiles and walks on.

Later that day, at the airport on my way to Paris, I am compelled on a whim to buy a *mezuzah*. I walk over to the duty-free shop and immediately find what I am looking for. The woman shows me a pink-gold Sephardic scroll containing a parchment incribed with one of the names of God. It is six years since my first kabbalistic experiment on the dining room floor. I fear that my contact with Madame Ariel has made me superstitious, but the delicate Oriental beauty of the talisman appeals to me. On takeoff I ask Noah to put it on for me underneath the wooden rosary that I have never removed since Sue brought it back from India. As he clasps the *mezuzah* closed around my neck, the rosary suddenly bursts, all the beads scattering wildly, irretrievably, under the seats of the airplane and through the aisles.

When I arrive home, I find that my proposal for a book about Tagore has been rejected. Months later I meet with an editor of a large publishing house who expresses interest in a book about Jewish mysticism. To research the subject properly I must return to Jerasalem in the spring. Reluctantly, I embark on a new pilgrimage.

Madame Ariel was my first link in the secret network of kabbalists. Working with her gave me easy access to the world of the Jewish mystics from then on. Narendra had freed me of my spiritual naiveté; Madame Ariel freed me of spiritual prejudice. Her little garden encompassed all. Once I had opened my own psychological windows, I felt that nothing would ever again remain hidden from me. I even discovered Jewish mystics in New York, and their language was no longer obscure. I continued meditating with Narendra one day a week and spent the rest of my time reacquainting myself with Hebrew texts. Surprisingly, several Kabbalah classes were being held throughout the city, and I sought them out in the hope of recreating my experience in Jerusalem. What I had found intuitively now had to be corroborated by tradition.

In an upper-story living room of a small two-family house in Brooklyn, I learned for the first time of the existence of a kabbalistic cosmology. The class consisted of a mixed group of young men and women, some like Nissan Rosenberg's "returned" hippie Jews, but older and more serious — though their sidelocks were recent additions to beards grown in India. Only the women hadn't changed; like the yeshiva girls of my childhood, they wore head-scarves and talked only of marriage and new babies as they gathered on an ancient sofa with popping springs. The women reminded me of the Beth Rachel School for Girls; they were as unfashionable as the heavy green wool sofa that scratched at my legs, placid and ornamental, like the purple bas-relief throne reserved for their teacher, a young Breslover Hasid named Reuben Gold.

The most liberal and therefore most suspect of Hasidic groups, the Breslovers had braved the jeers of the establishment and opened their classes to women. It was mainly for this reason that so many secular Jews were gathering at their open doors. Their founder, Rebbe Nachman of Breslov, a great-grandson of the Baal Shem Tov, was known for his free and joyful teaching, his acceptance of all who wished to learn his way of meditation. Though they are called the dead Hasidim because no disciple has ever been able to fill Rebbe Nachman's place since his death more than a hundred and fifty years ago, the younger American Breslover Hasidim try to maintain the liberal mystic ideals of the master.

Reuben Gold was then developing a reputation among seekers in the Hasidic underground. A heavyset scholar in his thirties, he entered the room, making sure to greet everyone with a personal nod and a smile. Wearing the inevitable skullcap and heavy glasses of the yeshiva boys I had known throughout my childhood, Gold, I saw immediately, would never make a splash as a guru. He possessed none of Nissan Rosenberg's flamboyant charm and displayed no inclination to sing or chant us into religious ecstasy. With the smell of cooking chicken wafting in over his shoulder from the doorless kitchen, Reuben Gold soberly opened a big black book and peered silently at the Aramaic text. The class waited with suspended breath as he began reading aloud and translating for us into English. At first he seemed tight and uninspired, but gradually, with the encouragement of sighs and approving murmurs from the audience, he gathered courage and began interpreting the text with great fervor. I had come during the third week of an extended discussion of the mystics' version of the creation of the world. The name of the text was therefore unknown to me, but that didn't matter, for within five minutes Gold had developed a recognizably Oriental cosmology. In the ironical context of familiar chicken smells, Orthodox headscarves, and unseemly furniture, an "Eastern" Jewish mysticism appeared to be emerging out of Brooklyn. The hardest part lay in readjusting to its earthy, dualistic metaphors and its historical God. But now that I was no longer alienated by its "religious" mold and its scriptural tone, I could immerse myself as comfortably in "the Ancient of Days" as I once had in Narendra's "Brahma."

Gold explained how the Jewish God is both "here and not here" at the same time, and how He constricted Himself in order to create the world. No matter that God was still a "He," there were hints in the discourse of a feminine presence to come. First, however, we were to understand that by constricting His limitless being into limited form, God had created a vacuum. This constriction, called *tzimtzum* in Hebrew, resulted in a process of emanation during which God then divided Himself into a series of ten "vessels," which, because they were material and could not contain the Infinite, overflowed. It is these vessels and their overflow that comprise the created worlds and, with them, the divine attributes.

"Man's obligation, in response to God's compassionate constriction of Himself, is to refine his own material vessel by living a spiritual life, ascending to the higher worlds, and knowing God through the vehicle of Torah. In the Creation, God set the stage upon which to enact His goodness and upon which we enact our lives, recognize Him through the agency of our free will, and receive 'punishment' and 'reward' according to our actions."

Mentally translating Gold's kabbalism into Narendra's more familiar vedantic terms, I arrived at: the "play" of Brahma, or the apparent limitation of the limitless; man's instinctive search for his source through knowledge of the physical world, self-exploration, and expansion of consciousness; and the notion of karmic "reward" and "punishment" as the inexorable result of human action. The kabbalists, too, injected the image of play into a kind of hide-and-seek version of God's apparent concealment and man's effort to find, and serve, Him.

"A king needs a kingdom," said Gold, anthropomorphizing the need of the omniscient Knower to be known and recognized by its self-created offspring. "The way to the King appears when man, in imitation of the divine attributes, becomes perfect and thereby merges with the Infinite. As limited physical vehicles, we cannot understand the process and purpose of creation. Only by literally merging our will with God's can we attain perfect understanding." Here was the doctrine of "egolessness" that formed the heart of all mystical practice.

"To look at the universe and comprehend it through God's eyes, as it were, Jews have the Torah, their most accessible path to mystical experience. Since we are created in the divine image, that is, in imitation of the attributes that are themselves perfect and limitless, we too must 'constrict' our existence and aim it toward God by contemplating the Torah, the living manifestation of the divine will, the physical, psychological, and spiritual means for the Jew's enlightenment.

"God's will manifested itself in ten fiery spheres that, to us, represent His ability 'from a distance,' so to speak. Since divine will and ability are interwoven, we cannot know where one leaves off and the other begins. God's self-constriction of will resulted in *tzimtzum*, the first of the divine paradoxes delineated by mystics like Isaac Luria, Moses Cordovero, and Moses Luzzatto. Another paradox exists in the spiritual contradiction between God's omniscience and man's free will, a question that provides a purpose for human existence to begin with and to physical choice, or action in the world. In other words, we are presented with the stage and the sets; we adopt our roles — freely, to a certain extent — and, with our divinely inherited will, we choose perfection.

"*Tzimtzum*," Gold continued, "is God's direct supervision, His action in our constricted physical world. That is why everything here is for the good, no matter how 'evil' it appears. You must believe that everything literally happening in the universe is under the direct supervision of God and not within a general, overall pattern of events. Everything in the plan must occur. Only time is subject to change — depending on the spiritual activities of the Jewish people."

Here I resisted the impulse to raise my hand and interrupt Gold's discourse. Why had he suddenly interjected history, and why specifically a reference to the Jewish people, when all along he had been talking so eloquently about humanity? But I was an interloper in his world, so I decided to swallow my question until he had finished. Then I might catch him alone, in a corner somewhere, away from the innocent eyes of the female believers who were nodding contentedly at his every word. Perhaps, I reasoned with myself, I had not caught the underlying subtlety of the symbol. After all, if God could "constrict" Himself, the "Jewish people" could be a reflection of His activities here on earth. Surely, He'd used them for thousands of years to prove a point.

Licking his finger and turning a page, Reuben Gold said, "We human beings and our world were given just enough time to perfect ourselves as God's plan has determined. And justice is meted out accordingly. Since we are bound by matter and time, we observe only the outer shell of things — matter, as conforming to time. The inner essence of all material things, however, conforms to God and may be known — though not by physical intellection — for direct knowledge is the purpose of the Creation. Our problem, it seems, derives from the vacuum into which God filtered His own light. As the light left the center, the farther it went, the more material it became. So great were the glory and brilliance of God's light that it broke the vessels during the first Creation. (An event symbolically delineated in Genesis as a world populated by the angelic beings who, disastrously, married the daughters of men. Or, in kabbalistic terms, the overabundance of divine light interacting with ill-adapted gross matter.) From this first attempt at Creation a few early sparks of the light separated themselves and departed. God filled new vessels, this time working more slowly, for He wished to create a vacuum and fill it too quickly in order to create evil as illusorily 'separate' from Himself. A paper villain for the cosmic play. Nothing in the world is therefore intrinsically evil, only in the way it is used.

"Our purpose in all this consists of reuniting the original sparks to their source (or reconciling the apparent dualism) by using all that exists to confirm our existence in God. Willing players, we only come to the Absolute by recognizing it under the mask of this physical world — which only conceals the Absolute so that we may peel away the obscuring layers that divide us from it. It's the divine paradox.

"All secular knowledge, all invention, all creativity, art, science, emerge from those departed sparks of holiness. And since the sciences themselves partake of the inadequate secular knowledge derived from man's reasoning faculty, his physical brain, they are inadequate to examine the Absolute. So-called supernatural power, too, comes from this extraneous holiness embedded in the sparks. Philosophical questions about God emerge from the vacuum where He is hidden; therefore philosophy provides the bridge between the intellectual and spiritual worlds. Thus the Jewish mystical attitude directs us to remember always the transcendental in the ordinary." Reuben Gold removed his glasses and shut the big black tome with a thump.

Here was a perfectly outlined course in Jewish karma yoga, which allowed a glimpse of heaven in a grain of sand. At that moment it seemed unmatched by any other mystical system for reconciling ordinary daily life with spiritual practice. For years I had struggled with the problem of interweaving the transcendental with the everyday. Yet nothing offered by the remote life of the zendos and ashrams realistically served that purpose. If he chose, the Jewish mystic could use his daily prayers as three periods of forty-minute meditations — morning, late afternoon, and evening — without abandoning job or family. Tangible exercises whereby he could "imitate" God's attributes (that is, cultivate egolessness) existed in the performance of the *mitzvoth,* the six hundred and thirteen multileveled precepts he observed in the course of his daily life. The study of the esoteric Pentateuch was equivalent to jnana yoga, philosophical discourse that leads beyond intellectual reasoning to direct spiritual knowledge. Somewhere between the rabbinic legalism of the anti-Breslover establishment and the faddish sentimentalism of Nissan Rosenberg's followers stood a genuine kabbalistic interpenetration of the sacred and profane worlds. The only remaining knots were the gnawing selectivity, the persistent "Jewishness," the punitive God of history, and the question of women, to whom most of the essential precepts and communal prayers were closed.

"Why did you specify the *Jewish* people when you mentioned God's plan?" I asked as I tried to edge Reuben Gold against the door as the meeting dispersed. But my question got lost in a welter of shouts and greetings, and he eluded me. The overpowering smell of chicken soup rolled in from the kitchen like a heavy fog. Ethnicity threatened to smother me — as always. With the indentations from the scratchy sofa still ripe on my legs, I rose quickly and headed for the front door. In the kitchen, a young woman with rosy cheeks leaned over a huge aluminum pot and ladled soup into two rows of bowls lined up on a table near the stove. On my way out the door I noticed that the table set in the large, open foyer was covered by the same checkered linoleum my grandmother had used on weekdays. In Brooklyn, nothing changed.

In Jerusalem, on the other hand, ethnicity was somehow not inappropriate. There it required no tortured attempt to translate the mystical experience primarily because the Hebrew language is itself a simultaneous medium for spiritual *and* ordinary daily life. Moreover, the very "Levantinism" despised by most Europeans and Americans put Jewish mysticism into its proper Semitic context. The food, life-style, light, and landscape of the city were virtually the same as those that inspired the kabbalistic metaphors in the first place. Despite surface changes, twentieth-century Jerusalem was still dedicated to the spiritual life above all else. During my second visit, therefore, Madame Ariel's Oriental idiom no longer appeared quaint. When I told her that I was officially in Jerusalem to research material for a book on Jewish mysticism, she immediately arranged a series of informal meetings with various kabbalists and Hasidim. How she did this without once ever stepping out of her house I will never know. Yet Madame Ariel's invisible hand disclosed a city teeming with mystic devotees. Esoteric painters and kabbalistic biologists rubbed shoulders with granola-producing Hasidim; the variety of cultures, preoccupations, and theories occupying Madame Ariel's Jerusalem was dizzying — a mystic banquet.

I spent one afternoon visiting a French writer whose parents had been members of a celebrated Algerian mystical community. In a pleasant apartment, surrounded by two or three darting cats (they never remained still enough to count), I exchanged notes in awkward French with Monsieur René Gilbert. Looking more like a retired museum curator than a kabbalist, the tall, stooped Monsieur Gilbert autographed his slim book on Hasidism and shyly handed it to me. Our conversation rambled in fits and starts until we found common ground at last in our admiration for the Baal Shem Tov. As his enthusiasm began to show, Monsieur Gilbert lost his initial shyness and was soon talking animatedly about the legends inspired by the founder of Hasidism. I missed a word here and there, but nodded at the proper intervals and even managed to interject a few tentative opinions.

"How does an Algerian kabbalist come to be so involved with European Hasidim?" I ventured as tea was served.

Monsieur Gilbert rose from his chair, walked over to a glassed-in bookcase, and reached for one of the sepia photographs clustered on top.

"This was my parents' teacher, George Fanon," he said, edging the photograph closer to my side of the table and pointing to a splendid, white-bearded, prophetic figure in robes.

"George Fanon was a prominent Polish kabbalist who, on foreseeing Hitler's rampage, traveled with his wife to Algeria, carrying with him many secret Hasidic manuscripts." Monsieur Gilbert cocked his eyebrow and added conspiratorially. "Would you like to see them?"

"Of course," I gulped, caught by surprise between sips of tea. "Frankly, I am amazed that you would show them to me, a stranger."

"But you are a friend of Madame Ariel's," he replied matter-of-factly as he rummaged through a box and came up with a packet of photocopied pages.

I eagerly scanned the awkwardly translated English aphorisms he handed to me, but soon gave up. They were too heavily rhetorical, too reminiscent of theosophical tracts reverberating with the wings of celestial beings to hold my interest. The texts contrasted jarringly with my image of Monsieur Gilbert as a scholarly, cultivated Frenchman with his feet on the ground.

"How do you use this material?" I asked, momentarily overlooking the occult edges of René Gilbert's life.

"I spent my entire childhood in the company of spiritual masters whose only purpose was to climb the ladder of the spheres to union with God," he said, pointing to the packet of Fanon's aphorisms. "The problem lies in making his techniques accessible to a new age. My own small meditation group consists mainly of young people who have returned to Judaism from forays into Zen and other Oriental disciplines. What Fanon offers is a very practicable *Jewish* form of meditation, which employs Jewish images like the tree of life, the spheres containing the divine attributes, the pillar of fire guiding the Exodus. My group is presently engaged in translating Fanon in the hope of publishing a book that will spread his teachings to Jewish seekers all over the world."

"Fanon looks a little like an Indian yogi named Sri Aurobindo," I said distractedly. "Did you ever hear of him?"

Monsieur Gilbert eyed me intently and said, "Ah, but didn't I mention that Sri Aurobindo's companion, the Holy Mother of Pondicherry, was my mother's closest friend?"

"What?"

"Yes, the Holy Mother is an Egyptian-born Jewess who studied with George Fanon. Then, of course, as you know, she became interested in the East and left for India. But she was a student of Fanon's Kabbalah long before that."

"Everybody's Jewish," I sighed.

David Castel, a studious young Jerusalem kabbalist originally from Paris, agreed to meet me in the home of a married friend (since he was single and Orthodox, it was unseemly for him to spend time alone with me). Surrounded by roller-skating children, we sat across from each other at a large table, leaving enough modest space between us to satisfy even the most rigorous of the precepts dictating social behavior between men and women. Castel was reputed to be the finest traditional scribe in Jerusalem; his meticulous Torah scrolls were coveted as much for their aesthetic beauty as for their scribe's saintliness. Mystic scribes are supposed to retreat from the world, fasting, taking ritual baths, and adhering to strict standards of celibacy, before setting to work. Being unmarried and strikingly handsome probably made it even harder for Castel, who pored over some books as we talked in order to avoid looking at me directly. For his friends' sake (the couple were "regulars" at Madame Ariel's Sabbath gatherings), he had agreed to be interviewed, but his hasty lecture was designed to leave no doubt in my mind that our meeting was taking place against his better judgment.

"Jerusalem is the only place now for true Kabbalah," Castel said breathily. "No one is practicing it outside. Kabbalah is not 'mysticism' but rather a scientific, logical study of the faculty beyond the intellect. Realizing our true humanity since Adam's fall, we are making it up, so to speak." He paused, his hands moving about nervously.

"Kabbalah can't be practiced alone in this century. It is a communal effort, the responsibility of the Jews who are living in their own community, on their own spiritual ground — the center of spiritual power, Jerusalem. The Kabbalah of the Ari* is the only kind that applies to our age. His form of concentration is a particular study to be accomplished by each individual kabbalist in his

* Isaac Luria, a sixteenth-century master who lived in Safed, Palestine.

own way — according to his specific destiny and role in the life of the Jews and the world — when he truly understands and performs *kavanna,* concentrated intention. The technique can only be learned from a spiritual master. It does not concern itself with ecstatic states; it is not like Hasidic, yogic, or Christian mysticism in that it teaches the kabbalist that it is impossible to become one with God, and it does not seek communion with Him. For this kind of kabbalist there are no supernatural events; he is a plain, observant Jew living the commandments and following the Torah — that is, the essence of Torah, which is Kabbalah. He must first be prepared as a talmudic scholar, for the unlearned cannot study the Kabbalah.

"Prophecy is different. That comes through Grace to the totally purified man. Kabbalah is social, human, political. It can do harm if used incorrectly; it could harm the working of the entire world. Hence, it is secret, practiced by a few.

"In this pre-Messianic age we live in now, the prophets are 'fools,' uttering prophecy in obscurity, prophecy mixed with foolishness." Castel folded his hands and blushed. Having removed their roller skates, the children were drinking milk in the kitchen. I had been dismissed as a credulous, misinformed woman whose best move would be to stop muddling around in mystic bypaths that were too intricate for my limited spiritual capacity to chart. Relieved when I refused the coffee offered by the woman of the house, the scribe got up and left the table. He had done his religious duty by warning a spurious American intruder away from the Kabbalah.

I looked at my watch and saw that it was six o'clock, then suddenly recalled that it had been a fast day for the devout, who were commemorating the destruction of the Temple. Castel had probably been hungry as well as agitated about talking with a strange, secular woman. He returned to see me out the door with a noisy child clinging to his trouser leg. Castel smiled at the boy. There would be no buses running in Jerusalem on the Day of Lamentations, and I would have to walk more than a mile back to Madame Ariel's house, where I would politely say that I had conducted a satisfactory interview.

"I'm sorry for bothering you on a fast day. I had forgotten," I apologized, backing out the door. I was humiliated by his contempt, and my face was hot.

Castel merely nodded.

Alert to the rules now, I left him standing in the doorway, careful lest I further breach the precepts by offering the Orthodox kabbalist my hand in farewell.

On the fourth of July, I climbed a hill high above Jerusalem in the hope of welcoming the Queen Sabbath with the Breslover Hasidim in their converted Arab mansion. The ocher stone building, with its porticoes and magnificent ornamentation, was a perfect piece of Levantine architecture, courtesy of the Turks who had lived there not so long before. The Hasidim inside were equally Levantine: voluminously bearded, dressed in striped silk caftans, white stockings, and black pumps. Rebbe Nachman's anarchistic Israeli followers were praying as the fancy struck them, facing in all directions, moving about, walking up and down the aisles, nodding, swaying, clapping hands — the ecstatic antithesis to Reuben Gold's "scientific" Brooklyn discourse. Mini-versions of their fathers, little boys with dancing sidelocks ascended the reader's platform carrying oversized prayer books, eating sunflower seeds, or dreamily picking their noses.

Relegated to an empty women's section, whose high, opaque windows were posted with signs forbidding one to "open the windows and peek," I pushed open the window and peeked just in time to catch the ceremony welcoming the Queen Sabbath. As God's immanent earthly presence, "companion" of the community of Israel in its exile, this female aspect of the Divine (unlike her human counterparts) was permitted free and joyous access to the synagogue. Indeed, the Hasidim were so delighted at her entrance that they turned en masse toward the Western door, singing and loudly clapping their hands in welcome. Someone passed around a small silver vial of snuff; each Hasid took one or two sniffs, rolled his eyes, and, inspired by the pungent aroma, stamped his feet harder. A little of the fragrance wafted over to the grim, darkened women's shelter, offering the lonely exile a vicarious sniff of the

Queen's perfume. At the end of the service, all the men joined hands and danced in a circle around the reader's platform. A ruddy blond Hasid with a paunch outlining his multicolored, striped caftan caught me pushing the window open still wider and screwed up his face in an angry grimace. When I ignored him, he shook his finger at me without so much as missing a step in his ecstatic dance. Deflated, I went outside for air. Mr. Paret, the neighbor Madame Ariel had enlisted as my translator and guide, approached me at the steps, where I stood gazing into a tiny cell that had been carved out of the bottom of the stone front porch. Inside, with a book, a candle, and a bed for company, a little gray man who looked at least a hundred years old sat rocking in meditative prayer.

"Shabbat *shalom*," Mr. Paret greeted me. "Did you like the service?"

"Whatever I could see of it," I said glumly.

"I warned you about that," said Mr. Paret, smiling. He was an observant Jew himself, but a man of wide-ranging interests who got up before six every morning to don phylacteries — and perform hatha yoga exercises afterward. A retired businessman-scholar with a leaning toward mysticism, Mr. Paret divided his time equally between studying kabbalistic texts and performing favors for people. Madame Ariel had recommended him to me for what she called his "open-mindedness and sweet temperament." True to her description, Mr. Paret traipsed around Jerusalem with me uncomplainingly, translating for sometimes as long as four hours without a break, wheedling me into places that a secular woman alone could never hope to see, and generally lending credibility to my enterprise. His sharp wife was, in fact, beginning to balk at our frequent excursions. Madame Ariel, with her sixth sense for such contingencies, was busy preparing an alternate guide offstage.

"Who's that little man in the cell?" I asked.

"That's the sexton; he's been here since the Breslovers took over the building. They say he never speaks, that he may be a little dim-witted."

"Just like the Baal Shem Tov. Does he live down in there?"

"That's his watchman's station. I think he lives upstairs in a small apartment. But to tell you the truth, I don't know much about him."

Disappointed by the lackluster Hasidim inside, my fantasy had already transformed the old sexton into one of Castel's divinely "foolish" prophets. "Do you think we'll get an interview?" I asked, now depressed and eager to leave.

"I hope so. I think I've almost convinced Goldstein, the synagogue representative. But you had better leave the talking to me."

Presently a group of Hasidim trickled out of the synagogue. One of them, an enlightened intellectual from the look of his trim auburn beard, red cheeks, and tortoiseshell glasses, recognized Mr. Paret and raised his hand in greeting. Encouraged by his appearance, I started to move forward, but my guide gave me a wordless signal to remain standing where I was.

After a brief consultation with Mr. Goldstein, Mr. Paret returned and said, "He'll only talk to you out here for a minute or two, and with me as an intermediary."

"Okay, when in Breslov . . ." So it was only the American Breslover contingent that had opened its doors to women.

Mr. Goldstein took a few steps in our direction and stopped about four feet from where I stood. Mr. Paret stationed himself between us, opening the conversation in Yiddish. With his face averted from mine, in the most outlandish interview I had ever conducted in my life, Mr. Goldstein responded to my relayed questions about the role of Kabbalah in contemporary Breslover Hasidism through neutral lips.

"The sect does not practice Kabbalah," came the first muffled reply. "Although Rebbe Nachman himself knew all kabbalistic practices deeply and did perform them, he prohibited most of his Hasidim from learning them, relegating them only to one, whom he personally selected."

Mr. Paret interjected a point in Hebrew that I missed. Mr. Goldstein only shook his head and continued on his party-line track.

"The Breslover Hasid's single purpose in life is to love God with a full heart, to connect himself with Him in everything he does, but particularly through ardent prayer, and in joy, never sorrow.

Dancing keeps the feet warm, and with warm feet and heart one must pray. Breslover Hasidim worship 'with the heart and with the mouth' — that is, with love and with singing out to Him. They have no practices for meditation or for achieving mystic communion, although some great ones have accomplished this. But those men died more than fifty or one hundred years ago."

The party line evidently did not encompass discussing *hitbodedut,* Rebbe Nachman's unique and exclusive form of spontaneous outdoor meditation, at least not with strange women. Without so much as a divergent glance to acknowledge my presence, Mr. Goldstein wished Mr. Paret Shabbat *shalom* and returned to the synagogue.

"Where's he going now?"

"Now is when the fun really begins," said Mr. Paret. "They eat, drink, and rejoice with more singing and dancing. But they won't let us in."

"He just recited that little speech to put me off. I'll bet they're practicing some kind of elaborate ritual in there right now, but they certainly won't show it to outsiders, especially not women."

"Could be. But I really don't think so. I'm sure you're aware that the tradition bars anyone who is under forty, unmarried, and *female* from studying Kabbalah."

"It's typically Jewish," I said. "That same 'tradition' has also confined women to a pedestal of ignorance and, adding insult to injury, labeled it *ayshith chayil,* 'woman of valor.' "

"Hasidism, as a viable practice, died out in the nineteenth century. You wouldn't be planning to bring it back single-handedly, would you?" Mr. Paret smiled ironically.

I shrugged.

"Come, let's go."

I followed him down the dark, steep slope leading to Bar Yohai Street. For one yearning instant I looked back at the brightly lit synagogue windows, then at the flickering shadows against the narrow cell walls beneath the porch. The old sexton was still bowed in meditative prayer. Whatever their secrets, the Breslover Hasidim were still the only ones giving open classes. One day, I promised myself, I would penetrate the deeper mysteries of my kabbalist ancestors — here, in Jerusalem. But now was not the time. Moving carefully downhill toward the lights encircling the Valley of the Cross, I left the dead Hasidim to their Friday night rejoicings.

I desperately wished to reconcile my obstinate individualism with my gnawing search for ethnic identity. I had spent years straining my legs and back into the lotus posture, eating abominable oatmeal with chopsticks, waking at dawn and washing my body with icy water in the hope that I might hear the sound of one hand clapping. I had been mesmerized by the siren song of the white-robed Sufi and sprinkled with Tibetan holy water as I touched the ancient feet of exiled lamas. But no Jewish master had welcomed me with open arms. My traditionally Orthodox childhood had been an ethnic harbor, its lighthouse beam only an illusion of safety. I truly believed what I had been told: I was "chosen," at once a child born of a priestly nation and, inexplicably, an exile, persecuted by the *goyim* for being a Jew and despised by the Jews for being a woman.

My entire past, with its warm, candlelit Friday nights, my mother reading aloud from the Yiddish newspaper over *her* mother's heavy oak dining room table as the perennial chicken soup fog pervaded the house, conflicted with my wanderlust, my perverse fascination with the "graven images" of the East, and my public love affair with its "strange gods." To compound the alienation, mine was a secret heritage, an oral mysticism transmitted to an esoteric circle of initiates who were themselves considered outcasts, so separate and distinct from the normative Jewish experience that they were periodically hunted, beaten, and excommunicated by their own suffering family. Kabbalists were looked upon as blasphemers who dared to entertain notions of uniting with God. Eventually, they were hounded into retreating, leaving behind only a scattered legacy: several labyrinthine texts that shrouded their secrets in esoteric metaphors, a handful of venerable rabbis to mumble the chants by rote, and no overtly practicing masters. I could search for years and find no one — despite my own Hasidic ancestors, my just intentions, and my spiritual smile. Yet, despite all the wasted hours I had spent in bowing my awkward head before the Buddha, it still seemed worth continuing my pilgrimage homeward.

Jews are forever engaged in a compulsive examination of their spiritual condition. It makes them both interesting and pesty. I never heard a Hindu or a Buddhist ask, "What is a Hindu?" "What is a Buddhist?" But, even in Israel, I never heard the end of the long debate, "What is a Jew?" Perhaps it was in part to flee from that ancient dilemma that I had turned eastward. I simply placed the nuisance of my religious identity on a dark shelf in my mind and brought it out on an occasional High Holiday for ceremonial purposes. Then I quickly stuffed it back among the other abandoned memorabilia of my youth, haunted by its pitiful rattling, leaving it ever undefined. I railed against Judaism for its dry, legalistic obsessions, for its failure to disclose to me its juiciest heretical secrets.

Even the chief Sephardic rabbi of Jerusalem feared the charms of the East. He publicly admonished the thousands of naive Jews who had been attracted to foreign beliefs that were opposed to the holy Torah, and he warned against pagan rituals like meditation and guru worship.

What exactly, I wondered, did the chief rabbi mean by "the holy Torah"? How did the dry reading of the Bible and a few outmoded customs connect us to the living cosmos, put us in touch with ourselves? What did *he* know of meditation, this guardian of "Jewishness" who probably could not distinguish between a pagan and a pundit? Nevertheless, something from the dark, hidden shelf inside me rustled in response to the phrase "pagan rituals"; it evoked a winter long past, when the earnest young Jewish face of a friend with radiant Semitic eyes reflected my own as together we prostrated our bodies and took refuge in the Buddha one cloudy afternoon on Riverside Drive. We had perhaps fled too far east too fast. And now the old Jewish myths, invested with new "Oriental" significance, beckoned me to return. I stood knocking at the door with my traveling pack in one hand, but no one was home.

The manuscripts I was then perusing in the Hebrew University library promised great revelations. Some listed various jumbled techniques for meditation on the letters of God's Name, while others described long inductive formulas for ecstatic trance, with due warnings against chanting incorrectly and crippling specific bodily parts. In "real life," however, the kabbalists I met were all denying mystic transport in favor of humble worship or extolling logic and science.

Surely, I pleaded, Madame Ariel might at least provide me with *one* miracle worker.

"When the door is opened," she answered, "it will be the right one."

In the meantime, she continued to send me on daily outings. In deference to Mrs. Paret's growing restiveness, Madame Ariel suggested that for my next interview I engage her cousin, Dr. Lilianne Hayeem, herself an observant Jew who attended the women's classes given by the Moroccan-born kabbalist I was scheduled to see the following evening.

Encouraged as much by Dr. Hayeem's demure wig and long-sleeved dress as by her perfect Hebrew and pervasive intelligence, I set out to find Rabbi Bassani in a shabby block of flats inhabited by poor Oriental Jews. Like the housing projects in Spanish Harlem, the featureless gray complex where Rabbi Bassani lived with his family of ten was seething with volatile activity. Tough youngsters in skin-tight pants smoked and spat on the corners of unpaved streets. Bony cats scrounged for garbage in open tins, and angry shouts escaped from open balconies along with the odors of fried cooking.

It took a while for Dr. Hayeem to find her way since the stairwell lights were out. I followed her with some trepidation as she climbed to the third level of a drab gray cinder block of flats. At the sound of our knock, a girl of about ten opened the door a crack, revealing a kitchen with a narrow cot containing an old woman who babbled forth an incessant senile stream of Arabic, Hebrew, and French. Dr. Hayeem exchanged a few words with the child, who then ushered us into the flat, past the infirm grandmother, and into a large, cheerful dining room with a ballroom crystal chandelier dangling precariously from the middle of the ceiling. A one-year-old in a loose diaper walked around and around the dining room table, sucking a lollipop with rapt concentration. Despite the apparent disorder, the flat turned out to be immaculately clean and not at all depressing.

Dr. Hayeem was about to ask the child to locate the rabbi when she was interrupted by a fashionable pregnant woman with carefully manicured and polished fingernails. She greeted us in a mixture of Hebrew and French, then led us upstairs to another flat, which served as the rabbi's private study. Seating us on a broad red silk divan, she left the room briefly and returned with two glasses of amber tea stuffed with green mint leaves. At that moment the rabbi entered and motioned for us to remain seated. After addressing Dr. Hayeem first, he casually introduced himself to me. Rabbi Bassani was a large and spontaneous man of about fifty with outsized features and narrow Chinese eyes. Refusing the tea his daughter offered him, he sat down directly across from us on a black leather chair, placed his large, red-knuckled hands on his knees, and, unlike the Breslover Hasid, looked directly into my face as he launched into his enthusiastic description of his life's work.

"I'll speak without your translation, Dr. Hayeem, if you don't mind," he said in French. "If you don't understand me, madame, just interrupt." His open smile won me at once.

"So, I hear that you want to learn about the Kabbalah, is that right?"

"I'm working on a book . . ."

Rabbi Bassani shifted his weight and leaned farther forward in his chair. "Kabbalah is a living study, not merely an intellectual one . . . a lifetime practice, the final aim and end of Judaism and Torah. Do not take it lightly," he warned, but his tone was gentle. "The emulation of Moses is the purpose of every Jew — that is, cleaving to, and knowledge of, the Divine. To begin to study Kabbalah you enter by means of three primary texts: Psalms, Ecclesiastes, and Song of Songs. These three degrees of apprenticeship cure the individual of worldliness and the attraction of the eyes for 'outside' desires. They provide the necessary preparation in ridding us of our selfishness. Meditation on these texts turns one inward toward 'charitableness' and transforms the *ani,* the I, into the *ayin,* nothing. Is that clear so far?" Rabbi Bassani paused and held my gaze, appraising me.

Dr. Hayeem stretched her neck and peered at me nearsightedly. The light from a large, unshaded lamp was reflected in her glasses, making it difficult for her to see. Rabbi Bassani told her to change her seat. Now that she was out of the rabbi's direct range of vision, she raised her eyebrows, visibly disturbed at his frankness in the company of two women. In her car, Dr. Hayeem had lectured me about my proper role, assuring me that she knew the rabbi's philosophy and warning me that it did not make room for women who wished to practice the Kabbalah. She had become restless during Rabbi Bassani's opening words, and it was now obvious from the prim expression on her face that she could barely restrain herself from bursting out with a torrent of unspoken questions about her religious confusion.

"I understand you perfectly," I said to the rabbi, ignoring the doctor's little gasp at my boldness.

"Can we bring you some more tea?" Rabbi Bassani asked her. Dr. Hayeem could only manage to shake her head.

"Now, when the eyes close to the material world and gaze inward toward the soul," the rabbi continued enthusiastically, "the soul goes through a process of purification that allows the ears to hear the sound of God during the recitation of the Shema, the declaration of God's unity with His name. The essence of that declaration allows man to 'hear' God." Rabbi Bassani illustrated his discussion by pointing back and forth between his eyes and his ears. "Once the vessel has been purified by the proper study of Ecclesiastes and Psalms, the soul is capable of love and longing for God. This stage is represented by the Song of Songs, where the mystic is finally admitted into His inner chamber."

To Dr. Hayeem's horror, I asked the rabbi to teach me his method.

"Yes," he replied simply. "How long are you here?"

"Two more weeks."

"Oh." Obviously disappointed, Rabbi Bassani thought for a moment. Then, his face lighting with optimism, he said, "Well then, keep in touch with me by mail. I will start you off with a correspondence course." He smiled, then turned serious: "But you may only begin when you have found two youngsters under the age of ten to whom you will teach it also."

Puzzled at his condition, I retracted a bit. "Let me think about it," I said.

Rabbi Bassani folded his hands over his ample belly and watched my face for a sign. But I was obviously unprepared to give him what he was looking for. Dr. Hayeem, in the meantime, had turned bright purple. Rabbi Bassani spoke again.

"The youthful search for mysticism in the West is, for the most part, only another stimulus in an already overstimulated culture — another toy, another food, or 'candy.' The search for visions and other such spectacles are not at all like the commitment to self-purification that marks the path of the true mystic. By this I do not mean self-mortification. These young people are seeking to escape from a world that is being brought to a final catastrophe by egoistic leaders who cannot see things that thoughtful people see clearly. Even nonmystics who think clearly are making use of man's faculty to visualize in thought what will be the result of his action."

I was reminded of Madame Ariel's self-revealing visualization technique. "You mean psychologically?"

"I mean more than psychologically. I am talking about foresight — literally. The kabbalist can see so deeply into thought that he sees 'future' results because that kind of *seeing* erases time so that future, past, and present become one."

It was only when I found myself once again out on the street that I realized that I had forfeited my first real opportunity to study and practice the Kabbalah with a teacher. Rabbi Bassani had offered me immediate apprenticeship, with no secrets, without even the demand for rigid observance of the precepts. Despite Dr. Hayeem's warnings that he taught women only superficially, Rabbi

Bassani had treated me as an intellectual equal. Yet I had hesitated, making him think that I was just another American looking for "candy." This rabbi had all the right credentials: He was a normal, earthy family man with a good reputation and a healthy Jerusalem following; there was nothing secretive about his teachings; he integrated Kabbalah with every aspect of his own life and thought. He spoke French clearly. I knew enough Hebrew to read the Psalms, Ecclesiastes, and Song of Songs under his direction. Yet I was somehow not up to the offer. Perhaps his final analysis of the "youthful search for mysticism" best characterized my own superficial commitment and capacity. I could convince myself that I was there to find the sources for a book, not a guru. Instead, I berated myself for being so hasty in leaving.

"I can't believe what he said to you," Dr. Hayeem said, speeding through the vacant streets at midnight. "What a great opportunity — he actually offered to teach you himself. You should be honored. I am amazed," she murmured, more to herself than to me.

"I am honored. But I can't stay. To really learn, you must commit yourself for an extended stay, and I can't do that," I said lamely, realizing for the first time that I was confused about my real reason for being in Jerusalem and anxious to return home.

But Madame Ariel had arranged several further interviews, and our own early morning "exercises" were invaluable as always in helping me sort out the chaos engendered by too much searching. I had given up my pretense to scholarship and was doggedly, even grimly now, dedicated to unearthing and pursuing kabbalists. To what end, I wasn't sure. But when anyone asked me, I became suddenly articulate, hiding behind my mask of "indifferent research." The morning meditations in Madame Ariel's garden, however, were flooded with images of paths not taken and angelic beings mouthing words I could not hear. As long as it remained secret, Kabbalah was safe. When the locked treasure chest showed the smallest sign of opening, my first impulse was to flee. In the spring and summer of 1975, I spent every day rushing about Jerusalem with pen and paper, interviewing, reading, microfilming precious manuscripts — and inwardly agonizing over what I was doing there in the first place. Only Madame Ariel kept me from splitting apart then. One day I grew so agitated over my "real" purpose that I decided to consult Rabbi Gaon, a renowned miracle-working kabbalist who held court every morning in the heart of the busy Jewish market.

With Mr. Paret again drafted into service, I rented a car and headed through the narrow alleyways in search of the Oriental synagogue housing the Yemenite holy man. We missed the actual street three times before Mr. Paret located the obscure sign we had been looking for. I parked haphazardly, front wheels on the curb near a wall, on the opposite side of the winding narrow road behind the awakening market. In the spacious courtyard beyond an alleyway, a woman swept the threshold of an ancient stone house painted the same Mediterranean blue as Madame Ariel's gate. I looked into the open door behind the woman and was startled to see a radiant old man in striped silk robes and a high white satin skullcap sitting motionless behind a table.

Something in his appearance — the flowing white beard, smooth brown skin, and clear black eyes — jolted me out of context. Seated in the peaceful early morning courtyard in the middle of the market, guarded by two weeping willows, the holy man could just as well have been a swami receiving petitioners in Benares or Rishikesh. For generations, his Yemenite grandfathers had been sitting in that same stone house, performing wonders at eight every morning.

The cleaning lady finished sweeping, went inside, and shut the door between Rabbi Gaon and me. Mr. Paret found a bench and invited me to sit down.

"Impressive, isn't he?"

"Amazing-looking man. How come you've never heard of him? You're from such an old Jerusalem family yourself."

"But we're Ashkenazi. The two cultures rarely mixed in my time; the Sephardic miracle workers, and even many of their religious customs, are unknown to us. And no doubt ours are foreign to them."

"Strange."

"It's part of the diasporic confusion. We'll get over it as soon as this new generation starts intermarrying. It's happening already."

"And the mysticism? Is that different?"

"No, that's all originally Oriental, only the Hasidim brought Kabbalah to the West, but the original comes from right here."

A teen-aged yeshiva boy appeared at the rabbi's door then and began praying. Ten or twelve people were already gathered around us in the small courtyard; some were signing their names in a ledger that the yeshiva boy had set outside the door on a wooden lectern.

"I think we ought to sign in. It looks like first come, first served," said Mr. Paret.

He walked up to the door of the rabbi's consultation room and engaged the yeshiva boy in conversation. A religious girl in long sleeves and dark cotton stockings (despite the July heat) bowed again and again from the waist in prayer, her face turned toward Rabbi Gaon's synagogue, which stood opposite the courtyard on a high balcony. While Mr. Paret chatted in Hebrew with the rabbi's disciple, I climbed the stairs and looked into the open doorway of the synagogue: no more than a neat, orderly room with a central altar and circular pews lined with plush Oriental cushions. A typical Sephardic synagogue, with mystic mandalas, signs of God's permutated Names drawn in the shapes of hands, seven-branched candlesticks, and long almond-shaped eyes. Down in the courtyard the petitioners were arriving, people of every variety — from the most fanatically Orthodox, dark-skinned Oriental Jews to girls in halter tops and blond couples from Tel Aviv wearing jeans. A one-eyed woman puffed on a cigarette, her head wrapped in a gypsy turban. Many elderly Oriental women like her filled the yard; they were tough and querulous, fighting for a position on the rabbi's list, shoving toward the door as names were called. It was eight-thirty. Everyone in the packed courtyard was eager now; even the modest praying girl rushed at the opening door with the rest of the crowd.

Mr. Paret stood aside and beckoned me over to where the young disciple in charge stood with the big ledger. "Don't worry, we'll get in when we're supposed to. I told him about you and put your name on the list. We're third from the man inside."

"Do you study Kabbalah?" I asked the mild-mannered boy with the sidelocks and flowing fringes.

"Oh, no," he answered quickly. "Too many have gone insane with Kabbalah. I am contented to serve the rabbi." He rotated his forefinger at his temple to emphasize the dangers of such mystical studies.

"Does the rabbi teach Kabbalah?"

"To a certain few, I guess. But most of us perform the correction prayers for the souls of those who come to him for help and advice. His disciples pray twenty-four hours a day so that Rabbi Gaon can help the callers who come from all over the country and abroad. When done properly, these kabbalistic prayers have the effect of purifying the souls of the petitioners and allowing them to benefit from the rabbi's intercession with the higher spheres in their behalf. Our only part in this is to continue reciting the formulas for purification."

"But why don't you want to study Kabbalah? Is reciting formulas enough for you?"

"Only certain minds are capable of studying Kabbalah. For the majority, like me, it is enough to serve God with love and devotion and to be fortunate to have such a holy man for a master," said the yeshiva boy.

The door opened; a short, taciturn man in laborer's overalls stepped out and was immediately surrounded by the pushing crowd. The yeshiva boy stopped talking with us only long enough to call the next petitioner, one of the angry crones who had been wringing her hands and complaining near us under one of the willow trees.

"He has cured the terminally ill, foretold death, arranged marriages, and correctly predicted births for barren women." The boy proudly listed his master's accomplishments. The old woman emerged from the house bearing a little white paper, which she waved back at the room behind her, crying and blessing the rabbi as she went. From inside, the seer's calm voice reassured her, gently urging her to go on to her work and not to worry. Her son was going to be all right.

I did not have a chance to voice the flow of questions engendered in me by the remarkable scene, for the boy called my name next, and I found myself hurried inside by the shoving crowd behind me. In the darkened room Rabbi Gaon sat behind a long wooden table covered with paper receipts like the one the old woman had carried out with her. Mr. Paret whispered that they were payment slips for the living expenses of the disciples who continually performed the "corrections." In the open room to the left was an improvised bed covered with a white sheet, flanked by two or three hard wooden benches. As the rabbi sat bent over the little white slips, Mr. Paret and I looked around.

Seating himself on the bench near me, opposite Rabbi Gaon, Mr. Paret pointed to the improvised bed and whispered, "The boy said that the rabbi sleeps only two hours a night on a wooden bench there."

On the wall behind Rabbi Gaon I was astonished to see a vivid reproduction of Van Gogh's whirling midnight suns.

The seer turned his perfectly tranquil face to me and said, "You are from New York."

"Yes."

"And what do you want?"

"I am working on a study of Kabbalah and I very much want to find someone who will teach it to me."

Rabbi Gaon flashed a brilliant white smile at me. "Surely your work will serve to bring the Messiah."

The conversation was not going as I would have wished. I could not be sure whether the rabbi was not given to using such dramatic figures of speech with all foreigners or whether he had really intended his remark for me specifically. I was not able to clarify his statement, for he was now bombarding Mr. Paret with rapid-fire questions in Hebrew about my life, questions that Mr. Paret could not answer for lack of information. Rabbi Gaon did not seem interested in the answers anyway, for he replied to them himself with advice for my future, saying that my work on the book was really a vehicle for unraveling spiritual knowledge from myself. With the help of his directive prayers, Rabbi Gaon promised, my book on Kabbalah would assist in spiritualizing the world in preparation for the Messianic Age.

Before I realized what I was doing, I handed the rabbi three one-hundred-pound notes and received one of the little white slips in exchange.

"We shall say corrections for your soul as well as for the soul of your book." Having completed the transaction, the rabbi waved me out the door into a pack of anxious petitioners who hurriedly shoved me out of the way, Mr. Paret following swiftly behind.

"Next!" called the yeshiva boy without recognizing either of us.

In the street beyond the courtyard, an irate shopkeeper stood with his fists clenched in front of my car. I had parked at the entrance to his stall, he said, and he could not open the iron grating over his shop because my front wheels were blocking the narrow space between the street and the thick iron padlock to the grating. He had lost an hour's worth of business and it was my fault. The man was furious, and if I hadn't been a woman, I think he would have punched me in the face right there. As it was, he stood cursing me in at least six foreign languages, despite what I felt to be the small trace of holiness still clinging to my aura from making contact with the great seer just across the road. But the shopkeeper did not seem to feel it. In answer to my apologies, he spat on the sidewalk at my feet and banged his fist on the windshield as I drove away.

"The corrections are starting to work already," I said ruefully to a white-faced Mr. Paret.

"Maybe you'll let me off and I'll walk home. I have to think about all this. The Messiah . . . You'd better think about what the rabbi said, too. And don't take it so lightly. I had a very strong feeling of being near someone special back in there. I'm generally skeptical about 'miracle workers,' but something in Rabbi Gaon's face, his eyes . . . I don't know. You may be getting in deeper than you think. Kabbalah is not for the curious. I want to get out and walk. It's been a very emotional experience for me."

"And very confusing for me," I said, pulling up to the sidewalk in front of a small park. "Maybe we should talk it over together."

"No," said Mr. Paret. "I'd like to be alone now, and I advise you to go home and do some thinking yourself." He got out of the car with a very preoccupied look on his face. Looking in the rearview mirror, I saw him walking toward a small cypress grove. I remembered Dr. Hayeem's violent response a few nights before. Now I'm making everyone around me crazy, too, I thought as I pulled away and headed toward Madame Ariel's house.

That night I dreamed I was in a center housing the greatest rabbis in the world. In the huge complex of schoolrooms, offices, synagogues, and cafeterias, I sought the greatest of the miracle-working kabbalists, but I was not sure why. Dressed in prayer shawls and skullcaps, officials in charge of the center guided each visitor to his or her proper place. As I was a woman, they naturally took it for granted that I had come to ask the great rabbi's blessings for my family. Worried that this was not the reason, that I had lied to gain entry, I walked along the corridor, certain nonetheless that when I saw him I would know what to ask, but feeling that it was better to let them think I was there for a blessing.

A disciple of the greatest of the rabbis guided me down a staircase, pointed the way, and left. I mistakenly entered a friendly cafeteria, where many students were eating. Excusing myself when they looked up, I hurried out and walked on to the nearest open office. I looked inside and found a youngish rabbi sitting there, a rather ordinary Conservative rabbi who was talking about Jewish philosophy into the telephone. I thought, He's not what I'm looking for. Very intellectual and all that, but no miracles. As I left the area, I passed by a bench in the hall where several young women were seated. One of them told me that she was still a student, but that she was waiting her turn for instructions from the Great Rabbi. She pointed to the office where I had just been, and I said, "That's not him." She merely shrugged and did not seem to know the difference. I walked away from the bench and searched around by myself in the basement complex of offices.

Making a sudden turn, I entered a room and found an old man with a long white beard who was wearing a black hat. Without a word, I walked in and sat down.

It was the Great Rabbi. In a low voice he told me that he had been waiting for me, that all my interviews with the rabbis upstairs were only an excuse to get to him on the pretext that I needed his blessing and his advice.

"You can have blessings and advice, if you wish," he said, but you don't need them, for I know all about what you are doing and looking for and what you have devoted your life to. I know all about Philo and Sri Singha and all the other teachers and gurus you have seen, and I know why you are here, and I will help you —"

The next morning, before I could tell her anything about my dream, Madame Ariel urged me to rush back home and dress up in properly respectable religious garb. She had hurriedly arranged an interview for me with Yehoshua Bloch, son of the late Isaac Bloch, whom Gershom Scholem had called the last great kabbalist of the twentieth century. One of the rabbi's female students, a brilliant professor of history and a punctilious observant Jew, had, after much coaxing, consented to bring me to Rav Bloch at eleven o'clock.

Sylvie Aaronson was a large-boned, formidable woman of about thirty-four. From the moment she got me alone in the car, she bombarded me with questions about my background. Why wasn't I religious if I was so interested in Jewish mysticism? Why did I waste my time with a secular woman like Madame Ariel who could teach me nothing of any value about the Jewish tradition? She herself would settle for nothing less than a *real* Jewish master once she'd decided to assume the Jewish path, "and in no other place but Israel," she stated pointedly. Every sentence contained an attack lodged at my superficiality. For her part, Sylvie had made up her mind in advance: Rav Bloch was directly descended from the legitimate, rabbinical, Mosaic line, while Madame Ariel was a mere self-styled guru. As a scholar and serious Jewish seeker, Sylvie would brook nothing less than the "tradition" and from no lesser being than the Rav Yehoshua Bloch.

Duly chastized for my capricious and "illegitimate" spiritual ties, I followed the straight-backed Sylvie into Rav Bloch's modest flat in the Orthodox quarter of the city. Perhaps she thought she was being dutiful to the tradition by at last introducing me to the right path. I could imagine no other reason for the disapproving Sylvie to have brought me to her master.

My first reaction to the son of the great kabbalist was shock. The tiny ancient sage with the white beard, mischievous burning eyes, and the black hat was exactly the old man in my dream! My heart thumped furiously. I noticed almost nothing about my surroundings, forgetting even Sylvie as a handsome, black-bearded Yemenite disciple of about twenty ushered us into the waiting room and instructed us to sit down. My first glimpse of the Rav at breakfast behind a half-open door had so dislocated me that I was conscious only of the sound of dishes and silver clattering under running water in the kitchen. Sylvie continued to harass me, now focusing on the proper behavior expected of me in the Rav's presence, but I saw only her pink headscarf and her moving lips and heard nothing but running water. The disciple did not reappear for what seemed an interminable length of time. Then he simply pushed open the door with the corner of the tray containing the breakfast dishes and very informally guided us into the Rav's study. I had expected the "son" of the great master to be middle-aged; in her entire harangue, Sylvie had mentioned nothing of his age or appearance. The little man in his eighties who beckoned me over to him and asked me my Hebrew name was slightly hard of hearing, dyspeptic, but otherwise keen and extremely good-humored. Our first encounter consisted largely of stock-taking. He considered my respectful fake Orthodox garb: my long, dark cotton stockings, long-sleeved blouse, and wide cotton headscarf; then he asked my family name and proposed talking in Yiddish, a language I understood, and that Sylvie, fortunately, did not.

I studied his surroundings. The small, cluttered sitting room full of photographs of his father and various dark-bearded masters, the informally strewn books and papers, the faded sofa covers, popping springs, and shabby brown chairs did not befit the greatness of the legacy. I remembered that rigidly Orthodox Jews did not permit photographs; only a few days before, a Hasid in the market had tried to break Noah's camera when he aimed it at him. Yet the Rav Bloch was surrounded by photographs. He had more surprises in store.

"Tell her not to be afraid and to sit closer," he ordered Sylvie in Hebrew.

Trembling, I pulled my chair close to the table at his right. His black vest and ample beard smelled of nutmeg; his eyes searched my face for a long, penetrating minute. I felt suddenly dizzy in his presence.

"Talk to him about anything you like, but don't discuss mysticism," Sylvie warned me in English. "He doesn't discuss mysticism with strangers."

I took a deep breath and leaned close to the Rav's ear. "What does Rav Bloch think about Kabbalah?"

He giggled slightly. "Kabbalah?" The Rav's eyes twinkled, and a pair of tender, young, smooth hands emerged from under the sleeves of his black silk caftan, waving like little flags. "There is no other mystique for a Jew who wishes to know God than to return to the homeland," he said in Yiddish. "Living in exile is an 'illness,' a fracturing of the body-soul-mind complex. That is why all you Jews living abroad are searching for God with such difficulty."

Almost before he had finished, I replied somewhat impatiently, "I've had this argument with other rabbis, and they always tell me that other traditions are not equal to the Jewish tradition. I'm tired of hearing how superior we are."

From the moment we opened our first discussion, I found it easy to speak absolutely candidly, even impertinently sometimes, to Rav Bloch. It was as though everything I had held in abeyance, all my complaints, self-hatreds, and annoyances with the Jews could come pouring out in his presence, shamelessly and without fear of reprisal.

"All these Eastern practices you people are trying have nothing intrinsically wrong with them — except that they are not yours! If you took a good look at yourself, you would see that you are your-self a transplanted Oriental who has been trying for generations to adapt, without success, to Occidental ways. That is why you are so eager to turn toward the East; it's in your blood, in your soul, this desire to return to the land of the prophets, where you will find your true identity." Rav Bloch spoke with great energy and in a loud voice, interspersing Yiddish with Hebrew.

"No gymnastics are needed, only a study of the Torah that goes beyond mere intellectual learning, a kind of concentrated prayer that can only be achieved in a Jewish setting, by degrees of purifica-tion, only in a state of ecstasy that combines soul, mind, and body rather than one that cuts the soul from the body. What you are reacting against, and rightly, is the rigid halakhic [legalist] point of view. You identify Judaism with those who call themselves religious but who have busied themselves with making idols out of the Law. Taking the personal God and transforming Him in their own childish image, these so-called observant Jews are less knowledgeable about God than the atheist. At least he sees God as no-thing. And that notion is closer to the truth than all the idol worship that passes for prayer among the Orthodox.

"Halakha is the outer shell; Kabbalah has to do with *neshama* [soul] and *ruah hakodesh* [holy spirit]; and these entail a way of life that combines casting one's lot in with a 'nation of priests,' actually *living* the commandments and Torah without any special meditations of a 'mystical' kind. It is rather a mysticism of place." The Rav stopped talking and held my gaze in silence.

I did not agree with or quite understand everything he had said, but my mind was too agitated to formulate any intelligent questions on the subject of mystical nationalism. What was happening be-tween us had little to do with philosophical speculation or religious disputation; it was rather like a chemical interaction. I felt we were communicating more directly from brain to brain, that he was using my question and his discourse only to make the deeper, unspoken contact I was then feeling through my pulse and skin.

"Come back," said Rav Bloch after a silent interval. "We have to talk more. How long are you here?"

"Only a short while, two weeks or so."

"Come back every day. I'll be happy to continue our discussion. You come with her." He addressed Sylvie directly for the first time since we had sat down. "Your Hebrew needs improving," he said to me with mock disapproval.

Sylvie obviously hadn't expected him to ask me back. "I won't be able to come each time," she said.

"No matter. You can come alone." He nodded at me. "There will always be someone here who can interpret." Then, pausing a bit, he added jovially, "Do you speak French?"

"Yes," I answered, thinking he was still making fun of me.

"*Bon. Au revoir.* I speak a little French, too, as you can see." The Rav stood up — and extended his hand to me! Afraid of transgressing the rules now embodied by a glowering Sylvie, I tentatively offered the master my sweating palm. Rav Bloch immediately grabbed both my hands and pressed them hard. "I really am glad you came, Penina," he said, addressing me familiarly, as if long accustomed to calling me by my Hebrew name. "We have some old, unfinished business between us. We can teach each other many things."

I groped for the door in a daze, trying to thank the Rav in any language that came to mind. I looked back and saw that the venerable master was following me out onto the landing in his carpet slippers. "Remember to take off that ridiculous outfit you're wearing and dress the way you normally do when you come back," he called out. "Ten o'clock in the morning."

I was elated. In my own ludicrous and tentative way I had found my teacher.

That night I tried to explain my feelings to Noah, but I was inarticulate. No great intellectual exchange had taken place; Rav Bloch had promised me no system, no teaching; we had not "meditated," nothing particularly "kabbalistic" had passed between us — nothing except the odd coincidence of the dream and our hastily arranged meeting. Yet I sensed that even if nothing tangible emerged from our future discourses, merely being in Rav Bloch's presence would teach me all I needed to know about Jewish spiritual practice. Fight him as I might, Rav Bloch had reached the deep "Jewish" portion of my soul. To prepare for the two-week struggle ahead, I gathered all his father's books I could get my hands on and spent the next twenty-four hours reading about the old kabbalist's mystical speculations on "returning" to Judaism.

The Hebrew word *teshuvah* means both "repentance" and "return." The old Rav Bloch preferred the latter meaning to the idea of repentance for sin. According to him, human striving toward God represented liberation from the desire bound up with action. Like the Hindu notion of karma, or action produced by desire, Rav Bloch's interpretation of "evil deeds" also referred to human enslavement to past habits, which, proceeding cumulatively, enmesh us in a net of mechanistic responses that result in destructive action. The impulse to "return" means that the will has determined for itself a new direction, a dehabituation of the old character that opens us to "purification" and prepares us to receive divine illumination.

Unlike the usual dualistic Judeo-Christian concept of sin, Rav Bloch's philosophy endorsed the mystical, universal view: "Sin," or "evil" action, destroys the unity between the individual self and universal existence. "Perfect repentance," in his words, could only be achieved by uniting ourselves through silent contemplation — in suprarational states of consciousness — with our highest potential, as symbolized by the "worlds within worlds." The work of the kabbalist therefore consists of delving into the secret meanings of the written Torah and acquainting oneself with its esoteric cosmic laws, studying the map before embarking on the exalted, but dangerous, voyage. Unlike ordinary intellectual work, this study requires perfect physical and ethical purity, egoless commitment to truth, and, above all, sacrifice of the self to the Torah (divine way).

The old Rav made a great point of emphasizing sin as "desire" that, in grasping outward toward the things of the world, obscured the tranquil mind required for kabbalistic inquiry. To this end, he reiterated the need for establishing perfect equilibrium of mind and body before indulging in contemplation of this kind. Uniting one's soul with the cosmic soul is, for Jewish mystics, a literal event. Since each "sphere" symbolizing the created worlds bears God's emanated attributes, meditation on them induces a state whereby the "soul" leaves the "body" behind, as it were. Bereft of its spiritual identity, the body is thus entirely open to whatever remaining evil qualities exist there. This intense concentration, during which the mystic literally transcends his ordinary, identifiable self and becomes infused with divine power, is, as David Castel had hinted, potentially harmful to the entire world. When the mystic resumes normal consciousness and finds that his body and ego are consumed by their normal desires, a terrible spiritual struggle ensues. Hence, the continued warning and secrecy of the kabbalists, whose experiential knowledge of these states has taught them the dangers at first hand.

The pieces were beginning to come together. That was why Rabbi Gaon's yeshiva boy worried about losing his mind with too much kabbalistic study. And why Rabbi Bassani had expressed his doubts about the Western mystical fad. It was truly a lifetime dedication to study — in the most profound sense of that word — to preparing the body, the will, and the mind (as Narendra had shown me in his way) as an athlete would prepare for the Olympics. You didn't just read a few books, sit down on a prayer cushion, light some incense, and "get enlightened." The attitude was inseparable from the goal. Intensive meditation too hastily indulged in resulted in a pleasant drowse at best, or, at worst, in madness. In America it was only too easy to work up fake ecstasy, to be "hypnotized" by chanting, and to fly high on drugs. The initial impulse toward sacred experience had to be accompanied by the will to refine one's character, to work to create a balance between heaven and earth so as not to fall into the abyss dividing them.

Rav Bloch had probably taken the teaching of "elevating by degree" from his father. Most aspiring mystics, even some among the great ones from the past, could not climb too high too fast. Over and over, the sages warned of entering contemplation unprepared and being "burned" with too much light. The real "secrets," therefore, would only be taught when the master, who had himself experienced the knowledge contained in the spheres, determined that the student was truly ready. For the kabbalist, the entire system has been perfectly and economically drawn. Our life here is no less significant than our divinity. Indeed, it is the keystone of the divine. Transcending our human limitations is no more relevant than using our human experience in the world. Thus, the old Rav Bloch cautioned against leaping ahead of the level at which we find ourselves, not only for fear of losing life or sanity, but because every degree, even the first, contains an important sacred teaching without which we could not comprehend the upper stages that follow.

Marked by an admixture of intuition on my part, infinite patience and love on Rav Yehoshua's, and a growing mutuality of language, our lengthy sessions together became the highlight of my remaining days in Jerusalem. I wore my "normal" costume — jeans and a polo shirt — shocking none of Rav Bloch's disciples, whom I often met in the waiting room. He was surrounded for the most part by a new breed of yeshiva boy: sunburned, cheerful, and less mortified by the sight of a female student. Nothing like their pasty-faced counterparts in Mea Shearim, yet they were all studying to become rabbis. Most of them would never think of bothering with Kabbalah, yet there was an unmistakable air of spiritual dedication about even the youngest of Rav Bloch's boys. His female students ranged from long-haired, aesthetic types to robust peasant women in heavy sandals. I amused myself while waiting in the outer room by drinking cherry squash and joking in broken Hebrew with Yakov, the master's chief caretaker-disciple. In the course of the crowded days I spent with Rav Bloch, I became acquainted with all sorts of people who had sought him out for advice on everything from where to marry to whether or not to convert to Judaism. His door remained open until well past midnight, when huge bus-loads of young men spilled out onto his doorstep after classes in Jewish philosophy. He ate only one meal a day, prayed early in the morning, and almost never allowed his doctor to come in while he taught — though the man came every day on time and paced nervously outside with the Rav's medicine in hand.

I saw old rabbis kiss Rav Bloch's hands; and once I even saw him kissing his dearest, most brilliant disciple in a moment of such mutual spiritual clarity that the two of them backed out of the door to the study and onto the street before realizing where they were. The sight so touched me that I cried. Rav Bloch embodied a love so intense that for many of us students it became tangible, an electric spark emanating from a handshake, an arrow of light in a smile.

One day a pair of Hasidic visitors appeared, dressed in black from head to toe and with the usual long sidelocks and flying fringes. Taking one look at me, sitting on the bench outside the door, they covered their faces with their huge hats and hurried inside to a room reserved for the Rav's yeshiva boys. I waited a long time that day because, as one boy told me, an important government man had come to discuss a political problem with the Rav. Presently I heard scurrying behind the door. Yakov, who had gone to buy groceries, was not available for his usual task of seating the visitors in order. Suddenly Rav Bloch himself came shuffling out, the two frightened Hasidim before him.

"What's going on out here?" he called loudly, cupping his ear.

The two young visions in black rushed up to explain that they could not possibly tolerate waiting in the same room with me, not even if there was the wall between us. With that, the Rav took each of them by the collar and hustled them out into the street.

"What was that?" I asked, barely containing my laughter.

"Nothing. Stupidity, that's all," he said, wrinkling his forehead with the familiar interrogatory grin he reserved for me; then he returned to his political visitor.

At Madame Ariel's suggestion, I once brought along an American hippie Hasid, one of Nissan Rosenberg's disciples. The meeting was touching and comical at once. Emmanuel the angel, as Madame Ariel called the young man, sat staring in bewildered bliss at "the great Rav Bloch." We were then reading Rav Isaac Bloch's book *The ABC of Spiritual Life,* an extraordinary little dictionary in Hebrew that outlined the various levels of consciousness on the Tree of Life, starting with *ahava,* love. The moony young Hasid could barely answer the Rav's inquiries about his background and interests.

"Who is your teacher?"

"Nissan Rosenberg. Has the Rav heard of him?"

"Ah, yes. You do a lot of singing and dancing," said the Rav, his eyes twinkling with irony. Often in our talks, precisely because I had spouted so effusively about my Hasidic ancestors, Rav Bloch (who descended from their rationalist opponents) went out of his way to downgrade Hasidic ecstasy. His own sharp, intellectual approach to spiritual life left little room for blank minds and aimless trances. Illustrating the difference between real contemplation and superstition, he delighted in telling me stories about credulous Polish Hasidim like Moishele, who once mistook the bellow of a prankster for the call of God.

"It seems that this Moishele had so longed for the voice from heaven that he sat all night under the eaves waiting to hear the summons again. The prankster, in the meantime, not satisfied with shaming his benighted neighbor by gathering the villagers on the roof to watch the game, now brought with him a huge bucket of dishwater. This time, as Moishele awaited the call, the prankster went up to the roof, shouted as usual, received the plaintive *'Hineni'* — 'Here I am!' — and, to the merriment of the villagers, poured the dishwater down on poor Moishele's head. You would think that the naive Hasid would have seen through the joke by then; but no, so credulous was this Hasid that he cried out with joy at the blessing that had been bestowed on his head. No less than the celestial hosts themselves had seen fit to purify him with a ritual bath!"

Leaving Moishele's young American counterpart to his ecstasy, Rav Bloch turned his attention to the lesson, talking mostly to me. During the discussion about love for the entire Creation, however, Emmanuel emerged from his trance and startled us both with a sudden question.

"Are we to love the *goyim,* too?"

"Of course the *goyim,* too. Every created thing," answered the Rav emphatically. I recalled his reasons for practicing vegetarianism and smiled. Rav Bloch avoided animal flesh because, as his kabbalist father believed, during the time of the redemption (which he seemed to feel was near at hand), meat eaters would have to answer to the renewed souls of the creatures whose blood they had tasted.

"What about Hitler, then?" insisted the newly awakened angel.

"You can't understand the meaning of Hitler," replied Rav Bloch quietly. "On a certain level even Hitler can be comprehended in the plan of Creation. It's a deep mystery; don't bother with it."

"But Hitler!" Emmanuel repeated with astonishment.

Resuming his mischievous twinkle, the Rav waved his hand in the air and said, "Okay, you can hate Hitler if you want to."

As we left, Emmanuel bowed his head before the master. "I know that the Rav is a *kohen* [priest]. Will he consent to bless me?"

I had never thought about asking for a blessing, although Yakov had informed me of the Rav's special priestly status with great pride. But watching the Rav place his hand on the boy's head and recite the prayer moved me suddenly, and I asked for one as well.

"It isn't necessary for you," he replied almost reprovingly. "Being a *kohen,* I am blessing you continually, whether you are in my presence or far away. Ours is an old connection, as I told you on the first day," he said, verifying my dream.

Rav Yehoshua Bloch was not without his enemies. His overtly mystical stance and his acceptance of secular students and women did not endear him to the traditionally Orthodox hierarchy. Indeed, there were rumors that one particularly fanatic leader of a Jewish, anti-Zionist sect had placed a curse on Rav Bloch's descendants. Some even went so far as to blame the death of his only child on the malediction. Rav Bloch evoked only passionate responses. I never met anyone who felt neutrally disposed toward him; people either expressed awe at his saintliness or unmitigated disapproval of his mystical nationalism. One morning I read an article in the

Jerusalem *Post* in which a noted scholarly opponent referred to the Rav as a modern "Sabbatai Zevi." This was tantamount to labeling him a dangerous fraud, since Sabbatai Zevi, a seventeenth-century apostate and pseudo-Messiah, nearly single-handedly destroyed the European Jewish community with his mystico-national crusade. Shocked that a reputable Orthodox scholar would publicly accuse *any* Jew of practicing the orgiastic, heretical techniques of the notorious Sabbatai Zevi (and even more so Rav Bloch, a rabbi with a worldwide reputation for profound spirituality), I showed the article to Yakov before my appointed class.

"Should I tell him?" I asked.

Yakov took one look at the name Sabbatai Zevi and rolled his eyes. "I don't know. What do you think? Maybe not. It's unnecessary to disturb the Rav with such nonsense."

"I think he should at least know what irresponsible people are spreading about him. This amounts to slander, you know," I said, waving the newspaper in front of Yakov's nose for emphasis. Although I hardly agreed with all of Rav Bloch's nationalist principles, I loved him enough to want to protect him from what I saw as the calumnious assaults of his enemies. At that moment, the study door opened and Rabbi Weiss, the treasurer of Rav Bloch's yeshiva, came into the waiting room. He usually spent one morning a week with the Rav, going over the institutional accounts. The Rav would sit in front of a mountain of checks and money while Rabbi Weiss called out the names of the donors. It was really an amusing sight, watching him nod disinterestedly over thousands of dollars, then come to life with a smile as one of the students interrupted him with a preplanned knock at the door, giving him the excuse to shoo the well-meaning Rabbi Weiss and his collected monies out of the study until the next mandatory accounting morning. Earthly goods meant nothing at all to Rav Bloch, perhaps because he was close to ninety. Yet, judging from his flat and his indifferent personal possessions, I expect that he had always shunned the material world. The only trace of pride he exhibited in tangible things was in his father's letters. These he kept in a long, brown-paged, dog-eared ledger. Occasionally, to illustrate a point in our discussion, he took out the long ledger, moistened his forefinger, and pushed rather than turned the gossamer pages to the exact letter he had in mind. Remarkably, the Rav did not even wear reading glasses. He merely lifted the text close to his chin and read, loudly and correctly, every word. Works like the *Zohar* (the classic textbook of Jewish mysticism) he seemed to know by heart. Motioning me to a special, glass-covered bookcase (with a missing left pane), he called out explicit references like: "That black volume over there, number four, page twenty-six, paragraph three." The Rav was indefatigable; we sat and studied and talked and argued and read sometimes for as long as five hours without a break. When he saw my head nodding and my body slumping against the back of the chair, he would shout out to Yakov in the next room for tea.

I brought him a bag of cookies once, then hesitated to give it to him at the last moment, remembering that Orthodox rabbis didn't eat gifts of food brought by nonobservant Jews. Without so much as examining the ingredients listed on the bag, the Rav grinned delightedly, tore open the top, munched happily, and pushed the bag toward me. I had very carefully chosen to buy from the kosher bakery on his corner, but Rav Bloch couldn't have known that. Yet he trusted me implicitly. Little gestures like that impressed me deeply. All my past experiences with Jewish orthodoxy had been bleak, life-hating, and condemnatory. Guilelessly, by *being* the commandments rather than by merely *fulfilling* them, Rav Bloch penetrated the accumulated bitterness of years in a matter of weeks.

During these intermissions, we usually chatted through an invited interpreter and drank sweet tea from glasses. Sometimes Noah came along just to bask in the Rav's presence. At tea, Rav Bloch told him amusing stories about world-famous visitors, itinerant Hasidim, his kabbalist-father's curative powers — all with no apparent significance. Then, a day or two later, Noah would be walking along in the street and he'd suddenly stop, fling his head back, and laugh, the meaning of the Rav's parable — directed particularly at Noah's unspoken question — dawning on him like the suddenly remembered punch line of a joke. For Noah, Rav Bloch was the Jewish version of the absent roshi.

Rabbi Weiss was furious when I showed him the article with the Sabbatai Zevi reference. "No, no, don't show it to him," he whispered, fearful that the Rav would hear. Just then, however, Rav Bloch pushed open the door and said, "Who is out there?"

To distract him from the fuss over the newspaper, Rabbi Weiss replied, "It's the professor from New York."

Poking his head around the door, Rav Bloch saw me and burst out laughing. "That's no professor, that's only Penina," he said, simultaneously deflating my hard-won scholarly identity and teaching me about the insignificance of titles. Similarly, when he picked up the newspaper and was informed of the ignominious comparison between himself and Sabbatai Zevi, the Rav shrugged his shoulders, pushed up his wide-brimmed black hat, assumed the naive look of a mischievous troll under a bridge, and said, *"Nu, mayle,"* which defies translation but means roughly, "So what can I do about it, and who cares what people call me?"

Once seated at the study table, he turned serious. "I have some important things to tell you today. Not so much for your book, but for yourself, personally, just so you don't misunderstand these teachings. It is all very important business, these discussions between the Rav and Penina," he said. "Maybe together we can clarify things."

I wondered whether he was not still joking but hardly had the chance to ask, for he continued to speak, indicating with his hand that he did not want me to interrupt him with questions.

"Judaism is the heart in the body of nations. Not chauvinistically, like Germany under Hitler, but cooperatively. Each created being, each nation, has a function. Every single nation bears an archetypal, autonomous function as part of the body of God. To find your place as an individual within a nation is not to deny the existence of other individuals and nations, but rather to work as a healthy body works when all the limbs and nerves and organs are operating as a unit. The foot does not ask to be the heart; the brain does not ask: 'Why am I not the liver?' Analogously, when you accept having been born as a Jew, or a Buddhist, or a Christian, you accept not only your given identity as part of the pattern of the Creation, but the identities of all the other individuals and nations as well. Finding your identity as a Jew, as part of the Jewish nation, the earthly reflection of the cosmic heart, requires preparation. First, the elimination of the confusion, the shame, the self-contempt perpetuated by exile and persecution. Then, spiritualizing your life — not by indulging prematurely in meditational practices and exercises, as people are trying to do today. They are experimenting with dangerous things, leaping toward the highest degrees on the spiritual ladder before they have even begun to integrate themselves mentally and physically in this world. Not by fragmenting yourself even further from the universal plan, as you do when you live like an American, feel like a Jew, and pray like a Hindu. Do you see what I mean, Penina? I am not talking about chest-beating nationalism. I am not talking about killing off the Arabs and marching into their homes. I am trying to show you how we must integrate ourselves personally, socially, politically, here on this earth, before we indulge ourselves in practices that have to do with God's business, practices that can trap you by diverting you from your true path to unity, the total communion with God that you are looking for. The danger is that those practices become an end in themselves.

"That is why I have not answered your complaints about not being given any *practical* exercises. I am against the study of techniques like Abulafia's permutations of the Hebrew letters, since there are no such masters around today to give people the advice they need on these matters or to judge the level of their spiritual accomplishment and future possibilities. So what I teach is the 'straight path,' taking one's place in the Jewish community and, thereby, in the created world; going from life-discipline to discipline of the intellect. Learning everything possible about life in this world before approaching the higher worlds is essential in this path. On each level there are natural laws, even in the realm of the 'supernatural,' and those laws must be learned before you attempt to walk there. Or else you will be hurt.

"The path I teach, Penina, helps to bring light into the confusion and darkness rather than throwing the disciple into the shadows without any weapons and telling him to fight. It's a question of gradually increasing the light, refining the human vehicle, the intellect, and then the spirit that lies beyond intellect, so that more and more light can come in and reduce the darkness, so that, at the right time, there is no darkness at all, only everything flooded with light."

In September, on the day before my scheduled flight home, it occurred to me for the first time since I had begun studying with Rav Bloch that I might never see him again. In two weeks we had discussed Spinoza, Freud, Jung, the Baal Shem Tov, and Maimonides. Not to mention his father's mystic texts, each sentence elucidated, mulled over, cherished, and ornamented by his own delightful commentary. It was a slow, monumental procedure, this "straight path"; I hadn't made more than my usual tentative commitment, more than the first shaky step, and I was leaving again. Rav Bloch might not live out the year. How could I rationalize shifting him into a corner of my head until the next summer vacation? Was I going to treat this demand for an entire life's dedication as just another "trip" — in every sense of that word? Yet staying in Jerusalem was impossible.

Although he must have sensed my upheaval, the Rav acted no differently from the way he did on any other morning. He opened one of the large volumes lying on the table in front of him.

"The difference between mysticism and magic . . . Yes, let's talk about that. Did you know that there were esoteric societies during the Babylonian period that interpreted metaphysics as the scientific study of the faculty beyond the intellect, what I referred to the other day as 'supernatural' power? In these societies, long before the sixteenth-century Maharal of Prague, the rabbis were creating 'golems' through the force of concentrated thought. Telepathic phenomena represent the point where science borders on parapsychology and metaphysics.

"The Rambam [Maimonides], in spite of his 'rational' exoteric writings (which were designed with the easily confused masses in mind), was himself fully adept at kabbalistic, or so-called mystical, techniques. But there is no 'mysticism' at work in all these examples. When a human being begins to develop his spiritual power, apparently 'supernormal' qualities accompany him; but these are really nothing more than a function of the higher reaches of brain. The force and intention of his thought are changing, becoming more and more concentrated, not intellectually, but spiritually. He can begin to 'read' people's characters, for example, because he is no longer in need of intellectual evidence, which is limited. This is only the beginning, a minor stage in the spiritual person's life. There are lower orders of the same 'talent': Take the telepathic ability of those who have no control over it, people who are born with it — like the man from Cleveland who came here and could tell me exactly where I had bought my hat, and even described the kitchen of the place where I was born, perfectly, down to the last detail. He was no great sage, only a businessman with a freak talent. This is not the same as the power of an *ish gadol* [great man]. The rabbi of Prague, remember, not only created the golem, but also discovered one of the mountains on the moon. He was a noted astronomer. Yes . . ."

I must have looked puzzled, because the Rav reiterated the fact with a weighty nod. "That mountain on the moon bears his name in honor of his discovery."

Rav Bloch patted my hand. "All is possible in God's Creation, Penina. Even that we should meet. Everything and everyone here is on a continuum . . . We all know each other."

"I'm leaving tomorrow," I said sadly.

Rav Bloch closed the huge tome and looked at me thoughtfully. "Will you be back next year?"

"I hope so."

There was a knock on the door. "Open!" called the Rav.

"There's a big class waiting outside," Yakov said, stepping into the room.

"One minute," said the Rav. Yakov smiled at me and said boldly, "See? If you lived here, you could see him every day."

"When are you coming back?"

"I think after spring."

"When?" The Rav cupped his hand to his ear.

The gesture recalled his age and vulnerability, and I grew tearful. "After Passover sometime, I suppose. I still have research to do."

"All right, then; you'll send me a copy of the manuscript?"

"If I ever finish it . . ." I thought of Rabbi Gaon's young men standing at their prayers night and day for the sake of my soul and for the soul of my book. "I forgot to tell you . . . I went to see Rabbi Gaon, and he said the book would bring the Messiah."

Rav Bloch chuckled; shaking his head from side to side, he said, "Nu, why not?"

I could tell from the familiar ironic twinkle in his eyes that the Rav didn't believe in the seer's "corrections" — nor in my bringing the Messiah.

"So, Penina, we'll continue our clarifications after Passover," he urged.

Quite without planning to, I reached out and hugged him. "May I have a photo? At least a picture?"

The Rav held me to his thin, old man's chest; his great, nutmeg-smelling beard scratched my cheek. "You don't need a photo, a physical reminder. We have a spiritual connection, a link now between soul and soul."

Embarrassed before Yakov's satisfied grin, I planted a hasty kiss on the Rav's cheek and ran out the door into the waiting room, where I was engulfed by a band of noisy yeshiva boys. Only after closing the rickety gate behind me at the end of the walkway did I gather the courage to glance back. Beautiful, dark-bearded Yakov stood waving to me from the top of the stairs.

"See you next year, God willing."

TWO

3

India — Extracts from Letters to Noah

I WAS STILL KNEE DEEP *in paperwork and research by the spring of 1976. Late that summer I traveled again to Jerusalem to meditate with Madame Ariel, locate kabbalistic manuscripts at the Hebrew University library, and study with Rav Bloch. The work was exhausting and, except for my sessions with Madame Ariel, almost exclusively intellectual. By the time I returned home in the fall, I was so tired of scholarship, Kabbalah, and everything "Jewish" that I would have gladly dropped the project entirely. Jewish mysticism, I felt, was nothing more than a collection of faded, unintelligible Aramaic scrawls, ghetto legends, and biblical crossword puzzles. It would take a more patient temperament than mine to piece it together as a comprehensible living practice for the twentieth-century layman.*

At the nadir of my despair, I received a call from my friend Aaron Breit, inviting me to attend a conference on Mind in Kashmir. A psychiatrist and a disciple of H. J. Shastri, Aaron traveled frequently to India in both capacities.

"You'll be the resident writer and kabbalist," he said. "The others will be mostly Indian intellectuals, scientists, and a musician and poet or two. Maybe even a yogi."

"What will we do there?" I asked.

"Talk. What else do you do at conferences?"

"Intellectual stuff?"

"Yeah, but in a maharaja's palace," Aaron said tantalizingly. I was intrigued as much by the casualness of the proposal as by the prospect of fleeing from the esoteric morass of material cramming my work space. At that moment, India seemed exactly the right antidote. Without hesitating, Noah, who could not take time away from his patients, encouraged me to make the trip. I rationalized the hiatus in my research by saying that it was a good time to visit Sue, who had by then committed herself to two years in the Vedanta ashram near Bombay.

So, in January of 1977, with a bag full of vitamins and pills, I flew to India.

13 January 1977
New Delhi

It's almost six P.M. and growing night very quickly. I can only see sky and, to the left of a high, faded pink sandstone verandah that resembles some crumbling ancient battlement, the rest of the enormous Ashoka Hotel, which (although I am tucked off into this left-hand blind corner) appears to offer a magnificent view of something that sounds like bus and car horns in the distance. Big black crows (?) circle the chimney and surrounding sky of this immense fortress. It is odd, finding myself half-asleep all the way on the other side of the world from you. And though I am exhausted, I already want to relate everything about the flight, my responses to the feel and smell of India, so I'll keep sending you queer, jagged letters like this one, jottings really, of what is happening to me here.

The twenty-two-year-old Italian yogi sitting next to me on the flight from Rome cried "Magnifico!" and sucked in his breath as he peered out the window. With shining eyes, hardly eating a bite throughout the whole eight-hour trip, he wrote his impressions in a leather pocket notebook. Finally, he grew too excited to write and turned to me for a few ecstatic words in fractured English. He had read *Autobiography of a Yogi,* it seems, and was instantly converted to the spiritual life. From the instructions given him through a correspondence course offered by the Los Angeles Center for Self-Realization, he practiced kriya yoga, a form of chanting and breathing meditation. "But now," he said, leaning forward to accept the Chiclet I offered him, "I must go to the source. India . . ." He breathed the word "India" with a sensual sigh, as Italian mystics ever since Dante have breathed the names of their elusive female guides. So the Roman yogi and three of his friends (seated, mercifully, two rows ahead, since one played a continuous medley of loud Italian rock on a tape recorder) were off to Allahabad and the Kumba Mela in search of enlightenment.

"Are you traveling for spiritual reasons?" he asked charmingly, to which I professorially replied, "I have been invited to participate in a philosophy conference in Kashmir."

On that note, we made a tacit peace of sorts, and he exchanged my Chiclet for a handful of pignola nuts that were very fresh and delicious. At the airport, he helped me remove my heavy shoulder bag, then disappeared in the mob along with his three shiny-booted, rock-playing friends.

(It is six now and the sky is very quickly darkening.)

The Indians appear very much like Arabs at first; more bureaucracy. Even the porter would not consent to take my bags out the door until a small green card stub had come down from customs, allowing me out of the building. That is part of traveling in a dictatorship, too, I suppose. Madame Gandhi's picture is everywhere, along with little pep-talk signs, telling people to do their job efficiently for a better India. The nodding, spitting squatters, many of them illiterate, either ignore or cannot read the pep talks. The customs officers and bank clerks behind the money-changing grilles are like their counterparts everywhere: phlegmatic with an occasional touch of sadism. These clerks alternated between being very nitty and very solicitous, as the whim took them.

The man in line ahead of me, a bald Australian, was interrogated as a potential CIA spy, although he looked just like the credit manager he claimed to be. But the Indian official in the maxi-coat with the gold buttons had simply taken a dislike to him and was refusing to allow his luggage to accompany him even as I was leaving. A clump of American shaven-headed Hare Krishnas were also fastened onto for questioning. (Maybe customs had received a tip about a bald-headed smuggler.) Seems a lot of dope gets in and out of this country under the folds of saffron robes. I admit I did not feel sorry for them; there's something revolting about their white-skinned, well-fed flesh pretending to be Indian. The *real* Indian passengers on board were, in fact, no more spiritual than a group of salesmen and their wives from Des Moines. They smoked, drank, and ate beef while the American sadhus dined on chickpea curry and sat cross-legged in meditation during the Peter Fonda movie, which the *real* Indians heartily enjoyed.

Outside the customs shed, in the damp, dark, five A.M. cold, more squatters wrapped in puttees and woolen head shawls sat spitting and waiting. With a volatile porter's help, I searched for my travel representative and found, at last, Mr. Singh, a young Westernized Indian in a blue down jacket. A smiling, alert-looking chap, I thought, someone I could at last really communicate with in English. But I soon found that the blue down jacket and Sixth Avenue swagger hid only another literal-minded Indian. Unlike the Arabs, who are multileveled, subtle, and quick, the Indians are uncompromisingly phenomenological people, which is why everyone calls them childlike. In every transaction — whether it be pouring tea on your leg in a restaurant or losing your luggage in a hotel — they have no room for nuance, no Greek anthropocentrism here. It's infuriating and liberating at once.

14 January 1977
Kashmir

Contrary to Mr. Singh's gloomy predictions, and with much fuss and bother over my alarm clock at the tight airport security check, I took the four A.M. mail plane to Kashmir and flew alongside the Himalayas. They are as I imagined they would be: mystical, awesome, unending, and godly. They flow with grace alongside heaven's basement, snowcapped and spiritual rather than foreboding — like the Jungfrau. Compared to the masculine Alps, the Himalayas are soft and welcoming; definitely feminine, they accompany the green vale of Kashmir rather than tower over it. True, I must have been influenced by all the stories about enlightened holy men sitting cross-legged in their snowy crevices; yet, as a pure phenomenon of nature, without any mystical ornamentation, the Himalayas are "religious" mountains. The ubiquitous "crows" that fly even as high as the Himalayan foothills, I learned from Mr. Singh on my departure, are called Indian bustards.

Enraptured, I stared out the porthole window of the chugging propeller-driven airbus alongside an American couple who turned out to be Harris and Eleanor May, fellow participants in the conference. He is a tall, sardonic California neurophysiologist; she appears to be European in the graceful way she takes second place to her husband. We were joined by a chunky, very proper Indian with iron-colored hair and a British accent who offered me a blanket against the cold and simultaneously introduced himself as R. V. Patel, a professor of religion at University College, London.

Only minutes after we landed in Ramnagar, the site of our conference, we were confronted by a procession of six scrawny barefoot men carrying a freshly dead corpse on a stretcher. One man blew a horned pink conch shell while the man behind him cried out over and over again what Professor Patel translated for us as: "Only God's name lives forever." It wasn't until I got to the motel where we are being put up that I remembered where I'd heard that cry before: in the Shema, when we Jews declare God's eternality with His name ...

At supper Professor Patel warned me against traveling to Allahabad, where my Italian acquaintance and one hundred million other pilgrims were gathering in honor of the Kumba Mela, a once-every-twenty-year-or-so festival that is astrologically determined. Priests and sadhus emerge from every nook and cranny and cave in India on this occasion, which marks the meeting of the Ganga and Jamuna rivers, the earthly reflection of the intercourse between the

Creator and His consort. Anyway, Patel assured me that I would be crushed instantly and left to be swallowed up in the mire on the banks of the Ganga, where eleven million people were immersing themselves every hour on the hour. Dr. Minar, a Bangalore psychiatrist who arrived for supper on the afternoon flight, reinforced Patel's warning with the news that cholera was already spreading at the pilgram site surrounding the city. Harris May advised taking malaria pills and staying away from the Kumba Mela, too. As Madame Ariel says, I am "emotive" and "suggestive," so I took the pills and the advice and vowed to stay away from Allahabad.

Supper conversation ranged from Harris May's assertion that the Tibetans were the best people in India to a contentious cross-cultural argument between Patel and just about everyone else present (except for Eleanor, the eternally feminine peacemaker) about Indian emotional life. Dr. Minar, who, it turns out, organized the conference, talked at length about his study of so-called primitive healing techniques among the aboriginal southern Indians that he found (to his educated surprise) were as successful with local village schizophrenia as Thorazine is back in the States. He should know; he has worked for the past ten years with the World Health Organization and was trained at Harvard. A typical Indian admixture of linear-logical and visual-emotional approaches, Dr. Minar appeared slightly more inclined toward treating patients with scrapings from the bark of trees and a few potent mantras than with capsules and electroshock therapy.

Patel, wearing his Uncle Sam hat now, protested that since the decline of Indian culture (to which he traces everything from Aryan Nazism to the use of ketchup in curry), the country had fallen irretrievably into a slough of bigotry, prejudice, and greed. Harris May prevented an argument by describing his colorful train journey through the Himalayas; he fascinated us all with details about the street poets of Darjeeling, who gather large crowds around them when they recite impromptu stories in Hindi. Old grannies, workers, all kinds of townspeople, rich and poor, will stop to listen to a tale of the young Krishna at any time or place. Harris says it's part of the "eccentric charm" of the Indian character.

Alone in my unadorned room, I sat musing over the discrepancy between words about India and its charm and the realities of life in the street. It is brutal, really — like the open trough of filthy, excremental water running down the gullies in the main roadway of Ramnagar. I tried to picture the mythical interplay between street poet and townsfolk audience, to imagine Krishna, blue and gilded, romping among silver-eyed peacocks, but could only recall the throat-choking fumes of burning cowdung patties, the unpretty poverty. And no "charming" cover of religious or mystical "compassion" could prettify it for me. We, after all, could listen to the street poet, snap photographs of Tibetan vendors, discuss consciousness over elegantly spiced food, and fly home on swift "iron birds." It suddenly appeared bizarre to be sitting among open suitcases next door to a Bunyanesque California intellectual and across the hall from a foppish comparative religionist in an Indian replica of a Holiday Inn (now frigid despite the noisily blowing heater propped up on a table and aimed at my stiff red knuckles) overlooking the Dal Lake, the maharaja of Ramnagar's semi-Gothic, semi-Victorian palace across the way — no, obscene, really, when down the road a few miles people were hacking away with TB and God knew what else, picking at their various sores, and trying desperately to turn a dollar. How could even the most detached saint maintain his "compassionate equanimity"?

I can no longer romanticize India — mystic or no. I cannot shed Madame Ariel's "being in life" no matter how reclusive I might feel about this web of illusion we call the world. I sense her good Jerusalem prayers around me, protecting me like Jacob's tent. And, as always, I think of you, and affectionately pluck your Buddha's earlobe.

This morning the maharaja took us on a tour of his estate. Pointing to the surrounding Himalayan peaks, he asked, "How do you like my lovely palace?" Stupefied by the vast, snow-decked mountains that were now visible from the sweeping half-moon terrace behind the palace, we could only drink our coffee and bob our heads up and down at everything the raja said.

White-gloved, turbaned waiters served tea and coffee English style, from silver urns into translucent porcelain cups. (I expect the gloves were just as much for sanitary and caste reasons as for style.) Even the cookies were English: your favorite McVities's sugared biscuits. The raja likes to dominate the conversation and, raja-like, demanded perfect attention throughout our first, social, encounter. In fact, the Indians in the company, even the most learned and distinguished of them, respectfully deferred to his every gesture. (He is, after all, a favorite with Madame G. and could one day come in handy should they ever find themselves in jail for saying the wrong thing to the wrong person.)

The Asian counterpart of a spoiled and vain American merchant prince out of an F. Scott Fitzgerald novel, the maharaja of Ramnagar took his philosophy degree in England. He is more than a dilettante, however, and fancies himself a spiritual seeker whose power and wealth favor his karmic struggle to educate mankind for the future. So, as a result of a visionary glimpse into his "ultimate purpose" on earth, the raja decided one day to embark on the search for "consciousness" with the same competitive fervor he had once displayed on the polo field. His dark, brooding Moghul features make it hard to ignore what he has to say; and he dominated the first conference meeting as he had dominated the introductory tea, offering "suggestions" rather charmingly and taking it for granted that his suggestions would not be rejected.

The biologists and psychiatrists spent most of the opening day tussling over the "mechanistic model of the brain."

The raja interrupted impatiently, "May not man be surpassed through further brain development? Dinosaurs, too, once ruled the earth and did not foresee their own extinction."

The distinguished Dr. Krishnagar, tweedy, bespectacled, just back from two years at Harvard, responded, "Man's further evolution cannot be physical but must be mental; it is consciousness that will change. As Aurobindo said, 'Supraconsciousness is the new evolution.'"

Professor Patel wrinkled his nose with distaste, hunched his shoulders, and spread his arms out on the table in front of him. "It is the intention of yoga to abolish the mind, not to expand it to better 'functioning.'"

"It is unlikely that new structural development of the brain will occur, except perhaps through environmental influences. Evolution, as you are referring to it, may be cultural rather than biological," added Dr. Gopal, a likable psychiatrist in a marine-colored turban.

At this, Professor Sanjay, the plump, boyish physicist, perked up. "Isn't it a question of quality versus quantity? Learning new ways of doing things, not necessarily *more* ways? Of refinement of the nervous system we now have, rather than new additions?"

"Have we yet determined that the mind is tied to the brain?" asked Dr. Konarak, a dapper physiologist in a midnight blue suit.

"Buddha speaks only of points of consciousness, no known entity called mind. Do we grow or expand with an immediate understanding or experience of mind pervading all without need of a physical entity?" asked Professor Patel, eliciting an answer from no one.

"Biological evidence shows that neocortical layers of brain are expanding in circuitry and are therefore developing more connections," replied Dr. Krishnagar politely to Dr. Konarak over Professor Patel's irately bobbing head. It was apparent that Patel had made a nuisance of himself from the start, which endeared him to me all the more.

"Yoga is an alternate way of consciousness," interposed the raja, one arm rakishly stretched out behind him against the back of his friend Krishnagar's chair.

"The mind, when it looks at itself, is already limited," came Aaron Breit's double-binding drawl.

"That is so," said the chain-smoking poet Bhandari. "As Huxley said, 'Brain is a limiting function which reduces the terrifying light.'" He sent Aaron a self-satisfied grin.

Then, somehow, the talk degenerated into a crossfire of quibbles about *siddhis*, supernormal powers. I could just imagine Narendra here, laughing them out of the room. The raja, always focused on power of any sort, talked animatedly about "manifestations" from mental realms into physical ones. I confess I turned off at that point until Harris May's calm, sardonic voice rang out to my left: "I'd like to suggest that we discuss the conjunction between physical and experiential research before we go off into a lot of anecdotal stuff."

"Especially since the mind is itself fragmented and likes to get bogged down in aimless ruminating," Aaron responded, evoking laughter and ending the meeting on a down-to-earth note.

At lunch I made friends with a Swiss psychiatrist named Greda Thorberg, a handsome woman of fifty or so, who has been working in a mental hospital in a Himalayan village for twenty years. Tonight, during one of the innumerable Ramnagar electrical blackouts, she invited me out onto the terrace of her room and recited Hindu myths about all of the constellations visible overhead. Finishing our tea in the dark, we talked about our yogas and meditations and whatnot. Dr. Thorberg found her path here in India twenty years ago with an old Kashmiri Moslem teacher who has since died. From what I can tell in such a short time, her guru did a very fine job. This woman is the only person at the conference — Western or Eastern — with the recognizably cheerful tranquillity, the unmotivated selflessness, of the true yogi. Eminently practical, yet full of folk wisdom, Dr. Thorberg taught me how the Tibetans sleep to keep warm: face down, knees on the bed, elbows nearby, head tucked between the shoulders, and body all scrunched up. It works.

A wonderful thing happened at the maharaja's tea yesterday. After an initially boring discussion about neurology versus free intention, we found ourselves on the terrace, face to face with a group of mischievous spider monkeys. This cocky family with very human features frolicked on the roof overhanging the buffet, frequently stopping to stare down at us with exaggerated curiosity. Suddenly their leader, a brute with a big fluff of gray fur and a bushy tail, impudently turned his rear and noisily peed down into the silver ewers, at the same time drenching petit fours, linen napkins, servants, and narrowly missing the maharaja himself! It was a colossal moment; eminent scientists and scholars laughed with embarrassment, the raja looked bemused, and the spiteful monkey tittered at us all from behind his hand. That is India, a place where nothing, and therefore *everything,* is sacred.

The second great surprise took place just as Dr. Gopal was about to read his paper on phenomenology. It was early in the morning and I was barely awake; my head nodded sleepily over my notes on the polished rosewood table. Gopal was saying something about Edmund Husserl when the door burst open and Swami Krishnananda, the chief guru of Sue's very own Bombay ashram, appeared without introduction. Orange robe and all, he thrust his way into the room with no apologies to the crestfallen Gopal and took the seat nearest the raja, who, from his languid response, seemed to be awaiting the arrival of just such a deus ex machina to challenge our growing restiveness. Krishnananda is thoroughly pointed, bespectacled, rowdy, and obnoxious. His continuous mugging fell on the group like a flattened Sammy Davis routine. Without being asked, and after taking one swift look at Gopal's paper over the speaker's shoulder, he drove straight ahead into a set-piece lecture on mind. Even the maharaja shuffled in his seat.

"Mind, ah, uh, you might say," Krishnananda's singsong voice resounded throughout the room over the occasional scratching of the two Sikh stenographers' pens, his arms making wide circles in the air around his head, his gold watch casting dazzling sun dots on the walls and ceiling. "Mind is thought," he finally blurted out. "Thought, ah, can never be without an object. Thought minus objects equals pure, ah, consciousness." Krishnananda laughed a high-pitched, cackling laugh and continued his Englishman-with-a-head-cold discourse. "Consciousness objectified is, ah, mind. Brain, ah, is equipment, a misapprehension of pure consciousness, what we, ah, call *avidya* in the Vedanta. Pure consciousness can, ah, only be experienced; it cannot be expressed. The movement to, ah, *samadhi* is a gradual movement through, ah, stages of consciousness."

No wonder Sue has written that she can't stand him.

The chemistry professor challenged Krishnananda on a vedantic point, and there ensued a long string of witticisms punctuated by "ahs" that I did not bother to follow. This swami is a pedant. He could not be the reason Sue came all the way to India. He could not be why she stays down in that ashram wearing white saris and eating half an allowance of milk and lentils in celibacy though she is in her sexual and artistic prime of life. I can't wait to ask her when I see her in Bombay.

Harris May must have read my mind, for he passed around a note that alluded to Krishnananda as "Sammy Davis, Jr." The analogy was impolite but, in a showbizzy way, undeniable. When you really took a look at the swami's gestures, his gold trinkets, and his habit of being on the verge of breaking into song, you felt you might as well be sitting in Las Vegas.

At last the maharaja discreetly got rid of the talkative swami. But the stage had been set for tension, which was bound to erupt no matter how hard the dignified Krishnagar, in his capacity as second chairman, tried to suppress it. Harris May, with his corduroy slacks, California beads, and independent researcher's brain, should not have been expected to tolerate the raja's high-handed Brahmanism for more than one session. He blew up after a lull in the exchange — actually, as Dr. Minar and Dr. Konarak were exploring the notion of consciousness in lower animals.

"I just can't agree with you guys about all this superconscious stuff. It doesn't strike me as significant when matched against studying what we've already got right here, now. We know little enough about the mind from even the most sophisticated neurological and physiological research data — my colleagues here will bear me out on that — so why begin with superconsciousness?" he bellowed into the maharaja's face.

"Always pragmatic, you Americans," the raja answered condescendingly. The Indians in the group looked away and fiddled awkwardly with their notes.

"I think what is at issue here, the primary controversy as I see it," interposed Dr. Konarak, "is whether the mind is a function of the brain, or whether the brain is a tissue through which the mind expresses itself." That took some of the pressure off and landed us back in a group controversy between the materialists and the idealists.

The afternoon proved tamer but no less interesting as a lesson in East-West dynamics. This time it was I who blew the whistle on the maharaja's "supermind." That nonsense was really threatening to get out of hand and ruin the whole conference. Even Sanjay the physicist, whose paper postulated from quantum theory the desire for an ultimate homeostasis of mind, seemed to efface the entire spectrum of human effort, toil, suffering, art, degradation, and nobility — leading us from earthly existence right up to the bland, ignoramus grin of the transcendental Maharishi. I piped up.

"This nihilistic propaganda sounds like another version of the Marxism I was exposed to in college. Just follow me, buddy, and you'll have bread — or, in this case, 'superconsciousness,' in the name of the perfectly equilibrized, blissed-out superfew."

Aaron Breit shot me an encouraging *okay* look. Thorberg glanced up from her writing pad and sent a big smile across the table. Surprisingly, the physiologist Konarak raised his thumb and forefinger in perfect agreement. For one half-second it seemed the room was about to break into applause.

The raja frowned but chose to ignore me. At tea later, however, he approached me and said, "You seem to think that Indians don't ask questions, that only you Americans are searching for answers." But before I could reply, he turned his back on me and embarked on a conversation about Indian miniatures with the artist-in-residence.

The next sessions gathered momentum. Then, miraculously, the raja was called upon to leave for some "pressing political reasons." (Who but an extrasensory yogi could know that Madame G.'s government was toppling? And the maharaja's career with it.) Free of all social constraints, the Indians at last opened up. Under Dr. Krishnagar's calm, informed guidance, we in fact began the exchange of ideas for which we had gathered in the first place. Dr. Marthanda, India's most prominent neurosurgeon, also thinks that man is in a crucial phase of biological evolution. Like all these Indian intellectuals, he feels that we are somehow poised on the brink of a great evolutionary mutation for the good.

"Physiologically," he said, "we have reached a stopping point, but psychologically, mentally, we are prepared for new, perhaps transcendent, forms of activity." Contrary to the radicals, he indicated that the evolutionary process *conserves,* rather than rejects, its past while developing. His picture of the brain (on which he operates daily — for free, Thorberg tells me — in poor Indian villages, where he enjoys a reputation as a saintly "family doctor" despite his princely origins) expresses its "localizing tendency, which is coexistent with unholistic functioning." Or, as our friend Aaron would have it, the normally "fragmented thought process."

"Dropping the self," said the poet Bhandari, "allows new or more 'grammars' to appear in creativity. Poetry is a limited experience in comparison to yogic experience."

Dr. Gopal, himself a published poet writing in Sanskrit, asked, "Is creative experience something coming from *inside,* do you think? Or is it plugging into the 'outside' wealth available to us when our antennae are set out?"

His psychiatric colleague Dr. Minar responded, "Creativity of every variety involves the need for self-expression. It seems to emerge, like the yogi's ecstasy, from one-pointed concentration and a sharpening of sensibilities. Both have in common the existence of no particular goal; it's rather an activity for its own sake. At certain stages of the process, each stroke or note, or moment of meditation, precedes the one that follows almost without the artist's or yogi's effort. Conscious poets have predefined goals."

"It's a question of inspiration versus perspiration," said Gopal, chuckling.

"I suspect that the moment of creativity is a fusion of outside — or environment — with inside," added Dr. Marthanda.

That night at the bar, an excited and voluble group of conferees passed around a bottle of cognac and continued the discussion, interlacing it with guru gossip — as their counterparts in New York might discuss literary celebrities and film stars. These scholars have traveled the height, depth, and width of India in search of *the* perfectly realized guru. Only the musician Rama Barati, himself a practicing tantric yogi, claims to have found one. The rest is all gossip. Today there are six or seven superstars among the gurus, and the Americans have "spoiled" them all. The *really* great ones, my new friends were quick to assure me, are all dead. I have been supplied with a shopping list from Benares to Bombay. Gurus await me in caves, at temple entrances, and above cigarette factories. Yet I am not inclined, I think, to follow it through. I have trodden that path before, and I am tired.

18 January 1977
Kashmir

The conference ended last night with a glorious sunset over Vaishna Devi, three grand Himalayan peaks visible from the palace verandah. The Indian sun's exact shade of salmon pink can never be caught by pen or camera. One moment the snow-covered caps are suffused in a warm orange dusk, and the next, as if some vast unseen Siva had switched off the current by blinking his eye, night falls.

Aaron Breit summed up the cause for the antithought faction by reiterating his pejorative characterization of thought as a "pleasure of the mind, a manifestation of desire." With his typical emphasis on "detachment," he sounds as if he is condemning rather than describing normal human activities like thinking, loving, and wanting approbation. Aaron cynically defined the "search for bliss," represented by the yogis of the group, as "an attempt to obliterate the separateness, the isolation of individuals. Bliss, ecstasy, God — they are all an escape, a manifestation of spiritual ambition," he concluded icily.

Harris May was more lenient on the "spiritual dimension" in man. He said that it was not "higher" (as the raja had emphasized), but rather that it was complementary to ordinary consciousness, or perception, which he defined as "the making of distinctions."

"In the spiritual dimension, distinction-making stops and unboundedness reigns. A subject cannot make distinctions about itself; it *is*. As subject, it fragments the ordinary world; while in the state of unbounded unity, it experiences holistically. The importance of attaining the spiritual dimension, as I see it, lies in gaining perspective on the world of intentional activity, deepening our understanding of our ordinary world of experience. Not running away from thought or cutting it off. That we could do with one blow from a sledgehammer. We are all agreed on the goal of unifying the fragmented, subjective view of the universe that dominates our life, but none of us seems to agree on the mode for achieving it."

"That's because we're looking subjectively," Sanjay called out. We all laughed. "What interests me is the transformation that is necessary to holistic experience."

Then, for the first time since we began, a gaunt man with long fingernails who had never removed his white mohair coat spoke up. His name, Aaron whispered, was Udyagar; he was a biochemist from southern India. I had seen him a few nights before, talking in the motel lounge to a young man with a long scarf who smoked incessantly and was reputed in the district for having disciplined himself through yoga practice to live without sleeping for a year. Needless to say, Harris May, Greda Thorberg, Aaron Breit, and I had many good laughs over that one. Nonetheless, Professor Udyagar was a serious, respectable person, though his Indian open-mindedness toward even the most ridiculous occult speculations was, like his ever-present white mohair coat and his mandarin finger-nails, a trademark. One thing about Indians: Every spiritual path is taken seriously, even the phony ones.

Professor Udyagar surprised us all by giving a personal account of his adventures in meditation. An Advaita vedantist by disposition and a scientist by profession, he referred to the *Upanishads* as an "experimental report," which scientists of the past left for re-testing in the future. The experimental model, according to him, had been clearly set out by the forest sages of ancient India and was there for all of us to try on our own bodies and minds. Mind, by obliterating itself in its present condition, as it were, was capable of evolving into a higher mode. The mental experiments delineated in the Vedas — designed to suppress all intellectual, sensory, and ruminative functioning — had to be carried on all the time, sleeping or waking, working or relaxing. The techniques he divided into Patanjali's yoga system (which, he said, was more dangerous in its lasting effects on psychology and physiology) and philo-sophical speculation advocated by the vedantists. The way of analysis taught by Shankara in the ninth century, he felt, was less dangerous than yoga and, when carried to the outermost limits, brought one beyond the heights of thought to suprarational realms. (Shades of Rav Bloch's "straight path" through the intellect by degrees.) Employing what he called the higher self as witness, or what kabbalists call self-reckoning, Udyagar claimed to have watched the phenomenon of thinking all the way to the end of thought.

It was fitting that this queer, shy man had the last word, for none of his talk was speculative; he was the only one in the room bold enough to admit having experimented on himself. The rest of us had merely indulged in harmless intellectualizing about events that were actually very important in our lives. But we were reticent, worried about our reputations, and afraid of being called mystical instead of scientific. Udyagar, on the last day of the conference, when it was too late, opened the door to its real theme: *our own experiences of our own minds.*

Dr. Krishnagar cleared his throat. "Yes. Ahem. You might say, ladies and gentlemen, that understanding the atom may resemble child's play next to studying child's play itself," he closed humbly. We politely applauded, and it was over.

Professor Udyagar's aloofness, his mandarin fingernails, and his persistent white coat had put me off. At the end of the conference I wanted to thank him for his honesty, but I couldn't because he reminded me of some kind of mad wizard, and I was a little afraid of him. Instead, I tried to pick a fight with Aaron as we sat in the lounge drinking beer.

"Why are you a disciple of H. J. Shastri?" I asked ungraciously.

"Because he doesn't give out any hope."

"That's just the reason I hate him. He's curt, hard, mean."

"Are you saying that he doesn't pay any attention to you and you resent him for it?"

"Don't pull that 'insight' analysis on me. He's mean. Period."

"What kind of teacher *do* you like?"

"None. I'm a misanthrope. I couldn't even talk to Udyagar because I didn't like his looks. Who knows, he might have been my guru in disguise."

"Is there anyone you trust?" Aaron persisted.

I thought a moment, took a sip of beer, and said, "Little old men with white beards who squeeze your fingers when they are making a talmudic point and who aren't ashamed of contact."

"What?"

"Nothing," I said, finishing my beer. "I'm just kidding." I wondered what I was doing in India. I wondered why I had left Jerusalem and Rav Bloch. I wondered whether I would ever stop wondering.

Today we toured the Siva temple and the great Vishnu temple and encountered more "consciousness" there than we had at the entire erudite affair back in the Ramnagar Palace. These Hindus have embodied Madame Ariel's *rêves* everywhere around themselves so that "ordinary" life is carried on within the framework of every possible manifestation of God imaginable by the human mind. There are fish men, lovely ladies with a thousand heads and hands, monkeys (like our peeing friend of the previous day), and a vast, pulsating landscape of conscious, unconscious, and superconscious realities. Worshiping life on all its myriad levels, planes, and worlds within worlds, to the extent of dressing it up in fancy five-and-dime jewels and polishing its wooden fingernails, is, I grant you, a primitive externalization that the Jews condemn as a distraction from the nonembodiedness of God. But seeing Oneness in its every possible manifestation, contortion, and variety when you ride your bicycle to work every morning, like seeing the ambling cows and the people washing themselves down in a filthy street that is suffused with religous feeling, forces "sanctity" into this life; in India "sanctity" is neither an abstraction you must leave your home in search of nor something you celebrate only once or twice a year. Indian "holiness" is a daily event, and its regularity tends to push the dualism of everyday experience into the Infinite from which it came.

Personally, I am not moved by the religious ritual here. I can't understand how Sue from Brooklyn prays to Ganesh, the elephant god, at four every morning in her ashram temple. I, a non-image-making Jew, an admirer of Hindu religious "technology" — that is, meditation, yoga, mindfulness, self-reckoning, and earthy spirituality — am in sympathy only with the "theater" of it. But that's decaying, too, I am afraid.

The ritual at the temple is short. The priest chants, lights the candles, addresses his speech to a shiny ebony statue of a giant Vishnu, the Creator, then greets the god's consort, Lakshmi. He throws flowers and oil around the statues and us. We in turn are handed flower petals, which we are instructed to throw at the feet of the gods; then the priest hands us oranges, which he blesses with a jet of holy water from a conch shell. He anoints our foreheads and tongues with hot clarified butter. It is all very Catholic. I feel odd talking to a statue, and the hot butter scalds my tongue.

Escorted around the temple by one of the priests, I search every little "house" inhabited by one manifestation of the myriad manifestations of the Divine: Ganesh, Hanuman, Bharata, Krishna — gentlemen with moustaches and turbans, veiled and unveiled ladies, monkeys, parrots, elephants, snakes, tortoises — everything indiscriminately tossed together in the cosmic salad that is our created world. The whole Hindu pantheon is there, dressed to the nines by the local priests and faithful Ramnagar devotees. Vishnu's temple is spotless, white, cold marble. Siva, on the other hand, being a destroyer, lives in a wild, shabby place on a desolate hill. Inside, we are forced to remove our shoes and walk barefoot across the freezing stone floor into pools of mud and water as a bulbous, rusty bell clangs away in our ears. Through two arched doorways we make our bone-chilling tour until we find ourselves at last in the inner sanctum, where two immense, erect phalluses carved of pure, transparent rock crystal are being washed and sung to and dressed in flower garlands by three elderly women in saffron saris.

Greda Thorberg whispers that the local Kashmiris believe that the peepul tree guarding the Siva temple is so sacred that if you urinate near it, you become insane. She says she even has some patients in her hospital with this bizarre "case history." The Siva lingam is a very potent organ. Interestingly, Greda considers herself a Sivaite and, with easy familiarity, takes the priest's sandalwood forehead scrawl and the almonds he feeds her as Siva's "gift" to his worshipers.

I decline. I am cold and less impressed by the moustachioed, roguish Siva than by his stunning crystal phalluses. Nevertheless, I continue to admire the remarkable flexibility of the Hindu mind, which is primitive enough to worship trees, yet sophisticated enough to worship the unity in all of life's multiplicity. Yes, even I can envision myself at some point in my life developing a favored aspect of God; I might feel comfortable, for example, asking boons of Shakti, the all-encompassing Mother. But — and this includes even the monkeys, charming elephants, and various dragons — my guides make a point of reminding me again and again that these multiple forms all reflect only *one* power, the Brahma, which pervades all. Unlike the anthropomorphic Greek pantheon of hedonistic and capricious gods, these Indian nature representations paradoxically bring you back to the emptiness behind form, the playful in the serious, the one in the many. Every element is included here, every day, month, planet. It's as complicated as the kabbalistic cosmology. Except that the Indians have compressed the cosmos into the manageable shorthand we Jews call idol worship.

When I left Siva's house, I felt that I had been walking through one of Madame Ariel's exercises, face to face with the archetypal collective unconscious of the human race.

In the afternoon, the maharaja's aide crammed us into a big old bus for a trip to Dal Lake, a local tourist attraction in the mountains. It was quite chaotic, really. Most of the party had to catch the evening train and didn't want to go. But before we had a chance to question or register protest, we were herded onto the bus and were climbing uphill along skinny mountain roads flanked on either side by terrifying chasms. I was face to face at last with the Himalayan ravine of my phobic meditative visions. Fluffy green trees, mustard seed flowers, and surprising moments of green patch marked the risky course of our journey. Even as high as nine thousand feet there were cows, gentle spotted creatures who knew just how and when to get out of the way of the determined, tight-lipped bus driver going uphill in second gear at fifty. The aide, Mr. Kumari, informed us en route at one point that we were only seven miles from Pakistan and, though we were not to fear, that the stretch of scrub brush to our right was a favorite hiding place for infiltrating snipers. Nobody so much as blinked. Indeed, the hills around us were alive with barefoot Indian army men and lazy green halftracks.

In the mud flats below a bridge leading out of Ramnagar, men in loose dhotis were throwing buckets of water at buses and trucks in a futile attempt to perform what we think of as car washing. Sanjay the physicist remarked with a nostalgic smile, "In my childhood in Kerala, I saw the same kind of old men washing elephants exactly like that. I guess these are India's new elephants."

All along the road, fatalistic signs urged motorists to be careful: LIFE IS SHORT ENOUGH, DON'T MAKE IT SHORTER. Wall announcements held out the promise of a thousand rupees for anyone who would "Report a Smallpox Case." Mud hut villages higher in the mountains were neat, their primitive main streets cleaner than the paved road leading into Ramnagar. The higher we climbed, the more orderly the scenery; farms, children, women, and livestock here were less frayed than the town dwellers below.

Conference members exchanged comments about the scenery, academic anecdotes, tourist information, political gossip. We spent over two hours on that rattling heap of bus before they let us get out; it didn't matter where we were by the time we unbent our cramped legs. Even the sight of the clear, peaceful expanse of mountain lake shining like a mirror in the sun did not take the edge off the grumbling. A frisky black mongrel puppy leaped at our heels, following us to the porch of the neat pink bungalow where our invisible hosts were said to be fixing us tea. Out on the grass, we clustered in groups and joked about taking an icy swim. Barati the music professor, Harris and Eleanor May, and I sat together and growled about our hunger as we swapped travel stories. Barati wanted desperately to be invited to the States; May wouldn't have minded being asked to teach in Benares, he said. Excluded from their conversation, I gulped great batches of cold clear mountain air and watched the antics of a tethered goat with a little bell around its neck. I could hear Aaron behind me, clapping his hands together with delight and extolling the virtues of isolation in the mountain fastness of Kashmir. "You could write and read and just sit here forever without any interruption from anyone; the world outside would simply disappear."

Can you imagine Aaron Breit sitting in the wilderness without his *New York Times* every morning? He'd be back on the next plane.

Barati, an urbane Brahman with luxuriant silver hair and dressed in handsome tweeds, talked exclusively of bhang, a favorite Benares version of hash, which he takes mixed with rosewater, fruit juice, almond extract, and milk. A potent malted, don't you think? I declined his invitation to partake, especially after hearing him describe the innumerable bhang addicts who sit nodding for days on end in blissful idiocy on the streets of that holy city. Barati used bhang, he said, for meditative purposes. He practices some form of tantric yoga and finds the brew helpful in inducing eight-hour stretches of perfect concentration. Even H. J. Shastri's brand of self-observation, he said, can be attained immediately with the help of a bhang cocktail. "You quickly feel your *self* disappearing," Barati promised.

Harris May, always provocative, said he was more interested in inducing eight hours of perfect sex.

"Very good, very good," Barati laughed, throwing back his handsome Brahman head. "I must remember that."

Half-starved by then, we passed around some of the *prasad* we had been given by the temple priests that morning: oranges, bananas, apples, and a few peeled almonds — food from the gods. At last we were invited into the pink bungalow, a government "rest house" (though devoid of any furniture on which to rest), where we stood in line, jumping up and down in place to keep warm. A lone wooden table at the center of the room was spread with trays of hard-boiled eggs, chicken, tomatoes, and delicious, spicy french-fried potatoes. We gobbled the food like the monkeys on the raja's verandah. I stepped over to look inside the "kitchen," a nook filled by three barefoot Kashmiri men wrapped in cloaks and turbans who squatted over a charcoal fire on a stone slab brazier, frying endless portions of heavily paprikaed chips. I knew I would suffer for my gustatory daring, but ate the potatoes anyway. The sleepless young man in the long scarf remained glued to Professor Udyagar's side. Whenever one of the women seemed about to approach him, the young man lowered his eyes and sidled away. Later I found out why. Professor Udyagar, who had been interviewing him about his meditative techniques all through the bus trip, described the young man to Aaron as "rigidly celibate," then asked Aaron for his neurological and psychological opinion of such yogic practices. Aaron told him that the boy was probably severely depressed and insomniac. You see, it all depends on where you're from. In India, not sleeping or making love means you are on some strictly ascetic spiritual path; in New York it means you are psychotically depressed.

20 January 1977
New Delhi

I guess the dispersal of the group was too much for me. I threw up on the plane returning to New Delhi, ostensibly from a plate of rancid dhal, but mostly from nerves at being cast on my own all at once. Everyone I meet is amazed (and aghast) when I say that I am traveling alone through India. It just isn't done. By evening, though, I calmed down and was able to keep down a plate of mullignatawny soup. At the very moment I was being sick into a packet of tissues in the stopped-up cubicle toilet of the mail plane from Kashmir, Madame Gandhi announced elections. To say that our group was taken by surprise is surely an understatement. Many were now free to travel, to accept fellowships offered by the UN, and juicy prospects in the Persian Gulf states, free to talk, to breathe! The raja must have lost his job, because he disappeared after that first day of meetings and never returned to see us off.

Political life interests me the least of anything here. The Hindustan *Times* is cluttered with stories about new dams and tractors as well as insipid letters from and to the lovelorn. Sample: "Advice much appreciated on aphrodisiac designed to cure frigidity in new bride of fifteen years." Signed: "Frustrated Madras bridegroom." There is nothing resembling a news analysis, not even one perceptive comment on the dramatic turn of events in the Indian government. Perhaps all the perceptive people are in jail. There is almost no international news to speak of except for occasional four-line paragraphs devoted to mining catastrophes in Albania. Remember Spain during that Franco summer when we slept in the street in Marbella and you read the *International Herald Tribune* three days late in order to make sure that the world was still going around out there? Well, I'm just as socially isolated here.

Wish you were here to join me for a vegetarian burger on a bun, for which I am ending this letter.

22 January 1977
New Delhi

The unexpectedly long layover in New Delhi provided lots of empty spaces. As Aaron promised before leaving me to my own devices, watching the tricks and black holes of my own mind would be the most interesting tour India had to offer. Studying loneliness after all my witty companions have gone, reading a three-day-old *Trib* and finding everything out as it has already grown old, experimenting with the unreality of "time," I sit in bed in this fancy hotel with my knees drawn up to my chin, looking out over the terrace at a rolling golf course, where dots that must be humans are swinging sticks under huge striped umbrellas. It's drizzling constantly; everything is hiding under mist. Only the government buildings complex, lit up at night like the Coney Island steeplechase, reminds me of life going on out there. My first preoccupation is a persistent headache, then upset stomach and the promise of dysentery. I search for things to do with a vengeance: revise itinerary, call unhelpful travel agent, erase and repeat crossword puzzles, read Shastri's books on examining mind, eat, drink gallons of sugared tea.

Later, I visited Moghul tombs covered with stars of David, a symbol, my Indian guide told me, borrowed by the Semites from the Hindus. Here, everything came first. I received an antimony spot on my forehead and a garland of marigolds from a shivering Brahman priest in a poor army overcoat at a slick and overdecorated Hindu temple donated to the city by a steel magnate, appropriately, a devotee of Lakshmi, goddess of wealth. The religious circus is everywhere; it makes even the mad Breslover Hasidim easier to tolerate now. Worship is for the illiterate, the obsessional, the poor. The spirit informing it, encrusted by it, hardly exists even here in the place where it all, as they constantly assure you, began. Maybe the spirit is hidden in places known only to ourselves. Maybe it's an illusion after all. Reading H. J. Shastri and attending the carnival show into which he was born makes it clear why he knocks things over so violently. He is dealing with centuries of ignorance, chicanery, and superstition. Yet even Shastri talks only to the rich and Western-educated Indian. Imagine some untouchable coming up to shake *his* hand. It is unconscionable to tell howling bellies to stop and watch the vagaries of the desire-ridden mind. Dr. Minar discovered that among the fishermen in primitive southern villages, as he told us at dinner on his last night in Delhi. That is why he, of all the members of the conference, has a haunted, responsible look in his eyes. Like me, Minar is torn by a desire to see beyond the physical world, but his eyes will simply not turn inward at the sight of so many bleeding beggars, and his ears cannot shut out the cries of the suffering world, unreal as it may be. I understand the Jewish antiascetic bias better now, its insistent emphasis on the *klal,* the human community, as the way to God, without which there is no "enlightenment" at all.

India has depressed and confused me. It is in the God business, yet it is bereft of godliness. Take my tour guide, a young, dark-skinned version of Robert Morley; he spends half the time lecturing me on the condition of the state and the other half praising "spiritual India." With venom in his voice, he describes his schoolteacher wife's suspension, a punishment for his refusal to undergo a vasectomy after the birth of their third child. A disaffected "intellectual," jack-of-all-trades, champion name-dropper, sometime poet, and jewelry representative (who steered me into a carpeted clip joint and tried to convince me to buy my birthstone to ensure future health and prosperity), Mr. Sarai, like Profesor Barati before him, spent most of our time together trying to convince me to bring him to the United States.

"What is Delhi but a graveyard for ambitious emperors?" he sighed poetically, spreading his hands for well-practiced emphasis as we raced through the Moghul ruins. Bala Sarai (known as Bali to friends) is too preoccupied with life's immediate problems to take much time for religious musings. Yet even he stoops to venerate the stones in the temple as we enter. Hindus, even liquor-drinking, meat-eating atheists like Bali, have a religious tic that leaps out in moments of forgetfulness — and is as quickly left behind when they have replaced their shoes and taken leave of the gods.

The moment we were out in the street again, Bali resumed his cynical complaint. "Once they become comfortably established, the swamis don't want to part with the goodies bestowed on them by their rich patrons. The masses can't look to them for sustenance, physical or spiritual, any longer. These days they counsel an unhealthy fatalism that is responsible for much of the misery of this country. Others are 'apolitical' and see nothing but their navels and nirvana."

Bali spent most of my tour badmouthing India, swamis, politicians, and publishers who refused to buy his poems. Trembling with fatigue, I finally took leave of him at the door to my grossly overpriced hotel, guiltily handing him far too big a tip, a bribe for my release. Before I could turn away and flee from him, he quickly thrust a handsomely printed white card into my hands. I thought it might be an invitation or a business card, an advertisement for still another birthstone salesman. In the lobby, throwing myself into a plush lounge chair, I read it carefully. One side of the card said:

Happiness is a Flower;
NEVER BORN without a THORN,
PURSUE NOT it in Isolation,
It exists in the STRUGGLE of Life.

Bala Sarai (Bali)
Lecturer Guide

Phone: 755104   27 Ahdoo
N. Delhi
INDIA

Upside down, on the second half of the eccentrically printed card, were a group of maxims.

Education which is neither Job oriented nor religious is the seed of Future Chaos.

Humanity suffers because of the extravagant mood of the few; in Austerity lies the true existence of Humanity.

Time has got it [sic] own writings more powerful and detailed than the writings of any admitted man of the mortal race.

(*Bali*)

On the other side of the card was a poem:

Live like a Lotus is the advice of the Sages,
Shun materialism is the Voice of the ages.

Yet the Bud of Humanity is never allowed
to be bloossomed [sic] up.

O' Voice! of the inner conscience,
I look up to Thee — guide me, through the period of
transition.
Listen! O' Mortal of the immortal Soul.

Complexity of the Society,
Demands upon you — Weed out.
the Suffocating Grass around you,

Materialistic attitude is the only Solace to you.

Let not the Roots of Materialism
Stretche [sic] out to Strangle you."

(*Bali*)

I sat reading the oddly punctuated card again and again, tears filling my eyes. I detested the silken-saried women passing by me with their bulbous jewels and their slick-haired, Western-clad men. The real heart of India was crying out its ambivalent, starving, rationalizing squawk of spiritual and physical angst from Bali's half-educated, tentatively searching business/poetry card. How dared I and my intellectual friends sit in the lofty mountains discussing changes in consciousness, when right here on the streets ten million Balis depended on nothing less than immediate action? Meditation was suddenly irrelevant. "Materialistic attitude is the only Solace to you." What were those middle-class Dutch hippies doing up against the Janpath walls in the heart of New Delhi but making a mockery of the real suffering of the limbless beggars competing with them for alms? And we, too, with our flights from stifling materialism into ashrams sustained by the same rich devotees whose perfumed saris waved through the lush parlors of obscenely luxurious hotels like the one I was sitting in — we were no better. What games were we "spiritual seekers" playing at the expense of Bala Sarai, his unemployed wife, and their three children?

To punish myself for my more fortunate karma, my life's advantages, I returned to my room and resumed the boredom and misery of mind-watching. The guilt was awful. I had intended to go shopping for silk caftans and cashmere shawls in the government store, but I had been so chastened by Bali's card that my taste for beautiful things turned to ashes. The more bereft of experience, the more deprived of sensory input like sightseeing, talking, eating, buying, the more the somatic complaints increased. When the organism finds itself with nothing to do, no place to go, and no money to spend, it rebels by "getting sick." No wonder all those unemployed beggars downstairs were suffering from disease; it was as much their uselessness as their poverty that caused their bodies to work on themselves for stimulus. We are, as Narendra has told me many times, made for action. Inaction leads to sloth, and sloth to illness. I became his living example. Migraine and slight indigestion soon swelled into a pounding headache unrelieved by the strongest medication. Emptiness was fought by creating constant chores: taking notes, calling the operator and trying to make contact with Sue, taking accounts, rechecking itineraries already rechecked a thousand times, rewinding the already tightly wound alarm clock, sleeping dreamless, dark sleeps, waking up soaked with perspiration and freezing, going to the toilet.

In New Delhi I tapped the root of isolation and drank its bitter juice for the first time in my life. Though more comfortable than Bali (in my carpeted, heated room), I suffered his search for the constancy in activity that would shut out the emotional hunger, the cry for a recognizable voice that might acknowledge my feeble existence. Nobody in the world knew me during those moments, and nobody cared. The anonymity made me ill, an easy mark for death. I could have been lifted up in the corpse wagon with all the other anonymous street people of India and dumped on a mass funeral pyre, and not a single voice would call my name. I reached the stage where even blinking my eyes became an event, something to take note of, cherish. I sorrowed for the poor lost animal that lived inside me, for all the castaways down in the mazelike streets. On the golf course below my balcony, the miniature businessmen continued their game.

It is my true belief that I only recovered from my mini–nervous breakdown because I was sheltered and well fed. Receiving a timely letter from Sue telling me how much she needed and cared for me pulled me up out of the self-pitying grave into which I had thrown myself because of the turmoil engendered by Bala Sarai's, and India's, woes.

I suspect, judging from only a quick, superficial glance, that in Benares I have hit the *real* bedrock of Indian religious life. Ramnagar appears wealthy and chic by comparison. The first creature to greet me at the airport was an old yellow dog; many more bum dogs followed in his wake. The villages I passed on my way into the city were active, poor, the usual amalgam of humanity — cows, gnats, pigs, dogs, and even a camel resting in a shady corner, eyeing the goings-on with the irreverent detachment of a Shastri. The taxi stopped for a quarter of an hour at a railway crossing, and we were forced to roll up the windows despite the stench and the humidity because the clamoring children who cried and pushed for "baksheesh" would not stop no matter how many rupees we gave them. In front of the taxi, a huge caravan of trucks gaily painted over with Hindu gods, Bengal tigers, and religious graffiti held up both the animal and human stream of traffic that tried making its barefoot way through the running ditches alongside the road. Children squatted and aggressively did their BMs to tease us for not giving them more alms; one boy lifted his oversized nightshirt and naughtily waved his penis at me to register his anger at my lack of generosity. "He's a Moslem," the driver assured me, aware that I, a Westerner, was unable to distinguish at a distance what quick Hindu eyes saw in an instant. Aside from the Moslem exhibitionist, there was no sexual differentiation between little girls and boys; regardless of faith, they all shared the same wretched filth.

As I unpacked in my hotel room, I looked out the window and

noticed the sun for the first time in four days. A stunning raga poured out of a radio in the hotel kitchen; honking cars, jangling bicycles, baying dogs, provided an authentic background drone to the music. Judging from the familiar whine of the conch, someone outside was charming a snake.

Later in the day

This town is as poor as you can imagine, but something soft and warm about the air enables me to relax for the first time on this trip. I was right. There was a trio of snake and mongoose charmers, two older men and a boy, near the front porch of the hotel. They spent most of the afternoon trying to fascinate the busloads of tourists emptying every hour on the hour at the front gate. There were the invariable "holy" Americans, with their sutras and *Autobiography of a Yogi* tucked under the arms of their saffron robes, coughing phlegmily, but walking barefoot nonetheless to demonstrate their piety. I watched the equally "unholy" French rush off to tour the erotic sculptures of Khajuraho. Afterward they returned — or, rather, descended — on the hotel dining room like a horde of famished pigs, eating everything in sight and elbowing each other most ungraciously at the buffet table. A friendly waiter who had seen it all before informed me with a complacent smile that the French would soon be running just as quickly up and down the halls in search of a doctor to cure the results of their overeating.

Seeing me pushed aside from the buffet, the maître d'hôtel approached and asked if he could fix me a special vegetarian dish.

"Are you a rug dealer?" he asked kindly, perhaps to make conversation with the one lone woman in the hotel.

"No, a conference goer," I replied prettily.

"Ah."

It was probably the maître d'hôtel who, feeling sorry for me, had informed the front desk that I was an important person, for when the guide came to fetch me, he was waving a card with my name on it and the letters VIP alongside. My Benares guide is the antithesis of the ceaselessly complaining, endomorphic poet of New Delhi.

More in keeping with the temper of the holy city, this young man is small, dark, and wiry, with deep soulful eyes — one of which is swollen with a great angry red sty.

Determined from the moment he greeted me in the lobby to give me the entire tourist spiel, he led me very cautiously through the mud to my car, probably because he was impressed by the mistaken VIP business at the front desk. I did not disabuse him, I confess; after my bout with loneliness in New Delhi, I could do with a little VIP treatment. The animal has to live, too.

Against the wishes of his older brother, a physician who had offered to support my guide and his family through medical training, this true lover of India has moved wife and family from his well-to-do situation in New Delhi, has refused to become a doctor, and has chosen instead to "seek happiness of the heart" through the religious spirit that, he is convinced, runs through the city of Benares.

"Here," he said, glowing with religious sincerity, "you do not wake early to rush to the office, but to rush to worship."

Alternately sad and optimistic about the glory of India, the young devotee nestled into his thin jacket and pointed out every Buddhist rock and stone and statue, explaining to me with heavy sighs how the Moslem invaders had reduced the great Indian nation. My guide's hopefulness emerged from his unshakable belief in the country's most powerful commodity: its religious life. Though coming at it from opposite sides of the fence, we agree on that.

Sarnath is Buddhist; away from the clamor and color of so many gods, goddesses, flowers, and symbols, it is like taking a cool drink of water after eating an enormous curry buffet. Buddhism is cool; Hinduism is hot. If I ever decide to follow a discipline outside Judaism, it would be Buddhist, for I am naturally inclined toward its doctrine of emptiness. The deer still roam in Gautama's deer park. Faithful Tibetan pilgrims circle the great stupa housing the Buddha's remains, uttering prayers and turning prayer wheels exactly five times. Then they repeat the procedure around the peepul tree, a graft from the original Bo tree under which the Buddha was enlightened. The Buddhists are not worried about going insane. A delicious, cool Buddhist breeze plays at the spot. It is still the sixth century here. Asoka is emperor and spiritual life is flourishing. The Moslem hordes have not yet arrived. The American sadhus have not yet been born.

I walk with my guide through the ruins of the splendid monastery where the Buddha taught, now covered with grass and flowers, layers of stone forming foundations here, pillars there, Buddha's very own teaching seat under a canopy of stone . . . and more Tibetans, whole families rotating prayer wheels in unison. It's hypnotic. Two young lamas in distinctive purple robes smile at us as they pass. An American sadhu, black from wandering under the hot Indian sun, wrapped in a dhoti, barefoot, indistinguishable — except for his handsome midwestern American looks — from the beggars who block our path and spit at our feet when we offer them nothing, offers me an unmistakably sexual glance and breaks the spell.

Despite the heavy dose of spirituality, my guide was compelled (according to tourist ritual and guide regulations) to stop at the local tapestry emporium, where a ten-year-old boy sat weaving myths in a windowless room. After being duly admired, the boy grew petulant suddenly and asked for a rupee a look. To save my solicitous guide any embarrassment, I went through the inevitable almsgiving and buying ceremonies. In the car, he apologized for having to take me there as part of his job.

"In two or three years, when you return, you won't recognize Benares," said the guide, his eyes shining with excitement. "The building has begun; they are already placing telephone and electricity cables under the street." All this as we passed the gruesome little sheds that pass for shops and homes, meandering feral dogs, and street urchins who brush against the legs of half-naked madwomen and water buffalos. *Why should this be?* reverberates inevitably in my head. The fields are blooming with wheat, mustard flower, barley, rice. The earth is so rich, really.

Part of me, the missionary, I guess, wants to teach the ignorant here how to read, how to protest, to conceptualize, to argue with the rajas. There is too little abstracting ability among these poor Hindus and too much living in abstraction among the well-fed, educated ones. An article in the Hindustan *Times* this morning described a study of villagers' consumption of alcohol and drugs — equally high, if not higher and more habitual, than that of the rich. Landowners use opium on their laborers because it makes them work faster and better. Heads of households pass the drinking habit down to their children. Farmers are burned out by the time they reach twenty. The major difference between villagers and city folk who indulge is that villagers (1) don't do it to escape from conscious anxiety or depression but out of "custom," and (2) they, unlike the city addicts, generally have no desire to quit. They don't regard dope as a vice but as a part of life. So there you are: Feelin' fine is everybody's goal, refined or crude; Oberoi Intercontinental or village liquor shed featuring local gut rot and Benares bhang.

Like Harris May, I too now prefer the Tibetans. They are always trim, smart, neat, well put together. They smile as they walk toward you on the street with their heads held high; they seem to be sharing a humorous secret with the gods. In a Tibetan temple, a group of young monks is seated on the floor. One lama, also a novice, is standing at the center of the room, challenging the others. Whenever someone debates him from the floor, he retorts with a loud clap from a stick and a victorious laugh, to which the assembled company responds with much good-natured shouting and belly-laughing. Two professors (older lamas) — one a portly, studious chap in spectacles who fingers prayer beads — squat in front of a massive statue of the Buddha and smile benignly on the rowdy proceedings. My guide asks what is going on, and the portly professor replies, "A seminar." Wonderful! Who would ever dream, "a seminar"? I think of my own terse discussions of Joseph Conrad and my frustrated mornings lecturing to nodding speed freaks posing as college students, and I am moved to awe. Great gaiety pervades this temple, which is decorated from floor to ceiling with blue, yellow, and red prayer wheels, tangkas, wall paintings of every Buddha imaginable, and ritual objects even you never dreamed existed. The enormous gilt Buddha, wrapped in yellow gauzy cloth, the dean of faculty, smiles down on them all. Nobody minds when we take off our shoes and step inside. Nobody approaches us for alms. Surely Buddhism has something to say for it. It hasn't the frenzy, the mass hysteria, that pervade Hindu shrines, only the peace inherent in the Buddha's smile and the cool, calming hint of his dispassionate presence.

Buddhism is masculine; Hinduism, feminine. All the erotic worship I have seen of naked women performed by semi-naked women, the adorning of Siva's phalluses with flowers, carefully, ever so lovingly bathing them — all the eroticism puts me in mind of Mexican Catholicism. Like my guide, I too understand that religion is not *part* of life in India; it *is* life. Every hour of the day, every day, is devoted to a different god. The ingenuity that is being invested in worship, adornment, myth-making — in short, the sheer energy that has gone into constructing the spiritual world — if rendered toward technology, could have made these people lords over the earth.

The Indian mother, in family and religion, reigns supreme. Idealized like her Catholic counterpart, saintly nourisher and cruel destroyer, bare-breasted seductress, she beckons hundreds of pilgrims every minute of every day into her temple at the heart of Benares, where "non-Hindu gentlemen are requested not to enter." All women, however, are invited in. It is raining. Each time a pilgrim enters the muddy great hall, he/she rings the giant bell overhead to summon the goddess. So many come that the ongoing din is deafening. Mischievous monkeys swing about overhead, eyeing the lush coconuts, fruit, and rice brought before the Durga, Kali, the wrathful black mother. Women wearing thick silver leg bracelets and rings on their toes follow half-naked sadhus into the temple: a hodgepodge of sensuality and asceticism, humility and vanity. Beggars, wealthy Punjabis in white head-wrappings, gaily saried women from Kerala, Gandhi-mimicking clerks in dhotis — every conceivable creature of the Indian imagination worships the great mother. Every day of the year — no less than three hundred sixty-five days, are devoted to gods, goddesses, and mythological and historical events. The faces of the worshipers — some high-boned and beautiful, others worn with bad nourishment, age, and poverty — all bear that blank-to-the-world stare of people in the habit of religious surrender, the empty eyes shared by those bhang smokers Rama Barati described to me a few days (centuries?) ago at the quiet Dal Lake. I am enveloped by the god-intoxicated, yet I am as cold to it as to a stone. All the flower tossing, bell ringing, floor prostrating, and padding about barefoot before a benumbed priest who automatically daubs anyone who comes in front of him with orange ash stirs me less than the memory of six elephants I saw in New Delhi gently ambling along to the tinkling bells of a parade rehearsal. The "real thing" does not match the sudden ecstasy I experienced on hearing Rama Barati improvise his erotic ragas on the sitar in the Ramnagar Palace at evening. These cheap plaster representations of the gods, repeated over and over again in the temples, bear no resemblance to the splendid stone sculptures of the Guptas in the archaeological museum at Sarnath. Art triumphs over religion.

I am uninspired by the mad, barefoot rush through the muddy puddles to plead with the impassive gods for their intercession in the business of living. Neither the crowds praying at the Western Wall in Jerusalem nor Nissan Rosenberg's brand of Jewish *bhakti* nor this strident Hindu display inspires me to religious feeling. Though I don't condemn it for others, religious sentimentalism holds nothing for me. I study these numb faces (they could just as well be the Breslover Hasidim dancing in the presence of their Queen Sabbath) for a sign of the light that inspired their *rishis* to create the Vedas, but there is nothing. Just as there are no Baal Shem Tovs.

One wild-haired face smeared with sacred ash seems to hold the hint of something more, but at the very moment he leaves the temple, the holy man heaves a big spit right in the front courtyard on the stones inscribed with the names of the pious. Perhaps I am finicky. Yet it is hard to reconcile myself to the kind of Indian earthiness that permits a worshiper to blow his nose onto the same sacred steps against which he presses his forehead.

I am glutted with religion; part of me wants to run away while three quarters of me remain fascinated, gripped by the spectacle. When I was a little girl, my grandfather used to wrap me in his prayer shawl in the synagogue when the high priests blessed the congregation and you weren't supposed to look because God had entered. All my life I have hungered to lift that shawl and take a peek. But, almost reflexively, I pull down a curtain of fear when somewhere around the region of my heart I feel the urge to look beyond. (*No man shall see me and live.* Remember?) Yet, here in India, I am tempted to hurl myself into the flood, be swallowed up in the worshipful throng. It is the impulse of the lemming, perhaps the other side of the dry, experimental, mind-induced suicide fantasy growing out of H. J. Shastri's self-observation technique. It is easy to get lost in a huge, hysterical crowd, and there is enough body warmth to make the disintegration cozy.

I am an ambivalent mystic, indeed.

26 January 1977
Benares

How to explain the Ganges and its pilgrims? My shivering guide and I arrived at its banks on foot at four-thirty in the morning. Walking through the largest of the city's intersections toward the main bathing ghat, I learned to my amusement that my deliberate avoidance of the Kumba Mela had only brought the festival to me. Millions of pilgrims, having finished their devotions at Allahabad, were now descending on Benares for the final dip. Endless streams of barefoot devotees elbowed past me in the mud of the dawn rains. I decided not to flee but rather to do what I had dreaded for weeks in India — let myself merge with the crowd. Embalmed in filth, flesh, faith, and cow flops, I lowered my head and pushed along with the coughing, spitting masses, dodging sprays of red betel juice and tubercular phlegm. Beautiful women moved gracefully alongside me, entranced, weaving their paths toward the water side by side with ancient hags, toothless sadhus, and portly, bare-chested grandfathers proudly sporting their crimson Brahman's threads on their naked bellies.

At the ghat itself, with the gray expanse of river appearing in the mist, I forgot the crowd, the doctors' warnings about disease, my obsessive fear of being trampled to death in the mud; I grew deaf to the noisy loudspeakers emitting recorded prayers. Only the river existed now, peaceful, yellow and green, beckoning serenely in the midst of chaos. Once we reached its banks, the worshipers lost all sense of modesty, of personal identity; even caste was washed away in its consuming waters. Exposing their naked bodies to the freezing morning air, people on either side of me rushed forward to gather the holy water in their palms; then, pouring streams of it through their fingers, they made offerings to the rising sun. Murmuring Sanskrit prayers to Mother Ganga, importuning her to shield them from the sun's harmful rays, they pleaded with heaven for a fraction of its healing light. Some hearty souls performed yoga exercises. How mad it all looked here, knee- and thigh-deep in water, the asanas I have been doing for over a decade in the carpeted warmth of the Washington Hotel, Narendra's green studio, and my own living room. Long-, matted-haired swamis performed the alternate nostril breathing by taking in water and pumping it out rhythmically, their eyes slitted blissfully in the expanding light of morning. Old women with flapjack breasts exposed stood waist-high in the water and chanted to Siva, inches from oblivious yogis in silent meditation. A middle-aged man plunged into the icy water head first with a loud shout. The guide talked in chilled whispers about the healing properties of the Ganges. I didn't believe him.

At last the sun came up fully, greeted by the smell of burning corpses, squawking crows, ambling sacred cows, and ululating old women. And at that place of death, only a few yards from where the lively bathers immersed themselves, I obtained my first awakened glimpse of the bridge between living and dying. For the space of a second, I crossed it fearlessly, looked into its vastness with absolute equanimity, certain that it is truly no more than an entry into another phase, a natural "part two" to the "part one" in which we are now appearing. Telling me to put away my camera, the guide helped me settle into a flatboat and directed the oarsman to row us toward the cremation ghat. In silence we watched the tearless funeral procession, the quiet business of disposing of the impermanent ash that is left of us when we finish here. The eldest son reaches into the smoldering embers and withdraws his father's skull. At that moment, the god Siva appears. I know because I "saw" and felt him.

Here in India people are busy preparing for that bodiless transition as we in the West occupy ourselves almost totally with maintaining, adorning, and preserving our *bodifulness*. Oblivious to the noise, mud, spittle, and vomitus, Mother Ganga accepts all. She sanctifies the excremental vision, cures the sick, cleanses the body on its way through to the next world, and provides a lapping cradle for the dead, who cry out to be set free so that they may hear the secret mantra that Siva will whisper in their ears as their souls depart.

Plunged back into the reality of the streets, the moment poised between heaven and earth, the high spiritual gift from the god taken for an instant, disappears. Ordinary consciousness returns. Out of Mother Ganga's sight, we are once again thrust back into the earth's excrescences — without the water's purifying power. Narrow market lanes choked with pilgrims, dogs, pigs, cows, children, priests, are pervaded by the bitter smell of charcoal from burning street braziers. Skeletal bodies sleep on bedrolls in the roadway; they don't even bother getting out of our path. We continue to make our determined way along with the rest of the crowd toward the golden temple at the confluence of many tortuous lanes and alleyways. It is raining again. Nobody feels it. The throng is so immersed in its ecstatic pilgrimage from river goddess to temple goddess that people are oblivious to the mud, the rain, the disease, the sheer uncomfortable closeness of body on body. In the temple courtyard the usual flower vendors and sandalpaste, saffron, and antimony salesmen are flanked by soldiers. It is so terrifically crowded inside that people are performing their devotions out on the marble steps. The peaceful meditation at the river is lost here. Perhaps this is the answer to the discrepancy, the difference between worship, a communal, frenzied, noisy clamor, and meditation, which asks for nothing, wants no communion with any god or idea of God, but rests content with what it finds within the silent spaces of the individual heart. That has been Narendra's Indian gift to me.

Worship, like all craving, asking, repenting, belongs to every tradition. Mea Shearim fanatics, Mexican Catholics, Arab Moslems, all practice self-flagellation of one sort or another in order to assuage one or many angry gods. Call it Siva, Allah, or Yahweh — the impulse is whining, anthropomorphic; it restricts and insults the Infinite, this bodily need to confine its isolated terror to the province of worship. Compulsive *mitzvoth* for the Jews, *pujas* for the Hindus, endlessly rotating Buddhist prayer wheels; they are all the same.

"How many of these pilgrims meditate, do you think?" I asked my guide.

"Only the sadhus and yogis," he replied, "and when people grow old and come to Ganga to die."

This Kumba Mela morning has concretely illustrated for me at last the elusive boundaries between ritual worship and meditation, between silence and chaos, between the gallant noise of living and the dignified calm of death.

27 January 1977
En route to Jaipur

Siva exacts his price. You don't peek into his secret realm and get away without at least a scar. My fascination with his dark kingdom, my newly acquired Indian readiness to greet and acknowledge him, must have called the god down to warn me in a dream of the brush with death I was to experience the next morning. In the dream, a bearded man in a brilliant red turban was making his way across the country, murdering women. It was as if I were simultaneously writing and living in a film where, during the final scene, the murderer came to kill me in my room because I had identified him in a public place. In the last scene of the film/dream, the man in the red turban climbed onto a fire escape and entered my apartment through the open window. He was moving threateningly toward me when suddenly my humorous orange tabby cat jumped at his face, disorienting him, and thereby permitting me to leap to safety after her out of the window on my left.

In the morning I was met for the first time since I have been in India by a driver without a guide. I tried speaking to the young, mute fellow who presented himself to me, but he appeared to be drugged or unable to comprehend a word of my English. The car looked beaten up and dirty, different from all the bright, presentable cars that I had been driven around in before. All flights were delayed, said the man at the hotel desk; everything about my schedule seemed haywire. Reluctantly, I entered the car. As we were driving at top speed down the narrow country road, it occurred to me very strongly that the fellow was not properly judging distances between our car and the oncoming vehicles speeding past us. But all my warnings went unheeded.

I shall never forget the sight of the bus as it came barreling down on us, *its driver the very same bearded man in the red turban who was trying to kill me in my dream!* Before my driver could pull to the side of the road, the oncoming bus crashed into the rear right door where I was sitting and drove on wildly past us without stopping. The window to my right was wide open, and a rain of paint, chrome, and debris blew in. I might have been blinded had I not been thrust by the impact all the way over to the window on my left, escaping injury just as I had in my dream.

After all that, the plane was six hours late, and I caught the flu while sleeping on a hard wooden bench in the drafty airport lounge. Siva didn't kill me, so he had to settle for illness instead.

28 *January* 1977
Jaipur
(*After seeing the Taj Mahal*)

Going from Hindu to Moghul again is like crossing from one country into another. There seem to be oceans and eons between the religious throngs at the Ganges and the love pilgrims at the Taj Mahal. The cruel, rapacious Moghul emperors constructed superhuman structures in which to enshrine their wasted remains. Unlike the Hindus, they never did manage to accept death, and still less to incorporate it wholesomely into life. So it became a kind of stunning taboo; surrounded by marble, gems, peacocks, and architectural wonders, and totally unlike the open cremation ghats that belittle our physical mortality, the Moghul tombs celebrate matter. The Taj, though a mausoleum, must be entered barefoot, as one enters a Hindu temple. We have come a step lower — from worshiping gods to worshiping humans. Yet something of Emperor Shah Jahan's soul, something religious about his devotion to this woman, helped him to surpass his greedy egomania. A distorted parody of the feelings of the ascetics at the Ganges who surrender their bodies to the goddess, Shah Jahan's earthly, sensuous love prodded him toward the divine.

White, pearl gray, golden, pale blue-white by turns, the structure appears to move with you as you walk. Every doorway leads to another in the quest for immortality. And, like all India's wonders, it is set in the surrounding dirt track fields like a diamond on a dung heap. India is a giant anachronism, filled with the decayed and decaying glories of its warrior, priestly, and splendidly noble past. Spiritual ruins, erotic ruins, religious ruins . . . everywhere ruins. The Indians, touched by the kiss of the gods, have surrendered earthly interests and allowed even their worldly treasures to decay. I experienced the fatal seductiveness of Indian passivity myself; in my eagerness to overhear Siva's whisper, I, too, almost died. With eyes lifted ever upward and ears cocked toward songs from higher worlds, how can people groom their land, care for their livestock? These men and women are so captured by the spirit that they haven't so much as a thought to spare for "the future," for "planning," family or otherwise. Villagers are content to toil in the fields on prehistoric wagons drawn by pagan bulls; wells still pump as they did thousands of years ago. The same ivory-teethed women walk with shiny brass pitchers on their heads, their skirts tucked up to the knees, their laughter purling across the early morning fields like the water they draw from the well.

Moghul India is rightfully buried in all its egomaniacal splendor in this country of yogis, for it represents all the supple pleasures of the flesh and of this world. Hindu India is the renunciation of the senses in exchange for the bliss of immersion in the Infinite. The Jews are stuck with their feet on the ground and their noses aimed at the sky. The Hindus are perpetually aloft. Perhaps Sue was right to come here, where there are no distractions from God. For centuries it has been customary to meditate in India's caves and forests, mountains and monasteries, because the two opposing forces in human nature were (and still are) so starkly outlined here: palace and gutter, beloved wife and grinning skeleton. To borrow from Yeats, India has pitched her mansion of spiritual love in "the place of excrement," but her spirit is so intense that she doesn't smell the rank decay below.

Today was interesting not so much for its Rajput palaces, forts, and elephant rides as it was for discussion with my new guide, a Vedanta student, palm reader, and amateur astrologer. In Naga, scholarship and superstition sit strangely mixed. He is twenty-one, he tells me, yet he claims to be eager to hang on to the dying spiritual wealth of his culture — and to dip his toes into the twentieth century, too. On the ride to the Jai Singh astronomical observatory, he read my palm and told me I would probably die quickly, accidentally, at the age of sixty-nine. It's nice, the way Indians talk about dying as casually as we would make plans to see the Knicks play basketball in two weeks.

In the open-air observatory I had my first short encounter with an Indian fakir. It was an old, weatherbeaten face with clear brown eyes that appeared from under a thick white shawl in the lens of my camera as I was unsuccessfully attempting to photograph the entire observatory from the wrong angle. Then the voice, in clipped British English, directed me to the top of one of the stone instruments at the end of a narrow staircase. From there I got a perfect view of the scene, snapped my picture, and thanked the mysterious old man. Naga whispered that he had never seen the white-robed man at the observatory before, but that it might be a good idea to follow him, for he seemed to know his way around the place. We asked the old man if he would explain the instruments to us. Giving us a slight bow, he led us through the observatory, providing a detailed lecture on the mechanics of each stone instrument, sundial, globe, and astrolabe.

"So you see, without any machinery, three hundred years ago they could accurately read the skies," the old man finished, resembling one of the well-preserved instruments himself. Then he led us to the zodiac center, a series of stone pillars reconstructed on earth to mirror their heavenly locations, with their corresponding astrological signs engraved on enameled shields on the face of each pillar. As we approached my zodiac sign, I asked the old man if he was an astrologer as well as an astronomer. He merely answered, "It would be helpful for you to wear coral now, as you will not be enjoying good health for some time." Then he walked away without so much as demanding a rupee. (Of course it later occurred to me that he and Naga were in cahoots and would share the profits in the evening.) My clinging sore throat and flu bear out the old man's predictions.

30 *January 1977*
Aurangobad

I made friends with the wife of the manager of the very chic Western-style hotel where I am staying while visiting the caves of Ellora and Ajanta. Thinking I wasn't pleased with the gourmet meat dishes on the menu, she approached me at lunch when she saw me ordering the vegetarian platter. Somehow that got us into a discussion about yoga, and before we knew it, we were exchanging notes about the exercises.

"I've been doing them for two years now," she said, "alone, from a book. How about you?"

"About ten, no, twelve."

"*Achai*." The manager's wife looked at me admiringly. (*Achai* roughly means "ah" or "oh" or "I see" or "okay" in Hindi.) "No wonder you have such a radiant glow about you. Your face looks like that of the yogis, such youthful glowing skin . . ." And then, almost immediately after the barrage of praise: "May I come to your room after you have seen Ellora and show you my exercises, and you show me yours?"

"Of course," I said grudgingly, my throat as scratchy as a hair shirt. It was just like being little and naughty again, sharing and comparing preadolescent secrets.

Wouldn't you know, she brought her paperback copy of Walter Berger's *Yoga for Health* exercises?

"He's the most popular yogi in India," she said.

"Really?" That did my heart good.

And don't you think I gave her a Walter Berger yoga lesson right then and there — in *India!* She was especially interested in "smoothing the skin on the face" and (no different from my Great Neck housewives and toupéed gymnasts) in "getting rid of *this*" (pointing to a rather cute double chin) "and *this*" (likewise to hips and gently protruding stomach). "Living in a hotel, you eat a lot because you don't have to cook for yourself." We both giggled like two furtive teen-agers.

The exercise session proved her to be rather more limber than she looked, a bit off balance, and possessing no knowledge of how to breathe properly. I demonstrated and was duly admired. As I sat in the lotus position doing some "complete breathing," she gazed at me with radiant eyes and said, "Ah, you look just like a saintly yogi in meditation."

Oh dear, oh dear. What to say to these mad, god-intoxicated, childish people? If I were a shrewd Walter Berger businessperson,

I could bring spiritual life back to India in a kind of guru-in-reverse movement, teaching the age-old wisdom of Mother India to Indians.

Later, over cognac in her aquamarine-colored suite (complete with wall-to-wall stereo and deafening Xavier Cugat marimba music lacing our conversation), we talked confidentially about our lives, cultures, and respective feminist stances. Her name, she told me, was Rani, and she was terribly proud of herself for having defied her Hindu family and married out of caste — unforgivably — and to a Moslem, no less. As if to compound the sin, the couple was childless by choice. Her husband had been a major in the Indian army for many years before growing tired of the peripatetic life and opting for the managership of the big hotel. She was appointed head of housekeeping and so considered herself his equal. Both were, for India, highly salaried.

"This is a small town, provincial, not like Delhi, where I was born. But interesting people are always coming through here — like you." She lit a cigarette and pointed the dying match at me. I thought flickeringly of Emma Bovary. "Middle-class Indians are terribly caste-ridden, bigoted, and the women are slaves. I am glad I escaped the life of my two sisters."

"What about the rich? I saw them enjoying themselves all over Delhi, wearing halter tops, driving around in sports cars, and without chaperones."

"The rich can do anything here, short of murder — and even murder sometimes. The poor are nonbeings; they make three rupees a day for their backbreaking labor, live in four-foot-high straw tents; the intellectuals are all leaving the country because there is no future for them. Only the middle management people like ourselves and the shopkeepers stay on and act like the rich. Haven't you noticed that Indians are mad for jewels, colored saris, tape recorders, cameras . . . I would sell my soul for a special type of silk and lace panty a guest from Paris once gave me as a gift," she admitted candidly.

I drank my cognac and lamented in turn. "At the caves I noticed that the crowd waiting to get in appeared ready to eat my camera.

They stared greedily for a full half-hour; some of them even walked around and around me, studying it, all but reaching out to touch it. It was eerie."

Indeed, the very room we were sitting in reflected the pitiful Indian hunger for American gadgets and plastic ornaments, the obsolescent flotsam that we consume without so much as a thought about where it comes from, the waste, the expense. Rani's hunger for what had made me jaded caused me to feel ashamed.

Her husband came through the door then, unannounced. He was a handsome Moghul type with dark sheik's eyes, curled Siva moustachios, tawny skin, and cruel, thin lips. The husband did not bother to introduce himself (he seemed visibly annoyed at my presence), nor did he bother to hide his sarcastic disdain for Americans and, I think, for me in particular, as Rani forced us to meet. Liberated or no, I was a woman traveling alone, and no Moslem gentleman respects such women.

"Your country will cause the downfall of the planet," he accused me sharply no more than a minute after we had exchanged names. "With your nuclear bombs and shocking waste of resources, you have already begun the inevitable process."

Personally guilty and totally unprepared for his onslaught, I blanched, then hemmed and hawed a little about the Russians, and finally dared to mention India's own recent nuclear muscle-flexing.

"Take the British," he said, totally ignoring my reply. "They have discipline — a fallen empire, but to be admired for their self-control, not like your American slackness and pampering."

Rani shifted around uncomfortably on her aquamarine sofa, imploring him silently to stop.

I looked at my watch. "It's been really delightful," I said, not unsarcastically. Rani and I parted with a promise to resume our yoga lessons the next day, but we both knew that our short-lived friendship had ended. I saw her again at breakfast the next morning, when she formally nodded her head to acknowledge me as she would any other guest. It was as if our exchange of true confessions had never taken place, as if our mutual puffing and stretching in our panties was nothing more than a shared dream.

"The rich live such a fascinating life . . ."

"Take the British, not like your American slackness and pamper-ing . . ."

The chatter buzzes around in my head and causes terrible night-mares. It sounds trite, Noah, but I have seen and learned in India only that trees are trees and rivers are rivers after all, as the old Zen saw goes. I am indeed blessed to be who I am, born where I was born, of parents who raised me honestly, proudly, whatever the flaws of their tradition and background. I could not help but think of Israel many times on this trip, sick and corrupt as it, too, is, but nevertheless containing independent, uncowed spirits like Madame Ariel and Rav Bloch. Without idealizing it, I see Jerusalem from here as if for the first time. Such spirits inhabit India, I am sure. This is such a vast country that no doubt these "simple" holy ones, the legendary wandering sadhus in the Himalayan fastnesses, men like Greda Thorberg's teacher, do exist. I did not find them.

I am convinced now that all the tasks we must perform in our search for truth in this life must be performed by independent in-dividuals — on themselves, never on others, but in conjunction with others, and never in complete surrender to the commands of one caste or priest.

Ted Sonmayer, your psychiatrist friend from Mount Sinai Hos-pital, was annoyed with me last New Year's Eve, when I started to cry at the sad lot of all of us pitiful human beings — not just the street beggars of India then — while we drank champagne and watched the desperately cheerful mob at Times Square on television. Ted said he thought it "arrogant and life-hating" of me to feel "sorry for the poor creatures." He said, if I remember correctly, that mysticism had alienated me from real people living real lives. But he was wrong, and Buddha was right. Once you have felt the first pang of this disease called life, the "world," once you absorb its poignancy, its corruption, its love, highest aspirations, myths, and seductive dreams about its own perhaps illusory possibilities (which India permits you to do as no other place can, with her flying gods and goddesses, giants of creation and destruction, colos-sal animals, lithe sirens, and devouring mothers — in short, because she so openly displays the entire spectrum of the human dream), you can't help but wring your hands and cry, "What is this?" And then, "How did I get here?" And finally, with the Buddha, "How do I get out?" Two, three, or five people in all of human history, perhaps, found the answers. No one person, country, scripture, or philosophy has total claim to them, despite all the conflicting proclamations. The clamor is deafening. Truth, however, is too evanescent, too evasive and grand for any one country to have captured alone. India comes close.

Sadly, for me she has no gurus, only those I have myself created in dreams.

4

Breakdown

I STOOD BLINKING MY EYES in the fairy-tale lobby of the Taj Mahal Hotel in Bombay. The sun blared down on the colorful bazaar outside, emitting eighty-five degrees of welcome warmth to my cold, sick body. A Persian Gulf sheik in a white sheet brushed past me, swinging a gnarled shillelagh in his diamond-covered hand. Shaking a bell-bordered blackboard with GIBSON written on it, a waif in velveteen livery hurried by, calling out a name that sounded like "Diphthong." Feverish and ill adapted to the crush of luxury, the perfume, the perpetually revolving doors opening to receive the handsomest, most elegantly clad and finely combed human beings I had ever gazed on in this world, I stood like a refugee behind my bags. Still dressed in my heavy black pea jacket, black boots, woolen skirt, and plaid scarf, I must have resembled my Siberian grandmother arriving in the port of Jaffa; I was equally culture-shocked. Now the liveried waif seemed to be calling "Perle!" between cries of "Diphthong." I felt myself being tugged at roughly from behind and whirled around to slap whoever dared to pull me from the rainbow dream into which I had so gratefully fallen.

"Iora Patauqua!" Sue gave me the secret sorority greeting. "Hey, Brooklyn! I knew it was you from the outfit. I saw your back and said to myself, 'Who else but Perle would be standing in the Taj lobby in one-hundred-degree heat wearing boots and a pea jacket?' I'll bet those clothes are from Bendel's, too! You always did have the art of making riches look like rags. I might have known . . ." She went on, backing off and pretending to examine me with the same critical eye our sorority sisters had reserved for nervous candidates at rushes. "That *shmata* on your head is a Givenchy!"

"Sue! I . . . thought . . . you'd . . . be wearing a sareee!" I threw my arms around her. In her ninety-five-cent Indian cotton trousers and loose mauve smock, it was *she* who looked like one of the chic, arty types scurrying around on Bendel's first floor. Her dark hair was frizzed out in a fashionable modified Afro cut; she was tan, lithe, beautiful — even wearing eye make-up.

"I thought you were ascetic," I murmured. "I thought you'd be skinny, with rotten teeth, shaven head . . ."

She guffawed. "Typical of you and your fevered imagination. Hey, what happened to your voice? Laryngitis? I'm starving, aren't you?"

We could just as well have been standing on Greene Street in SoHo, deciding whether or not to eat health food or Chinese.

The desk clerk asked if I had a room preference. Sue leaned over and said, "She does. A room overlooking the India Gate and the harbor." Awestruck, I stared at her as she maneuvered my check-in. The juxtaposition of the old Sue and the new casual expatriate, of celibate and sophisticate, was disorienting; I settled into a dreamy state and allowed myself to drift.

"We can still do all the things you mentioned in your letter, can't we?" I asked her in the elevator.

"You can come to the ashram, but you've missed Swami Shankaracharya. He's off on a lecture trip in Madras."

"Oh." My voice dropped with disappointment. I had come around the world to meet Sue's guru, and he had left.

"Well, you can just extend your trip. It's no problem," she said offhandedly, once again evoking the specter of our divergent natures. Sue had the inborn knack for detachment; she could simply pick herself up in the middle of life and push on to the next, more promising pasture. Without being a dilettante or a drifter, Sue could walk off for years, committing herself to a new goal so deeply that she cut away career, lover, family, as if they were ripened wheat waiting to be harvested. She could even walk off without a tear from the cat she had cherished as if it were a child. I was just the opposite; I clung to friends I had outgrown and sentimentalized uncles I had never met.

"I can't stay," I said, as we dumped clothes and books and gifts out of suitcases all over the room. "I have to get back to Noah, and teaching, and my home."

"We'll save the heavy stuff for later, okay?" she said knowingly. "Let's catch up on gossip and food now. I brought my best ashram friend; she's downstairs. Her name's Wanda, she's from Brazil, and she's been very sick, so maybe you can give us some of this medicine you've got, and, by the way, did you bring me the Jewish prayer book I asked you for?"

I had carried the miniature chased silver *siddur* in the bottom of a nylon stocking deep down in my bag. On hearing that Sue wanted a "Jewish" prayer book, my father had hurried down to his special Hebrew book publisher on Hester Street and ordered the most delicate, most traditional prayer book he could find. Since she was an artist, he reasoned, Sue could be reached more easily from the aesthetic side of her nature. My father and mother had handed me the little book at the airport in New York with great concern. "Maybe it will make her Jewish again." My mother sighed. "Don't you let her turn you into a Hindu!"

I smiled, thinking of that poignant scene as I dug into the stocking and retrieved the *siddur*. "Here!" I held out the book defiantly. "I've come to make you Jewish again!"

Sue reached for the *siddur* and caressed the chased silver and turquoise cover.

"It's beautiful," she murmured.

"Made in Israel," I squeaked, my voice almost totally gone.

"Let's leave everything and go down to eat. Wanda is meeting us in the coffee shop."

Glad of the opportunity to avoid "the heavy stuff," I followed Sue out into the hall, listening to her chatter about life at the ashram.

"Did you bring a bathing suit?" She interrupted her monologue suddenly.

"No, only heavy clothes," I muttered. The thought of exposing my chilled, aching body to cold water was unbearable.

"Well, I have my bikini, and I'm going to the Taj pool even if I have to buy you a bathing suit to get in. I'm hungry for a little of the good life — you know, jet-set food and fun. I'm up every day at four-thirty, studying Sanskrit when I'm not attending Swamiji's classes, or fighting off the monkeys who share my terrace; hardly have a minute for taking a pee because the toilet's communal. You *will* let me have a long, lazy bath in your pink-tiled, real American bathroom, won't you, old buddy?"

Wanda looked like what I had expected Sue to look like. She was frail, about ninety-five pounds, with the pale glow of death about her skin, and she wore a white sari. Sue introduced us with a great flourish. After a huge lunch, the three of us took a tour of the city. In a Jain temple, Sue made a point of describing with great care the function of each of the plaster gods in the wall niches.

"These are my friends," she said gaily. "I talk to them every morning — especially the animals."

"I hope you realize that you're worshiping idols by bowing before these statues," I whispered, straining the last of my diminishing strength to the breaking point. I now wished that Wanda would go away and that Sue and I were sitting out on my terrace in the sun, gossiping, eating fruit, and watching the ships sail away from the harbor into the Indian Ocean.

"You were always too literal-minded, Perle. You don't understand," Sue hurriedly whispered back.

"I suppose it doesn't matter; OM TAT SAT, isn't Truth One despite what the sages call it?"

"There *is* only one truth, but there aren't many paths, as you like to think. If there's one truth, there's one path."

"And you've found it," I answered testily.

Wanda saved us from an ugly debate by developing stomach cramps. When we had flagged down a taxi for her, she leaned out of the window and urged us to have a good time.

"Thanks, and you feel better." I strained my vocal cords to speak but emitted only a hiss. I wasn't sure which of us would collapse first; Wanda, however, looked seriously ill, debilitated. When she had gone, Sue said, "I'm really worried about her. She was raised a Catholic, and her commitment to the Vedanta still smacks of that Catholic guilt, so she unnecessarily mortifies herself. We're not encouraged to be ascetics. Swamiji understands Westerners and their needs as opposed to those of his Indian students. He has even told her to eat eggs, but it's her own interpretation of the teaching that has hurt her health. Everyone here has to go through his or her own private questioning."

"You too?"

"Sure, me too. There have been times here when I thought I was losing my mind. Times when I wondered what I, a nice Brooklyn, Jewish girl, was doing here. It's all part of the questioning, the examination of the ego, learning about the false self-identifications we build up and call the truth." Sue eyed me pointedly.

We had reached the hotel.

"Cancel all your tours. Come out to the ashram and stop all this nonsensical stuff. Let's go down to Madras and see Swamiji; he'll cure you. You're still looking, aren't you? Still a tourist."

"Okay, no tour tomorrow," I said as I followed Sue into the lobby of the anomalous wonderland that was to house our three-day marathon of vedantic discourse and talmudic dialectics. After twenty-four years of friendship, Sue and I had to meet anew in India.

We spent the entire first day sitting cross-legged and recalling our past on the floor of my hotel room among open suitcases, orange rinds, sticky cups, prayer beads, assorted tourist trinkets, and breakfast leftovers. At night we ate a Rabelaisian banquet in the Taj Mahal's most lavish restaurant, still talking endlessly over the piercing strains of Indian music, nodding in tempo to silken Indian dancers, commenting on the couples around us like Hollywood gossips, giving and asking each other advice — everything from how to deal with ashram companions Sue couldn't stand to handling students whose anti-intellectualism was driving me out of teaching for good.

As we window-shopped after dinner in the hotel galleries, Sue turned to me without warning and said, "You know, in a way, ever since Dr. Yiu's Oriental Lit class, you've been shopping around, avoiding a commitment to any particular path because you're afraid you might have to give up the cushy life you have, all the familiar comfortable things around you, your precious intellectualism, because you're afraid to surrender yourself to someone who can guide you to real knowledge!"

"Is this a conversation to be having in the promenade of the Taj Mahal Hotel?" I said hoarsely. I was stung, ashamed and miserable because what she said was true. "*I will not serve,* and certainly not at the feet of any living person. I think you're here because you're in love with Swami Shankaracharya," I spat out viciously.

"Of course I am," Sue rejoindered calmly. "We all are. One girl in the ashram has even made a fool of herself by openly trying to seduce him." Sue's open, honest face made me want to lash out further, to cut ugly gashes in the impregnable, infuriating fortress of her dogmatic faith — and in my own envy of her.

"That's part of it, too," she continued quietly, impervious to my assault. "You just have to find the right teacher so you can get over it — like finding the right analyst, who won't run away and marry every patient who falls in love with him."

"What about Krishnananda? I find him repulsive," I said, still searching desperately for an instrument with which to prod Sue, to make her "normal" again.

"He's just the chief swami of the ashram, but he's not my teacher. Once you meet Shankaracharya you'll see the difference. You are just afraid of meeting a *real* teacher. It's easier to run around unmasking those you can't relate to so you can feel superior and sanctimonious at the same time."

The war continued late into the afternoon of the next day as we sat on the hotel balcony overlooking the Indian Ocean. Ships were tooting by; below us in the streets, gay wicker café tables were occupied by happy, well-dressed "normal" people who were discussing business, love affairs, what they were planning to do after the movies that night — while Sue and I tore into our respective souls with a vengeance.

At midnight she took her longed-for luxurious bath, her first tub bath in a year. I sat on the bed reading the prayers from the *siddur* to her in English. Suddenly I interrupted myself and said, "Why did you want this prayer book anyway?"

"Swamiji wants us to do a temple worship according to our own religious backgrounds. He says that we have to return home, that we who are not Hindus must continue to function as Westerners in our own worlds, in our own religions," came the steamy reply from the bathroom.

"I don't understand," I said wearily. "Why would you want to mix Indian temple *pujas* with Hebrew prayer?"

"Because Vedanta is Indian, it's taught in an Indian context, but the *Knowledge* is beyond culture. What I am racially, ethnically, in my blood, doesn't become Indian because I happen to have found the teachings coming from an Indian body in Sanskrit. I just never found the Truth coming from a Jewish teacher in Hebrew, that's all."

"What if you did? Would you have sat in some dumpy Brooklyn flat and learned it even though Brooklyn is less exotic than India?"

"I wish it were Brooklyn. I love Brooklyn; it's *you* who is all hung up about it. Why didn't you stay in Israel with Rav Bloch, for that matter, if you're so Jewish? He sounds like a real teacher, the only person you really seem to have related to with trust — at least from your letters I thought you had at last found your teacher," came Sue's soapy reply.

Lacking faith, I resumed reading the morning prayer very vigorously. "I'll teach you some nice services in Hebrew to read in the temple in front of the idols," I said viciously. "There's even one where you're supposed to prostrate yourself; that ought to be very comfortable. I used to lead the prayers every morning at seven at the Beth Rachel yeshiva. I would stand and freeze in the cold outside — I was the first to arrive — until one day the rabbi, seeing how trustworthy I was, gave me the key. I became the *shammas,* the sexton. I was so good, so holy a little girl at the age of nine, that I dutifully opened the school, placed the prayer books on the seats for the other girls, and prepared the ark, opened the venetian blinds, then led the entire service, my head fervently touching the lectern. I bowed so lustily, with such intensity, with such faith . . . Oh, shit!" I cried. "I am tired. See you in the morning."

I gulped down some cough medicine, threw myself on the bed, and, missing Sue's muffled reply, slept, dreaming all night that I was the lone student in a huge, Bauhaus-style auditorium, listening to Swami Shankaracharya's lecture on Truth. I awoke at ten the next morning to see Sue fast asleep with half the pillow clenched in her fist. Shankaracharya's saffron-wrapped visage smiled at me from the snapshot she had deliberately left on the night table at my end of the bed. It was as though he had personally interceded for her, urging me on to the enlightenment awaiting me in Madras. I had merely to throw over all the mundane and illusory attachments awaiting me back home, extend my trip, change my air tickets, and immerse myself in the void.

I washed, dressed, and ordered breakfast to be sent up. Then I began straightening out the room. I made a huge orderly pile of the indiscriminate chaos belonging to both of us. Sue's things and my gifts for her I placed in a shopping bag, including some of my warm socks and underwear and the cosmetics I knew she wouldn't find in the Bombay bazaar. I was still busy sorting out our respective belongings, differentiating between our lives, when breakfast came and Sue awoke.

"Teach me about Truth," I said. "If you have found something perfect, as you claim, teach me about it. I want it, too."

Smiling, rubbing her eyes, and looking exactly as she had at eighteen without make-up — swarthy, Mediterranean, Jewish — Sue said pleasantly, "Let's put it this way. You have been suffering from a long chronic illness, okay? I develop the same illness, and we travel around looking for doctors who can cure it. We're best friends for many years. You travel in several directions; you try Tibetan doctors, Sufi doctors, Yogi doctors. I, quite by accident, find the one doctor who can cure the illness on my first voyage out. Then, as your oldest, best friend, I come back and tell you I've found the *real* article, someone who can cure the disease we share. *And you refuse to meet him!* Not only do you refuse to have a consultation — I'm not asking you to submit yourself to his treatment — but, in the name of friendship, of all the years, all the sufferings we've shared in this illness, you don't even consent to meet him! What am I to conclude? Only that down deep you love the illness, you've become so attached to it that you don't want to exchange it for the cure."

"I'm not going to Madras," I said, pouring tea.

"Do you want to see the ashram?"

"No. Let's stay here and have fun."

"In a way I understand," Sue said quietly. "Life changes radically once you submit to the treatment. Once you've crossed the ravine you don't look back, and you're not the same anymore. You're close enough to crossing to know it. You can smell the mountain air; your toes tingle in anticipation of falling. Oh, Perle, why did you leave Jerusalem and Rav Bloch? You were so close! If that was your way, how could you have thrown it aside?"

"How could I have thrown what aside? I can't stand Judaism! I can't stand Hinduism! I hate religion!"

"All right. Don't see Shankaracharya. We'll spend the morning looking around the bookstores and the afternoon sunning at the pool."

Between lemonade and pastries, under the swaying palms that lined the hotel pool, I taught Sue how to sing the Shema phonetically. Explaining to her how vedantic was this prayer declaring God's inseparability from His name, I carefully emphasized every letter, every variation in tone at the perfect enunciation of lengths of vowels and consonants, pouring into my song every kabbalistic twist and turn and secret breath in an effort to present what I now saw as *my* truth before her. Fervently, Sue repeated the words and melodies after me. Religion, anyone's, came easily to her; she even swayed as she sang, as naturally as an ancient Hasid in some dark corner of his ghetto synagogue would bend and sway his body in his efforts to call down the mercy of his faraway God. Sue had been a rock singer. She had a sweet voice and picked up melodies easily. When I taught her how to bow from the waist at the proper moment in the prayer, she did so quite gracefully. After all, she had had much practice by the time I arrived in India.

"Judaism is all *bhakti,* all devotion," she said, leafing through the English translation facing the Hebrew pages. "Where is the self-investigation, the inquiry into the nature of consciousness?"

"In the Talmud, in the discourses of the Jewish philosophers."

"Is there a method for real people, not just scholars, to follow?"

"By discourse, you mean?"

Sue bit into a glazed petit four. "Mmm. Instructions like those given in the Vedas and in the Gita?"

"Plenty of rational discourse in Judaism." I sighed. "Too much."

"Too much emphasis on a personal God, judging from these prayers." Sue put down the *siddur,* closed her eyes, and lovingly absorbed the sun. Judaism didn't interest her.

"I'd better put oil on my face or I'll scorch." I rummaged through my bag and found a sandy bottle of Aloe lotion, unused since the previous summer at the beach. The sight of the bottle suddenly recalled Noah, his patient forbearance, his never-scolding, never-lecturing, never-guilt-evoking presence. "I have to go home," I said in a choked voice.

Sue opened her eyes and turned toward me. "Vedanta is as much a method for attaining liberation as it is a philosophy. In Swamiji's hands it becomes a practical tool for investigating the nature of consciousness, the true nature of self, the sacred — all simultaneously. Nothing is cut off from anything else: the world, God, faith, the I — and all this is transmitted as real knowledge, something you are and know yourself. No mumbo-jumbo mantras or levitating meditations — pure knowledge, like you know that you exist. It's the teacher that counts here because he transforms the student as he transmits the knowledge verbally, yet in such a way that he unfolds the highest wisdom from within the student himself — because we all contain it, *are* it — through his supra-intellectual inquiry."

"Then why do you have to worship in a temple?" I rallied.

Sue turned onto her stomach. "Ritual can be seen as an aid, a way of establishing an egoless attitude or an induction to the emotions. Let's call it an attention-getting device. Meditation is only used to focus and refocus the mind away from identification with thought and ego as the real I. Meditation on a statement like 'I am' isn't the same as those magical mantras in TM. Vedanta doesn't teach how to evoke visions but rather aims to know the self as Brahma — pure Being-Existence-Bliss. It's a nondualistic, nonsup-plicatory identification with pure Being. *Bhakti* is less sophisticated; worship is dualistic and therefore on a lower level in that it presumes a split between a personal God and an I."

"You sound like Rabbi Simeon bar Yohai."

"Who's he?"

"A Jewish swami in the Jewish Gita called the *Zohar*."

"Perle, I beg of you, come to Madras and meet Swamiji."

"I'm going home tomorrow, definitely."

"I can't believe it. Is it really that you've discovered a place for yourself through the Kabbalah, or are you just being as stubborn as usual?"

"It's funny how we've changed places. You've chosen such an intellectual, verbal path. And now I'm running away from words. I don't trust them as much as I used to. I have to go with my feelings, and my feelings tell me to go home. Maybe it is Rav Bloch. But I'm still filled with too much bitterness to learn from him now. I thought I was over with it, but I wasn't. It wasn't honest, staying with him under the pretense of gathering material for a book. I'd have to live his teaching just as you're living Shan-karacharya's, and I'm just not ready. Maybe I'll never be ready."

A quick breeze ruffled the palm fronds overhead. The sun was moving west. "I have to catch a three A.M. plane. What's wrong with these Indians, don't they fly normal human hours?"

"You should know by now that there is no 'normal human' anything in India."

"True. Let's have a big expensive supper. I love charging things at this hotel."

Sue readily agreed.

Our conversation that evening was sparse, swift, and conventional. Without stating it, Sue and I knew that our parting would be made easier if we remained as impersonal as possible. We would not be seeing each other for a year, and we wanted to remember our meeting without bitterness. We had both failed to convert each other.

It was still rather light out when I walked her to the taxi stand outside the hotel. The first star hadn't yet appeared, but the usual crush of cosmopolitan internationals surrounded us: Like the world, the Taj never stopped in its frenzied pursuit of pleasure.

"There are lots of monkeys and parrots at the ashram," Sue called out as she was getting into the cab. "And a cat I've adopted and named Banana. You'd love the animals; you'd love the place!"

"I miss you. Noah misses you. Come back soon."

We kissed hurriedly on both cheeks.

"See you later," Sue said, rolling down the window and smiling her shy, quirky, fourteen-year-old smile at me.

"See you," I cried feebly as I waved, my entire life encompassed in that moment by a never-ending string of arrivals and departures.

At six the next morning, after three hours of enforced sitting in a hermetically sealed jumbo jet that, despite hysterical attempts at servicing, never took off, I and over two hundred other frustrated passengers were shipped by bus to the Holiday Inn for a nap and a shower, courtesy of Air India. Sue had had her way. I couldn't get out of India. But it was that extra day that made me desperate to get home; it unhinged me a little, too. Brought closer by our anxiety and hapless irritation at the facelessly inefficient Indian authorities who were keeping us there, we passengers spent most of our time getting to know each other. When we arrived in Rome almost two days later, I was disheveled and numb. Claire Henderson, my Baptist missionary seatmate, walked beside me up and down the airport lounge as we exercised our legs, talking compulsively of her experiences in the jungle villages of South India. It was as if she had to recount every detail to me in order to verify the adventure for herself.

"We spent a month wandering as mendicants, spreading the Gospel, like new apostles," she said dreamily, the jungles already fading to pale green in her mind's eye. "There is something remarkable about those people, a kind of openness I know I'll never find in the West and that I'll miss very much when I get home." Claire's face was glossy with nervous perspiration, the eyes behind her thick spectacles moist with sleeplessness and culture shock.

I, the unsuccessful missionary, remained silent and let her talk.

"In the midst of all that disease and poverty, such generosity, such trust," she mused, more to herself than to me.

"Did they resent your efforts to convert them?" I couldn't resist intruding on her self-deluding dream. What right did she have to wander around India in this day and age "civilizing the heathens"?

"Not at all, not at all." She set down her coffee cup; the frothy capuccino painted her upper lip with a thin sepia moustache. "In one very strict Brahman village, where the people were so poor that there were no doors on their houses (they lived in grass huts on stilts), we were offered not only the best bedrolls and private space for sleeping, but the last chappati in the house and the single lime reserved for their dinner."

"The whole family, a single lime?" I asked, knowing that the Indians would give the skin off their backs to any wandering sadhu; it didn't matter that Claire was a heavy, bespectacled virgin from Iowa come to spread the Gospel to the natives. Religion, any kind, would do. It had put the Indians where they were and given them a proper rationale for their starving.

"That's right, and there were at least eight people. When we refused to eat, they wouldn't hear of it and grew terribly insulted. So we ate the poor ration. Believe me, I felt awful about it. Here they were, heathens, living very naturally the lives of real Christians. We didn't have to preach to them. They were living embodiments of Christ's love, despite our view of them as ignorant and superstitious. I'll never forget those villages above all else."

"So you liked India?" I asked as we boarded the plane for the next stop, Paris.

"Well, I hated it in a way, too," Claire admitted tentatively, her eyes practically closing behind her thick glasses.

"What?"

"The dirt, the disease, the gentleness that becomes crippling passivity, the kind of inefficiency that made us all fume yesterday on the plane — you know the kind of thing I mean."

"Yes," I said. "It's the meek getting even." But Claire was already dozing into her Bible and she didn't hear me. I curled up in my seat and slept dreamlessly.

In London I was roughly awakened by a prodding stewardess and the captain's announcement that we had once again broken down. Like a crazy woman trying to burst out of a straitjacket, I thrust my arms out of my coatsleeves and pushed the stewardess aside.

"I'm getting off this plane and going home," I said. Then, turning to Claire, who was still half-asleep, I shouted, "Come on, we're getting off. We'll catch a British Airways flight home."

"What time is it?" Claire groped for her Bible.

"Two in the morning, London time. Get up, Claire. We can't let this go on anymore. Remember what you said about the crippling passivity? The last lime?"

The blissful hippie in the seat behind us drawled out for me to "take it easy." His flat, self-satisfied voice and "spiritual" grin increased my fury, and I almost lunged at him.

"Claire," I begged, "what's going on here? Is everyone drugged?"

"Patience." She accented the word softly, Christianly.

"Claire, what's wrong with these people?" I cried, feeling suddenly like a desperate character in a science fiction film. But Claire had fallen asleep.

"No use appealing to any of them," said a blond woman coming down the aisle in her fur coat. "They're all followers of some swami who blessed the plane and told them they'd get home safely only on a plane he'd blessed himself." She had a hard New York accent. "My name's Helen Daly. I'm getting off. How about you?"

"This minute," I said.

There was no time for luggage, no time for anything but grabbing coat and scarf and purse and running from India without looking back. The airplane door closed with a final thud behind us. In the transit lounge we were met by a pointy-faced, tight-lipped British ground hostess who assured us that every ticket office was closed; she could do nothing but put us up in a motel near the airport until eight the next morning.

Helen Daly and I huddled together, jumping up and down to keep warm as we waited for a taxi in the freezing entranceway of the ghostly terminal. We were both too cold and exhausted to talk. In the taxi, I learned that she was a Westport art dealer who had gone to India on a buying trip.

"Don't worry. I'll back you up if Air India refuses to pay the motel bill and if there's trouble getting your luggage. I've been through this kind of thing before," she said, as she closed the door of her room across the hall.

"And those poor idiots are probably still sitting on that plane," I murmured half-aloud, my rage having rolled to a dead stop. Noting only the heavy flowered carpet under my feet as I kicked off my shoes, I removed my clothes and fell into bed.

At six, I bolted upright out of a dream and began to weep — first a pure, mindless wail wrenched from the blind newborn animal I had discovered in India to be myself. After a minute or two, sensory awareness came, bringing with it a glimpse of the real root of my misery, my increasing distance from whatever god it was I was searching for so vigorously. Like the old swaying Hasid, the ancestor I had belittled in my fantasies, I was lying alone in my room, weeping and pleading with God to show Himself to me.

Hadn't I prayed fervently enough at services, observed the rules of the system to the letter in order to obtain all that I had ever wanted in my childhood life: just one tiny peek, a glimpse of old woolly beard on His flaming chariot? So small and distant was I, so cut off from Him, so scattered and confused then . . . and now. Where to find this light that the books all said was as near to me as my own flesh and rapidly beating heart, yet as distant as the frozen stars? What indeed had I been doing in India, looking for yet another chimera? For a further set of instructions to guide me toward the paradoxical greatness and minuteness lodged in the very space I occupied, for avoiding the goal at all costs in my busy search for a system, a *reasonable, logical,* cold, and unloving way to know Him, or It — or myself, for that matter? Acquiring India had been like acquiring another academic degree. And I had worked equally hard at it. How could the unnamable be so far away and so much part of me, or I part of this unmanifest No-Thing? Sue's logic escaped me. How could this tricky phenomenon called con-sciousness have led me so far from the target, urging me to look for a system anywhere else but on the ground where I stood?

Tears and sobs mingled and flowed freely. Remembering Claire suddenly, my eyes fell on the Bible beside the bed.

"Oh, no, not that old trick," I said aloud, as my fingers ran ahead of me and opened it on their own. My head, too, seemed to be operating of its own accord. I had lost control over my will. Taking the book to the window, I read aloud from the scolding Jeremiah in the scant, drizzly light of a London winter dawn: *"Thou hast played the harlot with many lovers; yet return again to me, saith the Lord."* Startled, the tears ebbing, I continued further:

Truly in vain is salvation hoped for from the hills, and
from the multitude of mountains: truly in the Lord our God
is the salvation of Israel . . .

If thou wilt return, O Israel, saith the Lord, return unto
me: and if thou wilt put away thine abominations out of my sight,
then shalt thou not remove . . .

Set up the standard toward Zion: retire, stay not . . .

I am pained at my very heart; my heart maketh a noise in me; I cannot hold my peace . . . For my people is foolish, they have not known me.

5

Puzzling the Divine Acrostic

I HAD COME ACROSS only one kabbalist in the States with whom I felt compatible. Therefore, when I returned from India, my first symbolic attempt to tread the Jewish mystic path led me back to the home of Reb Yosef, an antiestablishment Hasid whose vast learning and liberal approach toward ritual had turned his Philadelphia congregation into a haven for secular outcasts like me.

When Noah and I pulled up to the massive old stone house, no one seemed to be occupying it; there was no sign of anyone to greet us. A few faded Volkswagen vans bearing California plates stood in the driveway; the deserted witches' cradles in the cluttered backyard reminded me of the cold autumn day when Reb Yosef, robed in nineteenth-century Hasidic caftan, fur *streimel,* and all, had placed me gently in the iron cage and pushed me with my eyes closed until I'd gotten high and felt my body leaving my head, and then my head leaving the earth. "I told you you'd love it!" He'd laughed and gone inside, leaving me alone among the newly awakened wrens. Now it was Passover, sunny and almost as cold as on that autumn day. Halfway around the great wraparound porch, a couple stood without speaking. The woman was dressed in biblical garb: long white muslin caftan and purple head scarf, like a modest and proper Jewish wife. With her pristine, un-made-up face, she resembled one of those eighteenth-century *Rebecca at the Well* paintings rendered by middling, pre-Romantic painters long forgotten. I felt tawdry and overdone with my rouged face and uncovered hair, although my Indian caftan and Noah's long hair bespoke tentative membership in this otherworldly fraternity. Always uncomfortable around aging hippies, I winced inwardly at their wordless greetings, the idyllic smiles and blank nods as we entered, as if Noah and I were emerging from a coarser dimension into their finer one. Our spoken hellos were intrusive, for speech, as their eyes told us, had no place among the angels. I enjoyed talking so much; my life was a veritable word garden. My contemporaries, these new Hasidim were so focused on the Divine they hardly talked at all. Sue had once called me "a throwback, nothing but a Brooklyn *yenta* at heart." I wished Sue were there to liven things up a bit, that she hadn't abandoned me to reclaiming my past.

Noah settled himself comfortably into an old armchair in the living room, where a dim blue light outlined Reb Yosef's collection of OM decals, candles, Tibetan tangkas, incense, the velvet-draped ark containing the Torah, and his leatherbound kabbalistic tomes. A barefoot girl sat in one corner playing a dulcimer; opposite her, a bearded Sufi played a different tune on a recorder; the melodies did not blend. Too many people here were doing their own thing in silence. Only the children talked. There always seemed to be children suffering with colds at these gatherings, barefoot children with stuffed-up noses and curly blond hair. Unlike their affectless parents, they were bright and forward, indulging in thoroughly grown-up conversations as they gazed straight into my face with eyes that pierced their own little wizened faces like the coals I had used for snowmen's eyes long ago.

One such child, a boy named Yoash, introduced himself in perfect Hebrew. "I'm four," he said, holding up four dirty fingers. "And I do magic tricks."

"What kind of magic tricks?" Noah asked.

"I make pennies disappear. But only when I don't think about it. When I do think about it, though, the magic doesn't happen," Yoash replied to Noah's astonishment.

Dressed in a long white robe and slippers, Reb Yosef emerged from behind an unremarked curtain. Were the Essenes so casual? We hugged. I was instantly aware of his huge, bearded, Dionysian presence, his soft, yielding body and fluttering rabbi's wings for arms. How pliant, how unlike Rav Bloch — that hard, tiny Puck to Reb Yosef's hippie Oberon.

Reb Yosef's wife, Rachel, big, mother-earthy in black dress and white apron, puttered in the kitchen amid a nest of communal pots, bowls, Mason jars filled with sprouts, sunflower seeds, dried fruits, dangling garlic and onions, nuts — the new vegetarian Hasidic kitchen via India and Nepal. More loosely clad beards and covered heads, more biblical Rebeccas with pitchers, babies slung over their shoulders, were cutting, chopping, and running water in preparation for the Seder. Aimlessly, I picked up an egg, which, Rachel informed me, was to serve as a symbol of the Paschal lamb. Feeling awkward (annoyed at the banality of the egg, the continuing need for even symbolic sacrifice, blood-letting), I dropped the egg to the floor. Luckily, Rachel had hard-boiled the eggs in advance. Her earth-mother foresight had warned her about the intrusion of manual morons like me in her Passover kitchen, about self-doubting Jews. She did not even bother to look over at me when I burst out with "Oh, Christ!" as the egg fell.

Life in Reb Yosef's big stone house was a biblical costume party, a collection of Americans from Oregon and Connecticut and New York and California playing at being Semites from Judaea and Samaria. Yet we Jews were somehow also out of context in that historic landmark quarter of Philadelphia, like the cathedral-shaped Conservative synagogue six blocks away that housed Reb Yosef's little room upstairs, a conciliatory gift to the "radicals." The same "uh-oh, wrong place" sensation here in the house that I got when I accidentally entered the Jewish cathedral service on a Saturday afternoon as I searched aimlessly for Reb Yosef's hidden room. The typically chic suburban matrons turned as one to look at me in my dirndl skirt, sandals, and bare toes. Quickly, the sexton lifted his prayer shawl and directed me to the floor above, his finger on his lips, as though the mere sound of my voice might contaminate the orderly bourgeois proceedings in King James's English. The janitor, an old black man, had been delegated to lead me upstairs. I noticed, smiling behind him, that he was wearing a white silk skullcap. On the second floor, in a stuffy classroom, Reb Yosef was trying desperately to conduct his "alternate Sabbath service" among screeching children and irritated, premenstrual feminists draped in prayer shawls and *tefillin* while academic leftists argued loudly in the background with Zionists in three-piece suits. *Do you belong here either?* I asked myself that Saturday as a braided girl in a peasant blouse handed me a *siddur* and a prayer shawl and beckoned me to join the ceremony on the floor. *Do you belong here?*

Above the apparent chaos was an element of ritual about the bustle in Reb Yosef's big house, a loving quality to the work in the kitchen that reminded me of the boy and girl monks preparing lunch at the zendo in the Catskills, but without their selfless discipline. For me, eating was just something I had to do in order to live, an act performed without much enthusiasm or art, but rather a necessity to be overcome. Noah and I frequently promised ourselves that we would someday switch to the eleventh-century mystic's diet of Ibn ben Paquda: nothing cooked, only dates, nuts, cheese, milk, fruits, melons. For Noah, who spent less than ten minutes at dinner before growing restless, life would have been much simplified by eating melons while standing upright. Laziness rather than conviction motivated my own flirtation with the ascetic diet of the Jewish mystics. In Reb Yosef's house, however, cooking was a serious business and eating a sacred function. For the Hasid, each bite contains a divine spark; every step in the interaction between human digestion and organic matter bears the possibility of releasing holiness and redeeming the world.

Rachel was not upset by my continued awkwardness in the kitchen; when I clattered the dishes, she merely looked at me briefly and moved on. The Matrona passing by; God's female presence. Yet, like all Jewish matronly presences, she bore an unspoken threat. Implicitly critical, she waited for me to make the first move, withholding her praise and approval until I had done something tangible to earn it. All these tough Jewish women, Orthodox or not, were basically cold — until one day their steam valves burst, and they exploded with a hiss. There was no appreciable difference between Reb Yosef's efficient and closed-mouthed young wife and the shrill rebbitzen at the Beth Rachel School for Girls. Both were ominous; both begrudged me my freedom, my nonhousewifely ways. Both made me feel like an intrusive kid about to break something, always on the verge of dropping an egg, of messing up — or worse, that I had already transgressed and gotten away with it because I had been born sly and wicked. The rebbitzen would always find me out.

This time I was saved from my fantasies of her wrath by the announcement that Maariv, the evening prayer, was about to be performed. I stopped peeling oranges and handed the rinds to a girl named Kitty, who now called herself Tova. The kitchen was full of ex-Barbaras now calling themselves Miriam or Chana. And, in the typically ecumenical style of Reb Yosef, some of the male Hasidim were Sufi Mahmouds and Kalims. There was even one Parvati thrown in to leaven the internationally flavored Passover table. I was relieved to be done with peeling and dropping things; nobody had spoken to me much anyway — the stranger with no Hebrew name. Noah sat talking in the living room–synagogue with an excitable blue-eyed girl named Sheva (probably Judy in real life), who had just returned from a week with Madame Ariel in Jerusalem. When he introduced us, Sheva kissed me as if she had known me forever. The atmosphere in the room weighed on me heavily. First there was silence, then suddenly a devotee would break out into a private hymn praising God in Hebrew, humming, chanting, groaning. Though hardly a word had been uttered among us, it was apparent that all kinds of religious outbursts were encouraged in Reb Yosef's unpredictable congregation. At any moment someone might launch into embarrassing ritual gestures without warning. Sheva's effusiveness, though welcome on one level, was suspect on another.

Contrary to traditional Orthodox procedure, the Maariv service was conducted with musical instruments. I sat cross-legged on a big pillow ornamented by a hand-painted lion's face. Reb Yosef, big and approving, newly robed in fresh white with priestly gold bands billowing down the front of his expansive chest, silver fox *streimel* on his head, led the chanting. A Sufi played a tabor; a young man named simply Kenny (oddly enough) played the violin. He wore an elegant black smoking jacket and a brushed hillbilly hat. The girl with the dulcimer now played the harmonium; a languid boy in a Sufi crocheted skullcap fervently plucked at an oversized guitar. It was all quite lovely. One of the barefoot Rebeccas took up the tambourine and shook it in time to the singing, and the bitterly familiar liturgy of the Beth Rachel School for Girls was transformed into the magic of potential ecstasy. The Shema, cried fervently by all the outwardly disparate Jewish beings in the room, had touched a common root. The children of Israel were returned again to the foot of Sinai, if only for a moment. For the first time in many years, I felt a stir at the declaration of Yahweh's oneness with His name. The songs of praise — partly in English, partly in Hebrew, set to Hasidic and modern folk melodies by Reb Yosef — now vibrated with hidden meaning: God was truly real, truly a feasible possibility as our little band joined to sing of His all-pervasive glory.

But when we rose to recite the silent Amidah, the oldest and most sacred portion of the service, the magic spell broke. Like little Yoash, I had *thought* about making the pennies disappear and so they wouldn't. Thought had carried me back to any synagogue anywhere, merely reciting Hebrew words at top speed to get them over with, to finish the prayers faster than the "show-off" Beth Rachel girls in my class. Others, too, were jolted out of their rapture as the music stopped. The men shuffled, hiding their boredom in coughs. The children whined. The women left to look after the food in the kitchen. How quickly the divine vision had faded — for all of us. Only Reb Yosef was unwilling to relinquish it; he worked hard to charge us up again, to recall the light from the divine sparks we had released with the breath of our prayers. Reb Yosef was not one to let go of redemption so easily.

Launching into one of his "Hasidic rap sessions," he initiated the soul-searching himself, speaking candidly about his own frailty, his personal search, about the difficulties and waverings he had encountered in scaling and experiencing each of the spheres on the Tree of Life.

"All the stages of Illumination are difficult to traverse," he said, "but for me, it's particularly *geburah,* the rigorous left hand of God, that is hardest."

I admired Reb Yosef for publicly admitting that he could not confront his own violence. Yet he struck me more as a man lodged in the sphere of *yesod,* the sensual realm associated with the moon, for he was all sense, generosity, touch, characteristically Jewish in his preoccupation with this world, his attachment to the flesh. Looking at Reb Yosef as he talked, I knew that we Jews were ecstatics by nature and that asceticism was far from us.

The Seder table was set and waiting. Women gathered in small groups to light the candles. The first Seder night, Reb Yosef proclaimed, was dedicated to faith, the second night, to healing.

"Will you devote this Seder to my friend Betsy, a convert, who is very ill?" I asked, half-expecting to be ignored.

Breaking with tradition, Reb Yosef skipped the details: her Hebrew name, her mother's Hebrew name. All the complicated Orthodox finery surrounding the ritual was shorn away, leaving only Betsy, a human being in need of prayer. Loudly he intoned the Meshaberach, a healing prayer for "Betsy, daughter of Abraham and Sarah," and we lit the candles in unison, drawing the brightness from the flames with the cupping motions of our fingers. Guarding the light in our palms, we closed our eyes and drew on the sphere of mercy.

The candle-lighting ceremony was long, silent, infused with

mystery. I watched the women around me swaying before the light, and I suddenly grew shy at the hint of awe that threatened to rise up from my chest. What I had tried to work up artificially when standing barefoot before Vishnu was happening quite without effort as I approached the menorah, placed my two candles in their holders, and lit the wick. All I could think of in the Vishnu temple was that someone had tackily polished the god's fingernails an ugly plum shade. How literal the Hindus were, and how abstract (too abstract) in their worship were the Jews. Still, Reb Yosef's Seder was less intimidating than the soaked, icy marble floor of the Siva temple, with its ominous crystal phalluses.

Noah and I were seated opposite Reb Yosef's end of the table next to a rapt, blue-eyed boy in his twenties named Mahmoud, an uncommunicative girl with a long, black Chinaman's pigtail, some giggly virgins, and the emotional Sheva. Reb Yosef instructed the company to order the Passover plate so that each symbolic portion of food on it represented a sphere on the cosmic tree. So! All those years it had been more than just a few bitter herbs to commemorate Israel's suffering in Egypt; more than a few hard-boiled eggs and walnuts and apples standing in for the bricks and mortar of the pyramids; more than the commemoration of a historical event that by now no longer personally involved me or anyone else around the table.

"Egypt, as the *Zohar* reminds us, actually represents the state of the ego in this subject-object 'fallen' world. Every step of our journey through slavery and the wilderness is an ascent along the Tree of Life to undifferentiated consciousness," Reb Yosef said, gleaming as his guests arranged their plates. The matzo — home-baked, crusty, as ancient and brown as the Sinai desert — was delicious. "We pile it on three levels, the levels of consciousness we must encounter on the way to enlightenment." Now he was talking my language. No other Seder had opened in this way. All over America, Seders were beginning with kisses and Passover candies, with flowers and handwashing. But none, I was willing to bet, with the planting of the cosmic tree.

Every facet of the Passover ritual was performed by both men and women in Reb Yosef's revolutionary house. Removing all jewelry, I washed carefully up to my elbows. Purified, at peace with the aroma of food, the glowing candlelight, the matzo tree, the Temple in miniature I had constructed on my plate, I blessed, then drank, the wine. Reversing the sequence of the Seder, Reb Yosef first encouraged the children to ask spontaneous questions about the ritual. My own father would have considered it sacrilege. But Reb Yosef obviously understood the restlessness of children, and he was aware that their interest would quickly turn to grogginess and that they would grow pesty before too long. The Seder was, theoretically, for the *children* of Israel: "Tell every generation of the flight from Egypt." Out of habit, many of us continued the tradition without question. In most American homes it had become simply a family "party," indistinguishable from Easter vacation. In some households they even celebrated it with bread on the table, perhaps because the ritual, like the holiday itself, was too long and ill adapted to modern secular life. I was accosted suddenly by memories of my grandfather brushing bread crumbs out of corners with two white chicken feathers, selling the household *bometz* to Gentiles for the course of the holiday, and then by a twinge of guilt. Although I did not eat bread out of long habit, I did not kosher the house or change the dishes, either.

The children in the congregation were clever and practical, wanting to know how the Hebrews survived in the desert without water and food and wondering about the welfare of the household pets their ancestors had left behind in Egypt. The adults at the table greeted their questions with approving shouts and laughter. Reb Yosef lit a long, elegant joint, took a deep, pleasurable puff, and passed it around the table. I inhaled and suffered a harsh kick in my lower abdomen. The grass was strong, maybe even mixed with hash. Was marijuana kosher for Passover? I wondered, wryly picturing my father's face. Then I became conscious of a bearded young man in an embroidered peasant shirt and gaily crocheted skullcap sitting just beyond Sheva; he hadn't uttered one word since we sat down at the Seder table. Without the help of the joint (which he waved aside when Sheva passed it to him), he was flying high on some kind of internal prayer.

Sheva turned from him and inexplicably handed me her Haggadah, a closely printed, tight Aramaic version of the text, with no English translation and entirely unrelieved by the usual cartoon drawings depicting the course of the Seder. I had always loved those cartoons — the fat, silly son who asked dumb questions about the Exodus, and especially the villainous, wicked son who said "you" and not "I" when referring to the Jewish people. A secret affinity with him provoked me every year to turn to that page first. Sheva's intrusiveness had prevented me from indulging my secret vice.

"Here, it's Rav Bloch's version of the Haggadah," she said, "and I think it's appropriate that you use it since Noah tells me you're his pupil."

So it was not Sheva at all who plucked me from the brink of sin but the long arm of Rav Bloch, extending all the way from Jerusalem. Why did Noah have to blab to strangers about Rav Bloch, especially when I was not really his pupil?

I meekly exchanged Haggadoth with Sheva and looked down at the unintelligible, unvoweled Hebrew of Rav Bloch's divine acrostic. No English. No pictures. Nothing to give me a clue of what it was he had to tell me.

"You read Hebrew, of course," said Sheva in the challenging tone of a Jew who did.

"Not well enough to plow through this."

"I'm sure Rav Bloch feels you read it well enough." Conversation concluded. Sheva's eyes were brimming with unspilled tears; she was slightly hysterical from having drunk rather heavily from the ritual cup.

The children, inevitably, grew bored. After hiding the *afikomen,* they sat and fidgeted throughout the prayers. What else was left for them but the prospect of picking their noses and whining, as Yoash was then doing? Even if he did understand the Hebrew, the story was too long. Centuries of persecution. Centuries of having his nose rubbed in the grownups' talk of slavery, redemption, being "different" from other people. Yoash stubbornly refused to ask the Four Questions. I didn't blame him; I took secret delight in his stubbornness, his refusal to belong. Reb Yosef instructed the company to sing the questions together, and the grownups chanted so loudly that they covered the sounds of Yoash's screams as he was carried, protesting, upstairs to bed.

With the prayers out of the way, we settled down to the serious business of eating. Most of the guests dolloped their plates with salad and stuffed themselves with matzo balls and vegetable soup. Then a long baked carp drenched in tomatoes and peppers was brought out for the few nonvegetarians among us.

Staring into a gleaming fish eye, I suddenly blurted out, "If they rebuild the Temple and start renewing animal sacrifices, this is one Jew they'll have to count out!" Marijuana had made me sassy and contentious.

Rachel replied immediately, her eyes sparkling, "There was a sensuous pleasure in watching the fish get clubbed this afternoon at the market."

Restraining the urge to smack her hard, I stared mournfully at the poor fish embalmed in tomato-pepper sauce; then, paradoxically, my mouth started to water. Rav Bloch had assured me that refraining from flesh food was necessary in preparing for the Messiah, the time when all souls would be revived and we would have to confront those whose blood we had shed for food. Then why the sacrifices? Why didn't two Jews ever agree on anything?

Reb Yosef mediated fuzzily between my unflinchingly puritanical stance and his wife's earthy eroticism. Grass had made him even gentler than usual, all smiles. I could not understand a word he was saying. Then the peasant spoke for the first time. "We must sacrifice everything within ourselves to God," he said quietly and firmly.

"Awareness of sacrificing is hypocritical," I answered. "As long as there is a sense of an I doing something — even something good, like placating God — you are still stuck in dualism." Unremittingly Asian that, especially among these earthbound Jews around their sacrificial platter of fish. Many rabbis sat in Jerusalem awaiting the day when the animal sacrifices would be resumed in the Temple. Better never to rebuild the Temple, then. Better never to have to argue anymore about Jews and Arabs with Ibrahim, my Palestinian friend.

"You Jews are mad for reconstructing the Temple. You want the Mount so that you can tear down the mosque and re-establish yourselves there in order to reinstitute the sacrifices. I heard it in Hebrew on the radio. Just where the Rock of Mohammed stands!" Ibrahim had screamed at me in a fury. Then he had jumped out of my little Volkswagen and created a traffic jam on the Jerusalem-Jericho road . . .

Reb Yosef interceded with an explanation, but his rationale was muddy and vague, and no one listened. Kenny left the table and lay down on the living room sofa with a rosewater compress on his head. Reb Yosef tried desperately to reunite his flock with a Hindu parable about faith and sacrifice and two Krishna followers, but the Hindus could not get us out of the touchy muddle our Passover had become. How far did symbols go? I wondered. Were they only effective as literal transcriptions of higher consciousness? Were the rabbis really waiting in Jerusalem for sacrifices? Hadn't they seen enough blood drench that arid and desolate sand? Even the masses were no longer under their spell. Again and again, the young questioned their stale rationale for the ancient laws; thousands had left the fold. Growing numbers of Hasidic women were boldly demanding divorces. The old answers just wouldn't do.

How dull, dull, dull . . . the questions I had rehearsed for twenty-five years, the hunt for the missing letter in the acrostic. Nothing could save religion, not even Reb Yosef's fine dope. And I had foolishly come to Philadelphia in search of my missing "Jewishness," which clung to me from birth like a caul. I had hoped for — what? To share in a mystic ritual, the renewal of a people brought together long ago (also against their will) by another Reb Yosef, with the blaring of innumerable ram's horns, lots of thunder and lightning, and great gloomy clouds parting to reveal the illuminated letters of the Great Name. And I had gotten no such thing. I had tried to hitch a ride to Sinai on Reb Yosef's ecstatic coattails, to take a short cut to the peace that passeth understanding. And I'd been given *pilpul* in exchange, the same old talmudic mania for questions and answers, for legalistic hair-splitting. To sacrifice or not to sacrifice? But if? I had taken the short cut that Rav Bloch would never exchange for direct experience. The joke was on me.

How peaceful only to sit with Narendra on his green rug in utter silence, observing the wafting mind. But I was a Jew, and I had to find a Jewish frame for sitting. How had the real kabbalists emptied themselves of all but the clear, penetrating One? Not with all the noise and paraphernalia rattling on around them at the Seder table, I was sure. Where, then, was the golden mean between dry rabbinic legalism and the shamanism of the embroidered peasant to my right who had once again lapsed into private ecstasy?

The argument dribbled into Hasidic parables — always the sure-fire solutions to the unanswerable, the Jewish Koans. Where had Passover gone?

Noah rose, extending his hand across the table to Reb Yosef. "It's a long drive to New York. I've got work tomorrow."

Sheva stood sobbing wildly among the coats in the doorless closet in the hall. As Noah helped me on with my sweater, Reb Yosef came up behind me, turned me around, looked into my eyes, and handed me a matzo wrapped in a napkin. "It's for Betsy, part of the sacred matzo over which we said the healing prayer. Have her eat it." We kissed. The matzo had suddenly redeemed all: the sacrifices, the chaotic and indolent life in the big house, the puerile ecumenism.

"Happy Passover," I smirked.

"Gut yom tov, dear *Perele,"* Reb Yosef saluted me in grand-fatherly Yiddish. He was a man of wide gestures, multileveled, disorganized, human. I loved him dearly for a moment. Then he closed the door and was forgotten.

Noah breathed a deep sigh and looked up at the star-filled sky.

"You never see a galaxy like that in Brooklyn," he said, recalling a joke from our distant courtship.

"You sure 'nuff don't," I replied, tucking my hand in the crook of his arm. Together, we felt our way down the path toward the car. Reb Yosef had forgotten to switch on the porch light, and neither of us could see a thing.

6

At the Edge

DEEPER INTO SPRING. Again the long, intricate trek to the brink of the dread ravine in my meditations, this time with the added disorientation of a blind woman deposited in a prison shaped so asymmetrically that each time I felt around its walls for a door, I bumped into yet another wall and hurt myself. Inside me there lived a perpetual silent scream. A noisy chorus of Babel sometimes rendered advice: "Stop setting up a further delusion. Stop blocking your head with notions. Stop and see." The Babel was followed by an illusory silence that really all the while teemed with images, bits and scraps of recipes for enlightenment, formulas guaranteed to draw love and admiration for my nauseating "commitment," my "sincerity." The quest made my physically sick. I felt it again as I had the year before, in my belly, as a black hole; the old, by now nightly, familiar sensation of myself shrinking down into nothing more than my heart, a fist-sized blob of throbbing red tissue, the bleeding, sorrowing heart in the Rosicrucian drawings one found on the back covers of astrology magazines. The nightly sensation always reduced itself to sorrow; a place where "I" was nothing more than a giant teardrop about to spill out of the throbbing little heart called "me," which did not want to be annihilated no matter how much it blabbered about enlightenment in public, which was so sad about the confusion that she shrank and dried up — like Alice in Wonderland getting smaller and smaller. At last she condensed into an image of sorrow: the Mater Dolorosa. To this, Narendra only replied, "The ego dies hard."

H. J. Shastri, dapper but trembling with age and poor health, seemed more tender in the spring of 1977. He had already prepped us, put us through the pre–delivery room mechanics, stripped us of our street clothes and gotten us into our examining gowns, propped up our feet, and instructed us to lie back and push. Shastri urged us on and on: "Push." "See it." "See it now!" "For God's sake, see it!" The seminar was bigger and more openly emotional this time. We could just about feel the heads of our own identities emerging from our guts; but then, no, it was always a false alarm, a false push, nothing but air and self-pitying moans, nothing delivered. We simply could not give birth to our true selves but landed back where we started, dry heaving, sweating, asking Shastri for a drink of spiritual water to cool us. But, old taskmaster that he was, Shastri would not even so much as sprinkle our lips with a droplet of his enlightened insight. Instead he wiped the spittle of excited effort from his own mouth with one of his monogrammed linen handkerchiefs. It was not his fault; he had been trying for two years in a row with us, but we were bad followers. He was on the verge of giving up; we could not, or would not, go with him all the way.

Again in our own sessions, with Shastri absent, it was easier. There were the usual psychiatrists, physicists, and biologists to guide us. These people, were, after all, the new Levites preparing the stage for the high priest. We humanists in the audience clung to their dogma; only the scientists could mediate between Shastri and ordinary mortals, for we had chosen to worship with reason. Sanitized in mind and spirit, we were uncomfortable around the bloody-handed, knife-wielding high priest whose awesome words threatened to chop away at us, sacrificing our hearts and feeding our egos to his Truth. We needed the scientists as buffers.

In Shastri's presence I found I was no longer uncomfortable with the word "God." I had come full circle. Now words like "Void," "Truth," and "Absolute" made me squirm in my seat.

For three days we submitted our tender egos to the steely knife of Shastri's insistent questioning. *Who is it that is angry when there is no memory? What has thought done to the earth?* Among ourselves the problem was all "out there," without urgency. We theorized, ate sandwiches, and told jokes during intermission periods. It was nowhere as lavish as the maharaja's palace, but it allowed us to believe that we were a truly charming group of people who were desirably alike: a community of sharp intellect and honest inquiry. Then Shastri entered and made us all afraid.

"Do you really see it, sir?" came the menacing voice of the high priest as he flicked at a spot on his otherwise perfect blue silk tie.

Why is he vain? I wondered. If there is no ego, why is he so damned vain? Yet, as I watched him, I soon came to see that there was in fact nobody walking around in that blue suit and tie. It was as if we in the room had collectively dreamed him up and put him on an invisible altar. When Shastri spoke, there were no intermissions, no sandwiches, no jokes.

On the second day of our three-day seminar my ego was tickled into response. "If we are machines, as you say, how do you propose we step aside from the program and free ourselves?" I asked.

"Yes, like an old gramophone, you're stuck going around and around. How do you get unstuck?" Shastri changed the metaphor and turned my question into a question — like an old rabbinical Jew.

A psychologist in a brown suit said, "When I think, am I projecting desire, time, space, and sequence?"

I thought I would shout "stop!" but managed to control myself. The Babel had resumed from outside; I tethered the scream. Then I leaned forward as I used to when I was a ten-year-old student at the Beth Rachel School — brazenly, draped rather than seated on the chair — the posture of challenge, humor, all to hide the weeping heart that followed me into my dreams every night. I wore a white sweater with a tiny red heart just above the left breast.

Instinctively right, providing a target for Shastri's merciless knife. Metaphors spoke better for me.

"Suppose," I said in a very loud voice, "suppose it is the most urgent thing in my life, this *seeing* things as they are, this clear vision of life you speak about — without all the history, hopes, naming, jealousy, and planning thrown up by consciousness into thought. But suppose we move away from all this theorizing. Suppose I'm just an ordinary person, urgent about this issue, and I'm driving my car and somebody cuts me off, and I biologically and instinctively react without anger, or naming anything, then how am I to achieve this clear awareness of my life simultaneously with the event? I mean, sir, how do I live in the middle of all this and watch at the same time in that untainted state of awareness without going mad?" I sat back, satisfied that I had snared him. Shastri looked at me benignly, almost with approval. Then, swiftly, with only one chop, he said, "All right, madame, but what *is* your life? What is the meaning of your existence?"

Again I felt the black hole in my belly. Could I blurt out the real answer in front of all those people? "A pulpy red bleeding heart that sobs each night at the sense of its impending annihilation and weeps over the mail every morning as it reads about the imminent extinction of every created thing, from daisies to dolphins?" *"Sadness, that's my existence, Mr. Shastri,"* I wanted to cry out, no, scream. *"Where's Truth? Where's God? Where is the field on which all we pitiable waves and particles are doing the dance of death? Why did you abandon us? And why can't I see you if I open my eyes wide? Could that be why there are black spots when I read lately, the mote in my own eye?"*

"I can't help but feel that you have the answer but you're not telling me," I said lightly, breaking the tension and making everyone in the room laugh.

As the meeting broke up, I watched Shastri shake hands with the psychologist in the brown suit. When I came up close, the old man looked at me wearily through the milky eyes of age. I wanted to thank him to be polite, to say something, but I just stared.

"Thanks for nothing" was what I really wanted to say. Shastri could offer no comfort, not even to a dying ego in its last throes. Rav Bloch would have given me a pinch on the arm and said, "Penina," and although that would not have solved anything at all about the problem of Truth, it would have bestowed a temporary peace.

I walked to the car waiting for me around the corner, joking with familiar faces, but I felt schizoid. I had stepped out of my everyday self just long enough to turn my head around backward, but not long enough to set it back on straight again. With Shastri, the world would continue to remain askew.

At the lamppost on the corner I was tapped on the shoulder. Turning, I saw the square-faced wife of one of the physicists. In what sounded like hurried Hebrew, I heard her say: "I like 'Penina' better than 'Perle.' "

"Thank you," I answered stupidly, out of touch with what I had heard against the street noises, still too preoccupied with my inner Babel, still grappling back in the seminar room in a far corner of my brain with the old dapper saint who possessed the secret of liberation but could not bestow it on me.

Seeing my confusion, the physicist's wife leaned closer and repeated, "Penina is more suitable for you than Perle. I'll call you Penina from now on."

I laughed a real laugh for the first time that day. It was as though Rav Bloch had done it again, been with me at the edge the whole time. As if he had disassembled his molecules like some miraculous Himalayan yogi and traveled through the astral ether into the body of the gentle woman who now stood and smiled at me on a New York street corner. Another foot-loose, Hinduizing Jewish woman who had felt compelled to slip into the mother tongue to express her compassion for my distress. She had called to me in Rav Bloch's language to tell me that I was not alone after all, that we were indeed spiritually bound.

My afternoon meditation with Narendra went badly. As usual, our time together was a mixture of the mundane and the sacred. But Shastri's effect had not yet worn off, and meditation only spun me farther out of orbit. Tears kept swelling up in my throat as Narendra talked on about Shastri's "dry discursive method." Fortunately, another student arrived early and I was forced to leave. Walking home, I marveled at my solipsism. On the one hand, I was the center of the universe, the axis of time, all space and all creation. At least the mystics' testimonies had told me so. On the other hand, I was only a speck of dust on the inexorable wheel of time. How to reconcile all that glory and all that vileness? Perhaps it was only "Penina" who had the secret.

At home a letter awaited me. One of Reb Yosef's disciples wrote from Seattle for advice about going to Jerusalem. Who, I wondered, would answer her: Perle or Penina? I agonized over the possibility of misdirecting not only myself, but others. I addled my brain, remembering Ben Zoma, the unprepared sage who had entered the Pardes, the kabbalists' garden of mystic study, and had gone insane.

Over a cheese omelette, in the same Lexington Avenue restaurant where I had taken black coffee as an antidote to Sri Singha's song four years before, I related my confusion to Noah.

"What am I to tell Dina Hirsch of Seattle about Jerusalem without being a hypocrite? I'm in New York. If Jerusalem had the answer, then what am I doing in New York?"

"I always told you to stay there and see, but you never listen," he said.

"I am too skeptical. In my heart of hearts I don't really respect anyone, you know. None of the lamas, swamijis, and gurujis . . . I even call Rav Bloch by a secret nickname. I'm an unregenerate yeshiva brat. I spend my life making fun of rabbis. Sue says it's a basic mark of disrespect, a lack of firm commitment on my part — making fun of Rav Bloch. Yet, in an unconscious way, I have in fact admitted my love and reverence for him precisely by adding a diminutive *i* to his name. *Blochiji; Swamiji* — get it?"

"You know my opinion," said Noah, already approaching the

cashier. "Either go back to Jerusalem and see or hold your peace forevermore."

Meditation became a torment. An insistent, disembodied H. J. Shastri questioned me endlessly as I sat on my cushion, curtains drawn, incense smoke spiraling around my motionless body.

Shastri: What have you been doing with yourself all these years?

Perle: Hiding under an opaque veil of middle-class normality with my dogs, housekeeper, teaching, and mildly eccentric Eastern leanings. It's all totally acceptable to even my most rationalist friends because I do it for "professional" reasons, like writing and teaching. Noah's older colleagues think it's "cute." They ask me to stand on my head at dinner parties and introduce me to strangers as the "resident witch."

Shastri: You even managed to sell the trip to India to your family. After all, you weren't like Sue, ready to bury yourself in an ashram and worship elephants. You were attending a respectable scholars' conference. They wouldn't have swallowed it otherwise, would they?

Perle: You're bringing on a lot of thoughts and images, you know. Right now I see a whole train of associations in miniature — my three-day high with Sri Singha, with his burning coal eyes and Ceylonese chirp that so knocked me out that I couldn't eat or talk until I'd slept him off for fourteen unconscious hours.

Shastri: It's because you're suggestive, madame.

Perle: If I choose to, right now I can see myself sitting next to Sandy and Philip Weisman. He's another Jew looking for mystical highs away from home. I hear he wears robes and has turned orthodox Moslem. No wonder, with his wife following Nissan Rosenberg around New York.

Shastri: If dancing makes you feel good . . .

Perle (shuddering): When I think of those Wednesday nights in that damp, drafty basement on West Seventy-fourth Street, six formidable black toughs played basketball under klieg lights out in the yard. And then being packed into someone's station wagon so that I could tell Nissan my dream . . . I have a crazy streak.

Shastri: Wasn't that the night you met the handsome Hasid who had once been a Chinese scholar at Columbia?

Perle: Yes. He said it was simpler to get to the top of the mountain as a Jew born in a Jewish body rather than as a Chinese Buddhist in a Jewish body. Funny, Rav Bloch said almost the same thing.

Shastri: And you believed the Hasid?

Perle: Sort of.

Shastri: You were always a sucker for handsome yeshiva boys.

Perle: That's true. At the Beth Rachel School I was the one who sneaked off during recess to cross the street to where the boys' yeshiva was. I was in love with a blond boy with the unlikely name of Levi Snow."

Shastri: Hmm. Follow that.

Perle: There's nothing to follow. You're interfering with my breathing concentration. I had a crush on Levi Snow because he had blue eyes and blond hair and he was a terrific boxball player. So, while the boys were reciting Gemarrah out loud, I'd climb up to the first-floor window and yell in, "Hey, Levi Snow!" Then I'd duck my head so they couldn't see who it was. I did this about three times, then ran back across the street to Beth Rachel. It was my little secret ritual. The girls thought I was the bravest kid in the world. Levi Snow thought I was nuts. He knew it was me because we used to buy penny candy in the same store near the two yeshivas, and he recognized my voice after a while. But he always modestly lowered his eyes. They instill that at a very young age in those yeshiva boys, not to look full in the face of a woman. Although at nine I guess I didn't really qualify as a woman. Just a pain in the ass from the Beth Rachel School, which was known for having the ugliest, but smartest, girls in the city.

Shastri: You are too full of personality, the identification of yourself with memory. Look at your mind, choked with memories.

Perle: Filled with spleen and old fury about the constrictions of Judaism.

Shastri: And far too emotional. You must be detached in order to get anywhere with this practice. You simply haven't got what it takes; you are too given to tears and expansion of the heart at the drop of a hat.

Perle: You are right. That happened suddenly, without warning, a few weeks ago as I read a line from the *Surangama Sutra* on a plane coming back from Toronto, just as the stewardess was serving me cocktail peanuts and tomato juice. A tear fell into the juice. You are right, I am terribly inappropriate. But Shastri, you've got to admit that it's an ordeal to practice your system of self-investigation. Three days in a room with you gives me a migraine. I try so hard to work each thought down to its component words, and then further to the source of each word, every letter, but it's too extreme, too tiring. It only makes me want to sleep. Then I go searching around hungrily for a little of Nissan Rosenberg's easy ecstasy.

Shastri: And Reb Yosef sends troubled Sufis to your doorstep for advice. Who are you to give advice?

Perle: My teaching job is folding up; my books are remaindered as soon as they're published. With all my education, I can't earn a decent living as a secretary. I'm cut adrift, sir. Ever since I started attending your seminars and reading your unbelievably boring discourses, I've become like one of Henry Wilkes's ripples on the great concrete sea. Did you know that my life is coming apart at the seams, that bus drivers call me at eleven-thirty at night to invite me to spend the next day with vedantic swamis? A Tibetan lama ate dinner at my house and claimed that my dog had belonged to him in his past incarnation.

Shastri: Rubbish.

Perle: And the dog practically followed him out the door when he called her by her Tibetan name!

Shastri: You're gullible. Easily mystified.

Perle: There are too many juxtapositions. It's gotten so that I can't tease apart the mahayanists from the vedantists from the Hasidim. And it's not only me. People I know, commune dwellers, are suddenly looking for an entrée into the stock market, and businessmen are joining Gurdjieff groups. Old die-hard rationalist colleagues in the English Department at school are into est and yoga. The fad is threatening to swallow me up.

Shastri: To whom are these experiences occurring?

Perle: To a translucent bubble floating first here and then there. Other people are living through me. For twenty-four hours after meditating with Narendra last week I lost my memory. There were odd lapses, like finding twelve dollars in my pocket that I was supposed to use for something three days before and forgot. The first century in Alexandria seems as real to me as last weekend in Amagansett. Keats and Blake are more embodied than my neighbor, whom I greet in the morning at the elevator, carrying her damned Bonwit's shopping bag as if it were the Holy Grail. All this because of you, sir. I fear for my sanity.

Shastri: One so-called reality is as good as another.

Perle: You tell me what kind of life it is to spend all afternoon at the local police precinct looking at mug shots, fixated on a file labeled Yugoslavians. My madness is attracting unsavory types.

Shastri: You are a disorganized female in spite of your intellectual cover.

Perle: The world has a haze over it since I met you. The other day I dropped a pile of Noah's shirts on the way to the Chinese laundry and then forgot why I was out on the street in the first place. My brother-in-law, an internist specializing in arteries, cautioned me about premature senility when I told him this.

Shastri (his image fading as I take four deep breaths and blink my eyes open): Settle for nothing less than discovering the true nature of reality. Only through absolute knowledge will you see that this world, as presented to us by our deceiving mind, is not *it.* Goodbye, madame.

(Shastri wades through the ether like a ghost through tar, like Claude Raines, the Invisible Man, making provocative footprints in the snow.)

Without getting up from my meditation pillow, I resolved to go back to Jerusalem.

THREE

7

Jerusalem Again

RAV BLOCH'S NAME TURNED UP one day in the *New York Times*. I was absent-mindedly reading an article about the troublesome Jewish settlements on the West Bank when the letters of his name suddenly sprang out at me. According to the story, Rav Bloch was no less than a "spiritual adviser" to Menachem Begin, the important political visitor of the past summer who had robbed me of my precious hour of Kabbalah study on at least two occasions. I closed the newspaper and put my head down on my arms at my desk. No doubt when I returned to Jerusalem in a few weeks I would find someone else, a thoroughly revised version of my old teacher who had so assiduously avoided all photographs, all publicity, all notoriety outside of his immediate circle of students and loyal associates. With my eyes closed it was easier to rehearse the hints, previously scattered about in his various discourses, that the Rav was about to go public and, for me, spoil his image. On the day before our last meeting, he had insisted on reading a nationalist political statement, a fiery and dogmatic proclamation that every last dunam of Abraham's soil must be occupied by Jews. I had covered my ears.

"Look aside when your teacher's human follies emerge — especially his politics — and stay with his Kabbalah," Madame Ariel had advised with her usual foresight.

But I could not look aside. I urged the Rav to continue with our lesson, for I had come to resent the nationalist encroachments on my precious "Kabbalah time." The Rav was adamant. He spent the rest of the afternoon outlining his plan for the land as an "energy source for Jewish prophecy." Though the argument was by then familiar to me, he insisted on reiterating it before I left. Based on a Platonic analogy describing the world as a human body (the kabbalist's Adam Kadmon, or First Man), the Zionist mystic regards each nation as representing a part, or limb, of the whole — with the Jewish nation at the heart, its land designated by Scripture, its anagogic "place" defined by its literal one. Rav Bloch painstakingly detailed the importance of each limb of this universal body, each in its place and assuming its proper function, as a vehicle for the Divine Plan..

"My enemies call me a chauvinist," he had said, "because they cannot understand this concept of selflessness. They see everything only with politics in mind, and that is why they miss the importance of cooperation between all the limbs of the world body, the importance of the Jewish people in assuming its function — as it has not done for centuries — as a nation of priests. Why can't they see that I am not speaking of a superior race but of a nation that has, en masse, witnessed the Revelation at Sinai? We are all bound to carry within our souls the spark of that divine source and we are bound to act in accord with that revelation in every phase of our lives — not merely for ourselves, the Jewish people, but for the sake of *all creation*."

"It will never work," I protested. "Mystical nationalism, thanks to Germany, is doomed in the twentieth century. However sacred your intentions might be, your philosophy, manifesting itself physically in your creation of new Jewish settlements on Arab territory, can only bring about the disastrous split in the cosmic body that you fear so much."

The Rav only shrugged.

I resumed in a softer, chiding voice. "But let's not waste precious time on politics. Let's talk about Kabbalah, please."

"*Narele* [foolish child]," he said, patting my cheek, "everything is Kabbalah."

We had then spent our remaining time discussing the importance of dissolving the ego through love for all created things, in stages, until the mystic was ready to embrace as part of himself all humans, animals, stars, planets, and finally, in an act transcending ordinary consciousness, the universe itself. The Rav said, "The mystic so enlarges his mind that it leaves its intellectual enclosure and becomes so refined, so full of light, that it experiences God intimately. Then, ritual, which you complain about so much, becomes inconsequential. But don't worry about it yet, Penina, you're not there."

I responded with a sad smile. "But we both agree that the usual observant Jew performs the rituals as obligations, as a way to bargain and plead with some God they've made up themselves, don't we?" I asked hopefully, fearful that the nationalist gap between us would someday separate us forever.

"This childish notion of worship comprises ninety percent of the orthodoxy in all religions. It requires great depth, great fearlessness, to understand God as No-Thing," the Rav replied gently.

I thought for a moment I had won, but just as we seemed to be immersing ourselves in the highest reaches of kabbalistic discourse, he returned again to the Jewish nation, the insistent sore spot that fell between us like a dirty black curtain. Why is he so irrational on this point? I wondered. In an otherwise impeccably ordered mind, the issue of Jewish nationhood stood out like an embarrassing tic. How annoying it all was to a universalist like me, who had despised nationalism since my sophomore year as a political science major at college.

The argument presented in the *Times,* complete with pictures and a graphic description of Rav Bloch blessing a newly formed dry, empty space he insisted on calling a settlement, became an ominous warning for me. A year had passed. I was far away from the shabby room, the glass of tea, the book-strewn table; divested of its cosmic urgency, Rav Bloch's dream of universal harmony sounded like the ravings of a truculent old fanatic.

Only Madame Ariel, the eternal mother, never changed. She still sat sewing in her garden as troops of visitors came, disclosed their hearts to her, lunched on Algerian vegetable pies, and went on their way. She had not even aged. When I came upon her by surprise on my return to Jerusalem in June 1977, she hugged me warmly, held me away from her for a second or two as she studied my face, and said, "You have learned a great deal through your work in the past year. Very hardly." It was her charming mispronunciation that made Noah and her husband, Zvi, explode simultaneously into contagious laughter that soon enveloped us all. We sat on the tiny rear terrace overlooking the Valley of the Cross, the feathery tall pines shedding cones with a gentle plop, the pink sheets on the terrace across the way flapping in the breeze like triumphant banners welcoming us back; and we talked on and on about India, Noah's career, Madame Ariel's real and feigned illnesses, earthquakes in China, sunspots, her grandchildren, and various "pupils." As we talked, I realized that I had devised the perfect spiritual practice for myself. In Rav Bloch I found the complement of my ingrained intellectualism, the path of the head, or what the Chinese might call the Yang, the fiery part of myself. Through Madame Ariel I allowed myself to express my heart, the female path of compassion — and not a little female vanity. Jerusalem itself was the central branch of the cosmic tree, the path of spiritual beauty where the very breath of God stirred the pines and sighed over the hills at the sun's descent.

Madame Ariel's husband confirmed my fears about Rav Bloch's changing style. "We too are shocked at his overt political face," he said. "He has even appeared on television, very angrily, demanding that his own personal choice for minister of education be accepted by Begin. Imagine, both men considered for the post were his disciples, but the Rav was very much against one of them. But, spiritual adviser or no, Begin ignored Rav Bloch and chose that man."

"What did the Rav do?" asked Noah.

"He went on television with a very angry face, shouting and pounding on the table," Zvi continued, illustrating with his own colorful Russian hand gestures.

Madame Ariel reached among a pile of papers and folders and removed exactly what she wanted from the chaos without so much as looking at it. Like Rav Bloch, she too seemed possessed of the capacity to "read" with her fingers. Her presence calmed me; I was no longer fearful and edgy about being psychologically stripped or manipulated. I had indeed worked on myself "very hardly."

Madame Ariel handed me a well-preserved Hebrew newspaper with a November date. The article she pointed out was set in the middle of a rectangular series of photographs depicting Rav Bloch in various moods. The text described rumors of his approaching senility, his demagoguery, all framed by surrounding images of an unsmiling, fist-pounding rabbi with a Shylockian beaked nose dressed in grim black.

I shivered, and Madame Ariel handed me her shawl. "This isn't the Rav," I said. "He won't even allow photographs to be taken."

"That's right," said Noah. "When we finally prevailed on him to let us snap a few pictures, none of them came out."

What was I to expect when I met with the Rav again? Had he and I parted on a humorous political disagreement that for him was no longer humorous? *"We are both going up the same mountain to the same peak, Penina, but you are coming up one path, and I am coming up another. It doesn't matter; we'll meet on top."*

Madame Ariel watched my face as I scanned the newspaper. "Don't worry. With you he will never be angry. But do not be disappointed if it is hard to see him," she said. Then she turned the conversation to talismans, for a prominent Israeli ceramicist had fashioned a miniature version of the high priest's breastplate as a pendant for Madame Ariel's birthday, and she was very anxious for me to see it.

"Each stone on the *urim ve tumim* worn by the priest symbolizes a corresponding stage on the mystic's ascent up the cosmic tree of spheres," I said, examining the pendant carefully to see whether the artist had been faithful to the traditional colors.

Madame Ariel eyed me silently. Only when it was time for me to leave for Rav Bloch's house did she speak. We walked together to the front gate, our arms around each other's shoulders. "It is good that you have all this knowledge in your head, but do not let it get in the way of your understanding," she said as she pushed me gently out the blue gate, then pulled her shawl around her and called the cats inside.

"In the destructive element immerse." I mumbled Conrad's baleful advice to myself as I drove into the dreaded Orthodox quarter of town. What would I have to sacrifice if I really wished to practice Kabbalah? My freedom as a woman? Worse, would I have to become like the girl just now crossing in front of me, evoking such deeply embedded ancient fury that I pressed my elbow down on the horn and frightened two black-frocked, bearded men into shaking their fists at the windshield. Defying impact, the furious Hasidim banged against the fender of the car as I passed, raising dust. The girl who had evoked the ill-omened encounter wore thick brown stockings, heavy-soled mountain climber's shoes, a navy woolen sack dress, and an outrageous pasty brown wig that hung down in limp banana curls to her shoulders. She was about twenty, blue-eyed, rosy-cheeked, and once perhaps vivacious and quick-witted. Undoubtedly she attended the *mikva* and cleansed herself after every period. Undoubtedly she had intercourse with her husband only in the dark with her clothing on, according to the male laws of talmudic modesty. Undoubtedly, too, she had a baby every year. I screeched to a halt, having nearly run over a scroungy gray and white cat. Could it be? Was it still alive? Noah and I had bet against the odds of a knowledgeable Jerusalem friend that the bony gray and white kitten occupying Rav Bloch's trash can the summer before would survive the year. And here it was: a tough, unbeaten emblem of my own stubborn will to survive against the indifferent acceptance of Rav Bloch's Orthodox community, the unlikely repository of all the kabbalistic secrets I wished to unearth. The hierarchy had distorted them under the veil of tradition, rerouting them by way of Poland, Russia, North Africa, and America; but they had survived nonetheless: the cat, the Kabbalah, and I.

"Hello, Bum," I whispered, as the ugly wonderful cat stared at me with an angry scowl, as if to say, "Don't you recognize a fellow kabbalist when you see one?" and then scooted lickety split under a railing (ducking a row of newly washed, dripping *tzitzith* on a clothesline) into its favorite trash can in front of the Rav's house.

I parked the car on an uphill slant on the familiar narrow street. Great nodding sunflowers in the Rav's front yard beckoned me — cynically, I thought. Everything in Jerusalem has a persona, even donkeys and sunflowers and inanimate stones. All creation is holy.

Wiry children in short pants, skullcaps, *payot,* and flying *tzitzith* played a very hostile game of soccer in the wide cul-de-sac in front of the yeshiva at the end of the block. An Arab bearing a huge backload of reeds suspended from a basket on a long leather thong called from house to house in guttural no-language. Could he possibly be selling reeds? In Jerusalem anyone can sell anything. I braced myself and walked boldly up the steps, down the path, and up the small staircase leading to the Rav's flat. From the open window in the neighboring house came the anomalous squawk of Jimi Hendrix's "Foxy Lady." *Everything is Kabbalah,* I recalled.

Yakov answered my faint knock. Madame Ariel's translator had arrived before me and was waiting on a hard, backless seat behind the door. His name was David; he had curly hair, spectacles, a distant air, and he was drinking lemon squash. The same old furniture crowded the waiting room, but the whole place, I felt instantly, had assumed a new aura. Even gentle Yakov was harder, more forward, speaking in good, clear English. He was still dear in his way, offering food and drink as he always had, but there was a new thrust to his conversation, an aggressive tag to everything he said about the Rav, Israel, and an ominous new phrase: the movement. On the walls were strident political posters; everything in Rav Bloch's flat reminded me now of the new Dharma kingdom some of the American Buddhists I had talked to were busy creating in the West.

"A Dharma kingdom?" I had laughed over a superb Chinese dinner in a knowledgeable couple's loft only three days before my trip to Jerusalem. "Sounds like the Reverend Moon!" Now I was sitting under the Rav's fiercely Zionist posters, and the idea of a Buddhist kingdom seemed tame by comparison. I frowned and perspired for a quarter of an hour in the anteroom. Even Yakov's offer of barley malt — an old joke between us — could not entice me to smile. Madame Ariel's David was tense and quiet.

The Rav, folded over a little into the collar of his shirt, wearing a vest, house slippers, baggy dark trousers, and shirtsleeves, opened the door and asked us in. Squinting at me, he allowed a long slow smile to appear on his face before he hugged me to him. The Rav looked paler, less high-spirited, but his eyes still gleamed with unquenchable fire. Once we were seated he turned his attention to David — as though a year had not passed between us, there was nothing to catch up on. He knew everything about me that he needed to know. There was David, the new factor, to consider first.

It had taken me a year to get over my impatience and jealousy over Rav Bloch's scrupulous attention to my translators. And that only came with the realization that he was studying very carefully anyone I brought with me before he could begin to discourse on the subject of Kabbalah. In the beginning, I had been so ignorant and belligerent about his "putting me off" (as I had complained to Madame Ariel) that I rocked in my seat with a hideous, impatient grimace spread over my face. Noah pointed it out to me once when we were driving home through the vacant, nighttime streets, and I suddenly understood what the Rav had been doing when he scrupulously quizzed my translators. He had only spoken about Kabbalah in front of those he felt warranted it!

"What is your interest?" he asked David.

"I'm confused about my Jewish path. I have studied other traditions; they seem more amenable to me. Yet I am an Israeli, born here, a Jew."

"I know, I know." The Rav shook his head. "And you are confused." Of course. I should have known that Madame Ariel had sent David along for his own sake as much as for mine.

"There is a difference between learning other traditions — a good thing — and being *impressed* from within by virtue of your birth, with your own message of the prophets, David," said the Rav, looking all the while into the young man's dark silent eyes behind his spectacles. "There is a difference between learning from outside and organically revealing from inside yourself what is already there. Isn't there?" Rav Bloch pressed David's reluctant hand. I squirmed and looked at the pictures on the wall.

"Nu, Penina." The Rav suddenly responded to my restlessness. "You have read all the great Gentile philosophers — Aristotle, Plato — you can show David the likenesses between his own tradition and the others. Did you ever read in the *Zohar* the section that states that the Platonic mode is closest to the Jewish one, that is, the mode of faith as opposed to the empirical mode of the senses."

I had no idea what the Rav was driving at.

"The Oriental philosophies also emphasize faith over reason," he continued knowingly, "don't they?" David looked away from the Rav's piercing glance. "You have studied these deeply, haven't you, David?" I watched Rav Bloch press the young man's bare arm with his long, hard grip until he left white fingermarks behind. "But every tradition demands a certain amount of preparation. Ours, according to Chayim Vital, sets the student on the path of love, merit, ethical behavior — what we call the gates, right, Penina?"

At last he was teaching again; having read David's degree of preparation from his very pulse, from the "organically grown" Jew beating inside David's Gurdjieffian chest, the Rav resumed his lessons in Kabbalah at a point not too far away from where we had left off the year before. The iron shutters behind him were locked shut. Not a splinter of sunlight came through the cracks. The torn sofa had not been repaired; only a white chenille cloth had been thrown over the gaping spaces as a concession to modesty. Even the voices of the wild yeshiva youngsters at soccer outside could not be heard. The world hung in suspended silence at the Rav's table as he expounded.

"Without preparation, Kabbalah cannot enter. The process is not a learning per se; you cannot read books and take exams and become an *ish gadol,* a great man. It is rather an enlargement of mind that takes place, as I explained to Penina the last time she was here." The Rav winked at me complicitously, as if pretending that the meeting had taken place only the day before.

"Did you ever hear of the Ari?"

David nodded.

"The Ari was a very great kabbalist, so great" — the Rav threw his head back so far that he had to hold on to his skullcap to keep it from falling off — "so great we can't even describe him." Then he turned to me again. "You read a lot about him this year, didn't you? Name some of the books."

I was being quizzed now, but I could not judge how seriously, for what purpose, or for whose benefit — David's or mine. I had forfeited the intimacy of a consistent relationship with the Rav and, anchorless, I would continue to flounder during his apparent changes of mood.

"I read Vital, Abulafia, Luzzatto . . ."

"Ah, so you've read Luzzatto." The Rav pretended to be impressed.

"And Cordovero."

"Wonderful, Cordovero. And did you understand what you read, Penina? Cordovero, you know, was a great genius, very difficult . . ." He lifted his eyebrows and revealed the old pre–*New York Times* mischievous twinkle.

"You're always laughing at me."

"Never *at* you, Penina." Rav Bloch turned again toward David, who now sat staring at the old man in a mixed state of wonder and confusion.

"On his deathbed the Ari gathered around him the greatest of his disciples, all men thoroughly steeped in Kabbalah. 'You all know nothing of Kabbalah even though the world outside considers every one of you a saint,' he said.

" 'What about Chayim Vital?' they asked. 'He is your first disciple.' The Ari sighed. 'Ah, Chayim. He knows a little more than nothing.' He said it in Spanish, the vernacular used by the Safed kabbalists at the time. 'A little more than nothing.' " The Rav chuckled and repeated the phrase in medieval Spanish. I could see that he was thinking of his father and himself.

"Preparation is most important," he continued. "Unless our minds are properly cultivated, their roots sunk deeply into their organic Jewishness, all the teaching in the world can only fall on barren soil." He pointed suddenly to the single-paned bookcase; it too remained in its original state of disrepair. "Take the Zohar—"

"Which volume?" I asked, standing up to my appointed task. Every one of the Rav's gestures now assumed deeper and deeper meaning; I wanted very much to be worthy, "prepared." If I could hurry to exactly the right spot, the Rav would see that my memory was keen (an indispensable prerequisite in learning how to permutate the Hebrew letters of biblical phrases into the names of God for chanting and meditation); if he held back and talked only of preparation, or rifled slowly through his father's letters, or repeated old stories, he was testing my patience further or pointing out my unworthiness.

"*Gimel,*" he said, watching my every move.

I located the third volume almost as soon as the command was out of his mouth. "You see!" I cried, childishly triumphant, "I told you I know!"

Four hours later, the hum of a large group of male voices penetrated the cracks in the door. The Rav ignored the noise. Plunging into a long, detailed rerun of a story he had told me before, he regaled David with familiar snatches of conversation: lost Oriental tribes of Israel . . . Japanese masters . . . on and on . . . so that I, who had heard it all before, slipped into a doze. Then he suddenly swayed over a book of his father's letters, selecting one I had not heard before, and the lesson was jumping too quickly for my drowsy mind to follow. The Platonists again, and the rumored association between the prophet Jeremiah and Aristotle, an example of the importance of exchanging cultural views, and, yes, I had heard it correctly — Swedenborg! What rabbi on earth besides

Rav Bloch would be incorporating Swedenborg into a kabbalistic discourse?

"Yet, David," I heard him say as I shook myself awake, "the Torah is the true *derech,* the true path of the Jewish seeker. For you it would be good to read Bialik, the poet never taught by the Orthodox rabbis." The Rav outlined David's path, sending me a grateful smile; after all, hadn't I brought him one more potential Jewish convert?

"And you ought to read my father's book *Light of Return* and the basic scripture of the Jewish people."

David sat popeyed at the bizarre list of reading materials compiled by the odd rabbi Madame Ariel had chosen for him. For a moment we thought the lesson was over, but the Rav leaped from the reading list to something new and — considering my morning discussion with Madame Ariel — shocking. With the buzzing yeshiva voices growing more insistent beyond the door, the Rav pushed aside the books in front of him and said, "Now Penina, let me tell you about talismans."

I nearly fainted dead away in my seat. Neither he nor Madame Ariel had a telephone. She could not have spoken to him nor sent anyone to tell him of our conversation before our meeting. She didn't even know the Rav personally, having only heard about him from newspaper reports and from her "pupils" who studied with him. He, of course, did not know her. Yet he resumed almost word for word the discussion on talismans that she had embarked on eight hours before. Now it was David's turn to drowse. It was as though, whenever he chose, the Rav could cause either of us to blank out on what it was he had to teach the other privately.

That morning Madame Ariel had tried to impress upon me that the power of the talisman really lay behind it, in the mind of the wearer, and not in the dead object itself. Now the Rav, too, was saying the same thing.

"There was once an adamant *mitnagged,* a rationalist, who was also a great saint. He lived in one of the ghettos of Eastern Europe in the middle of the last century, and although he had no use for

Hasidim, or magic, or mysticism, this very holy man was forced to make a talisman. The people in those small towns used to believe in the healing powers of saintly rabbis, and they frequently came to plead with them for talismans to cure the sick. As I said, this very rational *mitnagged* did not believe in such superstitions, but one woman came again and again to plead with him for her sick child, demanding that he give her a talisman. She bothered the rabbi so much that he finally made a *kmaya* out of a rude piece of wood, carved a hole in it, and stuffed it with a paper on which nothing was written. The value of the talismans among the ignorant, as you know, lies in the so-called names of God written on those papers." I nodded. David's eyelids were shut tight behind his glasses. The Rav held me by the elbow and went on in a low voice. "The *mitnagged* told the woman that if she woke up one day to find no letters at all on the piece of paper he had given her, it would mean that a great miracle had taken place and that the child would be cured. The woman waited for three days, then opened the *kmaya* and found the empty paper. A miracle! A miracle! All the ignorant townspeople believed in the great power of their rabbi. The child recovered — but not from the paper, do you understand?"

"Mmm."

Yakov knocked, announcing the assembled *minyan* for evening services.

"Let them wait," said the Rav, selecting one of his father's books from the stack on the table; then, moistening his finger, he turned to the chapter on talismans. Motioning me closer, he opened the book wide, and together we read his father's words:

There exists a tremendous initial force and power in the utterance of a great saint. Even a short phrase can move a mountain or dry up the Red Sea. But in a time of lesser men, the phrase degenerates until it is eventually appropriated by the ignorant who never knew the saint, never felt his power, only heard perhaps about his "miracles." The ultimate decay of the saint's power occurs in the hands of the evil ones, the so-called magicians and the demonic forces who aim at destroying the world. And that is how very high spiritual power, falling downward, comes to be identified with superstition and ignorance.

Then science and "enlightened" thinking, or "reason," comes, sweeps away the superstition (and with it, the remaining sparks of holiness that still cling from the time of the saint) until a few hungry souls begin to search for it again. It is a cyclical pattern. These hungry souls are born with the faint knowledge of the sound of the saint's word reverberating within their souls. They cannot translate it, are soon haunted by it, yearn for it so hard that they brook no obstacle in seeking it out. Then, if they are successful in their struggle, they hear it clearly and revive it, creating in the process a new science.

The Rav looked up and wagged his finger at me. "That 'science' is the one you are so eager to learn, the Kabbalah. And when the time is ripe, it will be revealed."

My head swam, but I was happier than I had been in a long time. There was no mystery. It was quite apparent now that all the searching in the deepest crevices of the Himalayas would never disclose to me what I was wearing like a forgotten hat on my own head. It all only *appeared* secret to those like me who were so distracted by their hunger that they continued to pass it by. Although it was here all the time, the Kabbalah, like all profound mystical truths, would continue to be misunderstood by the foolish, ignored by the materialists, and overlooked by traditionally "religious" people who were not sufficiently expansive of spirit to use it properly.

The esoteric Jewish wisdom I had accused the rabbis of hiding was only as obscure as the thickness of the veil of reason and "logical" thought I wore in front of my eyes. The holy reverberation of divine letters, implicit in every facet of the created world, was there all the time, waiting to be heard by those whose souls were tuned to hear it. There was nothing to strive for. No convoluted exercises were necessary now. Only to listen, and listen well. The Rav maintained that Hebrew was the language imprinted on my soul. Why not? Since I had been born into a Jewish body, it would perhaps be best to stop struggling against my identity. Climbing the first rung of the mystical ladder in Jerusalem might indeed be the quickest, least resistant way to begin.

The next morning, Madame Ariel invited a group of her pupils to a luncheon talk on Jewish meditation by Monsieur Gilbert, her Algerian compatriot. The tall, gentle kabbalist was still trying to figure out a system for combining Eastern models with the intense prayer and Hebrew alphabet permutation of the early Hasidim. The lecture, half in French and half in Hebrew, was not terribly successful. The American pupils nodded and fell asleep; the French looked as if they had heard it all before and knew better; the Israelis simply looked hungry. Monsieur Gilbert described the various Jewish historical schools that had advocated *hitbodedut,* meditation, as a means for attaining ecstasy. But the session was too scholarly and never managed to get off the ground; we all could have read the material in translation in Gershom Scholem's books. Wilma, a redheaded American journalist with little patience for anything but "direct experience," asked him to demonstrate his own method of meditation. The shy Monsieur Gilbert turned to me and said in French, "What does she say she wants?" I asked as blandly as I could for a short demonstration. Monsieur Gilbert only shrugged, played with his thick glasses, and said, "Tell her that we sit on Tuesdays in my home in Rehavia. You, I have already invited many times. You may bring your friend, too," he reproved. It was true; I had avoided the Gilbert Tuesday meditations because they sounded like a hodgepodge of imported Oriental and Jewish techniques. Most of the meditators were Americans and Europeans who had shopped for many years among the swamis and roshis as I had. Some, in fact, were still regulars at the zendo on the Mount of Olives. (I deliberately refrained from returning to meditate with the roshi for fear of complicating even further my very tentative commitment to the Rav.)

"Yes, but what is your format?" Wilma insisted, her pencil poised above her ubiquitous journalist's pad.

An American immigrant named Helen, a loyal follower of Monsieur Gilbert's, looked at her with disapproval. "We sit in a symbolic posture and meditate on a violet light as we chant in Hebrew," she said through pursed lips.

"Well, that's not saying much," Wilma sniffed.

Madame Ariel interceded. "We all drink tea," she said sweetly, rolling up the multicolored skeins of wool for the tapestries she had been busily sewing. Then she rose from her pillows, courteously shooed us all into the garden, and whispered to me that I was to meet her inside on the pretext of helping her straighten the chairs in the salon. (As if you could straighten anything in that dear cluttered museum of a salon that had become more of a spiritual home for me than my own sparse and orderly living room in New York.)

When we were alone inside, she said, "I observed you throughout the talk. I think, regardless of what you have told me, that your work with Shastri has been very good. You are right to try to establish clarity and awareness of your emotions and thoughts as he urges. But as you are too emotive by nature, we will work on 'centering' this summer. You must learn to remain in the center of your being no matter what is going on around you."

Madame Ariel had not lost her habit of making declarations in the middle of the most apparently innocent social occasions. How you cleaned crumbs from the table gave her clues about your discontent, your hatred of your job; how you washed a window or drove a car provided a testimonial to your frustration threshold. She once told a medical colleague of Noah's from New York that he suffered from "too much water in the body" merely by watching his pinky as he held his teacup. To another American, a die-hard rationalist academic, she observed, "Your eyes can kill your students, but your laughter soothes them."

One morning Madame Ariel gave a small group of her pupils a task in the form of a game. Six of us were distributed about the house to clean. As I detested any form of housework, I proceeded to balk and grumble and made excuses for leaving. Her response was to take a lovely embossed scarf from the magic chest of drawers in the front hall and wrap it around my head gypsy-fashion.

"You will clean the windows!" she announced with great delight at my ill-natured display. One or two others pretended to groan at their appointed tasks, but, I noticed, she had given no one else such an extensive job. It was hot; the sun shone through the windows at its most penetrating noontime angle. I was alone in the back, unable to converse or complain or gossip with any of the others, who had been permitted to work together in the kitchen or in the cool garden out front.

With my bucket, rags, and newspaper (Madame Ariel insisted that you could never get the best shine on a window unless you finished it off with newspaper), I started methodically from left to right on the row of ten windows that flanked the rear of the flat. The chore was made worse by the squeak of paper on glass, which sent chills racing up my spine, and by the newsprint, which blackened my fingers. I hated Madame Ariel, my fellow pupils, the windows, the task, and myself for being such a poor sport. I located a tiny transistor radio on a ledge behind the rosewood, turn-of-the-century piano in the guest room. Torn between Mozart and a noisy rock station performing an unsuccessful Israeli imitation of the nonstop American variety, I decided — spitefully — to turn on the latter. I turned the radio up loud, taking a kind of perverse pleasure in the insistent rhythms of the music that I never listened to at home. Already, as Madame Ariel would have said, I was "changing a tendency" — admittedly, out of aggressive and negative impulses; but the object of Madame Ariel's dehabituating exercises was to break the conditioned habits of her pupils' lives — and so I listened to loud rock music. Wilma, who had participated briefly in a Gurdjieff group in the States, compared Madame Ariel's techniques to the Russian master's "self-remembering" exercises, during which the student "stood outside," as it were, and observed himself as he carried on the ordinary activities of daily life. Developing such "witness" consciousness is an essential part of all Eastern disciplines, especially the Buddhist *vipassana* form, which stresses observation of thought as it passes over the screen of the mind like a movie. In all mystical traditions, such "witnessing" is believed to lead to *selflessness* and, ultimately, to the ego annihilation that precedes the full and unobscured vision of the Absolute. Madame Ariel's harmless exercises aimed at nothing less.

Soon I found myself working only in rhythm with the music, oblivious to all but the swish of the water in the bucket, the feel of the glass under the rags and newspapers, the warm sun penetrating my bare arms; at one point I had so forgotten myself in the activity that I started to sing. As soon as the commentary in my mind faded I lost all resentment, all notions about drudgery, housework, and the like. It did not matter that I was working alone and others had company; I felt like a cherished old friend of myself. It was strangely uplifting, as if I had stepped out through the shiny window and looked in at a pleasant woman in a gypsy bandana who was singing and cleaning.

But at the tenth window I lost it; the old reflexive tics of thought drew me back into myself and into the chatter inside my head. Perhaps it was the radio — a distracting commercial intruding on the rhythm of the music that had served, mantra-like, to lift me out of my usual self-conscious absorption in what I was doing. Whatever it was, I found myself barely able to lift my arms at that tenth window. My body was leaden; my spirits were lower and angrier than they had been when I complained at the start. I literally dragged the newspaper from one end of the windowpane to the other, dripping dirty water from the bucket all over the Oriental carpet, consciously making a mess. The streaked results of my labor now reflected a sour, tight-lipped face under a skewed kerchief. I looked exactly like the bitter Orthodox woman of my own worst nightmares. Shastri himself could not have done a better job of rubbing my nose in the mirror image of my violent, wounded ego.

I cursorily swiped at the window, lugged the bucket to the bathroom, and emptied it into the toilet bowl. Wringing the rags dry and dumping the crumpled newspapers into the garbage pail in the kitchen, I straightened my shoulders and walked out into the garden like a grinning marine. The other five pupils had completed their chores and were sitting in a circle around Madame Ariel, on her green and white garden chaise. As I appeared in the doorway, they all looked up at me as one and laughed. I could feel my face grow red and hot, my throat choking down one of the caustic remarks with which I usually tend to defend myself against the threat of criticism. Madame Ariel held up her finger, and the laughter stopped.

"We are not laughing *at* you," she said, echoing the Rav (everything happened in twos that summer in Jerusalem). "I merely used you as an example for our lesson today. I told the group that you would be fine until you approached the tenth window, but that your customary impatience would burst out then, and that you would become very angry — so angry that you could barely finish your job."

"But I *did* finish," I said hoarsely.

"Yes, because of your habitual single-mindedness. That is good; you are a fighter by nature. It is good to be a fighter, never to give up, but not combined with anger and impatience. The way you came out of the house, even the way you carried your shoulders and tried to look smiling with the wrinkled forehead — we had to laugh."

I was almost more puzzled by the absence of reproof in the observation than by the unqualified expression of acceptance on Madame Ariel's face.

"It happened to all of us differently," said Helen, "only you were the last and most obvious."

Weary of myself, I stripped the bandana from my head and sat down among them.

"But how did you know it would be exactly the tenth window?" I asked Madame Ariel, although I already knew the answer.

"Because I know you very well, *ma chérie.* Your stamina is written in your morphology, in your face, in the shape of your head. You must change your hair style if you don't wish to frighten people away, you know. Revealing such a forehead might terrify those who are not as intellectually gifted as you."

It was my turn to laugh, partly because of her typically "mystifying" encapsulation of a keen psychological insight, partly out of embarrassment. Without thinking, I brushed the hair down over my forehead with my fingers. This time, we all laughed together.

After much verbal fencing, the Rav at last agreed to work with me on a text by Moses Chayim Luzzatto, an eighteenth-century kabbalist.

"This is only the early part of the threshold at the first gate," he said quaintly, staving off any further inquiry on my part as he held the door open for me to leave. The book, though not particularly esoteric, was not available in all of Jerusalem. I combed the dustiest reaches of the most Orthodox bookshops in vain. I enlisted the help of my scholarly translators; I scoured the university libraries, but even there I found no trace of Luzzatto's instructions for novices on the "early" path to the threshold of Kabbalah. From the Gerber Bookshop on Ben Yehuda Road I at last elicited the promise of a copy at the end of the week.

It was about four in the afternoon the following day when I boldly set out for the Rav's house alone, without book or translator. It was going to be the only way, I decided, that I would learn anything at all about Kabbalah. The Rav vehemently refrained from instructing me in meditative practices; well and good, I had completed more than a dozen years of yoga exercises and ten years' worth of "sitting" by the time I had reached his door. Every time I asked him what I had to do, he replied, "Nothing special. Only prayer and the commandments." It was maddening. I could sooner fast for forty days than pray, sit for fifteen hours without getting up rather than adhere to the religious laws. As the Rav seemed more inclined to reveal the speculative Kabbalah, I resolved to content myself with whatever bits and pieces I could glean from his discourses and leave the "practices" for later. With Sue's guru in mind as I walked up the Rav's narrow lane, I rationalized that orthodox vedantists also minimized the importance of structured meditation in favor of the discursive form that brought the mind to suprarational knowledge.

The Rav took every opportunity to let me know that the practical Kabbalah did not interest him. Yet, what on the surface appeared to be the scholarly exposition of texts (along with his own inimitable digressions and wry parables) soon became, for me, deeply "meditative" experiences. It was so stirring merely to sit in the Rav's presence that I frequently found myself unable to talk to Noah for at least an hour when he picked me up afterward and took me to dinner in a nearby Moroccan dairy restaurant. On several occasions I burst into tears for no reason at all. At last I understood the story of the Hasid who, when asked on returning from a year with his rebbe what he had done, replied, "I watched him tie his shoelaces."

"It's strange," I had said to him as we stood in the doorway, "every time I see you I ask for Kabbalah, and your only response is laughter." Wordlessly, the Rav clutched my head in his hands and pressed my forehead to his heart. Then he roughly pushed me out the door.

When I arrived the following day at a quarter past four, that same door was slightly ajar. I looked around it and saw the Rav seated at the head of a large group of men, engaging in what Yakov might call "a political meeting." The mood was urgent; I felt instantly shut out, uncomfortable around "the movement," the Rav's other side. "It won't work out today," I mumbled aloud to the empty waiting room benches. The Rav had worldly issues, the future of the Jewish people, on his mind and no room for Penina. Yet the fighter in me forced me to sit down and wait nonetheless. I was soon joined by a patient yeshiva boy whose calm expression indicated that he expected nothing, that even to wait for the Rav without seeing him was sufficient spiritual nourishment for a real student of Torah. Soon after, two women arrived, a young swarthy girl of about eighteen and her head-covered, Orthodox mother. Taking modest seats in the corner farthest from the boy, they sewed needlepoint and chattered endlessly in Hebrew. The boy was smooth-cheeked. The bearded ones, I had noticed, were always more restless, pacing up and down in front of the battered cadenza in the hall and using the bathroom often. One such fellow, a red-beard, entered almost as soon as the image passed through my mind; then, as if illustrating my observation, he clenched and un-clenched his fists and bit his cuticles before heading for the bathroom. When he came out, he was joined by a short stocky companion in a yellow and black plaid sports shirt who diverted him with jokes.

Unknown to each other, the small band of disciples and advice-seekers sat waiting dumbly in the Rav's anteroom, their ears cocked for a scrap from the unintelligible murmuring beyond the door. Inside, the men of "the movement" were deliberating about the redemption of the Jewish nation. Why did the Rav have to go public? I wondered again, wishing I could explore the issue with the sewing women and the bland yeshiva student in an open forum. What's your investment in the Rav? I wanted to ask them. Do you think he wants to leave this life in a blaze of prophetic glory? Do you suppose he entertains visions of himself being swept up to heaven on Elijah's chariot? Why else would he be indulging in such grandiose nationalistic nonsense? The boy was now bent over a book, pretending to read as he plucked at his hairless chin. The two women stared at me with undisguised hostility, as if they had seen through my heresy. Even the room smelled sour; perhaps Yakov had spilled a bottle of vinegar in the kitchen and mopped it up carelessly. The strident political posters glared down at me from the walls: NO! TO THE RUSSIANS WHO ARE HOLDING PRISON-ERS OF ZION. Yet they were interspersed with the old reassuring photographs of Jerusalem; the scarred tables, the rickety chairs, the hard and backless benches that I had come to cherish were still there, along with the sepia portrait of Rav Bloch's papa, who still looked down at me through deep brown mystic's eyes. Were my waiting companions political or religious or both? Was I the only person in the room pretending to be a kabbalist?

These days Yakov was talking militantly of "spiritualizing politics." How did you spiritualize politics? One large poster in poison green and blinding white was inscribed with the number 1 in large black print. Was Rav Bloch advertising himself as number one? Alongside the odd poster was a picture of an angry group of marchers — members of the Messiah's conquering army? Presumably, from the latest newspaper accounts, they were marching toward Hebron, Nablus — and the redemption of the holy people.

Repelled, I turned my eyes away from the posters toward the Rav's door. Behind it, all worldly concerns disappeared when he and I sat together and battled to "unlock the gates." Madame Ariel had commended me for my single-mindedness; now the Rav had the chance to exercise her findings by trying my patience, almost as if each day was designed to represent yet another hurdle, another test of my worthiness to learn. With great difficulty I had reached Luzzatto's first gate; now I had no way of getting in.

I was waiting there again on the following day at four. And the next day, and the next. The zebra-striped tile floors writhed under my feet. Two hours passed. Newspapermen, political men, people with problems, poured in and out of the Rav's study, a motley stream rushing to gaze on the master, some only to glance at him for two minutes, to touch his sleeve. One old gentleman emerged after less than five minutes, weeping copiously into an enormous handkerchief. My own meeting with the Rav two days before had consisted of fifteen minutes of hand-clutching and fervent pleas on my part for more "substantive guidance" in my reading. But I had been pushed out the door.

"Is it worth my coming here anymore?" I pleaded with him time and again. "You just don't seem to have time for me this year."

"People must come here," he said, serious for one moment. "This house must always be open to anyone who wishes to come."

"Same time tomorrow?" I asked petulantly.

The Rav nodded. "Try. Always try."

I was still trying a week later without luck. It was Thursday; the rickety waiting room was crammed with secular people from Tel Aviv. An aggressive blond woman who needed no encouragement introduced herself to me as Binah Dor and launched immediately into a story about her "mission in life, which is to come here once a week from Tel Aviv, bringing the people to see this great master for advice, for conversion to Judaism, for a few kind words of wisdom."

I was so uncharitable as to feel like vomiting at her speech. With her bleached straw for hair, her décolleté blouse and husky smoker's voice, Binah sat for three hours regaling me with tales of suicide, heresy, and murder. Yet she was as much a disciple of Rav Bloch's as I was — perhaps a better one. She was as devoted to him as any of the bearded scholars of the Torah. And, unlike me, she was willing to share him.

"My job, as I see it, is to bring those who must develop their souls." She leaned close to me and said this in English between many tentative pauses. Blowing smoke into my face, she continued, "One famous Israeli film star, a total — how-do-you-call-it — *api-korus* —" Binah looked around for help.

"Atheist," I added.

"Ah, you know Hebrew!"

"A little."

"Very nice. This man has changed the actor's whole life — after only a two-hour conversation," she said, pointing at the Rav's door. "He is now studying on a religious kibbutz. He wants to be a rabbi."

"Very nice," I echoed her wanly.

The room was steaming. People leaned up against the peeling walls; several boys stationed themselves near the battered cadenza and stared at the pictures above it. Yakov hurried in with a bag full of soda bottles, nodded approvingly at the crowd, and disappeared into the kitchen. He was evidently satisfied that our presence was somehow contributing to the "spiritualization of politics."

My sullenness only encouraged Binah to resume her monologue. "The Rav has given me a great . . . compliment? Do you call it?"

"Yes." The uncertain stool wobbled under me so that I nearly fell onto the floor as I nodded my head. I could feel its hard wooden edges cutting lines in my thighs under my skirt.

Still undaunted by my blank stare, Binah continued, "He said I am his link with the outside world."

"His liaison officer," I said, turning to gaze longingly at the Rav's door.

"Yes, whatever that is." Binah laughed huskily. "Don't be impatient, no matter how long you must wait to see him," she urged, interrupting herself suddenly. "Have patience. He has told me how important, what marvelous things you write for the outside to know." Binah's green eyes swam with generous tears. "Just mention my name to Yakov. I come from Tel Aviv every Thursday, no matter the expense of the petrol. It is only to see him and to bring him those who must talk with him. You understand?"

"I do," I answered truthfully.

Binah's most recent Thursday charge emerged from the Rav's study with a radiant smile.

"My telephone in Tel Aviv, do you want?" Binah said, reluctant to part from me, her doubtful new case.

"I'll wait here every day, as you advise. We'll meet again, don't worry. I sit here for hours and hours." A twinge of bitterness must have crept into my voice, for she grabbed me by the arms and fairly pried me from my seat. "No! No! You must wait. Do not leave." Her companion pulled at her, but Binah pushed the woman aside. Backing piecemeal out the front door, she cried for everyone to hear, "You must stay for the Rav! For yourself!" Then she was gone. I was ready to crawl under the tiny stool with shame. All conversation in the waiting room had ceased, and all eyes were fixed on me. I cleared my throat, got up, and went into the bathroom. Putting down the toilet seat, I sat down, propped my elbows on my knees, and rested my chin in my hands. The window in the bathroom was open; a thin breeze crept over the high windowsill. On the mirror over the sink, a cockroach sat waving its antennae, enraptured by its own reflection.

Had I deluded myself into thinking that I had entered the "tradition"? The Rav stressed over and over again that there were levels of preparation to be accomplished before the disciple placed even his first foot forward on the path. And after that there was nothing to learn. At other times he indicated that there were tangible stages of awareness, "worlds beyond the intellect" that could only be traversed after long practice. Then he had confused me further by his allusions to prayer and the commandments as prerequisites to the whole process. *Love of God, mitzvoth, love of humanity, love of Israel, love of Creation.* What were these to me but high-sounding abstractions? I, who was not nearly as generous as Binah from Tel Aviv, could never dream of embracing so many worlds, of pouring out so much love. I was not "earthy" enough; I took spirituality too seriously; I was *avid* and wished to leap into unfamiliar realms before being tried and proven ready. The Rav had not yet taken me on as his student! For two summers I had been sitting at the threshold of his zebra-striped waiting room, testing my patience, my selflessness, my devotion, only to find that I possessed none of these essential qualities. According to Rav Bloch's "straight path," I would have to spend at least this lifetime as Penina, reordering my innermost nature before I so much as glimpsed the first *aleph.*

I felt oddly as if I were waiting for a lover. I could not leave the bathroom because I was in the grip of real anxiety now, a feeling that my imperfection showed like a huge ugly scar on my face, that all the people out in the waiting room were rival suitors, standing between the Rav and me. I shook with jealousy and palpitated, like the little girl lover of Levi Snow.

Finally, there was a knock at the door. I had been sitting in a passion on the toilet seat for over ten minutes; Yakov called my name in a loud voice. If I could have climbed out the narrow window and escaped, I would have — running and running across the street away from the jeers of all the yeshiva boys who knew of my shameful love. I opened the door and entered the waiting room with my eyes cast down at the floor. At the same moment the Rav, a stooped elf in a stained black silk coat, appeared at the entrance to his study. Crooking his finger, he called me to him. When we were alone with the door safely shut behind us, he replaced his skullcap with a new, broad-brimmed Dominican friar's hat, looking at me all the while as if to say: *I am putting this on for you. How do you like it?*

Melting with love, I said, "That's a nice new hat." I marveled at the Rav's power to provoke great gushing wells of love from some secret, unknown source inside me. My steely nature turned to jelly at the literal drop of his hat. My petulant questions, my sarcasm, died on my lips; my tongue was struck dumb. The Rav appeared indifferent to the emotional transformations taking place in front of him. He had probably suffered hundreds like me from the early morning hours on. Noah would certainly be amused when I told him that I had fallen in love with an eighty-eight-year-old man. And so would Sue. Love filled the room, a sticky, palpable substance clogging every corner, flowing almost visibly in the space between us, vibrating with his slightest movement. Was this the "transmission of guru power" that had driven so many receptive Americans to distraction? *It's sick,* commented my reasonable self. *You have traveled one heck of a long distance for a loving glance and a pat on the head from an old man whose politics repel you and, when all is said and done, who has offered you only a measly "introduction" to the Jewish mystical path. Now that the Rav has led you up to what he mockingly calls the entrance foyer, he isn't going to let you pass through the door.*

We sat and looked at each other in silence; the Rav smiled and rocked slightly in his chair. He might have been hinting that I was not to bother him; perhaps he had given me all he could. Perhaps he was disappointed when I told him my book was not finished. Then again, as Binah had implied, he might have been using me as a vehicle for recalling Jewish unbelievers to the "true faith." A clot of bile rose into my throat. I would not be anyone's missionary. I would return to someone like Rabbi Bassani for practical implementation of the techniques and I would forget the Rav's books and his endless "preparations." Yes, I thought, trying to avoid his stare, it's time to move on to another level with another kabbalist. Every teacher with whom I had studied had taught me something valuable, even the seeming failures. In my dream the night before, Narendra and I had been taking a long, circular walk around a marina filled with starchy white sailboats. We had talked informally about our families until Narendra said, "Madame Ariel, Rav Bloch, and myself are really one and the same."

The Rav interrupted my treasonous thoughts by answering the door and letting in a newspaper reporter. "I'm sure Penina won't mind . . ." I did mind, but I smiled a fake, unminding smile and went out into the waiting room to brood further.

Miracle of miracles, the Rav; he never tires, doesn't eat for eight hours, doesn't sleep but two hours a night; barely gets up to go to

the toilet. The stamina of an angelic host, the energy of the Sephiro-
tic worlds guide his way. We are moving up the same mountain
from opposing paths, it is true, but I am losing sight of him behind
the foreboding peaks of holy war. The voice coming from beyond
his closed door is contentious, a messianic voice with a mission that
cannot include me. He is subtly giving me my walking papers. It is
over now. I was too dense to understand Madame Ariel's warning.
"I saw him on television and I feared for you," she said. I should
have guessed from the story in the Times. *His portion of the teach-*
ing is finished. The signs are true; the books he recommends are
nowhere to be found in Jerusalem. Penina is no longer special. She
has been drowned in the murky waters of messianic redemption.

"Sit here long enough and you'll find everyone in the world,"
Binah had said. She was right. At that very moment an American
black man in sneakers opened the kitchen door. Without removing
his Ivy League cap and windbreaker, he stood sorting potatoes. I
thought I was making him up; dreaming and faint with hunger, I
had placed a friendly black man in the kitchen. But no, he was
there, talking to Yakov in Hebrew about the Rav's dinner. A black
Jew, cooking dinner.

The newspaperman came out of the Rav's study and gave me a
cursory nod of thanks. Yakov indicated that it was all right for me
to return to my lesson.

Noting that it was time for the doctor to arrive, I asked frantically, "Rav Bloch, how does one remain in a state of *devekuth* at
every moment of one's life?"

He looked at me meditatively, his eyes partly shut, his chin on
his palm. Listening very carefully to his own thoughts, the Rav
said, "Yes. First study, then concentration, then prolonged concentration." He seemed about to go on, but then started suddenly from
his reverie and dismissed me snappishly. "Come back at eleven on
Monday with Luzzatto's *One Hundred Thirty-Eight Gates to Kab-*
balah and Irgaz's *Guardian of the Faith. Shalom.*"

On Sunday night I dreamed I was following the Rav to the sta-
dium where the Maccabiah Games were being held. I had just
about caught up with him before the entrance gate when I was

distracted by a vendor selling gaily-colored pinwheels. When I looked up, the Rav had disappeared beyond the gate, which slammed shut with a loud iron clang. No matter what I did to pry it open, the gate remained shut fast.

On Monday at eleven sharp, Yakov greeted me at the front door, saying that the Rav had been busy teaching until two in the morning and that he was now asleep. I sat down on the front steps with my hard-won copy of Luzzatto's book in my lap.

Thoroughly beaten, I made my despairing way back to Madame Ariel's house.

"It is time to seek a new teacher," she said.

I had spent every morning before my classes with Rav Bloch performing mental exercises with her in her garden, exercises designed to reduce "emotivity" and to increase "centering." The meditations consisted of watching the highly charged, free-flowing images in my mind. I was shocked to learn just how mundane and dull I could find myself — nothing like the dramatic wheels within wheels of the first year in Jerusalem. When I approached the simulated quiet I tried to create as a "center," it became apparent that there was none. Where the "center" should have been were turmoil, regret, shame at having been "used as the Rav's vehicle and then tossed aside."

"Why do you see yourself as 'used'?" Madame Ariel asked.

"I could see it in his contemplative stare when he pushed me aside as he spoke wearily of study and concentration; with one eye open and the other half-closed, he sank into kind of a trance, as if he were appraising the face of a stranger. Then, abruptly coming back and flashing the old, ingratiating smile at me, he urged me to return with the books. I don't want to return. I'm tired."

"You have allowed yourself to love Rav Bloch in a way you never loved another teacher — another person — before. And that was very important. There is nothing to be ashamed of."

Madame Ariel and I sat in the shelter of her pomegranate tree dipping into a bag of her favorite bonbons, which had been dropped off promptly at seven-thirty that morning by a wealthy pupil who brought her gifts of food almost every day. The candy was very expensive and very delicious. It took us only half an hour to finish the whole bag.

"After my very first meeting with the Rav, I spent the entire night weeping as if my brains were about to fall out of my head. I couldn't explain it, not even to Noah. He unlocked a certain 'Jewish gate' inside without demanding anything in the direction of adhering to the despised ritual — and without condemning my other practices, which, for him, can only be considered worship of alien gods. I didn't withhold a thing from him — yoga, Zen, I told him all. Yet he somehow freed me to open myself to the whole notion of a *Jewish* mysticism without any of the old guilt and hostility."

"Didn't he tell you it was a meeting between souls?"

"I think maybe we've finished it."

Madame Ariel stood to all of her imposing height. She crumpled the empty bonbon bag and then girlishly licked her fingers. "See him as a friend. I think your learning period with him is over."

But it wasn't. I wouldn't let it be.

It was 104 degrees in Jerusalem almost every day that summer. While everyone else slept during the midafternoon siesta, I quietly eased the car out of the driveway and secretly returned to the Rav's house. This time Yakov appeared, yawning, at the door with his shirttails trailing over his trousers. Screwing his face up, he informed me that it was unbearably hot, that the Rav had been busy all morning at a circumcision, that he was intending to go to another circumcision the next day, and that he could not guarantee me an appointment.

"Try again in the evening," he finished gratuitously.

"Okay. Tell him I was here and said hello."

I returned to the flat as quietly as I had left it. Noah was stretched out on a chair on the terrace, a book dangling like a piece of soft sculpture from his fingers. Feeling like an adulterous wife, I tiptoed past him into the house, poured myself a glass of iced tea, and sank onto the sofa. I remained there for about forty-five minutes, watching myself "dream" in a state that was neither dream nor waking. In my head, I wound my way through the narrow lanes of the newly reconstructed Jewish quarter of the Old City, following a donkey that stopped at the end of a cul-de-sac before a house with a high iron grating. I stood in front of the house, alone on the street save for the donkey, but I did not go inside. Finally, tired of waiting for something to happen, I dismissed the image, rose from the sofa, and wrote a letter to my parents.

Later that evening, as Noah and I were eating dinner with Zvi and Madame Ariel, I was suddenly compelled to describe my "daydream." Madame Ariel opened her eyes wide. "*That* is where you must go tomorrow. Your inside gave you the information you needed; it was the true voice from the center speaking to you, the voice that speaks in images, not words."

I was about to protest, but Madame Ariel continued. "There is a young rabbi in the Old City who is very quietly teaching Kabbalah. I have heard of this from certain Orthodox friends. His yeshiva is undoubtedly the place you saw in your awakening dream," she said with great finality.

"*Voilà!*" shouted Zvi mockingly. "A new adventure."

"Do not make jokes. This is very serious," Madame Ariel replied.

I had never before been so fanatically driven as I was about studying Kabbalah during that return visit to Jerusalem. The interlude with Rav Bloch fueled my spiritual greed beyond even his wildest expectations. I was now determined to be the first secular woman to delve into the Kabbalah and practice its complicated meditations without observing the traditional Jewish Law. There had been female kabbalists, but all of them had been Orthodox. Eagerly, with superhuman energy that defied the scorching heat, I spent my days searching in the maze of the Jewish quarter for a dreamed-of yeshiva.

Through the narrow stone alleyways: a labyrinth of yeshivoth, houses, clotheslines, gardens, boutiques, and more yeshivoth — none of them kabbalistic. Plazas with newly planted scrawny trees, donkey shit, unfinished constructions amid pools of wet cement, screaming Arab workmen with furtive eyes. No one had heard of such a place.

A bearded Hasid in a hurry passed by clutching a briefcase.

"Excuse me," I shouted after him, "do you know if there is a kabbalist's yeshiva in this neighborhood?"

He averted his eyes and nervously stroked his beard. Looking off toward a distant corner, he said, "There used to be, but he died. Maybe his widow can help you. Her name is Gottesman and she lives across the street." The Hasid pointed to an unfinished building.

"Thank you." With the blood pumping noisily in my ears, I crossed over a pile of bricks and turned a corner, entering a long, narrow, walled lane whose roadway was filled with hardened donkey droppings and huge, gaping potholes. I bumped into an American tour group, every last man and woman wearing striped tennis hats, shorts, and carrying a guidebook. Instinctively I made a left turn at the end of the lane and came face to face with the duplicate iron grating of my "awakening dream." Above the grating was a gold-lettered sign on a black background, YESHIVA BNEI UZIEL, and above the tin mailbox, the name Gottesman in a rough, hand-lettered scrawl. Up the stairs and just inside an open door on the first landing, a woman in her late sixties sat in a straight-backed leather chair. She wore a stiff wig and a dark flowered dress with lacy cuffs. Her open living room had been converted into a wee synagogue. Books lined the walls; an ark embossed in gold with the tablets of the Law stood before the eastern window, through which appeared a dreamlike view of the spires and domes of the ancient quarter of Jerusalem, the Mount of Olives, and all the paths leading to the Dead Sea. Except for the ritual paraphernalia, the widow Gottesman's flat was a duplicate of the roshi's zendo only a mile beyond her window. She sat aimlessly, her chunky legs splayed in front of her, staring into space. Two ethereal, blue-eyed children, a pigtailed girl of twelve and a near-sighted boy of eleven, sat, also aimlessly, across from her. None of them acknowledged me.

"Rav Bloch sent me," I said crazily, still participating in a dream.

"Come sit at the table," said the widow Gottesman without asking my name.

"I understand your husband taught Kabbalah."

The girl snickered. The boy looked down with embarrassment and knotted the cords of his *tzitzith.*

"My husband, Rabbi Gottesman, was the right hand to Rav Berman, the master of Kabbalah who wrote all these books." Without turning her head, the widow pointed to the walls surrounding her. "The old Rav Berman was" — she paused, her eyes filling with tears as she looked past my shoulder — "as great as the old Rav Bloch, this one's father. Rav Berman worked together with my husband, interpreting the *Zohar* for the new generation of seekers, trying to bring the difficult teachings of the Ari to the understanding of the ordinary person. But he died in his prime, and my husband, Rabbi Gottesman, was left to try to arrange and organize a school. He even managed to find a place, a building for a yeshiva. He devoted his life, his health; often the family went hungry so that he could continue spreading the words of his master." Removing a handkerchief from the lace cuff of her sleeve, the widow dabbed at her eyes. Her worn face hardened. "And then this American came, this Rabbi Lupold. He seemed at first to be a sincere disciple of my husband's, but he soon began promising great promises — translating the texts, bringing the knowledge to America. And then one day he stole all the manuscripts and never returned. He stole them while we were sitting *shiva,* this American Lupold, for my husband, who died of a broken heart because he failed in his mission. Another one, in London this time, somehow got hold of the manuscripts and published Rav Berman's work illegally abroad. From every side, the Berman tradition was being sapped. My husband died in Safed, praying over the Ari's tomb."

The widow Gottesman looked up at me with the same clear, blue-eyed stare of her granddaughter. "Now we have very little left. Only the books and a few students who come to see my son-in-law, Rabbi Gideon — but he won't talk to a woman. You should see my daughter, Inbal Stern; she lives down the street on Temple Road.

She learned a bit from her father. But what can you hope to do for us now? Look where we have fallen to . . ." The widow Gottesman and I seemed to be continuing a centuries-old conversation.

"I'm a writer," I said. "I will make this public."

"That's not it; you've misunderstood." She shrugged wearily and resumed her complaint in the tired Yiddish of every Jewish widow in the world. "What will happen to us now? My husband is dead; it is all gone. Only my son-in-law, with his small group, is left. Nu! That is all that is left. What will you do?"

"I'll write," I kept repeating, "I'll write." Then I awkwardly dropped a fifty-pound note on the table near her lined fingers.

"That isn't what I meant." She sat passively, not touching the money and not returning it. The braided girl smirked.

"He so wanted the teachings to be known." The widow wrung her hands and broke into a wail.

"I'll see your daughter. Was it Temple Street, you said? We'll talk again. I'm sorry to have taken your time . . ." I stood and backed out the front door.

"What time? All I have is time now," she groaned plaintively, rigid in her chair, exactly as I had found her.

Past the ark with its blue and gold threads, East Jerusalem was being illuminated in pink by the descending sun. Across the road from the zendo I could see the painted green spire of the Victoria Hospital. How simple were the Zen Buddhists! How uncomplicated their tea-drinking lives and quiet enlightenments. No teary mamas, no clinging widows, no fake American rabbis peddling arcane manuscripts — nothing but one clean-shaven, sweet-smelling monk in flowing robes, putting one foot precisely in front of the next as the clock struck four in the hospital tower, chanting alone on his mountaintop.

I am in eye of storm, the roshi had said gleefully. A storm was a living event, not like the perpetual dirge of the rabbi's wife who waited alone for death, to whom she would no doubt complain as bitterly as she had to me. I fled for my life out of the desolate maw of her empty synagogue. *Don't let the rebbitzen get you.*

Out in the street, the late afternoon sun burned the Jerusalem stone. The Old City was treeless and barren, a rocky labyrinth oddly out of time, in keeping with the Kabbalah itself — what it must have looked like when all the mystical yeshivoth were in full flower. What were they trying to rebuild now, Rabbi Gottesman's dream slightly tarnished? In the weeping widow's lifetime, perhaps. Or in mine.

I was hungry. I ate in a small, greasy café perched on a hilltop not far from the widow's house. The restaurant, like the Kabbalah, was empty of customers, a fallen dream of once bright-eyed young men. Their voices had been drowned between the covers of unintelligible tomes amid the cries of too many children who clung to the long skirts of their wailing women. Still, Monsieur Gilbert, a new kabbalist all the way across town, was insisting publicly that the Kabbalah was being brought back to the Jews by women, the new priestesses.

I chewed on a french-fried potato dripping with rancid grease, knowing I would be sick, longing for sickness to grant me respite from my mad search.

Inbal Stern was easy to find. At the second landing of a handsome new house on Temple Street, I was greeted by a thirtyish woman wearing a nicely tailored navy skirt, an aquamarine blouse, sandals, and no stockings. Only the wig betrayed her orthodoxy. The face underneath was quick, intelligent, suspicious.

"My mother called and said you were coming." Her eyes were blue, piercing, full of questions; her skin pink, younger than her years. But her lips were primly pursed shut for fear she might blurt out the long, silent litany of inhibitions fastened onto her eager intellect. Her nose was long and sharp.

"Who are you?" she asked.

"I talked with your mother," I hedged. What was I doing there after all? Having left the Rav's familiar precincts, I had cast myself on alien ground; timid, self-justifying, at a loss for explanations, I remembered my jeans and striped polo shirt — the costume of the intruder from the unholy "outside."

"Sit down." She motioned me toward the dining room table. The house was interesting: a duplex with a staircase separating a lower-level study filled with books; to the left, the entranceway to the upper-level living room, dining room, kitchen, terrace — all modern, comfortable, middle-class furnishings denoting intelligence and taste; no Orthodox linoleum tablecloths, doilies, and dusty carpets. Inbal Stern's home was like mine: spare, neat — even smart. The hand of a modern woman, a soul sister, was at work there. Another girl and boy, also about eleven and twelve years old, were seated on a sofa, but this girl had softly styled, shorter hair and wore a dungaree skirt and a denim workshirt.

"These children . . ." I pointed.

"The ones at my mother's house are my oldest sister's; they're visiting from Haifa," said Inbal Stern, demarcating her territory and declaring herself different from her sister.

"Tell me what it is you want, Mrs. . . ."

"Perle Epstein."

"Do you have children?"

"No."

Silence. Inevitably. I had disobeyed the biblical command to be fruitful and multiply my kind, the children of Israel, a Jewish woman's most obligatory commandment.

An alarm clock ticked ominously on an overhead kitchen cabinet. My time was running out. On the wall opposite was a fine pencil sketch of a bearded Jew with a broad forehead wearing a skullcap.

"That was done by my husband," said Inbal Stern proudly.

Seeing my opening, I plunged daringly. "I told your mother I was a writer. I am just completing a book on the Kabbalah in the United States." I agonized over each Hebrew word. "Do you speak English?"

"A little." Her intelligent eyes gave her away.

"And do you study Kabbalah?" I pursued her before she could shut me off.

"Alone. I've studied the books from my father. But the rabbis do not teach me. They do not wish to teach a woman," she replied in halting, but clear English.

Our hands rested within inches of each other on the dining room table. I knew her very well, my sister . . . her relentless years of secret poring over books, catching scraps from her father's table, eavesdropping in secret on Friday nights from the kitchen, where she pretended to be engrossed in washing dishes. Her yearning was as great as any I had sensed coursing through the serious, bearded young men in long black caftans — her brothers, her sons, her husband — her captors. Inbal's face reddened, her lips tightening into an ironic smile.

"I study alone, and sometimes with a group of women. But my brother-in-law, Rabbi Gideon, is teaching the system of Rav Berman to a small group of men in my mother's house — the yeshiva. He knows very good. He is an excellent teacher, but he will not teach a woman. Maybe to talk to him, but not to learn."

"Rav Bloch taught me. I am a woman and not religious, but women are ready to learn; they *must* learn now. It is their time even to take it by force, to demand Kabbalah for themselves," I said passionately.

Her smile widened. I felt her with me, a conspirator like the rebels beside me at prayers in the Beth Rachel synagogue; the iron-willed brilliant ones who went off and learned in secret what was forbidden to them — calculus, art, biology — all subjects reserved exclusively for the men to whom they would later submit after shaving their heads, their yearning for wisdom dropping invisibly to the floor with their thick brown plaits. Contenting themselves with the instinctual life of the Jewish woman, the girls of Beth Rachel could hope to climb no higher than the heart on the cosmic tree. But I would settle for nothing less than the Crown.

"During the time of the Ari himself, in Safed," I ventured, openly aggressive now, "there were women kabbalists. We even know the name of one — Francesa. Maybe now is the time for such as Francesa to learn and to teach openly."

Inbal Stern appeared to be nodding in agreement — or was she shaking her head in disgust?

"What do you want to learn from here?" she asked.

"I want to learn something about Rav Berman's method for practicing Kabbalah. Until today, I never believed in its validity. You see, I came across some of his writings while researching material for my book, but only in small fragments. And I've seen privately published texts in English, bad ones."

"Yes, my mother must have told you about Lupold, the unauthorized translations. She has something personal against him."

"Well, so do I. That kind of rabbi gives Kabbalah a bad name." Inbal was not interested in my feelings about Lupold. Her face told me, however, that she was ashamed of her connection with him, the family secret. "It will be better for you to talk to my brother-in-law, Rabbi Gideon. He knows much better than I do. Ah, but he is leaving for Safed tomorrow. The memorial of the Ari's death is tomorrow, and he and his group will go to the tomb in Safed. I'll call my sister. They live near here, also in the Old City."

She went downstairs into the study to the telephone. Cupping her hand over the mouthpiece so that I could not hear what she was whispering, Inbal never took her eyes off me. "He is out," she cried. "You will have to call him yourself tonight, after seven." She scribbled the number on a piece of paper and pushed it toward me over the staircase.

I was not to be placated so easily. Unremittingly, I tried to pry her open. "But your mother indicated that Rav Berman had a method. Is it *hitbodedut,* meditation, like the Hasidim; or *kavannot,* concentration exercises, like what they do at the Beth El yeshiva, or Abulafia's letter permutations?" I tossed about desperately.

"No, we do nothing like that. Rav Berman's work merely clears up the difficulties in the *Zohar* through the works of the Ari. How we make ourselves more spiritualized, but not through techniques. We do no meditation like that," she answered stubbornly.

"But the *yichudim,* binding the mind to the higher spheres?" I pleaded.

"*Yichudim,* like all the other names, are only metaphors — no, excuse me, symbols for states of the inside of a person. They are not *things* or *forms* in themselves; they are events."

I paused to absorb her thought. No two kabbalists had ever agreed on where the literal and the figurative parted ways. Only

I brazenly sought to break through the ornately encrusted and enameled mythology . . .

"Here is Rabbi Gideon's telephone number. You call him."

"Maybe you and I can learn together?" I offered, knowing that it would never happen, that I only half-meant it anyway. On what common ground could we meet? That of our inhibited and hungry Jewish woman's past? That wasn't a good reason to study together. Yet I was struck by the feeling that she too throbbed at the visceral level, where knowing was more important than life itself. With great restraint, which had drawn her lips into a thin, pale line, Inbal Stern longed for the same peek at God that I was trying to claim with arrogant thrusts of violence, with the pounding of fists on the rabbis' doors. *If you don't let me in, I'll huff and I'll puff and I'll tear the door down.* Rav Bloch's rejection had turned me into a desperate, predatory seeker, a hungry ghost. He had disappeared beyond a gate in my dream. I had found Inbal Stern beyond a gate in my dream. Everywhere in the old Jewish quarter of the city were gates, stones, and doors, a maze at the center of which sat — who? Rabbi Gideon and the secret key to the Kabbalah?

I bid Inbal Stern good-bye, thanking her for letting me intrude on her privacy.

"Not at all," she said politely. "I hope you find what you wish."

Down in the street a man trembled and quaked over a pneumatic drill. They were rebuilding the old Jewish quarter with a vengeance, opening the yeshivoth that had rotted behind moldy slats and urinals for two centuries before the Six-Day War. I suddenly felt glad to be walking along Temple Street. Abandoned and faithless, I nonetheless reveled in being part of a renaissance of Jewish spiritual study on sanctified Jewish ground. With a jaunty step, I threaded my way through the maze.

8

Toward a Jewish "Yoga"

T HE EARLY MORNINGS WERE BEST for working with Madame Ariel. The heat was not so intense then as to make her seek refuge in bed, for she suffered greatly from what she persisted in calling a hole in her heart. Noah called it a mitral valve lesion and gave her frequent check-ups, which made her very gay and agreeable until midafternoon, when she wilted like a queenly lily. After she had finished her kitchen chores and prepared the evening meal, she fixed us all a cup of mint tea and explained her system to us as we sat together in the garden. Noah took many notes; I played with the cats, whom I'd renamed Gurdjieff and Ouspensky. When the sun grew too hot outside, we moved into the house; the heavy drapes and tapestries, the Oriental carpets and Chinese silks in Madame Ariel's flat often gave me the illusion that I was an ancient desert adept consulting a temple priestess in her inner sanctum. Then she would do or say something outlandish that served to draw me back into the world of everyday reality. Like the Rav's nationalism, Madame Ariel's quirky love of mystification kept me from becoming a "follower."

As Madame Ariel described it, meditative practice required a balance between active yearning and a passive acceptance of "grace," the equilibrium that permitted enlightenment to take place. Likening the mystical experience to a happening outside of time, she compared the relaxed mind in meditation to the condition of deep sleep.

"All defenses are lowered, will is let go, and Being is permitted to enter. But you are promoting this will all throughout the day. For example, prayer, though not totally concentrated, can permit it to happen, too. You go out of yourself . . . ecstasy."

To help her pupils promote continuous objective awareness, she advocated performing reversal exercises before falling asleep at night. Using an ancient technique first described by Philo, the Hellenic-Jewish philosopher, then modified by the Ari in sixteenth-century Safed, Madame Ariel instructed me to visualize the events of my entire day, starting from the last one before retiring. I was to step into conversations, assuming the role of the other person, using his or her voice, mannerisms, gestures — all the way back to waking in the morning of that day. Most of the time I fell asleep before launching a quarter of the way backward; I was often so spiritually drained from my unfulfilled pursuit of Rav Bloch that I dropped off before I could even visualize myself brushing my teeth in preparation for bed. But when I did complete the exercise successfully, I achieved astonishing results. One night, after having dismissed the interminable psychologizing of another of Madame Ariel's American pupils as "unbearably boring," I actually found myself entering into the young woman's feelings so strongly that I virtually became one with her. The imagined event was so jarring, the intensity of her suffering so great, that I bolted upright in bed, gasping for breath.

When I described the results of my "reversal" to Madame Ariel the next day, she said, "You were conscious, acute, and at the same time your organism was at rest — as in meditation. At the end of the day, when you are most passive, you see that the reversal is better as a visualization to take you out of yourself than a mere rehearsal of what has happened during the day in your memory."

"Is that why I felt Beth so strongly? Because *I* wasn't there?" I asked, still amazed at the simplicity and depth of the technique.

"Reversal distances you from your day; you look as an observer at yourself from afar," she replied. "I changed the kabbalists' technique somewhat when I tried it out with my twin brother during the war. We were separated, he in Paris, and I in Algiers. Before he left, we agreed to look up at a star every night and mentally send a message to each other by imagining that we had changed places. It worked throughout the war. Later, we would compare results through an occasional smuggled letter from one of his Resistance companions. One night I looked at my star and knew that he had died." Madame Ariel paused. "He was killed in a concentration camp."

"It was typical of you to gaze at a star. There's something very poetic about such an experiment," I said, trying to bring her back from her melancholy distraction.

Madame Ariel shook her head and shoulders like a cat and said, "By focusing on something high, like a star, you take yourself out of yourself easily. If I go high, or focus my attention at the highest point in my imagination, I can see and feel everything going on in all the universe."

"But those are metaphors," said Noah.

"I am a very practical one. I do literal exercises to concretize the metaphor. When you look up, the muscles around the eyes stimulate the activity of the brain; it is the same with Oriental practices that advocate concentrating on the tip of the nose while visualizing a lotus at the heart. Remember, we are both body and spirit, linked by nerves and breath."

Madame Ariel had a curious interpretation of the *mitzvoth,* the Jewish precepts. For her, the Torah was a living reminder of the Jewish nation in the world, a refusal to forget history. The individual performing a *mitzvah,* she said, became one with the universe, one with time, yet simultaneously leaped out of time. The physical act of blessing, then eating, bread connected one to the Creator on both the material and spiritual planes. The Jew's present life was a bridge between past and future as well; his place in the Jewish nation was thereby always linked with the events of the future. The Jewish destiny was, in her words, an "inexorable genetic fact."

"That is why I am here in Jerusalem. I could have stayed in Paris, where I was very rich, very known. But my Jewish destiny here demands fulfillment," said Madame Ariel, correcting me with unassailable finality when I characterized her work as secular.

On the ninth of Av, two years to the day of my meeting with David Castel, the kabbalist scribe, Madame Ariel suggested that Noah and I fast in commemoration of the destruction of the Temple.

"If you work on this day, no gain can come from your labors," she warned. "Besides, it will be a good way of breaking with habit — not eating as a disciplinary action, a *tikkun*, as the kabbalists call it."

To keep our minds off food, Noah and I walked to the Western Wall to see the famous holiday display of Jewish ritual styles. A group of strictly observant men sat with their bare feet touching the base of the wall, heaping ashes on their heads and chanting dirges out of Jeremiah's Lamentations. On the periphery, thousands of people strolled, looked, gossiped — the intensity of the "inexorable Jewish destiny" thinning out beyond the small circle of mourners. As one tourist put it: "The Day of Lamentations is an occasion to see and be seen, a kind of Jewish Easter Parade."

Jeremiah had called me back to Jerusalem, and once I was there I was still unsure about the applicability of *daat* (spiritual knowledge) in my own life. *Daati,* the word used to designate observant Jews, meant "keeper of knowledge," yet the pasty-faced, life-hating spectacle of men in black caftans moaning and groaning before the wall repelled me. *Daati,* for me, was an emblem, an artificial standard of "modesty," a raucous sign in the Mea Shearim quarter of Jerusalem inscribed with blistering admonitions warning the Daughters of Israel to maintain their modesty by refraining from dressing in short-sleeved blouses and walking through the filthy, gutted lanes of the ultra-Orthodox neighborhood in jeans. It meant devoting oneself to the strictest, most mechanical adherence to the ritual codes in every phase of ordinary life. It meant the death of all spontaneity. Jewish ritual orthodoxy was as bleak as the bleakest Calvinist admonition about hell. For Madame Ariel, the metaphor lived only because she was married to a socialist-atheist and was herself not particularly observant. For me, Jewish ritual orthodoxy meant tearing pieces of toilet paper off the roll on Friday afternoons in preparation for the Sabbath day, when you were not supposed to cut or tear even toilet paper for fear that you might be desecrating God's day of rest.

At the wall, I bowed my head and wrestled with myself, weighing the arguments, wondering if I, like Madame Ariel, could be a keeper of the knowledge in its truest sense, a spiritually whole, constantly attentive human being, without actually adhering to the laws of kosher food, the Sabbath, and "family purity." The Torah's four levels were meant to be scaled individually, and, as Yakov used to enjoy taunting me, one had to know the Hebrew language well in order to read Scripture. That was logical. In order to study the text as a kabbalist, to elicit the secrets from the Torah's fourth (mystical) level and soar aloft, performing the *mitzvoth* in the physical world — orthodoxy — was inescapable. And yet, despite the Rav's assurance that Jewishness had been inscribed on my soul by the prophets, and despite Madame Ariel's belief that it was physically imprinted on my genes, I did not really wish to practice as a traditionally Orthodox Jew in order to become a mystical one. A more deeply gnawing question sprang up almost instantly: "Do I dare forge a new way, one that would circumvent the rigid Law?" Would that route inevitably lead to Sabbatai Zevi and heresy? As I watched the *daati* women around me rocking on their heels, weeping and pounding the wall with their clenched fists, I knew that I was equally as fervent as they in *rebelling* against orthodoxy with every breath I took.

I refused to lament. But I also refused to assume foreign rituals, as Sue was doing in India. I could always take Madame Ariel's "short path," a secular practice that made no scholarly demands and posed no doctrinal prerequisites, but merely advocated "cutting with tendencies" and performing an eclectic series of meditations gleaned from the works of Taoists, Sufis, and old kabbalists read in French. The "short path" was a potpourri of Madame Ariel's natural intuitive gifts, a synthesis of Eastern and Jewish techniques applied to practical life. Her version of asceticism was even more delicate than the Zen roshi's: an occasional small warning against a certain spice, a hint at fasting, a suggestion of mental control in an almost playful atmosphere, every gesture geared toward watching habits and tendencies as they arose — without reflection, analysis, or rumination. Only then was her pupil prepared for living and acting — properly and immediately — throughout the multiple worlds on the cosmic tree.

"If it is not for life, I am not interested. I am in life," was Madame Ariel's motto.

And nothing could describe her more accurately: a French lady at home, cooking, entertaining, arguing with her husband; no traveling guru circus. To some she appeared eccentric. Mr. Paret's wife, for example, cornered me several times on the street and asked what a sophisticated American woman like me was doing every summer "in that strange occult salon of Madame Ariel's." To foreign visitors, she was a "psychologist," or an international "hostess." To neighbors and scholars and schoolchildren, she was an adviser, sometimes an enigma; to a passerby, she was a handsome lady reclining in a big flowered lawn chaise, reading an Agatha Christie novel under a pomegranate tree in a tiny gárden behind a blue gate. To her closest pupils, she was as valid a spiritual teacher as Rav Bloch. Though she had been living in Jerusalem for over twenty years, Madame Ariel barely knew a word of Hebrew. Her critics said that the gap in communication alone immediately disqualified her as a "Jewish mystic." Yet many Hasidim appeared at her doorstep for mental exercises and advice. Priests and nuns came, too.

It was the urge for "legitimacy" that kept me from truly becoming Madame Ariel's pupil. Rav Bloch satisfied my requirements on at least two counts: his father had been an acknowledged kabbalist, and all four levels of the tradition were at his fingertips. Rav Bloch's was the "straight, or long, path," fenced in on two sides by reason and intellect, and therefore not dangerous. Madame Ariel's path alone would not do for a Westerner like me, with my overemphasis on learning and my inhibitions about ecstasy. She was too direct, too biological, too feminine in her devaluation of the intellect. Her own imposing presence was the guard rail that kept her pupils from falling into the abyss; but if she should die there was no "tradition," no one next in line to safeguard them. I could not travel along Madame Ariel's path without the balance provided by a conservative male teacher. And I would have to find him soon. Abandoned by the Rav, I was now determined to forge my own Kabbalah from the bits and pieces I had picked up from his table, a Kabbalah that successfully combined West and East, logic and intuition, male and female — nothing less than what the *Zohar* itself prescribed: "MALE AND FEMALE HE CREATED THEM ... When is a human being called ONE? When male and female are present together and one is sanctified. Come and see, when there is unity of male and female and one's intention is to the Holy, then is he complete and is called ONE without imperfection."

Berman. The name recalled a scattered mass of gibberish that promised to open the secrets of the *Zohar* for the first time since the sixteenth century, when the Ari had revealed them in Safed. In an occult Fourth Avenue bookstore, I had scanned Lupold's grotesquely translated book on divine emanation and, condemning it as fraudulent, quickly put it back on the shelf. Now, pungent with new promises, the strange, crooked lanes of Kabbalah were again leading me back to Rav Berman.

When reached at last by telephone, Rabbi Gideon reluctantly agreed to a meeting. Armed with a map, Noah and I parked the car outside the Old City gates. It was seven o'clock, and the stars and midnight blue sky lent the ancient quarter a still and timeless aura that had been obscured by the blazing sun at midday. The new cobbled lanes of the reviving Jewish quarter were well lit and clean. Rabbi Gideon had said that his flat was near the Mizrachi Bank. We found the "Street of Angels" easily, but not number 12. The streets crossing it all trailed off into a dead end. We trod back and forth in circles for a few minutes, searching out Rabbi Gideon's nonexistent house number. The buildings were connected by a labyrinth of inner courtyards, ivy-entwined gates, and stairwells tucked away into hidden corners. Nothing was accessible directly from the street proper except for one or two shops, an art gallery, and the bank. Even the yeshivoth were hidden inside the walls of open plazas, which were newly planted with fragile saplings in huge earthen pots.

Noah and I decided to separate and reconnoiter the street from opposite ends. At the corner near the bank I saw a young, wispy, bearded fellow in shirtsleeves rushing toward me with the inevitable flying fringes escaping from his belt loops. All *talmidim,* religious scholars, rushed down the street in a frenzy, as if sitting for hours on hard benches engaged in prayer and study made them unbearably restless and driven. They were usually wan and wiry and, like this one and his bearded compatriot who had directed me the other day to the widow Gottesman's, always in a desperate hurry to flee from a woman. I hesitated to ask the boy anything. Then, gazing around the vacant streets, I decided that he was my only realistic chance for finding Rabbi Gideon's house.

"Excuse me, do you speak English?" I asked in Hebrew, though the boy immediately struck me as somehow American.

"Yes."

I charged right up to him, stopping him in his tracks, nearly pinning him against an opposite wall, and pushing him into a flanking spiral staircase.

"Do you know of a Rabbi Gideon? Where he lives?"

The young man caught his balance, pulled himself free, and, hastening past me, called over his shoulder, "Yes, I'm going there right now. I'm late for my class with him."

No longer surprised by Jerusalem "coincidences," I motioned to Noah at the other end of the street and rushed off, close on the boy's heels.

The young man with the flying fringes and the nervous face of a pursued bird led us into the crevice of a building that opened into a courtyard, past a shop that led into a stairwell. Number 12. We would never have found the place without him. Three flights up, before the open door of a flat on a separate landing that looked dizzily down into the street below, we found ourselves in an entrance hall that made a right angle and turned sharply into a kitchen terrace cluttered with plants and drying utensils. The view, even at night, was spectacular — a dark sky peppered with timeless stars, domes, spires, and terraced hills fringed by silver street lights. Noah and I gasped in unison at the unexpected beauty of it. The boy had disappeared. Turning back toward the door in the entrance hall, we walked brazenly into the small flat after a cursory tap. To the right was a brightly lit kitchen partitioned from the dining area and entrance foyer by a freshly constructed wall. (We could still smell the plaster.) A small living room was visible beyond that, then another partitioning wall and a small, narrow corridor that presumably led off to bedrooms and bath. The nearest open door off the hall revealed a room with a crib containing a tiny, sleeping form. Beyond the living room partition we heard the sound of chairs being scraped across a tile floor and shuffling to make room for the latecomer. Trying to remain hidden, I peeked around the wall and saw a group of young men seated around a table. Before I knew what was happening, frantic hands were reaching out and pushing two chairs — one around the partition for me, the second, out in the living room among the men, for Noah, the legitimate observer. I was being relegated to the woman's position beyond the wall without so much as a table to lean on. But before I was so unceremoniously "dumped in the dark" (as I saw it), I had caught a glimpse of a plaid jacket and some four or five young men's faces. Not one of them was forty, and most were probably too young to be married — which meant that Rabbi Gideon was at least flexible enough to have broken the first rules of kabbalistic tradition. I sulked in triumph: These mystics were not as Orthodox as they pretended. Suddenly there was more shuffling and chair scraping, and the rabbi appeared in front of me beyond the forbidden wall.

I was as astonished at Rabbi Gideon's youth as I had been at Rav Bloch's age. He was in his mid-thirties, with an oval face, clear blue eyes, chestnut hair, beard, and sidelocks, a ready smile, and a slightly puzzled look. Despite the black rabbinical trappings, with his skullcap pushed back over his wide, high forehead, Rabbi

Gideon looked oddly . . . Gentile! His nose, long and fine, did a slight dip at the end, almost meeting the reddish whiskers that curled toward his mouth. He gazed at me, smiling like a frank and friendly Viking; Rabbi Gideon was apparently fearless in the presence of women. Very politely, he informed me that his class was not yet over and asked if Noah and I would mind waiting outside for a short while.

We went out the front door onto the landing; sharing the one porch chaise stationed there, we sat looking out over the staircase railing into the street below. The muffled sound of the resumed lesson reached our ears through an open window in the kitchen. We sat listening for less than five minutes when a woman hurriedly appeared. Some invisible messenger had delivered the word to the rabbi's wife: There were guests in her house, strangers, and she was not there to greet and appraise them. A plumper, more placid version of her sister Inbal, Rebbitzen Gideon wore a flowered blouse and dark skirt and the usual stiff brown wig. She came at us billowing forth children who seemed to sprout from her sides, her waist, her arms, and her legs — like wild buds on a sturdy, upright stalk. I counted four coming up the stairs with her and three trailing after — girls in long, hand-me-down dresses, pigtails, curls; boys in short pants, more active than the girls, more clinging, and whiningly teasing their sisters. The rabbi's wife did not try to hush them or even to restrain their horseplay. She sat down in front of us on the porch railing and proposed a cold drink, which Noah and I refused. Unfazed by the clinging, clamoring mass still sprouting from her every limb, Rebbitzen Gideon enumerated for us her children's names, genders, and ages in order. One shy girl, a leggy beauty of twelve, stood off in a corner and stared at us. Though her long dress was cut to conceal her newly developing body, she unconsciously bore herself with the elegant aloofness of a fashion model. Like a tame deer, she hung back close against the wall, looking at me with her father's clear blue eyes. Her hair was pulled back from her face in a ponytail, revealing the kind of natural beauty that in any other context would draw admiration, wealth, and fame. Here, however, the girl was being groomed for housework and "family purity," destined to fade under her wig of stiff, artificial hair, her translucent pink skin to grow puffy with childbearing. The dreamer's eyes would exchange their faraway questions for the downcast lids of the "modest" wife. I recognized the symptoms all too well. Like her Aunt Inbal, this girl would never remain content; she, too, would burn for knowledge in secret.

Rabbi Gideon's wife was chatting amiably about the newest occupant of the much-used crib, a boy named Moses, already inured to the invading army of noisy children and whispering kabbalists several feet away. Though only four weeks old, Moses was obviously expected to adapt quickly to the din.

Presently Rabbi Gideon, lanky and slightly scoliotic, appeared in the doorway and ushered us in. The five young men dispersed quickly; one of them, dressed in military gear, retrieved his rifle from a corner, bid the rebbitzen goodnight, and hurried past us. Of the entire group, only the rabbi himself was dressed in a long black caftan, the trademark of the strictly observant Jew. The deserted table was set with a large bottle of Johnny Walker Red Label Scotch, platters of delicately iced cookies, and a tray of small silver goblets, some of which were still filled to the brim with untouched liquor. The lean, hurried fellow whom I had trailed to the house had been instructed to remain behind as a translator. At the table, he introduced himself to me as "Tony," an American boy, as I had guessed, "from Chicago." The rabbi asked me to sit at his right, Tony directly across from me, and Noah farther to my right. The rebbitzen scurried into the kitchen with her brood.

In stumbling Hebrew I recited my well-rehearsed purpose for coming. The rabbi screwed up his forehead in an effort to follow my rambling monologue; then gave up, signaling Tony to intercede. After the translation into Hebrew, he nodded but said nothing. Again I attacked, more earnestly this time, confronting him with the "heavy artillery" I had held in reserve: my intensive research, my yeshiva background, my attraction to other, "foreign" disciplines — provoking no surprise, no shocked gasp at any of my crazy-quilt past lives, not even so much as a raised eyebrow at the possibility of my search for "pagan gods." Finally, in desperation, I said, "I have had two and a quarter summers' worth of introduction to Kabbalah with Rav Bloch. Now I am in transition; I'm seeking the link between the introductory study of Kabbalah and the practice."

Rabbi Gideon listened carefully, leaned his head to one side, and asked if I knew Rabbi Lupold.

"I saw his translation of Rav Berman's work and found him to be a fraud," I said, shocked at his association.

Rabbi Gideon appeared amused. Shrugging his shoulders as if to disclaim or unburden himself of any such connection, he said, "I bear him no grudge."

It was my turn to go on the offensive: "Why? Does your yeshiva have anything to do with Lupold's teachings?"

"Not at all," he said with great good humor, though it was obvious that he — and Rav Berman's entire line of Kabbalah — had suffered much at Lupold's hands.

"Don't be worried about my being a woman," I suddenly blurted out, fearing that women and charlatanism were somehow connected in his mind. "I have never been turned away by any of the rabbis I approached for Kabbalah. I must do this."

"Those were great rabbis," he countered in Yiddish, by-passing Tony's confused efforts at hurried translation from English to Hebrew and back. "With small rabbis like me it's not as easy," the rabbi said candidly.

Though we were, literally and figuratively, from opposite sides of the world, Rabbi Gideon and I were not too far apart in years or accomplishment. It could only be in that context — as equals rather than as master and disciple — that we might meet. The problem of his maleness and my femaleness, as he tacitly implied, would be temporarily put aside. Having quickly formed a modest rationale for our being together, and seeing no reason for further discussion about it, Rabbi Gideon immediately launched into an outline of Rav Berman's teachings.

"You are already aware, madame, of the correspondence between the six hundred and thirteen precepts and the six hundred and thirteen bodily parts, are you?" he asked, his tone and manner now awkwardly formal.

"But not kabbalistically . . ."

"We'll deal with that when the time comes. For the moment, you understand that these bodily attributes must be coordinated with their nonmaterial counterparts, the spiritual vessels, and that this process occurs in stages, *madregot,* until we reach unity —"

"Yes, yes," I interrupted impatiently. "I'm up to my eyes in talk about the levels. It's a specialty of Rav Bloch's. I think it's the way all you rabbis keep interested people from really studying deeply."

"But if you wish to understand the Jewish way, you must realize, Madame Epstein, that unity cannot be pulled down forcefully through meditative or any other 'techniques.' I can't teach you to pray with the Ari's *kavannot,* nor do I perform Hasidic exercises to obtain ecstasy through prayer," said Rabbi Gideon definitively, his delicate white fingers locked together, the scent of cinnamon and raisins emanating from his chestnut beard, his eyes intently fastened on mine. "It is rather a question, as Rav Berman put it, of spiritualizing matter, of making ourselves — through the performance of the six hundred and thirteen *mitzvoth* and constant unfaltering awareness of the spiritual dimension in all the created universes — of making ourselves worthy of the divine influx."

Everyone, it occurred to me, was beginning to sound like Madame Ariel. "You mean it's that *physical?*" I asked incredulously, worried that my worst imaginings about Jewish materialism were all coming true.

"There are five levels of being in human nature, as you know from your reading." Rabbi Gideon counted them each out on the fingers of his right hand as he talked. "First, the animal; second, the intellectual; third, the spiritual; fourth, the living essence; and fifth, the unique essence, the one that binds us directly to the Divine. Through the *mitzvoth,* which are each designed for our physical and spiritual 'purification,' we ascend, becoming at each new level so much like the Divine we are attempting to reach that when we have refined ourselves both physically and mentally at the highest level, the fifth, we have no more work to do — the Divine automatically works through us, becomes us — no exercises, no techniques, not even prayers are necessary. All the exercises are only for the lower levels; they are designed to purify us, to make us more like the Blessed One."

Noah and Tony exchanged uncomprehending glances across the table. The rabbi indicated that I was to translate for them from Yiddish. When I had finished, the rabbi pointed to the plate of cookies. Noah took one. Rabbi Gideon tucked his right hand into the left-hand sleeve of his caftan and resumed: "The way of the heart, because it is connected with the emotions and therefore with the instinctual, animal part of man, is not as pure as the way of the brain, or the intellect, because the intellectual level of mind is closer to the spiritual."

"The Rav Bloch made a reference the other day to Plato, saying that the world beyond the mind, the realm of spirit, is an even higher region," I commented.

"You know that the word for that is *ruach*, 'spirit,' don't you?" He looked at me pointedly. The rebbitzen, a child hanging from her skirt, breezed past and disappeared into one of the bedrooms.

"And 'breath,' too," I murmured, but the rabbi didn't hear me.

"Torah is studied for reward in the world to come — or because the Jew simply wishes to observe the commandments of his Creator. Those are the dualistic, early stages of approaching God. But there is yet another level of study that results in *devekuth*, constant oneness with the Divine, which is the real purpose of our existence. Luzzatto, for example, says that this is the deepest and most significant practice for a Jew, the real purpose of studying Kabbalah: not only to serve God, but to *know* Him."

"That's what I've been driving at all along. But all you people seem thoroughly contented just to serve."

"What did she say?" Rabbi Gideon asked Tony. I had spoken quickly in a muffled voice.

Tony shook his head at me. "Do you want to learn something or are you here to fight?" he asked in English, addressing me firmly and clearly for the first time that evening.

Embarrassed, I hung my head. "I'll shut up. Tell him it wasn't important."

Rabbi Gideon had probably caught a word or two of our exchange, for he smiled broadly and said, "There are only a few really great spiritual beings over the course of centuries who have earned this privilege of *devekuth,* although it is the obligation and role of every one of us to live toward this end. So we begin on the outermost level, the one we know best, the physical world" — here he removed his hand from his sleeve and tapped himself on the chest — "which, even in its physicality, is moved by the spirit within man. Without that spirit even our grossest functions could not take place." Flexing his hand, the rabbi moved his fingers toward the cookies again, then, lifting his eyes toward Noah, he said, "Take," as if he had picked up Noah's wish for a second cookie from their shared physicality.

"Thanks," said Noah, passing the plate down to me and then on to Tony.

When the cookies appeared at his place, the rabbi refused them and lowered his eyes. "The kabbalist, when he reaches for a piece of food, is consciously aware that the pleasure assigned to his taste faculties is inherent in the food, the eating, the assimilative and digestive processes, and the nourishment afforded by that food — all of which connect him to God."

There it was again: the Jewish insistence that it was only in the "everyday world" that we could locate the Divine. Noah and I, munching aimlessly, habitually, on our cookies were living examples of the unaware. Rabbi Gideon's meditation, however, was an ongoing state of mind; it was taking place even then, while we were eating. As he talked and gestured, indicating the cookies, and then the bottle of Scotch whisky, "Jewish meditation" in action was being exemplified. Life, for Rabbi Gideon, was one vast prayer! I could not possibly endure such a practice, although for one split second the thought was tempting. I could align myself with his tiny community, find a safe harbor in the walls of the old/new Jewish quarter of Jerusalem; it was warm in his flat, cozy with all those children running about, a like-minded community of mystics whose only reason for living was so to sanctify the material world that the entire universe would become nothing but God. Not through ascetic withdrawal in an ashram or zendo, but through plunging, with heart and head, into the created world itself. The thought was tempting, but only briefly. There were too many literal *mitzvoth* to observe, six hundred and thirteen, and I had not begun to enact even one conscientiously! The rebellious yeshiva brat in me had vowed, in fact, to defy them all.

Rabbi Gideon and I were alike only in our souls; our cultural habits were entirely incompatible. He wore a traditional costume out of the nineteenth century, a quaint remnant of the persecuted Jewish past. I wanted a practice combined with a life designed for the present, for the world (also sacred and divine in its own right) of jet planes, America, birth control, streamlined kitchens, and a planet nearing catastrophic entropy too fast for *mitzvoth* to stop it. Besides, too many of the precepts were no longer even physically applicable, for they pertained to the Temple, which history had reduced to a symbol. Spiritually, according to Rabbi Simeon bar Yohai, author of the *Zohar,* each Jew had to "rebuild the Temple" within himself. Rabbi Gideon already seemed to have built the foundation; but what of his wife, who was so preoccupied with children and housework that she could barely maintain her small flat, no less contemplate so massive a project as the Temple? Judging from her angry frown as she moved restlessly from room to room (never having been asked by her husband to join us at the table), running water and clattering pots in the kitchen, the rebbitzen was beginning to resent our intrusion on her family time. I longed to invite her to sit down but didn't dare.

"Where is the meeting ground between metaphor and literalism in Torah? The mystics have obscured it too much for the rationalists, and the strict fundamentalist interpretation of Scripture is only a husk without a truly nourishing kernel, a center to give it spiritual meaning," I said, having decided to forget the ubiquitous rebbitzen for the time being.

"When you begin to study Torah for its own sake, you know," the rabbi replied; "nobody can tell you."

I made a sour face. "Kabbalists claim to build on the physical. The Eastern traditions seem to shun it; they see it as an obstruction to the finer senses and, ultimately, to Truth itself. I'm too engrained with those Eastern attitudes to accept book study alone, to believe that there is nothing to give up, nothing to do, nothing to change in myself through strict and repeated mental exercises or prolonged sitting cross-legged in meditation on my pillow. It's not as simple for me as eating a cookie. Can a person just sit and read Torah and *know?* Rav Bloch says that after learning and concentration — deep concentration — something else, something finer, enters the human vehicle — a higher consciousness, if you will. When does this happen, Rabbi? When?"

Rabbi Gideon picked up a small brown book from a pile of four at his elbow. "This is Rav Berman's introductory book, *Treasure of the Way*; read it and get some answers to your questions. If you manage to read and understand one chapter there, the one on *devekuth,* 'cleaving,' then you can come back here and ask me more questions. Remember, I don't teach women," he added shyly, "but you can ask me questions."

Tony shifted uneasily in his seat.

"I'm sorry, I didn't realize it was so late," I said, afraid of uttering another word lest Rabbi Gideon withdraw his circumspect invitation. "I'll buy the book. Where can I get it?"

"Here, take this one," he said.

"Let me pay for it." I fumbled through my purse for a bill. The rebbitzen stood, arms akimbo, in the doorway, a menace from childhood. Noah took out a check from his wallet. "Do we make it out to the Yeshiva Bnei Uziel?" he asked.

"No, no." The Rabbi laughed, waving his hand at the fuss. "It's only twenty lira. Don't bother."

Leaving the twenty lira on the table, I thanked Rabbi Gideon for his time and wished him goodnight. I tried to thank the rebbitzen, too, but she had disappeared into the kitchen.

With the help of my brother, who was then teaching at the Hebrew University, I managed to read Rav Berman's chapter on *devekuth* in five days. When I returned to Rabbi Gideon's flat a week later, I barely had the chance to stick to our bargain and ask the first question before he opened the dialogue himself.

"So you liked the book?"

"Yes. At least it's simple. Rav Berman feels that we must become desireless in order to see God."

"You'll have to read it many times to see just how deep it really is," he said, no longer concealing his pleasure at my continuing interest in his teachings. We seemed to have tacitly settled on Yiddish as our means of communicating, for the rabbi continued without breaking for translation. Making a big circle in the air with his finger, he said, "You see, in the thought of the En Sof, the Infinite, there lies the entire Creation. Light and vessel are united in En Sof; even the light of the En Sof contains the desire to give and to get, but there they are not separate as they are in our created world of matter, where desire to give and to get are split, dualistically opposed. That is why Rav Berman says that severance exists outside of unity. In the world closest to the Divine, all is radiance. In the graduated descent from the primordial light, there are three lower worlds, all radiating with that light in lesser degrees. Good deeds and purification of our bodies and minds help us re-ascend to the highest light to which we are bound. But ascending does not mean that we empty the lower levels of being entirely and fly up to the Absolute all at once.

"For the Jew, the secret of this gradual ascent lies in the nature of the Sabbath. When we prepare our bodies and minds before the Sabbath, we make ourselves ready to receive that radiant light in its purest form. That is why it is said that Jews receive an *ibbur,* an extra soul, on Friday nights, so that we don't burst from the plenitude, from the overflow of the divine light that comes down to us on the Sabbath day in the form of the Shekhinah. On the other hand, those who violate the Sabbath fill the void of the three lower worlds and thereby nourish the husks of matter."

"Is this symbolic, or are you hinting that one must become a Sabbath observer in order to be a kabbalist?" I interjected.

"I am only saying that before performing the *mitzvah* of the Sabbath, you must prepare. That is the *kavanna,* the intention, the concentration of the six days preceding the Sabbath, when the opportunity exists for all to ascend," Rabbi Gideon replied, leaving me to interpret the symbolism for myself. Like Rav Bloch, he was not inclined to proselytize about *mitzvoth.* To perform or not to perform them was my business.

"The human being is the image on earth of the 'Small Face' of God. Each *mitzvah* completed by man therefore corresponds to a part of that 'Small Face.' When we perform them all perfectly, we are indeed creating a spiritual body for ourselves, because we then truly resemble God. Plant a tree, then you have olives; press the olives, and get the oil. Pure oil can be put into the menorah, where it burns perpetually. You can't get light, only opacity, from a gross vessel. So, when we start on the way, the Torah is a vehicle for conquering materialism and self-centeredness. In later stages of Torah, the *mitzvoth* involved are designed to correspond to the higher, more radiant worlds that can only be seen through 'spiritual eyes.' That is why those *mitzvoth* are so *irrational,* so difficult for us at this level of understanding to interpret. They aren't meant for the human mind to analyze, to ask why, since there are no *reasonable* answers once you have surpassed reason.

"Nonetheless, when you study closely you can begin to see the patterns in the Torah: Sabbath, the holidays — all of these are 'corrective' lights that correspond to our spiritual condition. In the final phase of the created world there won't be holidays; only Purim will remain because it is filled with the most light."

"I'll have to wait for the final Purim before even beginning to complete this vessel for the Sabbath," I said ruefully.

"Perhaps not. The average number of incarnations before enlightenment occurs cover a course of two thousand years. Each of the levels of man's consciousness — animal, intellectual, spiritual, and so on — are the equivalents of different incarnations as well. I would say that you are an old soul."

"Is that where I stand in the Jewish calendar?" I asked, smiling.

Rabbi Gideon answered, "He who doesn't speak evil has the key. Teach your tongue to say 'I don't know.' Always 'I don't know' in the world of dualism, where it is impossible to reach the final energy point with the brain, where perfect knowledge does not exist. You learn to accept your limitations; they, too, are from God."

Vexed at my limitations, I asked Rabbi Gideon for the names of people he knew who were enlightened.

"When a person negates himself entirely he becomes one with the Infinite. But you can't stay like that, so you come back. It is a communication with God called, in Ezekiel, 'Running and Returning.' You know the reference, madame, I am sure. Rabbi Akiva was said to be the most adept at 'running and returning.' But if you wish to annihilate yourself as a human being, then you do not return, you willingly remain in the En Sof."

"Buddhists call it Nirvana," I leaned over and whispered to Noah, whose head had begun to droop at all the untranslated Yiddish.

"But the practice is to negate yourself, your desire, before each *mitzvah* in order to induce egolessness," Rabbi Gideon went on. "That is why there are marks above the letters in the Torah, the little crowns like the hairs on the human head. In moments of total self-negation — as in Torah study without the hope of reward or in the egoless performance of a *mitzvah* — you are one with the Infinite. Those little 'hairs' sit above the letters to remind you that you can be drawn up and then released downward again, that you can *run and return* without danger when you are without ego. When the kabbalist enters the condition of 'love' and 'fear' of God, he is also running toward God and returning from Him; it's another way of referring to the 'cleaving.' " Rabbi Gideon stopped. "Translate for him," he said, nodding at Noah.

When I had finished my condensed version of the lesson in English, Noah said, "Wow, this stuff is incredible! I think I'll become a kabbalist."

The rebbitzen was nowhere to be seen.

"The paths are both general for Jews and particular for individual Jews. The Torah must and can be appropriated from within ourselves." The rabbi paused and said awkwardly, looking at the wall opposite, "If a woman finds the Torah in herself it can't hurt. She should not be stopped from learning. Even the talmudic sages made allowances for such women, saying that they should not be barred from study if they were so inclined."

"That was tolerant of them," I commented with a hopeless sigh.

"What you need," said Rabbi Gideon, "is a *mitzvah* to counter each limb whose desire is to *get* and to transform it into a desire to *give*. Our human existence is usually so habitual that even the observant Jew finds himself performing *mitzvoth* without *kavanna,* without concentration."

"Like mumbling the blessing fast to get it over with so you can eat," I said from years of experience.

"Kabbalah takes you beyond that. The *mitzvah* performed according to the Law is like coarse bread. Kabbalah takes you to the fine bread, much much higher and finer. If you learn Kabbalah with a pure heart, you come to knowledge. The path of thought, leading to yearning, leading to love, and finally, to action — brings you to *devekuth.* Yet the same path, when turned downward, can lead to 'sin.' We are given the potentials, the limbs and the free will, with which to exercise those limbs. The same arm can either slay or embrace."

Rabbi Gideon was very warm and open that evening. His face was slightly flushed from the pleasure he took in discussing Kabbalah; quoting from Rav Bloch's father, he again reiterated the talmudic opinion on the subject of studious women. "You have a good head, I can see," he said, his face reddening at his own boldness.

"A waste of time for a woman, wouldn't you say?" I replied.

"Usually a woman's way is simpler, more direct, than a man's. She helps her husband to ascend by performing women's *mitzvoth,* which are equally important. The human being alone cannot do it; you need male and female together on a physical level as husband and wife in order to spiritualize love on the physical plane," said Rabbi Gideon, unwittingly corroborating my intention to find the combined male and female aspect of God within my teachers as well as within myself.

A rudely slammed door punctuated our talk. Rebbitzen Gideon stalked in angrily. "It would be better if her husband sat near you and she sat at the other end of the table," she said to her husband in Hebrew. Then, without so much as a nod, she slammed yet another door and was gone.

The open window banged wildly in its frame, but Rabbi Gideon remained calm. He sat for a moment or two, then turned to Noah and asked thoughtfully, "What do you do for a living?"

"I'm a doctor," Noah answered in Hebrew.

"And what do you think of me?" Rabbi Gideon asked.

"I think you are one hundred percent healthy."

"Healthy? And studying Kabbalah?" Rabbi Gideon teased.

"Totally healthy," Noah repeated.

"And what is your purpose?" The rabbi turned to me.

I stopped and fiddled with my pen, looked down at my notes, and said, "My purpose?" The Hebrew word he used could also have been translated as "profession," and I chose to answer to that. "I'm a writer."

"Ah."

"I used to teach in the university, but now I write." Rabbi Gideon raised his eyebrows.

Then, sheepishly, I added, "But my purpose is to repair my severance from the state of oneness. *Devekuth* is my purpose." I did not say that I had no inclination for performing *mitzvoth* in order to do so. I did not say that I could try to overcome my "desire to get" or that I could study Torah with egolessness. I could not say that I knew the answers to even the simplest questions; after all, the rabbi himself had advised me to reply "I don't know" to any query posed in this dualistic world. Coming as I did from a limited and impermanent place of constricted vision, "I don't know" was always true.

"So we must remember that the human image reflects the Divine." Rabbi Gideon resumed from the point at which his wife had interrupted him. "The highest world goes from the crown of the head to the mouth; the second world of formation extends from the mouth to the chest; the created world is situated between the chest and the waist; and the material world lies from the waist down. That is why the Hasidim place a band around their waists before they indulge in deep contemplative prayer — in order to define the upper and lower worlds."

Another door slammed. Again the window shivered in its frame. Exercising her wifely prerogative, the rebbitzen this time put an end to the Kabbalah lesson.

I spent the following morning with Madame Ariel on her rear terrace overlooking the pines. Working with her had the effect of honing my awareness of my own fluctuating mental waves to such a degree that waking life and sleeping life soon shaped themselves into an unbroken continuum, like the beads on my ill-fated Indian rosary. Waking life, I discovered, was as "symbolic" as dream life. Simple events occurred in Jungian pairs: A friend named Sheila Gideon arrived from the States the same day I started my classes with Rabbi Gideon; an imagination exercise with Madame Ariel in which I "saw" a snake, was followed by an event in which I saw an actual snake near a construction site in East Jerusalem; Noah and I had exactly the same dreams for five nights in a row. Yet there was nothing occult or supernatural about these experiences. So-called telepathic communication became as real to me as making a telephone call from the broken-down booth in front of the hole-in-the-wall grocery at Madame Ariel's corner.

The interconnectedness of consciousness — whether I was awake, asleep, in stupor, or hyperalert — was as real and palpable to me as eating my Jaffa orange every morning and feeling the *real* squirt of *real* juice on my tongue. It was at once liberating and too intense to be walking around in a human body with a mind like a glistening, sharpened razor. There was no longer any dividing line between the absurd and the rational. I woke one Saturday morning to find that the clip-clop of camel's feet was not taking place in my "sleeping" dream at all, but that a gaily clad, flesh-and-blood Bedouin out of the *Arabian Nights* was actually galloping down the main road to the university on a caparisoned camel. To live with the mental channel always tuned on "imagination" was like being on a perpetual high. After a month or so, I was ready for a vacation from the intensity engendered by the "awakening dream," as Madame Ariel called it.

"Why don't you declare yourself openly as a spiritual teacher?" I asked her one morning. "Your work is as profound a form of meditation as any I have studied."

"The difference between me and a guru is that I am always in life. I take people as they are, not to make them over into any set image prescribed by tradition. I only help them to find what is best in themselves, not to 'enlighten' them according to any external goal. You are having these so-called mystical experiences because this is what you are inside yourself. I only worked with what you brought; many years of yoga are responsible. Not everyone wants illumination — the majority doesn't." Madame Ariel was sewing a beautiful tapestry depicting the Garden of Eden. A golden tree overarched a globe representing the earth; the sun was formed of golden threads; blue and green birds seemed to flit between her deft fingers. She held up her thimble-covered thumb. "Don't tell Noah, but this is for him, an *image* of his attempts to connect heaven and earth," she said, pronouncing the word in French, *eem-age.*

"I think he already knows it," I said. Noah had confided to me a week before that "Madame Ariel is putting me in Eden."

"Why do you pretend to be a housewife?" I persisted. It annoyed me that she could balance herself so accurately at the center of the high wire dividing the sacred from the profane when I was so shaky at it, so intent on acrobatic tricks and meditations, and still so subject to falling.

"To help my students rid themselves of old negative habits without imposing any exotic notions on them, not in direct teaching, but as in a game, in *living*. Then they really find their own way; through the proper instincts of the body and with the natural rhythms of life, my pupils find the path to God."

I was astounded. Madame Ariel had never before taken such a religious tone with me. Her mica eyes were, as usual, looking through me. As she uttered the word "God," I got my first glimpse of her profound power.

That night, I dreamed of the "unique essence," the highest level of the human soul:

I walked through the maze of the Old City trying to find my way by touching the walls on either side of me. On the empty street there appeared a figure, a female Taoist priestess, who instructed me to "see" my thoughts as they occurred, palpably, and then to watch the thoughts of every passerby. With the priestess at my side, I walked to the middle of a busy thoroughfare and stood looking into people, a witness to the permanent flame that connected them to the fifth, and final, stage of consciousness. But when the priestess proposed that I follow her and see "still further," I refused.

"You are a Taoist and I'm Jewish," I said. "I can't put on your hat."

In an attempt to find out just *how* Jewish I was, on the Sabbath following my dream I went to a traditional morning synagogue service — for the first time in over twenty-five years. Lacking courage, I coaxed Sheila Gideon into coming along, promising her that I would be taking her on an "Eastern adventure."

"I'll go to any service," Sheila, a spiritual seeker of many years, replied. "I wasn't raised as any kind of Jew, so it's all the same to me." She was a passionate auburn-haired woman who was almost as avid as I for some teaching or other, but she was propelled in her search by even greater inner violence.

The two of us wound our way toward Rabbi Gaon's synagogue through the narrow dirt roads behind the marketplace. It was eight in the morning, but the sun was already hot, the streets filled with Sabbath observers dressed in their best silk caftans and pancake-brimmed mink Sabbath hats. Wives walked behind dignified bearded men whose hands were clasped behind their backs, a gesture of meditative concentration that made them look like nineteenth-century Polish prime ministers. Each one had a blissful, rapt expression on his face; their wives only looked downward with averted eyes so that you could not tell if they were contemplative or angry. Birds sang. There was an unearthly sweetness to the morning; again the lines between real and unreal, concrete and imagined, were beginning to waver. The tiny laundry on the corner before you turned in to Rabbi Gaon's road assumed a sharper, clearer angle than it did on weekdays. Jerusalem, like its individual Jews, was also graced with a Sabbath *ibbur*, an extra soul. My friend Sheila looked radiant; even she, an atheist, felt it. Her gait was looser, her eyes had lost their haunted look, and her auburn hair shone around her face like a halo. We walked in silence until we reached Rabbi Gaon's synagogue in the courtyard off the long alleyway. We climbed the stairs and looked inside. Three men stood talking animatedly over a large, ornate Torah scroll spread open on the lectern before the ark. They were so immersed in their scholarly dispute that they had not bothered to remove their prayer shawls, though it was obvious that the service was long over.

"Sirs," I called into the cool, dark synagogue. "When is your morning Sabbath service?"

A swarthy Yemenite with a woolly salt-and-pepper beard looked up and called back at me from before the ark: "You are too late; we begin at four so that we can say the Amidah as the sun rises."

"Some kabbalist I am," I said, leading Sheila back down the steps and out through the sunlit courtyard where, two years before,

Rabbi Gaon had predicted that I would help to bring the Messiah. "I forgot all about the sun."

We walked a few feet down the narrow dirt road, looking into the innumerable tiny synagogues dotting the residential quarter of the Jewish market.

"Here," Sheila said suddenly, placing a lacy handkerchief on her head, "let's try this one."

She was so forceful and deliberate in her choice that I did not resist but followed her into a small stucco house with aquamarine shutters. The front entrance to the synagogue stood wide open to the street and led immediately into the men's section. To the left, quite exposed, without so much as a waist-high partition, was the women's seating area. Hardly three feet from the open doorway, a young boy stood reading the Torah in an unfamiliar Arabic-sounding chant. When he paused to wait for the congregational response, he tenderly covered the open scroll with a filmy silk scarf — as if he were covering the modest face of his bride. I had never seen anything like that gesture before in any synagogue of my child-hood. Eager for something exotic to draw me back into the fold, I acceded to the five wrinkled women in flowered headcoverings who extended their heavily braceleted, jingling arms toward me in welcome.

The whole room perked up at our arrival; what had lapsed into a lackadaisical, ordinary morning service suddenly became infused with new life, a sense of performance. The old women passed us prayer books and shouted into the men's section for their husbands and sons to slow down the service for the sake of the new guests. Shelia turned red and stared down into the unintelligible Hebrew text that a plump grandma had placed in her hands. A toothless woman wearing magnificently carved rings on almost every finger passed me a gumdrop. I was amazed at the wild informality, at the shouting and constant verbal interchange between men and women, at the good-naturedness of it all. In spite of the apparent chaos, the worshipers never missed a line of their prayers. Indeed, all the shouting and gesturing and anthropomorphizing of the Torah scroll seemed to have brought the divine "Mother" more palpably into our midst. At the sanctification of God's name, the members of the congregation rose as one and rocked on their heels. As the Torah was lifted up in full view of the assembly by the young boy who had been chanting, everyone suddenly cried out: *"Shalom, shalom! Be Yisroel ve be olam!"* Peace! Peace! In Israel and in the world. The women ululated and threw kisses at the "Mother" as she was replaced in the ark. Some saluted her by tossing tiny white pebbles at her from their pockets. For a moment I felt I had been transformed, especially when the priests rose, covered their heads and faces with their prayer shawls, and blessed us, crying the benediction in an ancient Semitic wail that stirred me down to my shoes.

"I loved it," Shelia said as we walked away from the Oriental neighborhood toward my flat. The European worshipers in the fur hats were walking home, too. The big Sabbath lunch was waiting for them, and later the afternoon stroll, the visit, the snooze.

I felt the old, inexplicable synagogue nausea rising in my stomach and the pounding between my eyebrows. "It was different," I replied cautiously. "But I have the beginnings of a migraine anyway."

"I don't understand what you're doing here," said Sheila. "But now's obviously not the time to ask you. Your face is as green as that tree over there; you look as if you're about to puke."

Once home, I flopped, fully dressed, onto my bed and slept away the entire Sabbath like a drunk sleeping off a hangover.

That evening Monsieur Gilbert brought a group of his followers to Madame Ariel's house. I knew instantly that there would be trouble when I saw them enter: a motley hodgepodge of yogis, ex-Buddhists, returned Jews, and fashionable Parisians, Monsieur Gilbert's students — two sweet things in their twenties, one long-haired, slender sylph in a white toga and gold mesh shoes, a bourgeois lady from Tel Aviv covered with blue eye make-up and layers of expensive jewelry, an intense, abrasive Israeli painter in a purple shirt and Sufi skullcap who informed us defensively as he entered that he was "now living in Paris," and a black-haired giant of a man in white cotton trousers and Indian kurta who had a big black beard and kind eyes. Pierre, as the giant was called, immediately assumed leadership of the group. His prominent black eyes, forceful aquiline nose, and bulging muscles compelled our attention. Without waiting for Madame Ariel to introduce him, he informed us that he was a hatha yoga teacher in Paris, a follower of Swami Sivananda. Accustomed to the respect of smaller people, Pierre did not wait to hear anyone else's name before announcing to one and all in sententious French: "I have come here in order to understand Jewish mysticism. My search is meant to show that all the traditions lead to the same place."

The mercurial painter in the purple shirt instantly sprang forth and seized the spotlight. "Madame Ariel says you have written on Kabbalah." He gestured accusingly at me. "What knowledge do you have of the methods?" he ended with a sneer. "How do you compare Buddhist, Hindu, and Tibetan meditation with the Jewish system? Who are your teachers?" He ran on without stopping for breath. The painter was so volatile that even the threatening giant looming only yards away did not faze him.

"My teacher is Rav Yehoshua Bloch," I said with dramatized simplicity, aiming the bombshell straight into the painter's hostile face and enjoying every second of its stunning effect. A vast silence stole over the room. So, I thought, it's going to be a sparring match.

"He doesn't teach women," someone mumbled in French behind me.

The Tel Aviv matron pushed her chair close to mine. "Would you outline the contents of your book for me, please?" she whispered obsequiously as she pulled a slim gold pencil from an elasticized locket around her neck.

The resilient painter sprang to his feet. "Never mind the preparations, let her tell about a practice. Let her say what she learned from the Rav Bloch about meditation." The painter was slier than I had given him credit for.

"Do you expect to bring Jews back to the fold?" asked the sylph in the gold shoes.

Questions were raining in on me from every corner of the room. "I don't know whom to answer first," I said, aware that Madame Ariel was studying my every move under pressure.

"What can this accomplish in the way of opening the practice to ordinary people, and to women in particular?" cried out one of the sweet young things.

My hands were sweating; I swallowed my customary impulse to spit out something sarcastic and end the meeting then and there. Instead, I mumbled a few incoherent French sentences about my own attempts and minor successes at scaling the heavily guarded Jewish fortress, but I was alert at every moment to the expressions on the painter's face. I expected him to cry out irately at any pause in my fumbling speech: "Give her the hook! Get that phony off the stage!"

From the anguished looks on their faces, it was clear that Monsieur Gilbert's people had no time for Rav Bloch's venerable Jewish preliminaries to mystical experience. They were eager to jump up the ladder leading to Truth two steps at a time. Now. Before the imminent collapse of Western civilization.

"The time is right," I cajoled them. "The world *is* moving fast, but the Jewish system is as potent as the Eastern ones. It is more inaccessible because the Jews have wandered away from home for so long, and because they are forbidden from proselytizing."

"Can the Kabbalah be practiced by Christians?" asked the French beauty in white.

"I'm afraid not," I said reticently, fearful of being labeled a bigot out of Rav Bloch's messianic camp. "The Jewish meditation demands an integration with the entire life of the Jewish community — with the language, prayers, daily practices of the precepts and Law. Kabbalah can't be lifted out of the tapestry of Jewish religious life. It's not just a sitting practice available to anyone, like Zen. Unfortunately or fortunately, it's tied to a religion," I said,

TOWARD A JEWISH "YOGA"   271

acutely aware that I, who had made no commitment to the religion, had no business lecturing on Kabbalah.

The artist in purple was equally aware of my falsehood; he foamed at the mouth with unconcealed rage. I was determined not to let him talk, not to let him disclose in front of all those people who I truly was.

"The transcendent phase of Jewish mysticism leaves all sectarian limitations behind, but the means to that experience — I am almost convinced — are Torah and *mitzvoth;* they are the heart of Judaism, and by extension, of Kabbalah, too. If practiced by a Christian, then, Jewish meditation would result in sure conversion."

The French beauty looked very grave. Painfully, she rose and walked over to Madame Ariel, on her pillows. Then she turned and said to the room at large: "I am a Christian."

Mortified at my blunder, I turned to Monsieur Gilbert for help. "Am I wrong in saying that to practice Kabbalah one must be a Jew?"

"Absolument!" he said forcefully, and everyone in the room began shouting at once.

What were all these mixed Hindus and Buddhists and Christians doing in Madame Ariel's Jerusalem salon? I mused amid the din. Was this group the embryo of the synthesis of old Jewish modes and new half-breed doctrines from the East?

Monsieur Gilbert gently commanded the floor. "I invite you all to attend my next meditation group on Tuesday," he said in a loud voice, the Tel Aviv matron simultaneously translating for the non-French-speaking guests. *A parody of the UN,* I thought, and potentially just as harmful, just as likely to promote misunderstanding and war in the world.

"What's the address?" called Sheila Gideon, always eager for a new teaching.

"Seven Rue Palmach," replied the sylph in gauze. "Near the President's house."

The misanthropic painter leaped to his feet. "I say there is no Jewish path," he screamed, "no Jewish meditation at all! I spent a year myself with the members of the Beth El Yeshiva, praying according to the Ari's *kavannot,* and there was nothing there, just a bunch of dried-up old men praying over letters they no longer understood. Then I went to Zen, and that is where I found some *real* practice, not just mumbling for old men!" he finished, an ominous leer glued to his face.

What are you doing here? I wanted to ask him; then, looking at Madame Ariel propped against her pillows in silence, I checked myself.

"We all come from different backgrounds," the woman from Tel Aviv interrupted him majestically, her diamond-studded fingers held up against the painter's fury. "Not all of us have had Yehuda's unfortunate experiences with Judaism. I for one have worked with a woman kabbalist near Tel Aviv for three years now, and her work, which is certaintly Jewish, centers on Jewish practice as a living thing, as part of your work, your marriage, how you wake up and face the world in the morning. But first," she eyed the painter critically, "you have to get rid of your psychological hang-ups and turn your anger into love."

"I'm not sure I get the point of all this," said Wilma, standing up and getting ready to leave. "It sounds like est or something."

A nasal Israeli girl with a Dutch haircut tried to intercede without success: "We all believe differently . . ."

The rich matron added, more aggressively this time, "The Jewish way and the other paths that Monsieur Pierre spoke of are not going to the same place. Definitely not!"

Pierre stood menacingly and stretched to all of his six feet five inches. With nothing but the ultimate Gallic contempt on his face, he headed straight for Madame Ariel. Before long, he and his Christian mistress were engaged in a private conversation with their hostess, ignoring everyone else in the room. Factions from Monsieur Gilbert's group were buzzing and arguing in three different languages with representatives of Madame Ariel's force. The salon had been transformed into a battlefield. I retreated dizzily to a corner — as far away as I could get from the painter, who had rallied anew and seemed to be threatening a fresh advance in my direction. Too many diverse worlds squeezed into one small space: Madame Ariel's salon, Jerusalem, Israel. Strange to say, I felt awkward and weary among these "new age" secular pilgrims whom I had once identified as "people just like me" — easygoing eclectics who flew from country to country like spiritual bees, distilling a spot of spiritual honey from this teacher and that, something old, something new, something borrowed . . . mostly borrowed. Nothing genuine about the attractive, educated, arty people who, like me, had only contempt for the Orthodox gum-soled shoes and shabby dark caftans. I looked around, feeling out of place. I was reluctant to admit it even to myself, but I had been more at home with the sidelocked Rabbi Gideon two nights before.

Pierre and his mistress left Madame Ariel for the champagne punch and cookies. Taking the French woman's place on the low Moroccan hassock near the bed, I said in a whisper, "This is too much for me. I'm going."

"You see for yourself that Monsieur Gilbert has difficulty with his pupils. He is a truly sincere, kind man, but he can't help his people to combine their lives with their practices. The painter is a very disturbed one. Zen discipline is very good for such a *typus*. He came in determined to fight you."

"I know. And he got to me, too."

"Aaah, that is because you were not paying attention." Madame Ariel smiled. "You must make what is working on the inside work on the outside, as I have told you many times." With that she pretended to hit me across the hands. "You must bring me a stick so that I may beat you with it each time you forget."

I laughed.

"Do not laugh. I mean it. You must go into the town tomorrow and buy me such a stick," she said.

It upset me to see just how serious she was about that stick.

The Rebbitzen Gideon was softer on the telephone when I made my next appointment with her husband. Determined now to continue my discourses with Rabbi Gideon until my last day in Jerusalem, I told Noah that we would have to "appease the wife by dressing more appropriately."

"We're on their turf and we can't afford to offend them," I said, tying on my headscarf.

Noah looked at me queerly and said, "It's easy for you to play games, isn't it? Well, I suppose it's no worse than the zendo."

"It isn't easy; you're wrong. I'd sooner go to Japan and shave my head than dress up like this, but I have a job to finish."

The rabbi greeted us with a friendly smile that, at the sight of Noah's embroidered skullcap and my long skirt and kerchief, broke into an amused laugh.

"Today you look just like a rebbitzen," he said, gesturing toward his wife, who smiled broadly at the compliment.

"This is for you, both of you," I explained.

My ruse worked. Although the rebbitzen still chose not to participate in our discussions, she stopped slamming doors; Rabbi Gideon dropped the "madame" from his vocabulary. The mood, once we had changed costumes, was totally relaxed. Rabbi Gideon even brought up the subject of a kabbalistic regimen without my asking for it.

"I'll give you a forty-day program to outline to all your American Jewish friends who wish to practice Kabbalah," he said quite spontaneously. "First tell them to retire at eight in the evening and to wake at two in the morning. Then they must go to the *mikva* and immerse in the ritual way. On returning home, they meditate for half an hour by visualizing themselves as sitting alone with God in isolation and reckoning their deeds before Him. Then they must study kabbalistic texts in Hebrew. Groups of people should get together and learn Torah for a few hours before sunrise. During the day they must study Talmud and the Laws. Of course, they must perform the *mitzvoth* before even beginning the practice, Sabbath observance being the most important by far. And it is essential that they learn the Hebrew language."

"Oh, is that all?" I asked without disguising my sarcasm.

"Tell them that is the program," answered Rabbi Gideon, still deliberately avoiding the second person, but clearly directing his regimen at me. "There is no easy way around it. You see, unlike other approaches to Kabbalah, which speculate or go around the point, Rav Berman's teaching is as clear as a correctly drawn map. If a man knows definitely where an oil field is located, he goes right to it, and he can then take another person to it as well."

We bantered and argued that evening like old friends. But toward the end of the discussion, Rabbi Gideon became inexplicably defensive. Even his movements grew jerky; finally, his hands fluttering nervously in front of him, he said, "I know you are not going to like this suggestion, but I think that the only way to interest the people you are writing for is to begin by studying the books in the original. There is no short way to practice. The practice of any spiritual path requires a commitment to learn that path in the original language and to practice its teachings as they were practiced by the masters of the tradition. Many have come here from India after a long time there and much hard work on themselves — with no results. Many of those are now vigorously involved in Torah and *mitzvoth* — through the back door, as it were. They are enrolled now in yeshivoth here, in the Old City, everywhere. They have come out of hunger, great spiritual hunger." Rabbi Gideon mopped his face. He was pointing his finger at Noah and me, talking rapidly now and with great passion.

"It is as the old Rav Bloch predicted at the beginning of this century: The new generation of spiritual seekers, he said, would be so hungry, so violent, in their search for the lost sparks of holiness that they would tear the doors down to find it. The old Rav Bloch was right. As you know, these are the pre-Messianic times, the ending of the two-thousand-year cycle of incarnations that mark the end of an entire universal cycle. That is why the best and most eager come from the new land, America; you are among those who have had everything in the material and intellectual world. You are sated — not like the boys from the traditional yeshivoth; they are contented with their love of God, Torah, and *mitzvoth*.

They don't seek Kabbalah — only the discontented, the ones who have become very hungry and know what good food is, the best food in the marketplace. Like a man who will spend all his money on a beautiful pineapple in the *sukh* because his hunger is so keen; even if he knows he won't have money for a place to sleep that night, he will buy the pineapple. His instinctive knowledge of the finest fruit is so accurate, so important to him, that he will sacrifice everything to get it."

Emboldened by the rabbi's passionate outburst, I said, "But you turn them off by giving them *mitzvoth* and the *daati* way of life as a prerequisite — old, dried fruit. Especially when they can go to other disciplines and be taught to meditate right away." I was thinking of the haunted painter and his trek across Europe in search of a living practice.

Rabbi Gideon was so excited that he had to stop himself from plucking at the sleeve of my blouse. Recalling himself, he leaned back in his chair and said more quietly, "Meditation without preparation is nothing more than autosuggestion, a fantasy. Mishna tells us that it is impossible for a leopard to change its spots or for a black man to turn white — that is how difficult it is for us to change our animal natures. We are tied to this illusory world, which we only perceive as logical because of our innumerable needs. Take the German people — high culture, rationality, democracy. Who could dream that overnight this highly developed civilization would become a nation of wild beasts? We are trapped by the illusions of the world and driven by our nature. Like the mythical animal also described in Mishna, a creature tied by its long gut that grows from its navel to the earth. Those two meters of gut and the little space on earth providing him with nourishment are all he knows. Most of us are like that mythical animal. Working on changing one's nature, one's ties, and hunger for the material world are necessary before one is ready to see the highest realms. And we won't settle for autosuggestion.

"That is why *mitzvoth* are necessary. First, to do them as a child who listens to its father without questions, without even understanding why his father wants him to do these things. Then, as one grows and begins to understand for oneself, to *see* the transformation that the *mitzvoth* bring about in all the worlds, to gain the sweetest pleasure from Torah — then one has truly developed into an adult. One fully understands the *mitzvoth* and performs them with perfect knowledge of their meaning and their effects. Everything that was once only *discipline* is transformed into a connection with God. *Devekuth.*"

It sounded right, familiar. But the thought of practicing *mitzvoth* without questioning them was still unbearable. "Were all kabbalists Orthodox Jews? I don't think so," I suggested timidly, terrified of the surrender the practice demanded.

"Of course," said Rabbi Gideon, stopping for a drink of water. "Even the most radical ones — except for Sabbatai Zevi and the like, who really dropped everything in their madness. Although kabbalists like the Ari suffered from the persecution of the traditional rabbis, they too all started from the base of Torah and *mitzvoth*. I would be fooling you if I told you that you could dispense with the *mitzvoth*."

He looked at me with eyes full of compassion and added gently, "I cannot teach a woman, but I will not shut the door on you. I am willing to answer questions from the sources you study. But let me assure you, as soon as you learn the Hebrew better and familiarize yourself with the texts, you will no longer have to search for 'teachers,' you will no longer have to knock on people's doors for their interpretations or their approval. You will find the way by yourself. It is all there in the work, and in you. You will understand it . . . I promise you."

"I'm not sure," I said. "I want to believe you, but I'm not sure. Can I still come back? Can we talk more?"

"Only if you have questions. I will be glad to answer them," said the rabbi, yawning widely.

"I guess you have to be up at two," I said.

Rabbi Gideon chuckled in reply.

For some strange reason, the sight of his chestnut-colored *payot,* dancing at either side of his face as he looked down the stairwell at us, suddenly filled me with joy.

It had taken many weeks, but I was beginning to see the situation in Jerusalem more clearly; and with my growing insight there came a greater clarity about the spectacle of disciplines a would-be Jewish mystic could choose from. The way of the Sephardic mystics, embodied in the practices of Rabbi Gaon and Rabbi Bassani, relied strictly on ancient esoteric readings of the Scripture and liturgy in altered states of consciousness. The Hasidim, especially the school of Rabbi Nachman, granted a more open path, but it was no less prohibitive for a woman. Since ecstatic prayer — centered on the figure of a rebbe and a tight community of Hasidim — was its essential practice, I could only hope to catch echoes of the teaching from the male-dominated tradition into which I was born. There was a Rebbe Alter who gave weekly lectures to women in Hebrew about the life and work of Rabbi Nachman, but his female students were never invited to participate in the heart of the practice — praying and singing and dancing out in the wilderness. Whenever I approached a Hasid for guidance in group prayer, I was told, "God forbid I should seed the ground for another Sabbatai Zevi and his orgies."

What remained for me was the speculative path of Rav Bloch and the distant promise of Rabbi Gideon's spartan practices. The "seculars" who were searching for Jewish spiritual teachings hung between Madame Ariel's eclecticism and Monsieur Gilbert's bold attempts to bridge the gap between Hasidism and the modern world. Out of respect for his courage, I finally attended one of his Tuesday night meditations.

In Monsieur Gilbert's flat I sat on a hard-backed chair in a circle comprised of skullcapped men and women of questionable orthodoxy, listening to Monsieur Gilbert read for twenty minutes from a Hasidic text in Hebrew. Then we were told to close our eyes and sit for fifteen minutes more. When the meditation was over, Monsieur Gilbert instructed us to tell the group what each of us had experienced. As my turn came, I felt myself lapsing into panic. I did not feel the "Jewishness" of the experience; I did not even feel relaxed as a result of the meditation. Except for the induction in Hebrew, the group could just as well have been gathered in some studio in Carnegie Hall, meditating on the full moon.

"I'm sorry," I mumbled when my turn came, "I couldn't concentrate . . . too many thoughts."

A considerate murmur arose from the faces around me. The girl after me said she had found herself on Mount Sinai with Moses; a neurasthenic boy felt himself surrounded by light; Sheila Gideon, always brutally honest, said she was feeling smothered by the intensity of everyone around her. It was like "show and tell" in kindergarten. Presently, the testimonials began, and "show and tell" turned into a religious encounter. A young South African got up and confessed to having prayed with the Beth El mystics to no avail. "I complied readily with their demand for orthodoxy," he said, "but they never reciprocated with the teachings. They have their innermost of inner sanctums, yet the rabbis are teaching the mystical disciplines to so few that the Kabbalah is getting lost altogether."

Again sympathetic murmurs rumbled through the circle.

The Israeli girl with the Dutch-boy haircut assumed a pained look and said, "Apparently the ultra-Orthodox have determined just who is and who is not 'pure' enough to receive the teaching. Women — never! Even the most eager and dedicated young Israelis, who have demonstrated their sincerity, their intelligence, their willingness to die for their beliefs, are kept out by virtue of their modernism, or their lack of *mitzvoth,* or secular attitudes toward clothing, life-styles, and women."

"What we need is a Counter-Reformation," I whispered under my breath.

The South African pointed to his skullcap and said, "Even if we *do* adhere to the *mitzvoth* they don't want us. It was only Monsieur Gilbert who made me want to perform the *mitzvoth,* not out of slavishness or the desire to bribe the authorities with my goodness, but because he showed me quite clearly how they related to my practice."

It was an earnest young crowd that surrounded me. As each of them rose to speak I saw that, in spite of their exotic differences in background and their varying commitments to the Jewish Law, all had grown tired of the East. They were nonetheless half-time Jews who wished to gain access to Kabbalah through the back door as yet unapproved by the "kosher" rabbis. Some clung to their Hindu and Buddhist practices out of habit; others strove valiantly to grow a hybrid Jewish/Oriental plant. They were mystics and traditionalists simultaneously, yet an intransigent Orthodox hierarchy resisted their pleas for acceptance, for the rabbis had chosen to ignore the old Rav Bloch's prophecy that it would be the "seculars" who would wrest the Kabbalah from the moldering legalists, just as the Baal Shem Tov had done two centuries before. And, like him, the secular high priests would empty the secrets into the streets for every common, ordinary Jewish soul to practice as he or she pleased. The question was: When? And, would it make these young people bitter if they had to wait too long?

"Why do you feel compelled to do it this way?" Sheila Gideon asked me as we walked together after the meditation down the narrow, honeysuckle-thick streets behind Monsieur Gilbert's house. "Learning Hebrew, reading so many texts you get headaches, banging at the gates . . ."

"I feel like Sue's counterpart in a way," I answered, imagining my childhood friend in India, wearing her white sari, seated apart from the sweating Indian virgin boys in her Sanskrit class, celibate.

"But at least she's getting the teaching," Sheila challenged.

"Well, the Lubavitchers are giving courses in Kabbalah to men and women, and there's a French kabbalist who lectures in public to mixed audiences here. Except that in the Lubavitcher's case they put the women in a separate room and the lectures are piped in by microphone."

"Wow," Sheila said, scraping at her cheek with her fingers.

"Jewish men must be the hottest men in town . . . gotta find me one. They can't so much as look at a woman without impregnating her."

"You'd be tumescent all the time, too, if you couldn't make love naked."

Sheila looked at me with raised eyebrows and an ironic grin. "You mean the Bible doesn't allow foreplay?"

I guffawed. "Oh, how am I going to work this out?" I shouted, hopping on one foot down the street. "Why did Rav Bloch take me so far and then abandon me? And Rabbi Gideon . . . Do you know that he recommended that I visit the Lubavitcher commune and talk to some American 'returned' Jewish philosopher, a kabbalist of giant proportions? And do you know what your namesake said?"

Sheila shook her head and stopped in the middle of the road.

"He said, 'Go see Blumberg, but don't tell him I sent you.' "

"Is he afraid Blumberg will think you're having an affair?"

"Of course not," I moaned. "He's afraid that he may be sending Blumberg the pox! I might have my period on that day and who knows what can happen! All women are diseased, unclean, bloody, and subject to fits with the movements of the moon." I hopped and howled like a madwoman past the sedate Dutch consulate. Inside, they were having a party: Tall, blond Gentile ladies and gentlemen could be seen on the open terrace, drinking champagne and wearing smart thin clothes.

"I'm a woman. A disgrace. Do you know that when my American scholarly Hasidic translator and sometime buddy — a liberated physicist, no less — when he gave me the name of a great Hasidic rebbe to visit in New Jersey, he also said, 'Don't tell him I sent you.' "

"My goodness," Sheila said mockingly, her eyes blinking up and down like a Victorian heroine whose bloomers had just fallen into the street. "My gooooodness!"

Together we made a haphazard pair on our way to the café in the park, where we had agreed to meet Noah for a malted milk. "You are Typhoid Mary in the Jewish world," said Sheila.

"But I'm going to bring the Messiah," I said, feeling tipsy though

I hadn't drunk anything but tea at Monsieur Gilbert's. "Rabbi Gaon told me so. And I'm Rav Bloch's 'bridge to the outside world.' And I'm Rabbi Gideon's only hope in bringing Rav Berman's works out in English and French. Otherwise they would rot here behind the walls of the Old City."

"Your magnetism, your inescapable sex appeal." Sheila was enjoying herself immensely.

"Maybe it's phrenology, or magic — my oversized head. Even Rabbi Bassani said 'I'll teach you' on first sight. Do you think it would be a good idea to try him again?"

"Didn't you once tell me he was very Orthodox? Isn't he the one with the hundred children and the wife you never see?" Sheila plunked me out of my pleasantly tipsy state into the realities of Jerusalem life.

"Either it's all diluted for public consumption, or the great ones are too old and preoccupied or too entrenched in custom — or maybe they don't even exist. The Hasidim who were on the verge of revolutionizing everything only managed to screw up by becoming just like everyone else and dressing in those grotesque Polish clothes. Ah, Sheila, too bad the ancestral blood still beats so hard in my veins. Judaism is my strait jacket. Authoritative sources inform me that the Messianic Age is just around the corner."

We walked down the ramp into the park toward the lighted café. On the terrace, handsome young couples drank coffee and gossiped; Israel was nowhere near the Messianic Age. Why was I kidding myself? I watched Noah as he tried to convince a harried waitress not to remove the two empty chairs at his table.

In Jerusalem at least, the sides had been clearly drawn: Monsieur Gilbert's novices performed the *mitzvoth* — not fully, but with sincerity. They studied and meditated Jewishly, crowding themselves under Abraham's shield in the hope of a better mystical future. The Orthodox on the other side of town were barricaded behind their black caftans and tome-lined yeshiva walls, awaiting Armageddon. Long having forgotten the secrets of their faith, they spent their days devising new ways to thwart the secular government. Only that morning the radio had reported that the chief rabbi of Israel was seeking to introduce a law to bar Orthodox women from serving in the army. In July, an atheist was killed when his motorcycle crashed into an invisible wire that had been strung across the road by fanatics in preparation for the Sabbath. In the riots between the secular and religious Jews that followed, two people were taken to the hospital with serious injuries.

Those in the middle of the war between the Jews — the kabbalists who had earned their hard-won respectability by emulating establishment standards — were tentatively calling out their siren song to sharp-eared novices who could hear above the din. But only just enough to frustrate the disciples when they appeared. The kabbalistic middlemen were themselves fearful: They only opened the door a crack, then slammed it shut in your face.

Find your way for yourself. Read the texts; practice mitzvoth *and study Torah.* What did those puzzling instructions add up to? Zero.

"Again I repeat, why are you drawn to this path?" Sheila asked as we approached Noah's table. "If it's so rigid and so revolting to you to get up and pray every morning, or wash yourself in the *mikva,* why do you even bother going this far?"

"I really think Shastri is right," I said. "No rituals, no I'm-a-this and you-are-a-that — a woman, a Jew, a Hindu — nothing here but us human beings searching for wholeness. But the vehicle, Shastri himself, doesn't speak to me. I like the message but not the medium. And I'm not really a Buddhist. The Maggid of Mezerich moves me in my guts. Somehow I keep believing I'll get past the gates. It's because it's so hard that I do it."

But I wasn't sure I really believed what I had said. With only twenty-three years to go before the great *Shabbat,* the end of the two-thousand-year cycle preceding the Messianic Age, what were the kabbalists waiting for? They seemed to be playing games while every other guru in every other tradition aired the family treasure chest across continents. Rabbi Gideon insisted that he did not teach women, yet he encouraged me to telephone him with questions. Rav Bloch claimed that he and I were spiritual business partners, then cut me off as if I were a noisome traveling salesman.

René Gilbert, as kind, earnest, and generous as he had been with me, was a bit too catholic in his tastes, less fruity than Nissan Rosenberg in New York, but permeated by the same air of incompleteness. None had reached me like the Rav, the little troll in his cave under the bridge. Not even Madame Ariel, the fairy godmother on her silken cushions, could inject me with the faith I needed to "scale the pyramid to the top," as she put it. Though it was my own by rightful inheritance, the Jewish ladder had proven harder to scale than all the disciplines I had ever undertaken. It was like trying to climb on air.

9

The Women

O N A F R I D A Y M O R N I N G, in a crowded flat on the Street
of Pines, beyond a flower-fringed walk and a big iron gate,
I sit surrounded by book-lined walls; a fat tortoise cat licks
its paws on an old brown sofa under hastily strewn covers; more
books, magazines, papers, clothes, thimbles, thread, are scattered
everywhere. Rebecca Polakoff, a silver-haired, stout, and cheerful
naturopath, ex-Argentinian theosophist, and her daughter Gabriella,
a chain-smoking intellectual, fluent in six languages, sit around a
small sewing table and search with me through the mystic texts for
a rationale for performing *mitzvoth*. Gabriella is one of Monsieur
Gilbert's regular meditators; she attends every lecture she can find
on mystical subjects — French, Hebrew, Spanish, German, and
who knows what — she finds them all as they pass through Jerusalem on their way east, west, north, and south. She is as intent
in her search as I am and as congenitally hostile to the dreaded
prospect of orthodoxy; yet she is better equipped by temperament,
more tolerant. Gabriella is frustrated by Judaism, but she is totally
committed to it. Madame Ariel chose her as my translator for perhaps that reason.

So here we sit, reading Rav Berman's unvoweled text: a woman of seventy-five, her fortyish daughter, and I, a stranger, drawn together by our femaleness, our second-rateness, attempting to penetrate the deepest male mysteries of body and soul for Jewish enlightenment.

The old Rebecca looks up from the book at which she has been peering for over an hour; shaking her head in amazement, with tears glistening behind her glasses, she says, "Before you two gave me the courage, I didn't dare read these books." She makes a sweeping gesture at the heavily laden shelves, the same black tomes that line Rav Bloch's and Rabbi Gideon's walls. "And now, thanks to you, I am reading and myself understanding the books I began collecting twenty years ago."

Three women sitting close under a lamp in Jerusalem, stared at by a quizzical tortoise cat; outside, beyond the high dormer window, is a long empty clothesline — *umbilicus mundi* — linking us to . . . where? Further still, red-tiled rooftops, an olive tree, a pomegranate tree, mourning doves calling doleful songs and flapping high into the flawless blue.

"Doesn't the air of Jerusalem tell you something special?" Rebecca reads my wandering mind. She has followed my gaze out the open window. Her voice breaks her daughter's concentration, and Gabriella stops reading.

"What has all this to do with wearing *payot* and *tzitzith* and keeping kosher?" she asks.

Rebecca and I giggle. I stare down at the patterned tile floor and the endless heaps of books in four languages — yoga, Kabbalah, homeopathy — and I yearn for Rav Bloch to take me back.

Three women under the lamp, gathered from far-flung places, sit groping for the truth so that one of them may be equal to the task of approaching a teacher who does not teach women. Rabbi Gideon is forty years younger than the matriarch sitting at my left, yet only he can substitute for the venerable and inaccessible Rav Bloch. Madame Ariel's children and grandchildren have arrived from Paris, making her inaccessible, too. I am entirely on my own now, making my way through my own dreams as if I were wading through dark waters in a pair of cast-iron shoes. Accompanied by two uncertain women, a tortoise cat, and a lamp, I am at once teacher and taught.

That night my journey leads me through the ancient Sephardic quarter outside Tel Aviv. Noah and I drive down the poverty-stricken, cramped lanes with their row upon row of one-room stucco houses and corrugated tin roofs. I am searching for a rumored female kabbalist, a practitioner in secret. The address given me by Rebecca Polakoff turns out to be a ritual bath house near a synagogue in the heart of the worst of the slums. It is almost night when we arrive. By the time we have found the bath house it is nine-thirty, and the synagogue and bath are long since bolted. In a nearby house an open door reveals a scene from a Mediterranean genre painting: two men in undershirts seated around a dinner table, watching a blaring television set. Two rough, dark fellows eat while a dark young woman serves them briskly in deferential silence. To her the hairy men are to be admired, feared, served without complaint — as elevated as any great rabbi or student of Torah is to his rebbitzen. The Hebrew word for "husband" is *baal,* lord. The traditional Jewish way of life, the first *mitzvah* for woman, is to serve him. I conquer the urge to turn and run.

In a corner of the room is a blond teen-aged girl in shorts.

"You want the Dinah who works in the bath house?" she asks incredulously, as if no one worthy of her opinion would bother asking for a creature such as Dinah. The two ruffians turn to look at me. "Take her over," one says solicitously, unexpectedly gentle. "She'll never find it otherwise." To protect women, first family *mitzvah* of the Jewish man.

The long-legged blond girl hops on her bicycle and motions for Noah to follow her in our car slowly around the dirt lanes to the next street. In the dim corner lamplight, I see a mauve stucco house with aquamarine shutters. The girl gracefully leaps from her bicycle and calls at the shutters: "Dinah, Dinah. Someone here to see you." A muffled voice responds from inside. I am awakening a woman from her sleep. The shuttered porch opens, revealing part of the interior of the minuscule room that is Dinah's house. The light from the street catches a white pillow, a bed. A small woman appears, wearing a red-on-white polka-dot nightdress that she holds closed at the neck. Her right hand is bound by a handkerchief; around her head she wears a bright yellow scarf; dark tendrils escape from around her ears. Her lobes are long and exaggerated, like the Buddha's. Dinah has a high aquiline nose, a small delicate face, and brilliantly lively blue-gray eyes. We confront each other suspiciously under the street light.

"Rabbi Gideon's sister-in-law's student Rebecca Polakoff sent me," I say in French. Dinah replies shyly in Hebrew and then in French, saying that she knows nothing. All the while, however, she searches my face for a clue as to why I am standing here in front of her kabbalist's cell on a Friday night, why I have come all the way from New York to ask her about things she has chosen to keep secret from the world.

"I have been told you can teach," I say outright.

"I only work at the ritual bath around the corner," she says guardedly.

"I heard differently," I say. We are feinting, awkwardly testing each other. Suddenly she grows tired of the game and says with a bold smile, "I taught myself everything. Who are my teachers? They are the Ari, of sacred memory, and Rabbi Simeon bar Yohai. I learned from their holy books and from my own understanding. I didn't know a word of any other language but French when I was living in Paris after leaving Algeria. Then I taught myself Hebrew from ABC, and with a dictionary I began reading the holy books. I am a seamstress by profession." The light from the street illuminates her dancing eyes. "I am still in the process of learning. I do not teach anyone but myself. I study alone. Until recently, not even my husband knew."

"Do you practice any system of disciplines?"

She responds with a pursed smile. "I'm sorry I can't ask you in. I don't turn on the lights on Shabbat. Return perhaps tomorrow night and we will talk about these things. Was the yeshiva in Jerusalem you referred to Bnei Uziel?"

"Yes."

"The Gideon family?"

"Yes."

Her face grows radiant. "Ah. That family. So you study the Berman system?"

"I have only just begun to read a little and to ask Rabbi Gideon a few questions."

"But I study alone. Only the books are my teachers."

Noah steps between us and takes up her hand with the handkerchief bound around it. "What's wrong with your hand?"

Instinctively "modest" around strange men, Dinah withdraws it immediately from his.

"He is a doctor," I assure her, "and you seem to be injured."

"I have had three visitors from France, and I cut myself opening a tin while making dinner."

"Let me see," Noah says.

This time she does not resist him but spreads her fingers, revealing a darkened, jagged cut inside her thumb.

"Have you seen a doctor?" Noah asks.

"Yes, two weeks ago."

"But this is infected. Have you been taking medicine?"

I can barely keep up the French translations of Noah's hasty English questions. Dinah looks at me wide-eyed, like a helpless child.

"Tell him I have applied sulfanimide," she says apologetically.

"That's no good. You must apply peroxide, three percent diluted in water," Noah says.

Dinah nods her head obediently. She has understood the word "peroxide."

I recall suddenly that I have a bottle of penicillin tablets in my purse. "She looks really infected. Can I give her these?" I ask.

Noah is delighted at my find. "I'll never criticize you again for carrying so much junk around in your bag," he says.

Black lines have formed in Dinah's hand at the juncture where the cut must have taken place.

"Give it to her."

I remove the bottle containing thirty-five tablets. Dinah looks puzzled and yet seems pleased that these strangers falling in out of the night have journeyed from abroad to give her medicine and relief from her smarting hand. I turn around; the blond teen-ager is no longer with us. We are alone in the middle of the dirt road — Dinah, Noah, and I. She trusts us now.

"You'll come back during the middle of the week and we can talk of these things. On Shabbat I speak only words pertaining to Torah and Mishna. We can speak of all this during the week when we meet again."

Noah is insistent. "But you must now begin to take these pills every six hours. It is now ten-thirty. What time do you usually go to sleep?"

Dinah gives him a surprised look. "Nine."

"And awaken?"

"On Shabbat at six-thirty. On ordinary days at four-thirty, to pray before leaving for work."

"Then you must take one now, and another again at six-thirty this morning, and then around the clock, every six hours if you can." Noah presses her palm. "Does it hurt?"

"Yes, a little." She bites her lip.

"Make her understand that it is infected and that she must clean it not with sulfanimide but with peroxide, and that she must take all these pills in the next few days."

I relate the instructions in a mixture of Hebrew and French.

"Yes, yes," she answers wearily, "but will they upset my stomach? Must I eat first?"

"You can take them with a glass of milk or with some yogurt. They won't upset your stomach."

Dinah looks very young and very pretty suddenly. Clutching her polka-dot dress to her chest, she goes into the house and fetches a piece of paper in which to wrap the pills. I hand her the full bottle and show her how to open the childproof cap.

"Tell her to see her doctor again on Sunday, as soon as she can," Noah says.

"How old are you?" Dinah asks me bluntly.

"Past thirty-five," I say, immediately aware of her thought that I am under forty and therefore ineligible to study Kabbalah.

"You'll take all the pills?" Noah keeps insisting.

"Yes, yes. I understand. Please forgive me for not asking you in —"

"We understand, of course," says Noah gallantly, as if we were not really standing out on a dirt road in front of a row of one-room tenement bungalows in the most dangerous quarter of Tel Aviv but in front of a mansion in France.

Dinah is so gentle, so glowing with faith born of soaring mystical flights, that I am humbled in her presence.

"Are you good at mathematics?" she asks me, suddenly intrigued and loath to part.

"Terrible," I reply.

"Oh." She looks disappointed. "I am good at mathematics. My way is through numbers, *gematria*, the numerical value of the Scriptures." She adds the translation in French to make sure I know what she is talking about.

"I know *gematria*, but I am not good at numbers."

"Fortunately I have a good head for mathematics," she says proudly, still lingering. We have become instant friends.

As she finally turns to go, Dinah bids me more enthusiastically to return. "Let us talk over these questions together," she says, taking me by the arm. I feel I am dream-walking again, imagining the encounter as I sit in the book-strewn house on the Street of Pines. Gabriella is reading Rav Berman's declaration that the time for revealing the "tradition" is now, and I am hiding my tears. I blink and find that I am standing in the middle of a shabby lane with a hidden female kabbalist and I feel that I am about to cry yet again.

"I studied the books alone and got the teaching," Dinah says reassuringly. "First Hebrew, then following each word with a dictionary." Even her speech is dreamlike.

"Goodnight, be well," I say to Dinah's frail, retreating back.

"Shabbat *shalom*," she answers; then she stops to kiss the *mezuzah* on the porch opening of her dark little room.

Climbing upward toward Jerusalem, I see the city encircled by a halo. No street noises. My body is taut; it feels as if it is being pilloried by unseen hands. How will I find Dinah again? And Blumberg, the American philosopher whose only address is Kfar Habad, a village of more than a thousand Lubavitcher Hasidim? Perhaps all these secret people really know each other, like an underground network of kabbalists with an unwritten agreement to bar strangers.

Run, fly, return — like the *chayoth* of Ezekiel's vision. Come and go, says Rabbi Gideon; let your soul leave your body and unite with the Infinite! In this haloed city, his own father lies dying of cancer, and the rabbi can still talk of deserting the body without so much as a quiver of sadness. And I am hastily running and returning in search of — what? Whom? A tiny woman in a red and white polka-dot dress, a *mikva* matron? These obscure madmen and mystics live in ordinary houses and do ordinary things. It is impossible to find them, to pin them down. No ocher robes distinguish them from the grocer or the Hasidic bookseller or the seamstress. They are so much "in life" that I may scour the length and breadth of the Holy Land to find them with no results. I wonder how much longer I must stay — and if I have not already been defeated.

10

Approaching the Mitzvoth

MY INFORMAL "CLASSES" with Rabbi Gideon (disguised as social visits to prevent any of us from imagining that he was "teaching a woman") were the most clear and informative interpretations of the kabbalistic disciplines I had ever studied anywhere. The basis of the Jewish path, as it turned out, was antithetical to all the Eastern systems I had experimented with: "We shall do and then we shall understand," said the Semitic Jews, in contrast to the Eastern preliminary demand for understanding our place in the universe before taking action. Jews were enjoined to perform the *mitzvoth,* the six hundred and thirteen precepts outlined in Scripture, before undertaking the flight toward the Infinite.

Rav Berman's texts disclosed a cosmic order consisting of four interpenetrating, repeated elements: vegetable, animal, intellectual, and spiritual. These "qualities" inhered as much in the higher worlds as they did in the body and mind of man. The initial task of the kabbalist was to purify these elements within himself by unquestioningly performing the *mitzvoth.* This total submission of ego would then create in him a new spiritual entity called a *partzuf,* literally a new "face," which, in turn, energized the physical, moral, and mental body as it purified the desires and promoted egolessness. Then, and only then, was he prepared to truly under-stand the essence of the *mitzvoth*. "Torah and *mitzvoth*" were nothing less at first than a discipline constructing a "physical" ladder to God; each rung influenced its upper and lower neighbors all the way from the highest point of the cosmic tree (the non-manifest world) down to the worlds below ours.

"You must be willing to work from the outside in if you are to do it the Jewish way," Rabbi Gideon said. "From the physical world inward, not meditating immediately, but choosing a *mitzvah* and doing it perfectly to start with," he urged, his eyes darting from Noah's face to mine.

"You simply must commence by doing the *mitzvoth* because the outer event leads — literally — to the gradual composition of the *partzuf*. Without a spiritual body there is no understanding of the spiritual world. Everything here is reflected there. You must re-member this point; repeated practice of the *mitzvoth* improves their quality not only here, on the physical plane, but there." He pointed at the ceiling. "Meditation is a 'decoration,' an adornment to the *mitzvoth* themselves."

"How do you do practical work without understanding its pur-pose?" I asked, truly agonizing inwardly over the problem. My mind would not let me assume an irrational, seemingly compulsive discipline — unless, of course, it found that discipline attractive. Zen appeared neater somehow. Watching every flexing muscle of the foot as I walked in meditation, with the sulfurous Dead Sea breezes blowing in on my cheek, was a million times more appeal-ing than the prospect of immersing my body in Dinah ben Aviv's ritual bath.

"The understanding increases with your spiritual ability. Both worlds work on each other. With faith you attack the 'vegetable' automatic part of yourself; the most superficial layer of the *mitzvoth* is in operation at this stage. You learn how to be automatically selfless, doing the act reflexively, humbly — not because it will in-crease your high opinion of yourself, but totally without a goal. This first phase in performing *mitzvoth* lifts you from matter to spirit. It comes completely of itself, this reversal. I assure you, since the vegetable nature is automatic, it is the easiest to change. It happens of itself, from replacing an old habit with a new one."

"Must we do all four selves in one lifetime?" I asked, beginning to catch a glimpse of Rabbi Gideon's meaning. Translated into "working on a koan," an apparently nonsensical occupation for no reason whatsover, the performance of a *mitzvah* like "studying Torah for its own sake" appeared less crazy.

"The Talmud teaches you how to perform the *mitzvoth*," Rabbi Gideon went on, "but Joseph Caro clarifies it further, more succinctly, in the *Shulkhan Arukh*. You must remember that on the physical level the *mitzvoth* don't direct themselves to reason, which is part of the intellectual self, but strictly to matter, the vegetable and animal part of the human being. Within the realms of the higher reaches of the intellect (I don't mean the problem-solving mind here, but *ruach,* the 'spiritual intellect,' as it were), we are moving farther away from gross matter. The *mitzvoth* are a kind of short cut geared to refine human nature irrespective of time and place; modern or ancient, the *mitzvoth* are timeless. Since human nature is consistently irrational, the so-called irrational *mitzvoth* — like not drinking milk with meat, for example — are specifically designed to change us from material beings into spiritual ones. There is no such thing as *mitzvoth* being too 'old-fashioned' for modern man to perform."

At last I understood. *Mitzvoth* were exercises not unlike yoga.

"The more developed the *partzuf,* or spiritual form of a person, the more he understands of the corresponding spiritual worlds. Once he has cleared away the obscurity generated by desire, he can see Truth directly. From the study of Kabbalah, he learns the higher levels of the *mitzvoth*. In the names of God, for instance, in the permutations, too, there are many levels. The name *elohim* is the level of nature that corresponds to the *nefesh,* or animal quality of the human being. That is why in creating the physical world, God is referred to in Genesis as *elohim,* God of Nature," said Rabbi Gideon.

"So in changing instincts into spirit, in spiritualizing matter, the Kabbalist changes ego into selflessness until he reaches the end of *mitzvoth,* the end of Torah?" I asked, growing more enthusiastic.

Rabbi Gideon nodded. "All the way to the redemption, not only of the individual, but of all the worlds along the ladder."

A little cherub with chicken pox marks all over her face sat in his lap as he talked, her huge blue eyes staring hypnotically into mine, her blond curls damp with fever. A boy of about eight, wrapped in a prayer shawl, stood near the bookshelf praying silently, rocking back and forth on his heels, as intensely as a little old man. An older, dark-haired girl with the motherly air of one accustomed to caring for a brood lifted the chicken pox victim from her father's lap. Brought down to the physical plane by her homely gesture, I reached into my purse and brought out a roll of candy. Rabbi Gideon put up a warning finger.

"Are you sure it's kosher?"

I studied the label of the English mints, finding nothing more dangerous than the usual artificial coloring and gum arabic.

"It's from England."

"Then you can't be sure," said the rabbi. "They could use gelatin."

Part of the *mitzvoth.* No candy made with pig fat; constantly on the alert about refining the material vessel for God. I sighed and replaced the unopened candy in my purse. The chicken pox victim wrestled herself free from her older sister and stretched out on a wooden bench opposite. Presently, with her finger in her mouth and her tattered brown teddy bear in her arms, she fell asleep.

Rabbi Gideon's house was like the shoe in the nursery rhyme: a magical/practical place, where the spinning worlds within worlds dovetailed into the chicken pox world of babies and mothers-in-law, like the one the rabbi rose just then to placate on the telephone. The widow Gottesman's snappish voice was loud enough to carry across the room, above the head of the sleeping child and all the way to the table, landing squarely on Rav Berman's cosmic texts with an earthy thud. Rabbi Gideon shrugged, pushed his skullcap farther back on his head, and calmed his irate mother-in-law on the other end of the wire. Then he returned to the table, saying,

"Rav Berman was a simple businessman, you know," as though apologizing for his own living example as a man steeped "in life."

"When I get the time, I, too, try to refine my material vehicle by performing *mitzvoth* — imperfectly, I am afraid — and asking questions as you do. But you must forgive me; I am worn out and we must stop for tonight."

Without much success, I tried to read Rav Berman's discussion of good and evil on my own. After one sparse insight into the relationship between my material and spiritual self, I decided to try a kabbalistic device for eliciting answers in dreams. Before going to sleep that night, I posed a question, addressing myself in the second person. In another "mental voice" I asked, "What is the relationship between the self and the other?" Lying on my pillow, I emptied my mind of all but my question and fell asleep rather quickly. In my dream, I found myself in New York, alone in SoHo among the art galleries and shops, walking past Sue's apartment toward a scholarly conference in which I was to participate as a speaker. Aaron Breit and many of the other doctors and scientists from the meetings in Kashmir were also scheduled to attend. In the lobby of the conference building, a man distributed a variety of chocolates, but I could not eat any of them because I had not yet found my "discussion partner." I wandered farther along to West Broadway, toward Canal Street, noticing that despite the rundown factory exteriors, the interiors of the buildings were all smartly renovated and painted in bright saffron. Suddenly the thought occurred to me: This is not the neighborhood for you. You are alone.

As soon as that happened, Noah appeared on the street. "I was alone until you came," I said.

"What do you like most about being together?" he asked.

"Union," I answered, putting my arms around him and hugging him hard. At precisely that moment I saw and felt both of us, along with the buildings, the sky, the street, and other people passing us by, as moving forms, substances floating in space and time. I knew these forms intimately, passing in them as they passed, moving as they moved without stopping; and I knew also that all we moving forms had given ourselves names and that we had named all other surrounding substances and events that were really nameless, and that if it were not for the names we had pinned on the entire spectacle of moving, passing, and interpenetrating forms, there would be no need to wish to stop or hold on to the process. It was a splendid, if brief, nameless and bodiless participation in the great flow. There the dream stopped.

Emboldened by the experience, I returned the next day to Rav Bloch's house. In the waiting room this time sat a group of long-haired Israeli hippies wearing white knitted skullcaps; one of them played a guitar and sang "My Sweet Lord" in accented English. Their leader, a wild-eyed young man in shorts and sandals, talked to me at length as we waited. For an hour he bombarded me with his blissful quest for oneness, his efforts to divest himself of the narrow parochialism of Judaism, and his six-month meditations. It was as if the Rav had planted him there, a wild, mocking parody of myself.

"Religion is all one," mouthed the hippie. "Why are the Jews so convinced that they are first, that they are chosen?" he asked loudly of Yakov and me in a contentious voice that belied his embrace of all humanity as "one."

"You go inside with him," Yakov pleaded with me in a whisper when the hippie's turn came.

The Rav did not seem surprised to see me despite my deliberate week's absence. Nor was he puzzled by my oddly matched companion. He greeted the boy kindly, then, inviting me to sit in my old place at his side, asked the hippie for his "story."

In a few excitedly garbled sentences, the boy disclosed his intense suffering. He was twenty-three years old and he had lost all interest in his job, the army, life, and he had experimented with drugs as well as with meditation.

"Have you ever studied Torah?" asked the Rav in reply to the long, confused tirade.

Wildly looking about, on the verge of tears, the hippie repeated angrily twice that he had studied it in school, "like everyone else in Israel."

The Rav removed his hand from the boy's shoulder and sat back pensively.

The boy cleared his throat. "I have no interest in the God of history. I wish to find the God in myself and in others. I wish to make connections with human beings," he said plaintively.

"What did you learn from Torah?" the Rav persisted.

The boy, his hair loosely falling over his eyes, leaned forward on his mosquito-bitten thighs. "I learned of leading innocent animals to the altar, of slaughtering with knives and letting blood flow; of smearing doorposts with blood; of an angry, jealous God who loves sacrifices!" A fierce combination of terror and challenge, the boy stared rudely into the Rav's face. "Now *you* show me how I can learn anything about God from Torah!" he spat out impudently.

"I will teach you," said the Rav calmly, looking directly into the boy's heaving face. "You have been emptied of Torah; your soul has become empty of Torah, and where it used to be naturally imprinted on you there grew instead emptiness and void. And now that void is occupied by demons. You are ill, confused and ill."

"What kind of meeting is this?" screamed the hippie. "I've come here to ask you, the great spiritual master of the Jews, to show me the way and you upset me like this. How do you mean I am ill?"

"You are confused and ill, and that is all I have to say." The Rav turned his face away from the young man and looked at me lovingly. That infuriated the boy, and he cried out at me menacingly in English: "You practice yoga; you said so yourself outside."

"Yes," I replied, softly, afraid he would crack and run amok through the Rav's fragile quarters. "But have you ever read the Hindu scriptures, the Rig Veda, for example? It, too, speaks of sacrifices. The Bhagavad-Gita speaks of battle and killing. You must understand the tradition you choose to practice," I said, knowing that it was futile to argue; the young man was too coarse of spirit, too deranged to understand.

"What does he mean when he says I've made myself ill with these practices?" he asked incredulously, by-passing the Rav, who seemed to have turned to stone.

"He means, I think, that perhaps too much meditation has made you ill. It works on the nervous system, you know. It may be why you feel the need to leave your work, the army — in order to escape from life, as you told me before."

The Rav remained between us, immobile as a statue. Lamely, I tried again to explain to the young man what I did not fully understand myself. Something terrible and awesome brewed in front of me, yet, despite all my years of teaching young men like this one, I did not know how to cope with what I sensed was about to happen.

"How do I differ from her? She has done the same things I have — yoga, meditation, and for much longer than I!" screamed the young man in Hebrew, unleashing his fury at the Rav and casting accusing flames from his eyes at me.

The Rav suddenly came to life. Very softly, so we could barely hear him, he said, "Don't compare yourself to her. She is full of Torah, and she is normal, healthy. You are ill and cannot learn."

The young man could not fathom this. He put his face in his hands. "How can that be?" he murmured brokenly.

"You are ill and confused now. Come back another time. We'll talk again," finished the Rav, his clear eyes glittering, not with familiar kindness, but as if he were perched high on an unknown rung of the ladder of the Ultimate, confronting invading demons in another state of consciousness.

The boy was in despair. "I'm not pleased at all with this interview," he whined, getting up stiffly from his seat. "I don't know if I'll come back . . . ever."

"Nu," said the Rav, not moving, not touching him on the shoulder, as I had seen him do to all who came and went.

The hippie walked back to the waiting room in a daze. Compelled to soothe him, to give him something to fill his void, I followed him and reassured him. "The Rav Bloch treats everyone differently," I said. "Some he takes in close and others he pushes away. I know because he's done both to me, and it's for a reason, I am sure. Don't be hurt," I said unconvincingly. The hippie eyed me with fury, then gazed around abstractedly at the walls of the hostile room that had given him access to the great Rav Bloch, the last of his Jewish disappointments. He had been brushed aside, along with his so-called spiritual quest, as if he had been a flea at the great master's table, and he refused to be comforted.

I returned to find the Rav sitting in a trance exactly as I had left him, his forehead drawn into heavy furrows, his eyes unfocused, gazing across the table at the bookcase with the missing glass pane that housed the *Zohar*. At first I thought he might have suffered a stroke. Then I became frightened, terrified at the thought he might be dead. No lovable troll sat in the Rav's seat waiting to hug me or clasp the hands of his favored Penina. Suddenly there was a loud clap, as if lightning had struck the table, then a moment's silence followed by another resounding clap. I watched in awe as the Rav raised his right arm about a foot from the flowered-linoleum-covered table and slammed it down yet a third time. There was a brief interval of silence, and the terrible procedure began again: three more perfectly spaced, thunderously loud claps of his powerful right hand on the tabletop. Was he driving out the boy's "demons" from the room? I wondered, not daring to move. Was it possible that the poor, misled fellow had carried with him evil airs that had to be slammed out with the flat of the Rav's powerful hand?

Timidly, I made my way to his side. "What's wrong?" I ventured, sitting down close to him.

"Nothing," the Rav answered quickly. "I thought I heard Yakov outside."

I knew not to press the point. "Here are the books," I said stupidly as I pushed the Luzzatto and Irgaz texts at him.

"This one first," said the Rav, opening *Guardian of the Faith* and peering at the introductory pages. He bowed his face down close to the book and read quietly to himself, turning pages abstractedly, now and then getting keenly interested in certain portions and skipping hurriedly past others. The thick pages sometimes got stuck in his beard, and I helped him turn them past him in silence, wondering still at what had happened, frightened lest he misunderstand my impromptu connection with the hippie and be angry with me somehow. Five or ten minutes passed in silent page-turning; then the Rav rose from his chair without so much as a second glance at me. Opening the door to the waiting room, he went out into the front of the flat and returned moments later — followed by a pack of fifteen yeshiva boys.

I shut the book and looked up at him. The Rav walked over to the wooden wardrobe in his bedroom, removed his black "teacher's" frock, put it on, and shuffled toward the bench in his floppy checkered felt slippers. I stood and approached him. Lifting his eyebrows as if seeing me for the first time that day, the Rav said, "And so?" — as if to say, "We are merely passive instruments. What can we do?"

"I can't come back tomorrow," I shouted into his ear, pained and confused by his mercurial behavior. The yeshiva boys looked at me disinterestedly.

"When?" The Rav cupped his ear.

"Perhaps the day after tomorrow. Shall it be four? Five? Any special time?"

"We'll see," he answered noncommittally.

"Okay with me." Shaken, I pushed my way through the crowd of boys toward the door, clenching my teeth. I felt as though the Rav had kicked me in the stomach in front of the boys, and my bowels were crunching hard with rage.

Taking the steps at the front of the Rav's house two at a time, I hurried into the street. Noah sat across the narrow lane, waiting for me in the parked car. Seeing me come, he rolled the window all the way down, reached into the back seat, and presented me with a huge bouquet of flowers the moment I drew near. "Happy Birthday!" he cried.

For the first time in my adult life, I, who had always made such a fuss about my birthday, had totally forgotten it.

Better never to have been born, I thought bitterly to myself as I kissed Noah and jumped up and down with pretended delight in the middle of the road.

Gabriella and Rebecca Polakoff were very excited about accompanying me to see both Rabbi Blumberg and Dinah ben Aviv on the same day. They thanked me so effusively throughout the trip along the Jerusalem–Tel Aviv Highway that I grew distracted. Passing the exit to Kfar Habad, I took a wrong turn and ended up in a potato field. Zigzagging crazily through the upturned furrows, deep in manure, I came at last into the main street of the Hasidic village in reverse gear. Luckily no one was there to see. It was siesta time, and one hundred and four degrees in the shade.

Contrary to what I had imagined, Kfar Habad was a handsomely developed colony of houses, schools, and synagogues surrounded by green shrubs, tall trees, and sumptuous flowers. The Lubavitcher Hasidim and their families were living a cooperative socialist-religious existence only a few miles from modern Tel Aviv, just as the Galilean kabbalists of Safed had done in the sixteenth century. Their practice, well known since the eighteenth century, when Shneur Zalman, the first Lubavitcher rebbe, inaugurated his own brand of ecstasy into the Hasidic experience, consisted of meditative prayer and devotion to the living master — who today, oddly, lived in Brooklyn.

Rabbi Blumberg's house was a spacious beige sandstone villa. I only found it by getting out of the car and tapping on doors picked at random until I located one family who had heard of "the new Blumbergs from America." Since Rabbi Gideon had instructed me not to mention his name, I had spent much of the trip down from Jerusalem making up likely stories to justify my presence there. Rebecca Polakoff, whose white hairs belied her naughty good humor, had recently taken a fall and was furious at being forced to use a cane. "As if you haven't got enough trouble making excuses to get in," she said, responding to the outrageous permutations and combinations I was rehearsing for Rabbi Blumberg's benefit. "You had to bring along a big, fat, old, helpless cripple!"

"You're the only reason he'll let us in." I laughed, taking her elbow and propelling her ahead of me. If Blumberg was indeed a "Baal Teshuva," a newly returned Orthodox Jew from the States, he would be even more meticulously careful about greeting strange women. Only an elderly crippled lady like Rebecca Polakoff could in fact breach the immediate gap that faced us on the other side of the closed door.

Rebbitzen Blumberg, blue-eyed and very pregnant, answered our knock and let us in with the slightly sour expression of her kind. The rabbi appeared almost instantly behind her. He was about thirty-four, pale, almost sickly; curly, sand-colored hair dribbled in question marks from under his black hat. He wore a white, short-sleeved shirt that revealed very smooth, white, girlish arms. Seating himself at a table in his study, Rabbi Blumberg cast his deep, dark brown-eyed glance at me, drowning me in two heavy pools full of meditation and kabbalistic pondering.

"What brought you here?" he asked in perfect American English as we were seated.

A dark-haired replica of her father, his five-year-old daughter wandered into the room dragging a stained pink security blanket after her. Hopping onto the piano bench to my left, she lay down flat on her stomach and promptly fell asleep. Only occasional thumb-sucking noises reminded us of the child's presence. In the kitchen beyond the open door of the study, the rabbi's wife made the customary homemaking clatter. At the peak of the afternoon heat, after fifteen minutes of conversation in the study, the rebbitzen cried out her husband's name from the kitchen. Blumberg rose and left, returning soon after with a cobalt blue pitcher of ice water and matching cobalt blue glasses. The rebbitzen had taken pity on the old woman; I had been right in bringing Rebecca Polakoff along.

I went through my usual three paragraphs about writing a book in English about Jewish mystical practices. I was bored with my justification speech, but it had proven successful so many times before that I did not bother revising it. Blumberg responded to it well, and by the time it was over he had accepted the legitimacy of my intrusion.

"We are here at the recommendation of a woman in Jerusalem named Inbal Stern. She runs a small Kabbalah class for women," I explained, trying to skirt the name Gideon, but hoping the rabbi would make the proper mental connection. And I did not lie, for both Gabriella and Rebecca Polakoff had indeed spent some time trying to learn Kabbalah with Inbal Stern the previous winter. Mother and daughter sat, limp and perspiring, on the sofa across from the rabbi.

The interview consisted mainly of sporadic questions from me and low, hurried English replies from Rabbi Blumberg. It was a purely intellectual encounter, typically clear, typically Lubavitch in style.

"Meditation through prayer is the Habad way," said the American rabbi, resting his glance on the old lady, who was now nodding over her cane with heat and fatigue. Briefly, his eyes turned in my direction, and I stared back at him boldly, expecting him to avert them, but he continued to look at me as he talked. He seemed happy, in fact, to be exchanging opinions with an intruder from his old world. No doubt the Habad Hasid sitting before me had once sparred in the Columbia dining hall with secular philosophers in his abandoned past. His discourse embraced existentialism, phenomenology, Buddhism, and even the occult.

"The Jewish paradox," he said, pouring water from the blue pitcher and handing it to Gabriella, "consists of the ability to live as if we are dualistic beings in an apparently dualistic world. That makes permanent 'enlightenment,' such as you speak of with regard to Buddhism, impossible — because of the continuing process of creation of *things* out of the No-Thing."

Gabriella gulped her water and yawned. Rabbi Blumberg talked faster, more softly, of the deepest mysteries, of "cleansing souls in the River of Fire." Both Rebecca and Gabriella were asleep. I could barely keep up with him myself; he was trying to bombard me with too much information so that I would grow bored, give up, and go away.

"Enlightenment comes after we have made progress through our faith (which, for the Jew, is the ability even to die for the One), during which we forget all the sensory experience of our life, and then travel through a sort of vacuum tube of air, during which the soul is pulled up farther, until all contact with past experience is ended."

The child on the piano bench stirred and moaned in her sleep.

Ignoring my questions, the rabbi continued at a furious pace, his voice growing lower and lower, sweat flowing freely from every pore of his delicate face.

"Physical knowledge is all embedded in Kabbalah. Everything that is being revealed now through the advances of science is contained in the kabbalistic wisdom books, which describe the nature of the universe — physical as well as spiritual. When all is finally revealed in the physical world, the Messiah will come. As the Baal Shem Tov said, 'When Kabbalah is no longer secret, Messiah comes.'" Here he stopped for breath and a drink of water.

"Well then," I goaded him, "we must be ready for the Messiah, since even women are eager to study Kabbalah."

"We are living in a period when there are no inspired teachers, when distance from God has become so great that . . . this is a time of the greatest evil," he whispered tremulously.

"According to the Baal Shem," I persisted, "the Kabbalah must become the property of women in the end of days."

"When the Messiah comes there will be no distinction between men and women," Rabbi Blumberg corroborated shyly.

Rebecca Polakoff slept as innocently as the restless child on the hard bench at her side. Rivulets of salt water poured down my face into the crevices between my cheeks and nose. My back was soaked through; I was being cleansed in a river of fire. It was like discoursing in hell.

"One must be filled from within with the Torah, the Way. Ninety-nine percent of the men, as well as the women, don't feel it," said the rabbi, reminding me of Rav Bloch and the "void" hippie of the day before. Since the kabbalists all apparently believed that Jews were imprinted with Torah by virtue of their birth, the "training" I was seeking so assiduously could only reveal itself in me through unquestioning faith. And that was impossible, because every time I found myself confronted by a rabbi, I became swollen with questions. Questions spilled out of me like water out of a resuscitated woman on a beach. I lost all control. I had no faith, only doubt and the challenge born of doubt.

"The Messiah must be on his way," I said brattily, "because you are talking to one woman among many who plan to be in the forefront when the Jewish secrets are revealed." The discussion was over.

I left Rabbi Blumberg's house no more enlightened than I had been on entering it.

Gabriella and I took a spicy Sephardic lunch in a roadside café: tahini, baba ganoush, and falafel sandwiches, washing it all down with several bottles of Coca-Cola. Sparring with rabbis made me voraciously hungry. Rebecca sat with her elbows propped on the table, chastizing us for eating such unhealthy muck, assuring us that she for one preferred to starve rather than abuse her digestive system so cavalierly. She was very proud of her naturopathic knowledge and very stubborn, even fanatical, about food. Gabriella, on the other hand, thrived on cigarettes and junk food.

We reached the poor slum streets of the Atikva quarter at one in the afternoon.

In the light of the scorching Mediterranean sun, Dinah ben Aviv appeared even more pure, more raw and simple, than she had on the dark Friday night of our first encounter. Inviting us in, she could barely contain her pleasure and chattered with great verve and sparkle about our fortuitous meeting. Gathering the three of us around her kitchen table, she said, "I promised to tell Madame Epstein about my system of *gematria*," and immediately began drawing Hebrew letters on a napkin.

"This is the word *kas*, 'anger'; now see what happens when I permutate the letters very quickly according to their numerical correspondences." With amazing alacrity, she jotted several numbers near each letter, then, as if by magic, she transformed the word for anger into the word *mikva,* ritual bath.

"Through the purification by water, both in letter and in deed, one can change 'anger' into 'holiness.' "

Rebecca Polakoff had at last found what she was looking for. Wide awake now, she pushed her face close to Dinah's and said, "How did you do it? How did you get the courage?"

"I am fifty-one years old," Dinah replied artlessly (I had taken her for forty-five). "I have been studying for eleven years, since I left Algeria and came to Paris. I worked all my life as a seamstress, but when the search and subsequent study became my life, my air, my food, I knew that I must come to the Holy Land to continue. I have no children. My husband is a postal worker. He is not religious; he has no idea about what I am doing or why. I searched as you did for rabbinical teachers, but being less educated, less modern, I faced much greater obstacles and humiliations. Even bookstore salesmen refused to sell me books on Kabbalah unless I brought my husband to buy them. Finally I gave up on all the rabbis. I found in the books themselves what I was looking for. And now I am totally isolated; having renounced everything, with only enough food to eat and clothing to put on my back, I pore over my books. I learned how to get the answers to my questions the hard way, through experience, direct experience. Sometimes it was bitter — dangerous, even. I learned not to meditate while menstruating, for example, because I experienced terrible electrical currents along my spine in the presence of certain texts. I warn you, dear ladies, against doing this." She shook her finger with mock menace at Gabriella and me as she paused after her flood of confessions.

Everywhere around the kitchen table there were slips, fabrics, patterns, remnants. Off in a corner, an ancient Singer sewing machine announced Dinah's abandoned trade. Our presence had given her the opportunity to burst through her self-imposed silence.

In her excitement, she had not had the chance to order the flat. "Please excuse the mess," she said, offering us cherry squash. When her back was turned, the meticulous Rebecca inspected the glass for stains. Finding it spotless, she drank eagerly. The room was clean and cheerful in spite of the disorder. Almost inches away from where we sat was the big double bed Dinah shared with her unsympathetic husband. The refrigerator faced into the street like a huge, brooding sentry. Dinah flung open the shutters. Although the sun was moving west, the air in the room was stifling. It was a choice between privacy in the heat or exposure to the inquisitive passersby who stared openly into the room, and Dinah chose the latter. She was entirely without guile or defensiveness.

"I am planning to leave my husband soon," she said, her stunning confession punctuated by the sonic boom of a low-flying jet.

Gabriella and I stared at each other; Rebecca changed the subject.

"What are you reading now?" she asked.

Dinah removed several books from a shelf over the sink. Among them I noticed the Ari's interpretation of the *Zohar,* one of the most arcane and difficult of kabbalistic texts.

"I have read these many times, but I am studying this one in particular now," Dinah said.

"Unbelievable," Gabriella murmured admiringly.

"Even when I did not understand them, I continued reading. The Aramaic was not too difficult for me because I read Arabic, but mostly I am able to understand . . . intuitively."

"So all it is is reading," Rebecca mused, nodding her great silver head.

"No, no." Dinah frowned. "You must practice the *mitzvoth,* too. They are essential to understanding the Kabbalah. Even small things like covering the head and the body; the laws of modesty have their place. This did not come to me from the outside; nobody told me I must do them. I knew no rabbis; my husband is not Orthodox. I learned the reasons for the *mitzvoth* from the Kabbalah itself. I am not learned in Talmud, Mishna and Halakha, but I have grown to understand the precepts and their purpose in granting me this sweet closeness to God." At the moment she spoke, her face glowed with love like those of the female Christian saints in Renaissance portraits. The self-abnegating aura of love emanating from her face suddenly threatened me; I felt myself being swept up in it and drowned as I had been by the passionate intellectualism of Rabbi Blumberg's discourse only two hours before. I wanted desperately to withdraw from her as I had from him.

I changed seats, moving to an armchair at the farthest end of the room away from the table.

The women ignored me. I drifted away in thought as Dinah's voice went on, gathering passion in her attempt to convey her experience. I grew increasingly uncomfortable and ashamed suddenly at my closeness to her marital bed; I could see the rumpled imprint of her husband's head on the pillow, a man's sock thrown carelessly between the sheets.

Dinah must have sensed my embarrassment, for she called to me from across the room: "Your appearance with the medicine that night was surely a small miracle. Look." She held up her hand for me to see; it was pink and whole. "I told my husband that your arrival that Friday night was a sign. The cut, as you see, is completely cured."

A phrase from Rabbi Gideon's most recent lesson sprang to mind: "The entire Torah rests on faith. There is no other way. Learning Torah brings one to faith." It was exactly that vast and unadulterated faith that Dinah projected into the poor little room, a cosmic vapor from another, higher world — a faith I could not feel, a world I did not yet wish to enter.

"God created the evil impulse," Rabbi Gideon had said, "but He gave us Torah as the medicine to cure it. Torah takes away evil, it eliminates flaws. Learn Torah with *kavanna* toward acquiring faith," he had urged me. "The remedy for your stubbornness is Torah. If the medicine does not work, it means you haven't toiled long enough in the Way."

How ironic, I thought as Dinah chatted on. I am a medicine bearer who cannot cure myself. Sue was right; I am in love with my sickness.

In late August, Rav Bloch once again opened his door to me. Sheila Gideon was about to leave for home, and I had promised to take her to meet him before her departure. On a sleepy weekday afternoon at about four, having abandoned all hope, I was greeted at the front door by the Rav himself. He gave us both a big, disarming smile and said, "I am happy to see you." Once inside, he left us and returned dressed up in his finest double-breasted silk frockcoat. I introduced him to Sheila, and he took her hand, saying to me in Hebrew, "I am so happy that you have brought this one. I am thankful to you for this." Then he asked her the usual preliminary questions, the ones he reserved for his "lost" Jewish children: What she did, where she came from.

"She's a psychologist," I said, amazed that *I* was now translating from Hebrew into English and back.

"I'm a bit of a psychologist, too." Rav Bloch gave Sheila his mischievous smile and patted her hand. "How nice it is that we have met," he kept saying over and over again. "We are already dear friends through Penina, dear friends."

Eager to disabuse him of his hopes for Judaizing her, I said, "Sheila is a student of H. J. Shastri, an Indian teacher. We met at his lectures in New York and became friends. She has had no exposure to Judaism, nor is she interested."

"Shastri!" cried the Rav joyfully. "I know that one. I have studied his ideas a little. They are nice, full of clarity and depth, but tell her, Penina, that these same ideas are with us, too, that we, too, have clear and significant writings."

I was startled numb. My salvo had backfired. Rav Bloch smiled happily at Sheila, his eyes still clear, his hand trembling only slightly in mine. Energy passing to and fro between friends. Then, typically, he resumed a conversation that had been interrupted weeks before. As if there had been no agony, as if I had not wandered and sought and failed again, he looked at me and said, "So where have you been, Penina?"

Red in the face, I answered, "Over and over again I tried to see you, but you closed the door. I think our 'business' is really finished."

"Why? I am here all the time. I am not going any place," he replied innocently. "Our 'business' is never finished. I am always here for you. Anyway, what's past is past. You are here now and you have brought me this new friend and I am delighted."

Noah entered the room and greeted the Rav in Hebrew.

"Where did *you* learn the holy tongue?" The Rav laughed and nodded his head at Noah. Without waiting for an answer, he turned to Sheila and said, "What kind of meeting have you in mind?"

"He's asking you to meet with him." I turned to my friend. "Where and when, I'll never try to guess."

"Tell him I'm leaving in only two days," Sheila said.

"How long is she here?" the Rav broke in.

"Only two days more."

The Rav lifted his eyebrows high into his forehead. "Is this her first time in the country?"

Sheila nodded.

"And she liked it very much," I said, eager to assuage his disappointment — and partially because I was secretly gratified that Sheila would not appropriate my hard-won treasure. "She spent much of her time touring."

"Does she wish to come back?"

Sheila nodded vigorously this time. The Rav had made another conquest.

"When?"

Sheila and I talked a little in English while the Rav awaited her answer with undisguised anticipation.

"Tell him April," said Sheila. "Say anything to relieve the pressure. I don't know that I'll come back."

"What date? So we can make an appointment right now," said the Rav.

"Tell him April seventeenth . . ."

"Pesach!" Rav Bloch gleefully clapped his hands.

"What did he say?" asked Sheila, puzzled at the Rav's display. She was accustomed to Shastri's detachment and felt awkward in the presence of such Jewish demonstrativeness.

"Passover," I said.

"That would be wonderful," said the Rav. Then, again interrupting himself, he turned to me. "Did you ever read a book by a Frenchman named Barth, a young man who studied with me for a while, a book on mysticism?"

"No."

Suddenly the Rav got up and walked over to the windowsill near his bed. The narrow ledge was piled and crammed in all directions with packets of letters, pamphlets, correspondence of every variety in no particular order. He removed several letters from a voluminous pile. "No, no, that's not it," he muttered to himself, searching under another mountain of letters and dusty flyers. "I can't seem to find the book; maybe I gave it to someone else. I was saving it for you, Penina. Do you think your friend would like to see my Japanese correspondence?" he asked puckishly.

"I've already told her about it," I said tactfully; twice before the Rav had asked me about his Japanese correspondence. He seemed to be trying to fix unruly facts in his mind. It was curious: On the one hand he was sharp, humorous, and hale — but on the other, he seemed to have no room in his head for dates, explicit names, and past conversations. I felt a sudden mournful clenching at the heart: The Rav would be drifting away from us all soon.

"What about the world, Rav Bloch, what is happening? Are you optimistic?" Noah asked, rescuing us from the embarrassing pause.

The Rav shrugged and said, "It's fine as far as I can see. Begin is in office and he's an upright man."

"No, not politics," Noah said, "I mean the world." He made a sphere in the air with his finger.

"Ah" — the Rav looked up — "we can talk about politics, but as for heaven — God is there and everything is in order."

We all laughed.

"Where does she work?" Rav Bloch asked, turning again to Sheila.

"A clinic in New York, and she sees private patients, too."

"And she's leaving so soon . . ." The Rav shook his head with disappointment. "When she comes in April, tell her we will arrange a program of meetings." Then he seemed confident and satisfied, suddenly decisive. "Yes, in six months, when you return, Sheila, we will meet regularly and discuss Hinduism and the ideas of H. J. Shastri."

Sheila, Noah, and I stared at each other with disbelief. What a brilliant stroke! The Rav had said nothing to her of *mitzvoth*, nothing of Jewish tradition, not even a word on his favorite *bête noire,* the Jewish homeland. He had obviously decided to meet the "enemy" head first. What a subtle tactic for an aged man, one whose entire being was immersed in the Messianic return of Israel to its soil, its physical and spiritual home. Rav Bloch was *a bit of a psychologist,* indeed. Stimulated by the Rav's offer, Sheila asked, "What do you teach all the different people who come here?"

"Each is a world in himself. Many who come are confused, ill, needing advice — like your patients. Others, like yourself, are intelligent, educated people who are looking for something that the intellect does not offer. So we work, teaching each other, discussing, exchanging ideas about Hinduism and the like, seeing where we can both teach and learn. I begin with the level at which I find the person sitting in front of me; often with no goal in mind at all," the Rav explained. Then, looking at me, he said, "Tell her to come with Gabriella Polakoff, not with you."

He had probably detected some hidden affinity between the two women and, with his usual insight, determined that Sheila and Gabriella would benefit from the meetings together more than Sheila and I ever could.

"I understand," I said.

"You *always* understand, Penina." He pressed my hand firmly. "And when do you come back? What have you been doing?"

"I have been studying the works of Rav Berman . . ."

Again the Rav's eyebrows lurched high into his smooth, white crown. "An important man. My father and he had a correspondence."

Thank heaven, I thought. He's legitimized Berman for me.

"You come back with *Guardian of the Faith* next week." Rav

Bloch switched from Hebrew to French, a signal that the interview was over.

"What day?" I asked desperately. "What time?"

"Just come and we'll see," the Rav replied, his open-ended invitation unwittingly throwing me into the abyss. Again the cruel possibility of waiting, of long, fruitless hours on the hard bench in his front room. I fumbled for complaints in Hebrew, but found none.

"How much time have you left here, Penina?"

"I don't know, the end of the month, I'm not sure."

"There's time then," he said, satisfied.

"I have to go back when my book comes out. I have to be there in four months."

"What?" he asked.

I had made some sort of error. Again I repeated the sentence.

"Ah!" The Rav's tiny frame shook with mirth. Emitting a crisp dry breeze with the stirring of his body, he said, "You used the feminine form of the word for 'months' and came up with 'news.' So you have four news broadcasts before your book comes out, have you?" The old man roared at his joke. Then he stood and walked with us into the anteroom. Sheila waved good-bye to him at the bottom of the stairs leading to the long front walk. The Rav leaned his arms on the railing and gazed down at us sternly. Then he turned, and his tiny, dark-frocked form was gone, swallowed by the formidable doorway.

It was dark. The Jerusalem cats foraged in silence in the trash cans in front of the house. Noah opened the back door of the car for Sheila. As he unlocked the front door for me, an elongated shadow emerged from the long pathway to the Rav's house. It was Yakov, his white shirt collar brilliantly illuminated by the street light that had just flickered on. Holding his white, knitted skullcap on his head, with his white fringes flying, Yakov bounded across the road toward us like one of Chagall's yeshiva boy angels. With a broad smile, his black Yemenite eyes agleam, he approached my window and crouched down to speak into the car.

"Are you happy? You see him now." He shouted at me and then at Sheila. "It was good. Yes?"

Then, without even giving us a chance to reply, Yakov darted back up the stairs to rejoin his master.

Hannah Fox came just after Sheila Gideon left. Hannah was passing through Israel on her way to India, trying, she said, to absorb as much of her own tradition as she could before returning to her Himalayan swami and his brand of kriya yoga. Hannah was fluent in Hebrew and Aramaic; she punctiliously observed the Sabbath, even going so far as to light candles on Friday nights in the Himalayas and to study Hasidic texts alongside her Sanskrit Upanishads. Hannah was a religious sponge, so of course the opportunity to join me in studying *Guardian of the Faith* was too tempting for her to pass up. And although she was thin, anemic, and constantly exhausted as a result of her lengthy meditations and self-imposed deprivations, Hannah read with me for long hours in advance of her desired meeting with Rav Bloch. She even changed her flight plans and lengthened her stay by a month when she heard who my teacher was. From Hannah, I learned that the entire first portion of the book was a dialogue between a kabbalist and an anti-kabbalist in the style of the medieval Jewish philosophers.

When we entered Rav Bloch's study at five-thirty in the afternoon of my appointed day, the sun was already beginning its descent. In Jerusalem, an early sunset was always a sign of imminent departure, of the possibility that this meeting with the Rav could easily be the last.

I was surprised by Rav Bloch's cold greeting when I introduced him to Hannah. He searched her face briefly and then immediately selected a huge volume of Talmud as the source of his lesson.

"He's in one of his contradictory moods today," I whispered to Hannah. Unlike Sheila, she was openly Jewish. She had been educated in Hebrew schools all her life; she was proficient in Hebrew conversation — Hannah should have impressed the Rav instantly. I had told him nothing about her impending move to India, yet he must have "read" her as clearly as he had Sheila, whose deep Jewish identity smoldered like fiery Hebrew letters across her face. Hannah's skin-deep Jewishness could not fool him.

The Rav pushed his dog-eared copy of the Sanhedrin section of the Talmud under our noses and began to read out loud from Maimonides' commentaries on a particular selection having nothing at all to do with *Guardian of the Faith*. When he was three quarters of the way into the lesson, I realized that it was not for me but for Hannah that the Rav had commenced a description of "the three kinds of people who approach the Aggadic, or mystical parables of the Talmud."

"First," he said, "there are the simple literalists who worship indiscriminately anything they feel is holy. Then there are the so-called enlightened rationalists who believe nothing," he continued mockingly. "Finally, there is the deeper understanding of the intellect, which knows that there is a higher spiritual meaning in even the apparently gross or silly tales of the Aggadah."

Again the Rav tested his novices. Always forcing us outside the gate, always teasing, demanding that we "prepare" but never teaching us how — except in whispered asides and pregnant stares. Hannah was right to have given it all up and headed for India, like Sue. The keepers of the Kabbalah were not ready for the "seculars" whom they so claimed to admire. We were too quick and eager, too thirsty for them. Years of sitting at the gate would pass before any of the Jerusalem masters would let us in. Hannah and Sue had taken the quicker route. I, by default, had to remain. An invisible ball and chain bound me to everything the Rav Bloch stood for: the tattered little room, the linoleum-covered table, the piping bird chant of young girls praying early on a remote Brooklyn morning: *Modeh ani lefonecha,* sung by rote with twenty-four mechanical doll nods to match each word. I could not find any other way but this one. I no longer had the stamina to leave it.

"Those who study Rebbe Nachman of Breslov's way" — Rav Bloch interrupted the lesson suddenly and looked into Hannah's eyes with the same stern expression he had cast on me from the stairwell some days before — "must be one hundred percent pure, stable, whole in body and mind — or else the teachings can rebound on them and cause them to sin. It is the most dangerous way of all. That is why the Gaon of Vilna rejected the Hasidim, because he saw clairvoyantly into the distant future, when their ways would lead people like you to heresy."

I shivered. The Rav had seen Hannah's departure to India without her having uttered a word.

He thumbed through a great faded brown notebook on the table and lit at last on a sentence written by his father. "The search for spirituality, when performed by the improperly prepared, will destroy and darken the seeker despite his best intentions," the Rav read ominously, his voice quavering. Hannah lowered her eyes. The Rav shut the book, folded his hands under his chin, and smiled sadly at us both.

"I'm returning to the United States soon," I reminded him. (In Hebrew, the words are "States of the Covenant.")

The smile dropped away from the old man's lips. "No, don't call them States of the Covenant; *this* is the only Land of the Covenant, *our* covenant. Say instead *am rek,* empty land. America is a spiritually empty land."

"It is not an empty land for those who live there," I said quietly.

"It is empty for Jews. Jews must not be running all over the world; Jews must live here."

Again he persisted in throwing up the old forceful nationalistic barriers between us. Perhaps in his mind "nationalism" and "preparation" were one and the same. Perhaps he had rejected me because I had come for two years and refused to throw in my lot with him completely. He saw me as an interloper from an empty land, coming and going at my leisure, blithely writing books about what was to him the heart and essence of the Jewish existence. I was an onlooker who had insinuated myself in the guise of a seeker, and he was vexed at the intrusion. The lesson, like the masquerade, was over.

Yet, like a persistent lover, I refused to give up and returned many times after that day. Accompanied by Hannah Fox and Gabriella Polakoff, I tried again and again to squeeze the last precious drops of wisdom from the man I had chosen as my spiritual master. The Rav remained dispassionate.

Wearing a nicely ironed, fresh white shirt, he regaled me again with the story of the Ari's disciples who "knew nothing." Then he searched out a big old book entitled *Prefaces and Gates,* which, he said, was written by a friend of his father's. The author's knowledge of Kabbalah was so great that it prompted one of the old Rav Bloch's closest disciples to give his newborn son the kabbalist's name.

"At the naming ceremony, the proud father was just about to call the boy Shlomo in honor of the kabbalist when my father stopped him, saying, 'Call the child Simcha in honor of Rabbi Simcha, who is the greatest master of Halakha. Let his middle name be Shlomo, for the revealed Torah must come before the concealed.'" The Rav drove home his point with fluttering hands. Then he read aloud to us from *Prefaces and Gates,* Rav Shlomo's kabbalistic masterpiece.

The book was filled with prophecies of apocalypse, the revelation of esoteric wisdom, and final redemption in the twenty-first century.

Rav Bloch read next from Ezekiel, saying, "The Jews will have no choice in the matter of their redemption. When God has been sufficiently humiliated before the 'nations' by his straying children, He will literally pluck up the community of Israel by the nape of its neck and place it back in its rightful home." He glared at me.

Suddenly a tiny bug, disrupted from its long sleep among the dusty pages of *Prefaces and Gates,* rushed onto the page and scurried around the Rav's finger. He moved the book back and forth, trying to dislodge the bug without touching or startling it. Then he blew on it gently, jostling the book slightly in an effort to set the bug free. Suddenly Gabriella reached down and impulsively crushed the bug to death with her thumb. The Rav looked pained; shaking his head from side to side, he said, "Why did you do that? I was just telling you about the end of days and the redemption of souls, and you did such a thing."

Gabriella, crestfallen, had no answer.

Beyond the door in the spare study, three yeshiva boys from the United States were studying Torah and three young women waited in the hall. The entire city was filled with pilgrims like me, only more deeply committed ones. Already immersed in the spiritual life, they patiently awaited the redemption Rav Bloch was so certain of. It did not matter, really. To God we were like bugs. Religious or not, observant or not, "returned" or not, He would forcibly return us to our anthill or stub us out with His finger. Humanity was desperately hungry for religious "secrets" in times like these; but that, too, did not matter, for in the coming years, nothing would be concealed. God's name would be written in flames above Mount Zion for all of Israel and the world to see. Rav Bloch had tried to spare a bug that lived in the Holy City, for it too was meant to share in the days of awe.

On the day of my last visit with the Rav, I discreetly sat in the front hall eating sunflower seeds. More and more "returnees" to Judaism appeared; more people with psychological and spiritual problems sought the Rav's advice. At six-fifteen a tall, hearty, bearded man with familiar tanned features entered the room. We looked at each other and knew that we had met before, but neither of us said anything. Having worked up a sunflower thirst, I went into the kitchen for a glass of water. Yakov stood peeling potatoes at the sink. The big, broad-chested man entered after me.

"Even *I* must wait to see the Rav," he bellowed at me jovially. "Don't you remember me?" he asked.

I looked at him closely and said, "Now I know. You studied with Rabbi Miller and me the first year I met the Rav. We all sat around the little table in his bedroom."

"That's right. I'm Bader. You were the professor studying Kabbalah."

"Where is Rabbi Miller? I never see him — or you — here anymore."

"We usually come at night, but we are all very, very busy these days — the Rav, too, haven't you noticed?"

"Yes," I cried, eager for more of his good-natured consolation.

"Everything is so changed around here. At first, if you remember, there was always time for me — hours of endless discussion and study — and now I can barely get in to see him for five minutes."

"Ah, but now you are like me and like Miller — his two chief disciples. He knows you and he knows where you are, so you don't *need* to see him for such long hours. It's only when he doesn't know you that he worries," Rabbi Bader said reassuringly.

"But this year there are so many psychological problems — Israelis, non-Israelis, so many searching for a spiritual life —"

"So you noticed the change, too?" He smiled, twinkling like an oversized replica of his master, a young, tall, sun-browned vision of the Rav.

Squeezed tightly against the sink in the cramped kitchen, Rabbi Bader and I drank lemon and lime soda and chatted as Yakov continued peeling potatoes in silence.

"Even Yakov is in a darker mood these days," I said, knowing for certain that Yakov understood every word of my English.

"He is also growing older — like the Rav," sighed Rabbi Bader.

"Yes, it's all different," I said sadly. "I saw him get angry at a psychotic boy."

"Yes," the rabbi concurred. "He is older, too. But you have seen a change in the people of Israel, a change for the better?"

"They're less depressed — and more brutal," I said.

"That, too."

A boy in a khaki army uniform pushed open the kitchen door.

"He's calling you," he said to Rabbi Bader.

"Let this woman go in first. I can always see him, but she'll be leaving soon," said Rabbi Bader, exerting a gentle push on my shoulder. The crush out in the waiting room was barely negotiable. I squeezed through a phalanx of gawky adolescent boys in white shirts and waved my thanks at the bearish rabbi before entering the study.

The old man was in a hurry to say good-bye. "Why do you say you'll send me the book after it is already published? I want to see the manuscript," he ordered crankily.

"Don't worry. It's all history, no interpretations, none of the work we've done together. That will be for a later book, maybe."

He shrugged, peering into my face with an apprehensive smile.

"I may return this winter. I'll come and see you then, give you the book myself."

"After the fact, what's the good of that?"

"Are you angry with me?"

"No, never."

"May I write to you?" I asked.

The Rav was frail, but he clasped my hands so tightly that my fingers were numb.

"You don't need letters, photos, anything. I told you many times: Ours is a spiritual connection for always, an indissoluble link between our souls."

"*Shalom,* then," I said, embracing him.

"*Shalom,*" the Rav replied, wrinkling his forehead. "*Shalom,*" he repeated absent-mindedly as he pushed me toward the door.

I left without looking back, knowing that I no longer wished to wring the spirit out of him by force; I no longer needed to drain the old man of his power. My passionate involvement with Rav Bloch had mellowed, had become detachment. I was free to come and go as I pleased, to love him in *shalom:* peace.

FOUR

II

Running and Returning

I RETURNED TO JERUSALEM in the spring of 1978, determined to start my practice of the *mitzvoth* by observing the Sabbath. Of all my "Jerusalem guides," Madame Ariel alone remained steadfast. My rabbinic teachers had gently but in no uncertain terms refused to instruct me further in any kabbalistic discipline but textual study. When it came down to my practicing Kabbalah "in life," only the blue gate stood open. Madame Ariel shrewdly cast the heavy Sabbath task, with all its onerous past associations, in the form of an "exercise."

On the first Friday I cleaned the house thoroughly and grimly; my body and hair were drenched with sweat, my face with unwiped tears of rage and frustration. After all that time and self-discipline, I could still feel demeaned and abused in the Jewish woman's role of housekeeper. As the sun set I showered, lit candles according to the hour noted in the newspaper, set the table for dinner, blessed the wine and bread, and sat in brief meditation afterward. I slept until four-thirty and awoke to watch the sun rise. At five-thirty on Saturday morning, I attended services at a quaint Sephardic synagogue around the corner from my flat.

Downstairs in the men's section, an assorted group of Oriental men and boys sat around a long table chanting Sabbath songs. It was a gay, wild, theatrical moment; the melodies were so engaging that I hardly noticed that I was the lone woman peering down from the balcony until a wrinkled crone in a white headscarf appeared at the open door, kissed the *mezuzah* and the Elijah's chair fastened high upon the wall near the women's entrance, and, shaking my hand with her beringed, withered fingers, wished me a "Shabbat shalom." Steaming glasses of coffee and tea were passed around to each of the singers below by a man in shirtsleeves who performed as the waiter, while the worshipers at the table took turns singing passages of each chant with exotic trills and nasal legatos, much to the noisy delight of their companions. The unembarrassed kissing, the easy, unaffected pleasure these men took in praising the Sabbath, soon became infectious, and I found myself foot-tapping and swaying along with them. A second old woman in a headscarf arrived with a tray bearing a glass of black Turkish coffee, which she offered me with a "Shabbat *shalom*" and a friendly smile. More women in headscarves came at about six; one, wearing bangles and exotic earrings, ululated at the Torah in the ark, prayed with her hands wide apart and with her body swaying, and talked to God through the open window into the blue, early morning air of the holy city.

During the intermission, I leaned against a stone wall in the sunny courtyard, trying to observe my mixed and quickly changing emotions with detachment when a rotten-toothed woman with an evil eye approached me.

"This low Iraqi synagogue," she said contemptuously. "I only come here for memorial services because they say them later than at my own synagogue, the one up the street, closer to the market. I am Persian."

She seemed part of a strange, disjointed, devilish plot to confuse and disorient me, this muttering *djinn* squinting at me complicitously, reading my doubts. Insecure about my Hebrew, I merely smiled and shrugged.

"Tell me," she went on doggedly, "are you Orthodox? Do you know a nice Orthodox girl who might wish to marry my son? He is twenty-two, a yeshiva student who studies day and night in the Bayit Vegan Academy."

Why does he need a wife if he studies day and night? I wanted to ask the crone but didn't.

"I'm only a visitor," I said. "I don't know any eligible religious girls in Jerusalem."

The woman stepped back and appraised my silk headscarf and my American shoes.

"Tourist, American tourist from Chicago!" she accused.

"No, an Orthodox writer from New York," I said, barely containing a cheerless laugh.

"Why aren't you praying at the Ashkenazi synagogue, the big one on King George Street? What are you doing here with these Iraqis? All the Americans like you go to the big Ashkenazi synagogue. What are you doing here?" She moved toward me, her foul, rotten-toothed breath on my cheek.

"I'm Sephardic," I said, cutting her short.

Two men appeared as the witch started to ask me for my address. One was the sexton, a man in shirtsleeves with a gray, pointed beard whom I had observed from my window as he swept the courtyard of the synagogue every morning. The moment she saw him, the Persian demoness hurried off into the market labyrinth across the road. Robust, with a sharp nose, darting Oriental eyes, and reminding me of my grandfather with his huge all-encompassing prayer shawl, the sexton introduced the other gentleman as the leader of the congregation and himself as the *shammas*. Then he handed me a book whose jacket was the color of Madame Ariel's gate and said in raspy, Sephardic Hebrew, "It's the Torah reading of the week; you'll want to follow it as the cantor reads. He's a very good cantor."

The leader of the congregation, a tiny man wearing a big homburg and looking exactly like my grandfather's insurance man and synagogue companion, smiled at me broadly and disappeared into the men's section to prepare for the Torah reading.

"My name is Shmuel," said the sexton. "Come around to the

kitchen and I'll give you another coffee and some special Oriental cookies."

I had rediscovered the synagogue of my childhood.

Sipping sweet Turkish coffee and eating sesame cookies, I learned from Shmuel that he was "a bit of a kabbalist" himself, "an informal disciple of a great Sephardic master."

"I've written a book in English about Kabbalah," I said timidly, waiting for the inevitable male snicker. Instead, Shmuel raised his eyebrows and spontaneously invited me to join him and his fellow kabbalists on their upcoming pilgrimage to the tombs of the mystics in and around Safed. I was taken aback by his openness and a little fearful. I said that I would be glad to come.

The rest of the morning service was long and uninspired. Despite the cantor's perfect melodic rendering of the Torah portion, my attention drifted to the birds outside. I had no patience for the innumerable Deuteronomic injunctions against eating birds of prey and no sympathy for the intricate details of the slaughter. The song of the real mourning doves in the gutter of a neighboring roof made my chest feel heavy and brought tears to my eyes. I looked at my watch and saw that I had been sitting in the synagogue for five hours with nothing in my stomach but black coffee and two sesame cookies. The sun was yellow and hot, its earlier pink nacre glow against the Judean Hills turned to brilliant flame, its Sabbath morning magic gone. I resolved to return the next day with a small contribution and a request for a seat on Shmuel's pilgrimage.

I was exhausted and slightly nauseated when I returned home and found Noah setting out an ideal Sabbath breakfast of fresh challah, goat cheese, grapefruit, and coffee.

I ate, showered, and tried to nap the endless day away, but couldn't. At four in the afternoon Noah and I took a long walk across the city to visit with Rebecca Polakoff, who, sick with cancer, claimed to have "no interest in the world of the living." Her Kabbalah books had not been opened for a year, she said listlessly. Gabriella had simply lost the spirit for it when I left. The women were tired, beaten. I dared not ask about Dinah ben Aviv, but pictured her footloose and disheveled, wandering "for the sake of Torah," like her ancient, exiled master Simeon bar Yohai. I was tired, too.

On sighting the first three stars of evening, Noah performed the Havdalah service, praying over the wine in Hebrew with much difficulty, causing me to fret and scramble with my old impatience to part with the Sabbath. Real Hasidim clutched at the remaining Sabbath shreds, praying for the Queen to remain, but I couldn't wait for her to leave. The singing in the blue Sephardic synagogue beneath my window continued into the darkening night.

Later at Madame Ariel's, an American sociologist cast the I Ching oracle for the future of Israel. I felt schizoid at emerging so fast from the deep well of orthodoxy into the slightly mad, dizzyingly eclectic world of Madame Ariel's salon. A spiritual case of the bends. Yet, I reminded myself, it was under her tutelage, not the rabbis', that I had assumed the *mitzvah* of observing the Sabbath with *kavanna,* proper intention. But in her parlor, too, I sat inattentively, preoccupied about my inability to pray, musing over my lack of passion. I no longer cared about Judaism.

Nonetheless, I went early the following morning to the Sephardic synagogue to give Shmuel my promised contribution. The gates were locked. I approached a neighbor on his balcony.

"Nobody there past six-thirty, when services end," the man said curtly.

As I turned to go home, I saw Shmuel working contentedly in the courtyard. I hailed him with a loud "Good morning," and he opened the gates. Such a brown, hale, kindly face. Such laughing eyes, and my grandfather's gray beard and ruddy cheeks, too. I handed him the money. Again we exchanged names; he had forgotten mine and wondered what I was doing in Jerusalem.

"I'd like to see the Ari's tomb," I reminded him.

"Oh, but there's no room in the minibus," he said forlornly.

"But I have a car."

"Then you can come." He laughed as he scoured the coffeepot in the little sink behind the synagogue. "And maybe you can take two or three more holy kabbalists who've been left out for lack of space."

Somehow, in the middle of our plans for meeting the next day, we wandered further into a kabbalistic discussion. For two hours we remained locked in a conversation that, in any other town, time, or world, would appear absurd; in New York it would be insane.

"I am Shmuel; this is the *gematria* of my name," he said, permutating the Hebrew letters as Dinah ben Aviv had done in *her* mystic's cell a year before.

"The prophet's name," I replied, enchanted and amazed at my ability to flit in and out of Judaism in a matter of hours. All it took to retrieve my erring soul was a magnetic glance and the magic play of sun and shadow on a synagogue wall.

"I am a kabbalist in secret. I study alone, for twenty-five years, here, in the kitchen." Shmuel motioned appropriately toward the flame under the hotplate.

"Who are your teachers?"

"Kabbalah is not obtained from teachers. It's a gift handed to you at birth . . . from God. The yearning of the soul to study Kabbalah is not meant for all, only for those who have reincarnated many many times and have the message clearly imprinted on their souls. The rest here are good people. I am *shammas* here for fifty years in this synagogue, since I am a boy. My father was *shammas* first. He used to produce cigars in Iraq, but he came to the Holy Land and devoted himself to God. Several of his books are on these shelves."

We wandered from the kitchen into the synagogue, Shmuel removing an occasional book from a bench or a shelf on the reader's lectern: *"Brit Menuchah, Zohar, Shaar Ha Gilgulim,"* he murmured the mystic titles dreamily. Then, turning sharply, he looked at me and said, "But yours is the soul of a young man, a kabbalist in a woman's form — the reason you wish so hard to learn, you can't help it; the yearning is part of this incarnation for you. We — people like ourselves — always find each other. You have a great soul, I see, a great need. Torah is not enough for you; Kabbalah is the end and essence of our life here, and you know it. It does not matter about your being a woman, or a man, or an animal, or whatever. God has given you His gift of yearning for Kabbalah — and the capacity to learn it." We returned to the kitchen.

"Your soul is like a trapped bird, fighting and battering against the bars of its cage to find freedom. It's a great war in you."

The utensil shelf above the sink was filled with kabbalistic books. Shmuel pointed at them, saying, "Read the texts yourself and the light comes."

"But I have been looking for teachers." I protested against his simplicity.

Shmuel slapped his thigh and roared. "No teachers. Kabbalah can't be taught. It's inside. Study alone and it will come."

"You remind me of a woman I met, Dinah ben Aviv. She's a secret kabbalist, too."

"You will take me to her one day," Shmuel whispered.

"Do you all need to know each other?"

"We always recognize each other, but we study alone; it's a question of you and God alone, and that knowledge is not available in groups."

"But many of you know each other," I insisted.

"Yes. I have a young friend named Mercy; he's very stubborn and we always disagree. But he is a very dedicated kabbalist. As you are." Shmuel removed a snapshot from his shirt pocket.

"This is the great Sephardic kabbalist I mentioned last time. Such a man is divine; he sits and communes with God alone. Study and learning of kabbalistic books in a group is all right, but you must remember that it is only *textual* learning."

Recognizing Rabbi Gaon in the snapshot of the "divine" man, I said, "That man once told me that my book would help bring the Messiah." Shmuel looked at me with deep respect. "Then he saw into your soul. He saw your function in this incarnation."

"I think he was making fun of me," I said, trying hard not to succumb to my weakness for Sephardic mystification.

Shmuel was dead serious. "Rabbi Gaon is not one to make fun

of people. If he said that, he meant it. Not all of Simeon bar Yohai's books are even known. Why shouldn't you be preparing the darkness for the time of light?"

Resisting the impulse to reveal to him my own darkness, I said, "I just feel so alone in this search."

Again Shmuel laughed his scratchy wise laugh and slapped his thigh. "No fear. When you see spirit everywhere, there is no reason for aloneness or fear, no attachment to the things of this world, no fear in the world of perfect faith. Then you are friends with the sages; you sit and chat with Rabbi Akiva, Elijah, and Simeon bar Yohai — no problem."

We were interrupted by knocking at the gate.

"Maybe it's my husband. I've been away so long, he probably thinks I've gotten lost."

"It's not your husband," said Shmuel definitively, as if he could see through the iron doors. "I mostly study alone," he continued. "I have tried to teach some of the younger boys, but Kabbalah is not an intellectual gift, not a 'study' in the same sense that you study Torah. It is not like prayer, either; certainly not the kind that suffices for this congregation and most others. Kabbalah is best learned alone and in secret. People would laugh at you if you told them that Shmuel the *shammas* is a kabbalist. Most of them, even the most saintly observant ones, think it's crazy to bother with Kabbalah."

The knocking at the gate grew louder and more insistent. Shmuel opened it and let in a street sweeper wearing a blue smock and a peaked cap. He pointed to the big-featured newcomer with the protruding ears and generous smile, saying, "He's from Morocco, another kind of underground kabbalist himself."

The street sweeper responded with a long Hebrew barrage about the joys of living on the holy soil. Finally overflowing with emotion, he rushed up to the wall of the synagogue and kissed it. Then, removing his cap and turning to me, he said, "Do you speak French, young lady? You are from Paris?"

"No, America. But I speak French."

"Then let me tell you," he said in French, pointing at the

shammas, "you are in the presence of an angel, a real one," he ended in a whisper. "Shmuel is an angel come to earth to help human beings. You are a lucky young lady to have met him."

As always when my reasonable and mystifiable selves went into battle, I experienced an attack of heart palpitations. Shmuel, who did not understand a word of French, smiled pleasantly throughout the weird exchange. Then, collecting his bottle of tea, rags, and assorted papers in a plastic shopping bag, he shooed us out of the courtyard and locked the gate of the synagogue behind him. The effusive street sweeper took his leave, continuing to doff his cap and bow at us from the waist until he finally disappeared out of sight around a sharp corner.

Forgetting time, I walked through the narrow lanes of the Jewish market alongside Shmuel, who insisted on showing me in person the appointed meeting place for the journey to Safed the next morning. I was surprised to find that my secret kabbalist was a gregarious, well-known figure throughout the market; in the course of our fifteen-minute walk, he was greeted by Jews of every variety. Shmuel had a smile and a kind word for them all. Our subject was lofty — nothing less than direct knowledge of God — but his speech was simple, almost peasant-like, his tone excitable and serene by turns. We ambled through the narrow alleys of the market, avoiding cars, shoppers, Hasidim on their way to the study bench. I was transformed into an ancient kabbalist, wandering through the holy city at the side of an angel who had assumed the form of a man — the simplest, most ordinary man at that — in order to teach me how to teach myself, the lesson I was always forgetting: the most important lesson of all. Like my distant ancestor, the Baal Shem Tov, Shmuel too was a synagogue sexton who swept the courtyard in daylight and communed with God in deepest mystery during the night.

Defenseless suddenly, I poured out my soul to him: "You were right, I am at war. I am about to leave the battlefield; I am tired — too much struggling to find teachers — too much. I am not really Orthodox; it's a game I'm playing." I fumbled in Hebrew for the proper words in which to dress my despair, my sham. We had reached our destination and were standing out in the scalding sun at the entrance to an ultra-Orthodox hotel, our kabbalists' meeting place. Scurrying Hasidim, the ubiquitous black crows of Jerusalem, eyed us quizzically. The dwarfed heir of a great rabbinical dynasty stopped in his tracks to extend his hand to Shmuel and nod his head at me before resuming his dwarfish business. I felt myself faltering at the border between worlds, the old, uncomfortable sensation of landing in an alien place without the proper code words, ignorant of the language.

"No matter — Orthodox or not Orthodox. You must be strong-minded," Shmuel stated forcefully, angelically aware of my demonic struggle, my inborn tendency to stray from the fold.

"The evil impulse seeks to prevent you from breaking through the bars of the prison of this world. You have loved too much of the world, been too concerned with it. When you turn your thoughts and desires elsewhere" — pointing toward the cloudless sky overhead — "then you weaken the Angel of Death. He is a scavenger who hangs around lovers of the material world. Your desires only make him stronger and fatter, and the bars of your confinement tighter. When you weaken him with yearning for God, then the deadly angel leaves your side — and all fear leaves with him. With faith, with Torah — no fear, no war."

Longing to join the ranks of the faithful, I said, "But we have to eat, to work, don't we?"

"Yes, of course," Shmuel replied. "To earn a living and care for this body; I work for a living, too. But my major work is caring for the synagogue, the house of God, to see that all is in order."

I nodded obediently, ready to throw in my lot with the sexton and clean the synagogue, too. We walked away from the hotel toward the busy corner of Jaffa Road, where we would part for the day.

"I know all kinds of earthly troubles," said Shmuel. "But understanding of the true nature of things through Kabbalah helps you not only to endure your troubles, but to *use* them to see God. That is what He wants when He has given you the gift of yearning. I can see that despite the obstacles you have it, you are one of us."

I blinked my eyes in the blazing light amid the honking buses and the irritable shoppers who scraped at my legs with the corners of their net shopping bags. Although I half-expected him to have disappeared into the sky, Shmuel still stood there in front of me. Was I not really having this conversation with my innermost self? Had I not really made him up, my angel? But no, he was right there on the noisy corner, a human being in a brown, short-sleeved shirt carrying a shopping bag piled high with a tea bottle and assorted papers and shoes.

"Can we talk like this again?" I asked.

"Yes, of course. How long do you stay in Jerusalem? Till the end of the summer?"

"Yes."

"And where do you live?"

"Right around the corner from your synagogue. I can see you from my window when you clean the courtyard in the morning."

"Ah, my brother is your neighbor, and I am always in your vicinity," he assured me. "What do you say that I call out your name and your donation next Saturday?" Shmuel landed on earth with a sudden thump.

"No, don't do that. I'd like you to have it anonymously, no name. Just use the money for the synagogue as you please."

Shmuel looked thoughtful. Very softly and tenderly, he said, "You're sure no name?"

"I'm sure," I said, ever mindful of the irreverent past, when loud pledge calls rivaled the cries of prayer on Brooklyn Sabbaths.

Shmuel approved my decision. "Very well." We shook hands.

"Tomorrow in front of the hotel at six in the morning?"

"Yes, be prompt," he said.

"See you then." I floated away on my cloud of bliss, eager to inform Noah that I had spent the morning with an angel.

I found him in Madame Ariel's garden eating scrambled eggs and potatoes with her and Zvi.

Refusing lunch, I described my encounter excitedly. Noah interspersed my pauses for breath with questions; I sensed that he was growing enthusiastic about my secret kabbalist, and it pleased me.

Madame Ariel sipped her tea and watched my face as I talked. Almost as soon as I had finished, she said, "This is a ninety-degree turn from your usual way, which is cautious and down to earth, isn't it?"

It was as though she had splashed her cup of tea in my face. I withdrew instantly, asking Zvi for a cold drink in order to change the subject. I felt foolish, as if I had revealed a hidden defect in public and been scorned for it. How could I admit to her that what I now longed for most was precisely the courage to make a ninety-degree turn away from my habitual caution; my skepticism had gotten me nowhere. Under Shmuel's sheltering wings I could surrender my questioning ego to the elusive, abiding, irrational faith that I lacked and chat with the sages. And Madame Ariel was spoiling it all by telling me to be cautious. For years I had been plagued by mistrust of so-called masters. Even the great kabbalists were considered dangerous frauds in their own time. Who was to say what was real and what was fake on this mad and circuitous spiritual road?

I made a quick excuse for leaving. As I closed the gate behind me, I heard Madame Ariel's warning: "Be careful of this man and the people with whom you are traveling. Don't be carried away."

I thanked her petulantly for her advice, got into the sun-cooked car, and drove off without so much as a wave. I was determined not to be careful, but to fling myself wholeheartedly into the "mystical" spirit of the journey with new and intoxicating wildness.

I drove close behind the yellow and red minibus through the sere hills and maniacally curved roads of the Jordan Valley. Our first stop was Shechem, the tomb of Joseph. In the dismal Arab town, under a merciless sun, the faithful dismounted, entered a cave, and circled around and around the flat rock tomb inside, praying, chanting, and blowing a curved and elongated ram's horn. I circled behind the ragtag boys, bearded Hasidim, and Sephardic laborers who comprised our unwholesome-looking pilgrimage, fearing that Madame Ariel had been right. Then a magnificent old man in a black hat and caftan looked up at me, his eyes aglow above his white curls, and I felt justified in my decision. My passengers, a French-speaking, self-styled rabbi in platform shoes and pork-pie hat and his smooth-skinned wife, the fortuitously named Mazal (luck), were busy unloading their tape recorders and cameras from the back of my car. "Frenchie" came up behind me with his gear, opened a black leather briefcase, and revealed a bottle of cognac that turned out to be a transistor radio. The beautiful old Hasid with the long white beard resembled Santa Claus. Shmuel was busily dickering with the bus driver. I was surrounded everywhere by characters out of fairy tales and joke books: a Rumpelstiltskin with a long, curled gray beard, dressed in a cast-off jacket six sizes too large for his frame, a rope holding up his clown's trousers, wandered among the circling devotees selling candles, papers, anything. To the little boys he distributed candies; me, he constantly pestered with requests for "charity," holding out a besmeared yogurt cup, the remains of his midmorning snack. Catching sight of the persistent beggar, Shmuel hurried over, admonished him for bothering me, and escorted me back to my car.

My reverse gear stuck as we were turning out of the shrine's courtyard, and I kept the bus waiting in the blistering sun as I juggled frantically to back out. Five minutes went by, and nobody came down to help me. I looked into the windows of the bus, plunked down on the hot dust like some jettisoned hermit crab, and grew fainthearted at the specter of the scowling Orthodox faces and fist-shaking Hasidim inside. The driver, an easygoing Moroccan wearing a tiny knitted skullcap and speaking only slang English, at last jumped down to help me. Behind him, a huge, angry hulk in black stood shouting in the doorway that the female had brought the pilgrims bad luck by being allowed to come along. "Frenchie" shouted and waved the figure back into the bus, urging me to pay no attention. I was already on the verge of panic, and we had not even gotten past the first tomb.

"A snap!" cried the helpful bus driver, jostling the gear into reverse on first try. "No sweat," he grinned ingratiatingly.

"*Toda.*" I thanked him in Hebrew to let him know I was serious and not just some inquisitive "chippie" reporter from America.

From the way "Frenchie" and Mazal addressed me throughout the trip, it was evident that Shmuel had tried to pass me off as an important journalist from abroad.

The second tomb was a small domed heap of stones high in the Galilee, which we reached only after a parched, backbreaking drive through razored mountain roads. I never once looked out the side window, but kept my eyes fastened to the tailpipe of the bus in front of me. At the tombsite, we scrambled stiffly out into the field; this saint, Rabbi Abba Halavta, did not seem to interest the men very much, for they uttered only cursory prayers and seemed more intent on stopping behind trees to pee. A few halfhearted bleats from the ram's horn, a near brawl over when to start and stop the prayers, a stunning rendition of the Shema from none other than Rumpelstiltskin, and we were hurried back into my car for the hasty trip to Meron. Interested in Rabbi Halavta suddenly, I lingered, trying to work up some religious feeling by touching the cold stones and meditating with my eyes closed. As I moved closer to read the inscription on the surface of the tomb, I stumbled over a stiff, dead pigeon lying on its back with its toothpick legs in the air. A kabbalist's warning, no doubt; a symbol of the dead tradition I was seeking to exhume; an omen of what awaited me. Disgusted, I looked for comfort from my thermos and found that my coffee had grown putrid and cold.

The bus crawled doggedly up to Meron, and I followed. As we approached the base of the mountain where Simeon bar Yohai and his son Eleazar were buried, I was suddenly flung back to India. Hundreds of devotees walked, rode, bicycled, and jostled their way up to the domed Arabic building housing the remains of the *Zohar*'s author, the most illustrious kabbalist of all. It was the most rampant display of idol worship I had seen since Benares: women slumped up tightly against the rabbi's velvet-draped tomb, weeping and groaning, their cries bouncing from one damp wall to the next of the crowded cave. Losing myself in the morass of begging Hasidim, moneychangers, hysterical women, flies, black-stockinged children, and aimless hippies, I gazed impassively at the tomb and again tried to work up something resembling mystic ecstasy. The prayerful din swelled to an oceanic roar. I could not even manage a contact high. I hated every minute of it. The ever-vigilant Shmuel caught up with me as I was about to leave and asked if I was thirsty, if I wanted a Coke. Relieved at the excuse to get out of the brocaded tomb, I accepted his offer.

"You can pray for anything you want at Rabbi Simeon's tomb and you'll get it," he said on our downhill trek to the refreshment stand. Two tawny yeshiva boys in shirtsleeves were perched on a rock under a twisted olive tree, biting alternate chunks out of a greasy salami.

I squinted into Shmuel's face, outlined by a halo of painful sunlight. "There's nothing I want," I lied.

In Safed, at the Ari's tomb — the crown of our pilgrimage — I was pursued for money by a cripple wearing a black suit, black hat, and black glasses.

"You from America? You alone or with you husband?" asked the cripple, flashing an ominous row of gold teeth at my uncovered, un-Orthodox head.

"With my husband," I replied hastily. "He's over there." I pointed at the crowded tombsite, where some thirty men in black caftans huddled in prayer. The cripple licked his lips and wandered off amid the weeds and broken bottles interlacing the kabbalists' tombs. I stood and walked closer to where the men were praying. Candles burned crazily in the wind on the ghostly hilltop; tiny folded notes, pleas from the faithful, were stuck into every crevice of the Ari's resting place. A wax-encrusted stove had been soldered into the head of the tomb; I heard an occasional yowl from a fervent devotee who, in his ecstasy, had wandered too close to the flame. Moving around to see better, I came face to face with the black hulk that had shaken its fists at me from the door of the bus. Screwing its ogre's face into a terrifying scowl, it flailed its arms and shouted at me to get away. A fat boy in a long, striped caftan screamed the Shema over and over again like a madman; Hasidim trailing their wives and children in prams behind them hurried up and down the skinny paths leading to the tombs, jabbering in Yiddish. The graveyard was littered with glass and paper and birdshit: a mystic garbage heap. Not one of the faithful had thought to tend it, to keep it green and sweet-smelling. The new kabbalists were crude, given to tossing their empty lunch bags out of the bus window onto the highways; their clothing was stained and reeked of ancient sweat.

I had thought I would surely have something to ask of the Ari. Now the sight of his name on the desolate, weed-smothered tomb evoked only blankness. The ogre bent from the waist and joined the caterwauling of the mad boy in the striped caftan. I took the path leading away from the tombs toward the parking lot on the upper level of the kabbalists' cemetery. Two black-bearded devotees nearly fell off the steep mountain path in their efforts to avoid facing me head-on. I was tempted not to step back and let them fall into the littered ravine. Nothing to ask of the holy Ari. The aluminum tap of the cripple's crutches and the clink of change in his full pocket followed behind me as I fled from the fat boy's windborne screams. *Shema yisroel adonay elohaynu adonay echad!* At a respectful distance, a handful of women genuflected in silence, their lips moving in frenzied prayer. I looked down at the scene and suddenly fancied myself an old Safed kabbalist stretching his body prone on the tomb and talking face to face with the saint. As I turned the bend leading away from the cemetery toward the men's ritual bath, I caught a last glimpse of the wildly gesticulating ogre. But for the injunction against murder, that Hasid might have torn me to bits on the spot.

We stopped for lunch high in a pine forest above the city of Safed. "Frenchie" and Mazal spread out their picnic on a wooden bench at the base of a slope leading to the refreshment stand. Beckoning me to join them, husband and wife settled down for an elaborate feast of hard-boiled eggs, sardines, rye bread, cucumbers, and cheese. They were a devoted, earthy couple who seemed to be really enjoying the company of an intruder from beyond the boundaries of their restricted world. Mazal, who had been quiet for most of the trip, grew almost garrulous as we ate. Did I write for a big newspaper? Had I been to see the kabbalists in Brooklyn? She had heard there were whole communities of them living there.

"Frenchie," ever the mannered gallant, fetched us sodas and ice creams and cups of water from a fresh spring. Unlike most Orthodox husbands, he joked with his wife, publicly sought her opinion, and was unashamedly attentive to her every need.

"I'm not much interested in all that praying," Mazal confessed to me when her husband had gone to buy her a second ice cream cone. "It's too long; but I enjoy the journey. Do you have children?" she finished inevitably.

"No," I said, looking her straight in the eye.

"No wonder you can get so much work done," she said candidly. "With me, it's from the refrigerator to the stove and back again most of the day. That's why I look forward to trips like these."

"It's nice that you can get away," I said.

The bandy-legged bus driver approached our bench. "Let's get this show on the road," he cried with a self-satisfied wink.

"I hope this will be the last tomb," Mazal said boldly.

"I'm afraid not, missus; my people tell me there are at least two more in Tiberias, maybe three," said the driver, shrugging.

Mazal sighed, packed her leftovers neatly in a plastic sack, and followed her husband downhill. "Frenchie" seemed to have lost his earlier swagger; he plodded beside me, the ever-present radio silent in his pocket. I wished the transistor *were* a bottle of cognac; I could have used a mouthful of fuel just then.

We reached the tomb of Jonathan ben Uziel after a wretched two-hour trek over rocky mountain trails gouged out of the Galilean wilderness. "Frenchie" looked out of the car window at the dizzying flood three thousand feet below us and prayed. The twelve-year-old boy who had been deposited with us as a guide looked about to be sick all over the front seat. I drove like one possessed, steering the bumpy trails as if I were escorting my charges through hell. Two huge brown deer leaped out of the brush onto the road ahead of me as I entered a cul-de-sac in time to find the yellow and red bus backing away from a chasm.

"Close call!" shouted the sweating driver merrily out the door of the bus. "I wouldn't go any farther if I were you!"

We parked at last on a dirt trail in a grove of almond and palm trees. There was something decidedly different about this tomb: an eerie, almost palpable sense of its power. Jonathan ben Uziel had expounded so brilliantly on the secrets of Torah that flames encircled him and low-flying birds were immolated on the spot. Even the querulous Sephardim felt it and walked in silence. The prayer at ben Uziel's tomb was going to be fervent, I could tell. Everywhere rose the potent aroma of candle wax. Below the mountain a small cactus grove encircled a narrow trail on which could be seen a miniature Arab on a miniature donkey. We were about thirty-five hundred feet up, breathing the same heady air ben Uziel had breathed in his lonely hermitage of rock, olive trees, cedars, and cautiously circling birds.

A group of pilgrims who had arrived before us refused to make room near the cloth-covered tomb. Shmuel mediated; the ogre snarled; several Hasidim climbed the rocks and shouted their solitary incantations at the setting sun. Before long each side was singing louder, and competing shofars were blaring discordantly into the holy silence. Soon prayers gave way to angry words. Pleas for peace were ignored; more impudent shofar blasts punctuated the singing of the first group; an unearthly tenor voice rose above the chaotic roar, only to be followed by a defiant marching song from the yellow-and-red-bus pilgrims. Young boys took up the militant prayers with their own squeaky tune. I was now really alarmed at the prospect of a fistfight in the middle of nowhere. A din of Babel, not the glory of prayer, filled my ears. More verbal accusations were exchanged. No wonder the Kabbalah had all but disappeared from the earth; its sons had disgraced the graves of the masters with squabbling, begging, spitting, and pissing. Ugliness and spite now reigned in the land of the mystics. One young Hasid in white stockings and patent leather slippers split away from the haggling devotees in disgust. Rushing into a field of thorns, he pounded his fist against a rock and pleaded with the Almighty to intercede.

I sat on a broad flat stone some five yards from the fray, writing notes. Presently I felt someone standing over me and looked up, using my notebook as a shield against the brilliantly descending sun. The figure before me was tall, wiry, clad in black: a Yemenite boy of about twenty.

"Why are you writing?" he asked in Arabic-accented Hebrew.

"Uh . . . I am working on a book about the holy places in Israel," I said defensively. The boy's look was glassy, as if he might be on drugs, and I was afraid of him.

Hovering over me like a famished blackbird, he said menacingly, "Why aren't you praying, then? If you know these are holy places, then why aren't you over there with the rest of the women, praying?"

"How do you know I'm not praying?" I asked archly.

The boy moved closer, his face taut with indignation and the potential violence of ill-restrained sex. "If you wished to pray, you would pray with the women back up there, standing."

Warm spite rushed into my chest, urging me to lash out at the stranger. "I pray the way I want, and you pray the way you want — okay?"

From nowhere, then, Shmuel appeared. "What do you want of her?" he snapped at the boy.

"Nothing," said the intruder, backing away.

Mazal walked up close behind Shmuel; she looked tired and sullen, not at all the docile Orthodox wife she was supposed to be. "It's those Yemenites," she called aggressively at the departing boy. "They bully everyone; they always take first place for themselves."

"Are there any Yemenites in our group?" I asked.

"No, we are mostly all originally from Morocco and Iraq. And the old man with the white beard is the lone Ashkenazi."

Still shaken by the hostile encounter, I returned to the car. A squinty-eyed, red-bearded scholar in black trousers, a green shirt, and long fringes knotted into his belt leaned against the front fender. The sight of him displeased me, but I greeted him cordially. I had seen him running to catch the bus early that morning; he was the only devotee wearing sandals, and he had the sharp nose, narrow red-brown eyes, and wispy beard of a goat.

"It's all right; stay where you are," I assured him as he was about to move from the car.

"How are you enjoying the trip?" Redbeard asked amicably in American English.

Relieved to the point of tears at the familiar sounds, I instantly dropped my persona and, somewhat impulsively, said, "Oh, you're an American. Thank God."

Redbeard nodded and squinted into my face.

"This is the best of the tombs, don't you think?" I asked. "A real power spot."

"It's been quite an experience," he added sympathetically.

"How did you find out about the pilgrimage?" I asked.

"My wife read one of the posters and thought I might be interested. I've been living in Jerusalem for a year. I'm a composer," he confessed shyly, his eyes half-shut with the strain of peering into my face, his newly grown *payot* sticking to his temples in the moist heat. "And you?"

"Oh, well, I was told about this trip by the *shammas* at my synagogue. How are you enjoying it?"

"It's been quite an experience," he repeated. "Riding in that bus . . . I mean these Sephardim are really something. They're fighting with each other like mad one minute, and the next minute they're singing . . ."

"Must be fun," I said. An awkward pause followed.

"And you, what are you doing in Jerusalem?"

"I'm writing books about Jewish mysticism, Kabbalah . . ."

"Are you married? Living here?"

"Married. We're here for about three months. What do you do here?"

"I'm composing. I'm learning, too — studying Torah. It's been a wonderful experience."

"I'm glad someone's enjoying it," I said imprudently. "For more than two years I've been searching for kabbalists, from California to Safed, and the only real ones I've come across are those we visited in their tombs today." I motioned despairingly at the bowl of trees surrounding us.

Mazal opened the car door then, and my new friend leaped to his feet. "See you," he called, hurrying toward the bus. I was sorry to see him go.

The next shrine was a cave once inhabited by a legendary saint with a singular talent for making it rain whenever the nearby farmers asked him to. Another mad trip across the rutted, stony wilderness left me less than enthusiastic; I could no longer even pretend to myself that I wished to pray. Shmuel, however, was especially attached to the rainmaker, and he insisted that I accompany him. The oxygen level inside the cave was near zero; hundreds of burning candles in little glass cups were devouring whatever dank air we could breathe. The avid pilgrims were making it worse by stampeding six abreast through the narrow, bat-fringed mouth of the inner cave, where the saint lay buried. After lighting a candle and muttering something to Shmuel about how "nice" it was, I hurried out, taking in huge gulps of the fresh air wafting over from the Sea of Galilee a few kilometers below. I sat on a stone fence bordering the parking lot, jotting hurried impressions in my notebook. I looked up in midsentence to find my American composer friend standing before me with his shoulders hunched, his arms spread, and his chest heaving.

"I must tell you," he gasped breathlessly.

"Here, let me help you," I said, fearing that he was about to lose consciousness from having remained in the stifling cave too long.

The American pulled away from me. "Ever since we talked, I must tell you that you must stop writing about Kabbalah!" he shouted asthmatically. "You must never write another word about it because you are disordering and, yes, destroying the worlds!" His chest heaving mightily, the composer continued without letting me utter so much as an exclamation of surprise at the shocking turn in his behavior.

"You are a married woman, and your head is not covered! I have been watching you. You must stop right now what you have been doing," he yelled, his slitted eyes popping. "You do not observe the Halakha and therefore you have no right to put down another word about Kabbalah, do you hear me?" The composer moved toward me as if to strike.

Instinctively, I pulled back, raising my notebook before my face and nearly falling backward over the low stone fence.

"How do *you* know who I am, what I write, or what I observe?" I screamed back at him, my voice cracking with terror.

"You do not cover your head, and that means that you are not pure. All of you who do not observe the Halakha down to the letter and write about Kabbalah have destroyed the worlds, do you understand?" The American was on the verge of tears. I searched for Shmuel, for Mazal, for anyone to rescue me from the crazy man, but they were all still lingering in the infernal cave. Trembling, I screwed on the cap of my pen and closed my notebook. I would stare him down or be killed.

"You are endangering your life in the world to come!" he continued relentlessly. "In your impurity you are endangering the life of your husband, your children, your grandchildren — all those in contact with you! Every letter you have written has endangered everyone on this trip. I urge you to stop!"

My own slow burning rage was now fired by his impudence; the culmination of the day's insults — from the leering cripple, the black Hasid, and the Yemenite thug; Redbeard's arrogantly exposed fringes, his self-righteous assessment of my "purity" — unleashed two years of restrained fury. For a moment I thought I would slap him hard in the face, but I held back. The American composer, a born-again Jew, was plainly insane. My blood thumped in my temples so hard I thought they would burst. It was the same insanity everywhere. I hated it; I hated all the black-clad men who wanted to push me off mountaintops for being a woman. I despised the sex-mad Torah scholar now spewing his venom at me. He contained them all. I was sick, exhausted, disgusted, at the coarse extravagance displayed at the shrines, nauseated at the sight of baggy-trousered children with long *payot* babbling only in Yiddish — little Polish ghetto-dwellers so accustomed to the rank darkness their ancestors had lived in for two hundred years that they could not endure the Galilean sunlight, would never dream, like normal children, of rolling naked down its cool green mossy slopes. Was it this living death I had been searching for so avidly? Did I really wish to lower myself into these flea-infested, airless tombs along with the other shouting, jostling, grim-lipped women and tearfully plead for the Way? Did I dream I could perform *mitzvoth* to please Rabbi Gideon or the Rav Bloch — or myself, for that matter? I pictured myself immersed forever in the crude mob occupying the bus.

"Get away from me," I hissed at the American. "You get away from me this minute!"

Rumpelstiltskin, seeing me unguarded by Shmuel, ambled over and thrust his smeared yogurt cup under my nose. Startled, the American turned and fled toward the bus.

"*Tzdakah.*" The watery-eyed troll pleaded for charity, his fly buttons all undone.

"Here." I dropped all the coins in my pocket into his dirty cup. Against Madame Ariel's wise advice I had cast myself among beggars and madmen — and I was paying for it.

I said nothing to anyone on the trip down to Tiberias. Mazal and "Frenchie" wearily dragged themselves to the next two tombs, but I excused myself, claiming that I needed to rest for the long drive back to Jerusalem. Shmuel poked his head in the window of the car at the last shrine, the resting place of a miracle-working rabbi.

"What's wrong?" His face was wrinkled with concern.

"No problem." I jauntily imitated the slangy bus driver.

"Okay, better you rest in the car," he said, turning toward the mammoth synagogue in the tomb's courtyard. "We're going to say evening prayers here, so it will be a while."

"I'm going to write a little," I said, noting that it was already pitch black out. "I'll work over there by the light of the refreshment stand," I added, seeing Shmuel's dubious expression.

"As you wish," he said.

I had forgotten to bring along a sweater and was shaking as much from controlled hysteria as from the cold night air.

Alone and safe in my car, I watched the everyday antics of the refreshment vendor in his small booth. Transplanted again to the secular world, I viewed the man's every homely movement as a miracle; the mundane, nonprayerful act of setting empty Coca-Cola bottles into a case appeared beautiful to me, as sanctified a deed as any the miracle-working rabbi himself might have performed. Humbled by the man's easygoing normalcy, I forgot about taking notes. Suddenly a dark shadow flitted across my window, blocking the light from the refreshment stand. It was Redbeard, seeking me out again, as my protectors were at prayer. His face was aflame; he was wild at the mere thought of me, I could see; my impure presence was so powerful that it had lured him away from enacting the *mitzvah* of prayer. One glance, and I saw that he was ready to devour me alive.

Weary of tombs, shrill Hasidim, dwarves, and thieves, I boldly rolled down the window.

"Say, you!" I shouted at the shadow.

The American Torah scholar approached and looked at me with the same astigmatic, pained stare of before.

"Since you have been so generous as to share your information with me, I would like to return the favor and tell *you* something about Judaism. I would like to tell you that unless you are a *tzaddik* like Rabbi Akiva, whose grave you desecrated by your wild behavior today, you have no right to judge another Jew, no right to condemn his commitment to the *mitzvoth*. Did you know that the Temple fell because of people like you who walked around judging and criticizing their fellow Jews left and right — until the Romans came and finished them all?"

The American silently blinked and stared at me.

"And the second great sin you committed was humiliating another Jew. Being such a serious Torah scholar yourself, you no doubt are aware that humiliating another Jew is one of the most grievous infractions of the Halakha!"

My accuser bit his lip. "I didn't intend it as a humiliation. I was pleading with you to be careful about writing anything about Kabbalah," he murmured.

Unaware of the religious war taking place in front of his stand, the vendor went on rattling bottles and sighing as he bent over the soda cases.

"Well, I felt humiliated," I shouted indignantly over the clatter. "You have insulted a fellow Jew, and in a public, *holy* place!"

"I'm sorry," blubbered the American, backing away from me in fear. "But . . . but . . ." His wispy beard trembled; his chin worked up and down like a puppet's. "Please don't destroy the world!" he got out at last, and then he took off in the direction of the synagogue.

It was our last face-to-face encounter of the trip; but he managed to entreat me once again, from the window of the bus this time, as we pulled out of the courtyard in tandem. With the veins in his forehead bulging, he leaned out to the waist, screaming in Hebrew, "Please go and see Rabbi Mathias, in the Old City. Remember! Rabbi Mathias — he is the only one who can save you!"

I contented myself with an ironical smile; I could never see the American's Rabbi Mathias even if I wanted to, for the famed kabbalist had refused to talk with a woman, even by telephone.

"Frenchie" began humming a popular Israeli song. The boy picked it up, then Mazal, and finally I, too, was singing. We sang uninterruptedly for two hours into the terror-filled darkness all about us until at last we reached Jerusalem.

As I unlocked the door to my flat that night I felt light, buoyant, relieved of a great burden. There was no need for me to be anything but myself. I would no longer camouflage my intentions under the guise of a disinterested reporter or a "returned" Jew. Neither of them was I.

When I told Madame Ariel about my encounter with the American, she was not at all surprised.

"Most of the mystical scholars are mad," she said airily.

"Am I?" I asked, shocked. Perhaps I had really lost touch with practical life in all this avid searching.

"No." She laughed. "It's simply that the rabbis don't look carefully at the mental state of those who come to them. Many young men like the American you met are wandering around Jerusalem; studying day and night in the yeshivoth makes them even crazier than they were before they got here. Religion, when it is not integrated into life, can be very dangerous.

"I am reminded of a brilliant young mathematician from Morocco who was brought to me by my cousin Dr. Hayeem. He was a student of Rabbi Bassani's. The poor young man went mad as a result of permutating the Hebrew letters. When that happened, Rabbi Bassani did not want him around anymore, not to hurt the other students. So, eventually, the young man listened to Dr. Hayeem's advice and came to see me."

"All religious teachers abandon such students in the East; you either manage within the system or you go mad — and then that's *your* problem. The Zen Buddhists are kind enough to provide food and shelter for the monks who break down as a result of their strenuous meditations," I said.

Madame Ariel pursed her lips and shook her head. "Yes, I know about that. But to me each person's life is precious. I am a Sephardic woman in life, not an Eastern fatalist." She winked at me, smoothing her dress and lying back on her pillows.

"What happened to the mathematician?"

"I worked with him through mathematics, giving him visualization exercises to bring him back to the world of numbers, where he functioned so well in his work. I made him use his left brain, you might say." She giggled, always playful about the rational world of science. Madame Ariel fancied herself a scientist of sorts: Depending on her mood, she was a medieval alchemist or an ancient Hermeticist.

"The instability of the Orthodox mystics and the wild syncretism of the secular ones somehow make me retreat from the idea of any sort of 'spiritual community.' It's gotten so I can't tell the difference between those who are looking to Kabbalah as a sympathetic cure for mental problems and those who are really serious about knowing themselves," I said.

My travels had indeed made me aware as I had never been before of the pervasive mental suffering around me. The world of the mystics, like the world of ordinary people, consisted of troubled individuals who desired nothing less than to unite all the warring fragments comprising their lives — along with the added burden of cosmic awareness!

"That is why I have no telephone, no formal 'school.' I would be drowned by troubled people day and night," sighed Madame Ariel, whose profound inclination was to help them all.

I felt supremely at home in her garden that morning. A brief meditation with her resulted in a moment of perfect joy, which continued to glow inside me throughout the entire week.

Puffed up with new confidence born of my tiny little satori, I wandered through the Jewish market the following Saturday morning toward Rabbi Gaon's synagogue. I wished for nothing less than to pray among an entire congregation of kabbalists — on my own terms. The streets were still dim as I made my way up the stairs at the end of the alleyway leading to Rabbi Gaon's quarters. I barely poked my head in the doorway, catching a glimpse of twenty or so swaying figures covered from head to foot in prayer shawls, when I was stopped by a bearded, gap-toothed man who demanded to know what I wanted.

"The women's section," I whispered feebly. "I've come to pray."

The man came around behind me and roughly pushed me away from the entrance. "There is no women's section here," he snarled. "This is a kabbalists' congregation. Women are not allowed here!" Before I knew what was happening, I found myself being propelled by his huge, hairy paw past an open toilet into a kitchen. A little boy looked in at me groggily from the porch.

"What do you mean coming here?" the man whispered apoplectically. He seemed about to explode into a million pieces at the thought of my presence; it was his duty to keep me from profaning the tabernacle beyond the kitchen door, and he looked ready to knock me down if he had to.

"One in a hundred thousand men understand Kabbalah, so what do you, a woman, even think you are doing here?" he croaked, not giving me a chance to answer. From beyond the open kitchen door came the sound of stuporous chanting.

"I —"

"Women must not *dare* approach it. I have been studying for

twenty years, and I do not understand it — so much less you."
He pulled down a dog-eared copy of the *Zohar* from a nearby shelf.

"Tell me, what is this?"

"*Zohar.*" I managed a choked whisper.

Opening the tome to the section on Creation, he cried belligerently, "There! Go on and explain that to me!"

"On one foot? Or will you give me twenty years?"

"Now! Tell me right now what it means!" He pointed a gnarled finger to the Aramaic text.

"I've seen it before, you know," I said, backing off; now that it was light out I was sorry I had come. I wished I were back in Shmuel's synagogue, where it was safe. I wished I were not always sidetracking myself with "adventures." What to do with the rebellious yeshiva brat who could not resist bearding the rabbis in their dens?

"Where did you study?" My interrogator wrinkled his nose with disgust. His face was actually generous and open; he was some Sephardic child's jolly grandfather who brought boxes of toys and bags of candy. Whenever he visited her he affectionately pinched his granddaughter's cheeks. In the synagogue he tucked the little girl under his vast, winged prayer shawl. But the sight of a woman in his kabbalist's cell filled him with repugnance.

"I studied with a Hasid in the United States."

"Ach!" He impatiently waved his hand. "You understand nothing, you know nothing. A woman must not touch Kabbalah!"

"I've written a book."

"What kind of book?"

"On Kabbalah. It's my sixth book," I added extravagantly.

"On Kabbalah? *Nothing!* It's worth nothing!" The grandfatherly kabbalist stepped back, then came forward again. "In what language?" he inquired ambivalently, now interested in a freak posing as a woman who wrote books and had the nerve to come and tell him about them at four-thirty on a Sabbath morning.

"I didn't propose to explain it — just to describe Jewish mysticism for a lay audience, in English. You don't have to get so excited," I said pettishly.

"Nothing!" he repeated. "Just stupidity and uselessness — that is what you have accomplished." Then he softened suddenly; his eyes, his face, even his beard, lost their harshness. "I know that you want to learn Kabbalah," he said, really acknowledging me for the first time. "But you can't. I know about you, I have heard."

"I talked to Rabbi Gaon himself about my book." I forged ahead stupidly.

"And what did he say?"

I did not dare tell him. "He thought such a book was a good idea, that it was the right time for it."

Outside, the bluish light had turned gold; the birds woke and commenced their day in the courtyard in front of Rabbi Gaon's house. The kabbalist indicated that we move back onto the porch. Another bearded ghost backed out after us. Indifferent to my presence, that one crooned and shook and bowed at the ark all the way out the door and into the toilet.

"Bring me your book," said the grandfather. "Bring it here."

"But you don't read English. We can't talk about the book or about the Kabbalah because you don't speak English," I said.

"I read. I understand enough," he replied in English.

Below the synagogue, in Rabbi Gaon's bird-filled courtyard, the housekeeper appeared in her bathrobe. Holding a tiny, mewing red kitten gently in her palm, she leaned over a box containing a whole family of cats and placed the kitten at its mother's breast. Suddenly the chirping birds stopped singing. All was silent in the ancient court of the kabbalists. I stood at the top step with suspended breath.

"Come here with the book tomorrow," the grandfather commanded me. "Bring it to Isaac. Ask for me, I am always here."

"Thank you for your time. Good-bye." I headed down the stairs: it was my turn to be scarce.

Isaac followed me. "I want to read it."

I turned away from him. "*Shalom,* good-bye. I do not give away free copies of my book to anyone but friends," I said, hurrying off. I did not want his criticism, his approval, his interest, or his pity; nor did I want his brand of mysticism any longer. The early morning damp covered even the walls of the marketplace; every multicolored shanty was sweating. A black hound appeared from behind a garbage pail and snuffled at the cracks in the road. I picked up speed. From the far end of the narrow lane came the sound of chanting. As Shmuel's friendly synagogue came into view my spirits leaped high; the black dog disappeared in a littered alleyway. I crossed the street, narrowly avoiding the corpse of yet another bird: a freshly killed wren that had obviously been decapitated by a speeding car only minutes before. The head had been severed by a clean blood line from the fragile stalk of the bird's neck; like a tiny glass marble, it lay no more than a foot away from the body. I gagged, walked on. By the time I reached the outer staircase of the women's section and opened the synagogue door, I no longer had the heart for prayer.

At seven o'clock on Sunday morning, I went to Rabbi Gideon to plead with him to allow me into his group of practicing kabbalists. I found him with a dark man of about forty, poring over an enormous Talmud. Rabbi Gideon was in his shirtsleeves, a glass of tea at his elbow. When the two men saw me their eyes opened wide; they appeared to be in an altered state of consciousness, and it took them a few seconds to determine who or what had entered the room. Rabbi Gideon dismissed the man, who took his jacket and briefcase and, bowing his head at me, quickly made for the door. The rabbi's wife appeared to be out; not even one of his myriad children played about him. I had obviously interrupted a daily session of deep meditative study.

"Let me join your yeshiva; let me pray and meditate and study with you the way that man does," I blurted out.

Rabbi Gideon reached around behind him, removed his jacket from the chair, and put it on. "You cannot join the men," he said kindly. "Besides, you don't understand that we were created differently for a purpose; for women the way is shorter. They do not need so much prayer and study because they are constructed by nature not to require so many *mitzvoth*. Women are closer to God by virtue of their ability to create life through their bodies."

I must have blushed, for Rabbi Gideon asked me politely if I would sit down at the table and take some coffee or tea.

I refused and stood staring at him blankly.

"Can you make noodle pudding?" he asked suddenly.

"No, why?"

"Never mind." He shook his head. "Do this," he resumed, looking for a new departure from the embarrassing predicament into which I had thrown him unprepared. "Say one prayer each day; impel your husband to observe the *mitzvoth* and to study Torah. Send *him* to me. Continue writing your books to spread the word of Kabbalah into the world outside, and perform the women's *mitzvoth:* Shabbat observance, kosher home — you know them. If you do these with *kavanna,* you will be brought automatically to a higher understanding of their function in approaching God. You simply must accept the difference between men and women."

"My husband can't bear the way the Orthodox Jews treat women. He has no inclination to become a yeshiva student. The community of women you want me to join would mean the end of my joy in living. I can't do it," I said. "We will still be friends, won't we?"

"Yes, of course," he said. "You and Noah are always welcome here."

"Thank you," I said, hurrying toward the door, feeling shy and relieved at once. I had finally confronted Rabbi Gideon without hedging; I had told him outright how it really was with me — alone, without using Noah's indifferent presence as a pretense, without the rebbitzen, early in the morning, when he was unarmed and in his shirtsleeves. I did not want to reach God only through my body; I wanted a synthesis of mind, heart, body, spirit, soul — or whatever it was that comprised my total humanity. The Kabbalah was doomed, I felt, because it had not provided for women.

In my book I had rhetorically wondered why so many Jews were rushing eastward in search of God. From all that I had read and learned, I was then convinced that there definitely existed a "tradition," a Kabbalah that could be lived and practiced by Jews as well as Zen or yoga. But by the time Rabbi Gideon informed me face to face that it was my role to "impel" my husband and to refrain from pushing ahead any farther on my chosen way, I had begun to doubt if any viable Kabbalah existed at all. I feared having invented the notion to still an old call of Jewish guilt or conscience, and my most recent traumatic encounters with those who called themselves kabbalists only compounded that fear and urged me to put the old Jewish ghosts to rest. *"Can you make noodle pudding?"* was either a profound kabbalistic koan or Rabbi Gideon's final rejection of my mutant womanhood.

My close association with his family did, however, serve to change my initial prejudiced view of the rabbi's relationship with his wife. At first I looked upon her as his appendage. In time I found her to be his perfect complement: Rebbitzen Gideon was robust and practical; the rabbi was delicate in health and, though brilliantly witty, he looked to her often to corroborate his humor, to correct his facts — even going so far as to ask her in front of company to quote biblical and talmudic passages he could not remember. I often wondered whether they were not in fact studying together in secret. The Gideons, I concluded, were — on their own terms — as truly equal in their marriage as Noah and I. In no way did I ever see the rabbi treat his wife as a simple housemaid; both were equally surrounded by their numerous children as they worked, and both enjoyed the clamor. The Gideons had very clearly divided their external roles, but emotionally, and even intellectually, they were two aspects of one functioning unit.

Still, my doubts about Kabbalah were further corroborated later that week in deep conversation with a French biophysicist who had been studying Jewish mysticism for thirty years. Serge had actually moved to Israel in order to implement his studies in his everyday life as a Jew. Like Shmuel and Dinah, his unlettered counterparts, Serge felt that the study of Kabbalah was a personal affair, available from the discourses of the masters in their books and scattered manuscripts. Whether male or female, all one needed was tenacity and mastery of the Hebrew language; the insights, he promised, would come from the study itself. Serge prayed three times a day, using the Ari's meditative *kavannot* as vehicles for contemplation.

He had even begun to practice the *mitzvoth* in order to discover the secret levels of meaning behind seemingly ordinary acts like wearing a skullcap.

"Enlightenment for the Jew," he said, "is more a question of seeing and then spiritualizing matter — not denying the world as illusory. On the contrary, the Jew must live in it more deeply." For Serge the scientist, Kabbalah was a more rationally structured way of comprehending the universe than all the theories proposed by so-called rationalists. Nevertheless, Serge too felt that Judaism was in crisis. But he had cast in his lot with the Jews, and he was hopeful that out of the ferment something new and vibrant would grow. Like the Rav Bloch, he saw the future of Kabbalah reflected in the eyes of eager secular people like himself, who were hurrying the process along and bringing it to fruition even sooner.

I admired Serge for his vast intelligence, his humility, his comfortable Jewish identity; yet I could not be as hopeful as he. Out in the streets, even as we were talking, Orthodox and secular boys were beating and stabbing each other in a Sabbath brawl over closing off the roads to automobile traffic. The crisis was not in books nor was it in the future; it was already on, taking place physically less than a mile from the civilized, tree-lined street in Rehavia where we sat eating ice cream and contemplating the higher realities.

Perhaps in the world of the Kabbalah, "making noodle pudding" was synonymous with seeing God. I could not make noodle pudding; moreover, I did not want to learn how.

It was clear that I had reached the end of my Jewish pilgrimage. I told Madame Ariel that I wished to stop the Sabbath exercises. She looked up from her pillows and said, "My uncle, who was one of my teachers, a great Orientalist and expert in Vedanta, said that I should always go to the furthest point in my work. He encouraged me never to stop before I had accomplished all there was left to accomplish in that particular work. Are you sure you have accomplished everything, *chérie?*"

"All right, one more Sabbath," I reluctantly promised.

I went to bed on Friday night at about ten. But instead of falling asleep, I saw myself looking out the bedroom window into the courtyard of Shmuel's synagogue. A large circle of peasants was seated on the stone floor, the women in brown linen and white scarves, the men all recognizable Sephardic kabbalists in laborers' clothing. The group seemed to be excited about participating in some sort of lottery, for they were passing around slips of brown paper with much gaiety. Their leader, a blond young man of unearthly beauty, looked up and saw me gazing out the window.

"Do you wish to join the lottery?" he asked.

I nodded.

"But remember, once you accept one of these slips there is no turning back; you must accept the consequences."

I took the slip from his extended hand and immediately found myself at the center of the circle.

"What do you see?" everyone cried at once.

I looked up at the sky and saw a diamond horse poised above the circle leading a sapphire chariot. The delighted peasants applauded my vision.

"Now you are ready to come with me and see the reversal of time," the young man said. "But you must be willing to accept everything you experience on the journey, even if it means being dislodged and changing."

Agreeing to the terms, I followed him into a nineteen-forties roadster.

"Don't be afraid to look into the back seat," the guide said. I turned my head and looked into Noah's face — only he was plumper, a portly, benevolent-looking man of sixty! I started.

The guide touched my shoulder. "It's all right, don't be frightened," he said.

"Can Noah stay with us on the trip?" I asked. "This *is* Noah, isn't it?"

"Yes, only older, how he will be. He can stay," the guide consented, driving on.

We stopped in front of a department store, which I immediately recognized as May's. Puzzled, as I never shopped there, having always considered its merchandise to be cheap and shoddy, I hesitated when the guide told me to go into the store.

"What am I supposed to do here?" I asked.

"Go in and find one thing; I will wait for you in the car."

The older Noah sat mute in the back seat. Alone, I entered the store to find myself in the middle of a very odd hand-made crockery sale: Every last dish, pot, vase, and mug was painted in gold and bright saffron. I picked a mug off the shelf and, turning it around and around, saw that it was embossed with the prancing golden lion of Judah. I will buy that, I thought, and I took the mug to the cashier. There I encountered a straight, disciplined row of serious Japanese businessmen waiting to pay for their golf clubs. I looked at them with only passing interest, wondered what they were doing there, and continued on.

Outside, the guide was waiting for me in the roadster; seeing me with my golden lion of Judah mug, he gave a satisfied nod and motioned me back into the car.

Our next stop was a big, friendly, comfortable Victorian house at the center of a spacious green lawn. The guide led me up the front steps and into the house, where a family was gathered at a long, beautiful rosewood table for a festive dinner. The dining room was huge, with impressive wainscoting; everything was as perfect as it had been in my favorite childhood storybooks.

"I've been here before!" I cried out enthusiastically. "I know this house." And with that everyone dispersed. It was as though my shout had broken through a transparent veil that would have allowed me to see and hear everything going on in that house without being seen and heard in turn. I had forfeited my privileged observation point with my enthusiastic outburst, but I was still exceedingly happy in the house.

The young guide ushered me to a staircase at the right-hand corner of the large dining room. "Here," he said. "I must go on and you must take over yourself. I have passed through this phase, and now that you have agreed to join the circle and the lottery, you will go on as I have done. Walk in alone to the next room."

Fearlessly, I descended the staircase and found myself walking on a marble floor bordered on two sides by wooden stalls filled with exquisite chocolates and a variety of brightly wrapped candies. I touched my hair and found that I now wore pigtails! I looked down at my body and saw that I was dressed in the white pinafore of a little girl and that I not only looked like a child but that I actually felt and experienced the world around me as a child. Even more, all the childlike wonder and delight that had ever existed was now experiencing the world through me!

I reached into one of the stalls and ate a cholocate — the most delicious milk chocolate, exactly the sort I had adored eating in the movies; the big silver bags of cholocate kisses my grandfather brought on Fridays from the outdoor market; the very essence of chocolate inhered in every bite I took. There were chocolate-covered marshmallows, too, and chocolate graham crackers, which I had not eaten since I was ten. As I bit into the cosmic sweets, I experienced *perfection*. Angels sang, rainbows appeared, innumerable foreign colors striped the sky, and all around me there was nothing but wonder, delight, completion. The bodiless voice of my guide rang out from the heart of the angels' song: "This is the true gift the Torah wishes you to have — only sweetness, delight, and *joy*. This is where the Torah wishes you to be."

In this blissful state, I awoke into the physical world and washed and dressed in the dark. The familiar Noah lay sleeping on the bed, one hand tucked under his pillow as usual. Nothing in the house had changed.

As the sun rose, I went downstairs into the empty Jerusalem streets and headed for the synagogue. Shmuel met me in the courtyard as I entered the gate. I climbed up into the women's section, taking the steaming glass of coffee he held out to me on a tray. For several minutes I sat alone, waiting for the Sabbath chanting to begin. Nothing happened; the men's section remained empty; nobody came. Presently Shmuel appeared at the door of the women's section, his cheerful, robust, and clear-eyed face lighting up the emptiness.

"Where's the Saturday morning chanting?" I asked in a loud

voice that carried across Elijah's chair and bounced back at me from the ark.

"The early morning singing is over; we only did it for three weeks. Each synagogue in the neighborhood gets a turn; now they're meeting and singing across the street — don't you hear them?"

The faint, raspy sound of Sephardic chanting purled through the silent streets and into the open window behind me.

"But there was light in the synagogue all night," I said.

"That was my little group of kabbalists; we were reciting Psalms throughout the night; we do it every Sabbath of this month — the days of awe before Yom Kippur, when the heavens open and the Book of Life waits to be inscribed."

Not feeling "normal" somehow, I could only sit and stare at the *shammas*. Without waiting for my next question, Shmuel walked out the door and down into the kitchen. Almost a minute later he returned, carrying a plastic bag filled with cakes in one hand and a sack of candies, chocolates, and gum in the other. Between his thumb and forefinger, he had pressed a bunch of freshly picked wild herbs.

I could not really believe what was happening. My "dream" was literally being continued in my waking life. Shmuel divided the bunch of herbs, giving me half and holding the other half of the delicious, fragrant leaves before my face. The singing from across the street grew louder.

"These are for a blessing; you must inhale their sweetness when the Sabbath departs and you recite the Havdalah." He pressed the herbs into my hand. "And the candies — here, take — do you like Bazooka bubble gum?" He emptied the entire bag of gums and fruit drops and mints and chocolates onto the bench. No end to the delights Shmuel could pour for me; no end to the luscious scent of spices and the perfect love and bliss pervading his little synagogue. I had entered the court of the kabbalists and touched heaven without even knowing it.

"Take all the candies you want," Shmuel said, looking mischievous and angelic at once. "Oh, wait a minute." Again he vanished through the open door. The streets below were gradually filling with Sabbath observers; not one car horn could be heard in the roadway, only the clear sound of divine chanting. The women in white scarves were beginning to arrive. "Shabbat *shalom*." They saluted me, kissed Elijah's chair and the ornate bronze *mezuzah* on the door, and sat down with their inevitable old women's sighs.

Shmuel appeared in the doorway with a great toothless smile; he hadn't even bothered to put in his false teeth. In his right hand, the angel triumphantly held up a transparent bag bursting with multicolored spherical candies.

"Here!" He gleefully tossed me his prize.

I caught the bag and clutched it in both hands. Printed in wavy black and white Hebrew letters on the outside was the word "JOY."

Temple Israel

Minneapolis, Minnesota

```
IN MEMORY OF FATHER,
   HARRY S. BERMAN
        FROM
  MRS. JUNE BARRON
```